Taking Hold of the Real

Taking Hold of the Real

Dietrich Bonhoeffer
and the Profound Worldliness
of Christianity

Barry Harvey

CASCADE *Books* · Eugene, Oregon

TAKING HOLD OF THE REAL
Dietrich Bonhoeffer and the Profound Worldliness of Christianity

Cascade Books
An Imprint of Wipf and Stock Publishers
199 W. 8th Ave., Suite 3
Eugene, OR 97401

www.wipfandstock.com

ISBN 13: 978-1-62564-844-0

Cataloging-in-Publication data:

Harvey, Barry, 1954–

Taking hold of the real : Dietrich Bonhoeffer and the profound worldliness of Christianity / Barry Harvey.

xiv + 342 p. ; 23 cm. —Includes bibliographical references and indexes.

ISBN 13: 978-1-62564-844-0

1. Bonhoeffer, Dietrich, 1906–1945. I. Title.

BX4827.57 B445 2015

Manufactured in the U.S.A.

To Rachel Ann

Contents

Acknowledgments

DIETRICH BONHOEFFER HAS BEEN a constant companion of mine for nearly three decades. I have written on some aspect or other of his life and work on several occasions, the fruits of which supply both the framework and some of the content for the present volume. Even when I have not written explicitly about him, something he said or did frequently acts as a catalyst for my reflections. My interest in his life and work is both descriptive and constructive, as I seek to discern what his theology has to show and say to the church in our time and place. My aim is not simply to arrive at the best understanding of what he said and did in his context (though that is important), but to enlist his help in our efforts to spell out a theological grammar that is adequate both to scripture and tradition, and to the particularities of the time and place in which we currently live, move, and have our being. I hope that this book repays a small part of my debt I owe to a friend I did not have the chance to meet.

The title of this book is derived from a line from a poem Bonhoeffer writes from prison, "Stations on the Way to Freedom": "Hover not over the possible, but boldly reach for the real." The verb in the German is *ergreifen*, to seize or grasp, not merely to contemplate what is real.[1] The nature of reality, as Bonhoeffer understands it, is grounded in God's becoming human in Jesus Christ, and thus taking hold of the real gives fitting expression not only to his theology but to the course his life took up to the very end.

Writing a book, especially this book, is never the achievement of an isolated individual. I owe much to friends and mentors in the International Bonhoeffer Society, who welcomed me as a young scholar into their ranks and gave encouragement at innumerable points along the way. In particular I would like to express my appreciation to Victoria Barnett, Gaylon Barker, Mark Brocker, Guy Carter, Keith Clements, John de Gruchy, Wayne Floyd, Peter Frick, Clifford Green, John Godsey, Lori Brand Hale, Karina Juhl Kande, Geffrey Kelly, Michael Lukens, Nancy Lukens, John Matthews, Kirsten

---

1. *DBWE* 8:513 (*DBW* 8:571).

Nielsen, Hans Pfeifer, Jeffrey Pugh, Martin Rumscheidt, Christiane Tietz, Reggie Williams, Ralf Wüstenberg, Philip Ziegler, and Jens Zimmermann.

Family, mentors, colleagues, and students all make vital contributions, in many and varied ways, to what is finally produced. Simply mentioning them here does not repay the debts that I owe them, but perhaps it will suffice as a token of my appreciation. In particular I want to thank Philip Thompson, Mark Medley, Elizabeth Newman, and Douglas Henry, who took time out of their busy schedules to read and comment on a preliminary draft of the book. Their suggestions significantly improved the final result.

Friends in the Ekklesia Project (too many to mention here), whose love for the church is manifest in all they do and say, have blessed my life. I have also been gifted with students—graduate and undergraduate, past and present—who have consistently provided both the enthusiasm and the rationale for undertaking a project such as this. Whatever I may contribute to our common confession in the God of Jesus Christ with this book would not have been possible save for all that I have learned from and with them.

I must also express my thanks to all those at Cascade Books who helped make this book a reality. Jon Stock and the sisters and brothers at the Church of the Servant King have been dear friends for some time now, and the chance to work with Rodney Clapp on a second book project was a prospect I simply could not pass up.

My wife Sarah, son John, and grandchildren Lexus, Audi, Porsche, and Ella are my joy and delight. I shudder to think of what my life would be without the love, friendship, and support of my family.

I dedicate this book to my daughter Rachel Ann. She was two years old when I defended my dissertation, and I remember her greeting me at the door of our home with an enthusiastic "Hello, Dr. Daddy!" I cannot begin to say how proud I am of who she has become and what she has accomplished, and I look forward to what she will be and do in the years to come. To her and to all my family, friends, and colleagues, and above all to the God of mercy and grace, I give thanks.

Several of the chapters contain adapted material from previously published essays or books, and I gratefully acknowledge their origins. Parts of chapter 3 appeared originally in "The Wound of History" published by William B. Eerdmans, and have been adapted by permission of the publisher; all rights reserved. Portions of chapter 5 first appeared in "Accounting for Difference" published by Vandenhoeck and Ruprecht, and have been adapted by permission of the publisher; all rights reserved. Parts of chapter 6 originally appeared in Harvey, "Religion, Race and Resistance," published by Gütersloh, and have been adapted by permission of the publisher; all rights reserved. Portions of chapter 7 originally appeared in Harvey, "Life in

Exile, Life in the Middle of the Village," also published by Gütersloh; in Harvey, "Re-Envisioning the Wall of Separation," published by Regent's Park College, Oxford University, and adapted by permission of the publisher, all rights reserved; and in "Ransomed from Every Language," published in *Review and Expositor*, and adapted with the permission of the publisher; all rights reserved. Parts of chapters 4 and 9 were originally published in *Can These Bone Live?* by Brazos Press, and have been adapted by permission of the publisher; all rights reserved.

Abbreviations

DBW 1:   *Dietrich Bonhoeffer Werke 1: Sanctorum Communio*

DBW 2:   *Dietrich Bonhoeffer Werke 2: Akt und Sein*

DBW 3:   *Dietrich Bonhoeffer Werke 3: Schöpfung und Fall*

DBW 4   *Dietrich Bonhoeffer Werke 4: Nachfolge*

DBW 5:   *Dietrich Bonhoeffer Werke 5: Gemeinsames Leben/Das Gebetbuch der Bibel*

DBW 6:   *Dietrich Bonhoeffer Werke 6: Ethik*

DBW 8:   *Dietrich Bonhoeffer Werke 8: Widerstand und Ergebung*

DBW 11:   *Dietrich Bonhoeffer Werke 11: Ökumene, Universität, Pfarramt, 1931–1932*

DBW 12:   *Dietrich Bonhoeffer Werke 12: Berlin, 1932–1933*

DBW 13:   *Dietrich Bonhoeffer Werke 13: London*

DBW 14:   *Dietrich Bonhoeffer Werke 14: Illegale Theologenausbildung: Finkenwalde, 1935–37*

DBWE 1:   *Dietrich Bonhoeffer Works 1: Sanctorum Communio*

DBWE 2:   *Dietrich Bonhoeffer Works 2: Act and Being*

DBWE 3:   *Dietrich Bonhoeffer Works 3: Creation and Fall*

DBWE 4:   *Dietrich Bonhoeffer Works 4: Discipleship*

DBWE 5:   *Dietrich Bonhoeffer 5: Life Together and Prayerbook of the Bible*

DBWE 6:   *Dietrich Bonhoeffer Works 6: Ethics*

DBWE 8:   *Dietrich Bonhoeffer Works 8: Letters and Papers from Prison*

DBWE 9:   *Dietrich Bonhoeffer Works 9: The Young Bonhoeffer, 1918–1927*

DBWE 10:	*Dietrich Bonhoeffer Works* 10: *Barcelona, Berlin, New York, 1928–1931*
DBWE 11:	*Dietrich Bonhoeffer Works* 11: *Ecumenical, Academic and Pastoral Work, 1931–1932*
DBWE 12:	*Dietrich Bonhoeffer Works* 12: *Berlin, 1932–1933*
DBWE 13:	*Dietrich Bonhoeffer Works* 13: *London, 1933–1935*
DBWE 14:	*Dietrich Bonhoeffer Works* 14: *Theological Education at Finkenwalde, 1935–1937*
DBWE 15:	*Dietrich Bonhoeffer Works* 15: *Theological Education Underground, 1937–1940*
DBWE 16:	*Dietrich Bonhoeffer Works* 16: *Conspiracy and Imprisonment, 1940–1945*
CD I/2:	Karl Barth, *Church Dogmatics: The Doctrine of the Word of God*, Part 2
CD II/2:	Karl Barth, *Church Dogmatics: The Doctrine of God*, Part 2

Introduction: The Great Wager

Nothing, then, which Scripture says about Faith, however startling it may be at first sight, is inconsistent with the state in which we find ourselves by nature with reference to the acquisition of knowledge generally,—a state in which we must assume something to prove anything, and can gain nothing without a venture.

—JOHN HENRY NEWMAN, "The Nature of Faith in Relation to Reason"

"WE LIVE," WRITES DIETRICH Bonhoeffer, "in the time before the last things and believe in the last things, is that not so?"[1] We live, in other words, *in medias res*, in the middle of things. There is nothing novel in this observation, for this has been a perennial fact of human existence since our first parents were cast out of the garden. What is unprecedented, and what I attempt to account for in this book in constructive conversation with Bonhoeffer, is the distinctive character of the middle here and now. Prior to the sixteenth century there existed a recognizable consensus in Western Christendom about the origin, essence, and goal of this middle. The nonhuman world spoke of its creator's purpose and action, God was the central figure in the constitution of society, our everyday surroundings were imbued with purpose and direction, and women and men discovered the meaning of their existence from their place in this marvelous, mysterious cosmos.[2] This consensus has all but disappeared with the demise of the *corpus christianum*, leaving us with disaggregated bits and pieces of a once complex and integrated social order.

The intellectual, moral, and spiritual capital that had accumulated over the centuries was wagered on what Adam Seligman calls a new "authoritative locus of sacrality," grounded on a foundation of transcendental

1. *Wir leben im Vorletzten and glauben das Letzte, ist es nicht so?* (DBW 8:226, my translation).

2. Taylor, *Secular Age*, 25–26.

1

dictates rather than transcendent reality. A set of "'self-evident' truths . . . as amenable to reason as the principles of Euclidian geometry" displaced conceptions of truth revealed by a transcendent Being. The stakes were nothing less than our bodies and souls, together with the earth to which bodies and souls belong. Though its outcome remains to be seen, it is doubtful that this is a wager that humankind will win.[3] Christians are not exempt from this state of affairs; faith is no longer the default position that can simply be assumed. Indeed, in many ways our forebears were responsible for this situation. What is now needed, says Bonhoeffer, is the free wager of faith (*das freie Glaubenswagnis*).[4]

It is the desire to make sense of the venture of Christianity in the modern world that has fueled the interest of many in the life and theology of Bonhoeffer, who states that faith in Christ is the great wager that can never be safe or beyond question.[5] In what follows I attempt to think with him about the distinctive features of our own time and place. His description of the profound this-worldliness of Christianity in particular provides a social imaginary around which to craft a constructive approach to the church's engagement with a world come of age, and thereby to make sense of the peculiarities of the present as we strive to live truthfully before God and bear faithful witness to our neighbors.

Bonhoeffer's understanding of profound this-worldliness is best understood as a wager about human life that participates, on the one hand, in the life, death, and resurrection of Christ, and on the other, in the concerns and joys of a fallen creation. It stands in contrast to a second kind of worldliness, which he describes as "the shallow and banal this-worldliness of the enlightened, the bustling, the comfortable, or the lascivious."[6] The notion of profound this-worldliness may seem odd to those who assume that Christianity has always been primarily interested in what happens on the far side

---

3. Seligman, *Modernity's Wager*, 12–13.

4. *DBWE* 8:41 (*DBW* 8:24). With regard to the translation of *Wagnis* as "wager," see Green, "Pacifism and Tyrannicide," 45.

5. *DBWE* 8:41. In his address to an ecumenical conference at Fanø, Denmark, in August 1934, titled "The Church and the Peoples of the World," Bonhoeffer states, "There is no way to peace along the way of safety. For peace must be dared. It is the great venture." Though he is speaking here specifically about the way to peace, it applies equally well, *mutatis mutandis*, to his understanding of faith as a venture of responsible action. He goes on to state that "peace means to give oneself altogether to the law of God, wanting no security, but in faith and obedience laying the destiny of the nations in the hand of Almighty God, not trying to direct it for selfish purposes. Battles are won, not with weapons, but with God. They are won where the way leads to the cross" (*DBWE* 13:308–9).

6. *DBWE* 8:485.

of the grave. Bonhoeffer contests that presumption, which he sees as rooted in a desire to be delivered from the sorrows, hardships, and anxieties of earthly life. The proclamation of Jesus Christ in both the gospels and Paul's letters, and in particular the hope of resurrection, is not an escape route out of the tasks and challenges of this world. It instead "refers people to their life on earth in a wholly new way,"[7] where they seek to act in concert with the reality of God united to the reality of the world in Christ.[8]

Bonhoeffer's theology thrusts us into the middle of an ongoing apocalyptic drama,[9] a place that enables us to see all that is happening in the world around us as implicated in God's work of judgment and reconciliation in Jesus Christ. He lives and speaks to us as a witness to the fact that to participate in Christ, and thus to be performers in this drama, is to belong to those "on whom the ends of the ages have met" (1 Cor 10:11[10]), and thus the middle of our life's journey takes the form of the time before the last. Like Karl Barth, his focus is always the reality of God in Christ breaking into the world to set it aright, but unlike Barth he spells out God's activity in a way that includes our participation in that action. What Hans Urs von Balthasar says of the Apostle Paul applies, *mutatis mutandis*, to Bonhoeffer: "He shows how the drama comes from God, via Christ, to him, and how he hands it on to the community, which is already involved in the action and must bring it into reality."[11]

Bonhoeffer refuses in his theology to "smooth out the folds" of history by imposing an artificial sense of completion on it, or taking refuge in an abstract description of the world that claims an abiding universal significance.[12] Of all the figures in the Bible, he seems to identify most often in this regard with Moses. In an Advent sermon delivered in Havana, Cuba, in 1930, he says of the great prophet and lawgiver, "His life was a journey to the promise, a journey in hope through disappointments, tribulations, defeats, through apostasy and unfaithfulness; but he had a hunger for the

7. *DBWE* 8:447.

8. Returning to the earth in the power of the resurrection, as N. T. Wright puts it, often involves "dangerous and difficult tasks, up to and including martyrdom" (Wright, *Surprised by Hope*, 241).

9. As I discuss in more detail in chapter 1, though many might find the notion of apocalyptic alien in connection with Bonhoeffer, when examined in the light of recent biblical scholarship into the gospels and the Pauline letters it is altogether appropriate as a description of his fundamental theological imaginary.

10. Translation by Hays, *Moral Vision*, 20. Unless otherwise stated, biblical quotations are from the New Revised Standard Version.

11. Balthasar, *Theo-Drama*, 2:57.

12. Ibid., 2:54.

promised land that drove him ever onward." And yet, at the end of his life, at the hour at which this hope was about to be fulfilled, "God says: Ascend the mountain and die."[13] Bonhoeffer returns to Moses at the end of his life in the poem "The Death of Moses," declaring, "Through death's veil you let me see at least / this, my people, go to the highest feast. / They stride into freedom, God, I see, / as I sink to your eternity."[14]

Any attempt to think constructively in conversation with Bonhoeffer about our time and place is indebted to the work that many excellent scholars have done to situate his life and thought in their original social and historical setting, above all to the editors and translators of the critical edition of his writings in German and English, and also to the excellent biographies of Eberhard Bethge and Ferdinand Schlingensiepen.[15] At the same time, however, this aspect of the interpretive enterprise alone can never decide the continuing meaning and promise of his writings. At stake, as Bonhoeffer puts it in *Ethics*, "are the times and places that concern us, that we experience, that are realities for us."[16] He understands the logic of historical existence, which, as Oliver O'Donovan has observed, "is that living in a given age means having a distinct set of practical questions to answer, neither wholly unlike those that faced other generations nor mere repetitions of them."[17] The undertaking to which he devotes his life, and the one that we must now take up, is the question of how to understand the particulars of the times and places bequeathed to us by the God of Jesus Christ as both gift (*Gabe*) and task (*Aufgabe*).[18]

What concerns us now as members of the body of Christ has principally to do with the shape of profound this-worldliness in this era after the dissolution of the *corpus christianum*.[19] The need to think carefully and truthfully about this matter has never been more pressing, for we must bear witness to what God has done, is doing, and will do, in circumstances very different from what our parents and grandparents dealt with. Whether or not we are prepared to do so, the church in Europe and North America has embarked on "an expedition into lands as yet unknown."[20] Though not all of the familiar signposts have disappeared (and a few from the early centuries

---

13. *DBWE* 10:586.

14. *DBWE* 8:540.

15. Bethge, *Dietrich Bonhoeffer*; Schlingensiepen, *Dietrich Bonhoeffer*.

16. *DBWE* 6:100.

17. O'Donovan, *Church in Crisis*, 45.

18. See *DBWE* 1:278 (*DBW* 1:189); cf. *DBWE* 6:180.

19. *DBWE* 8:485.

20. Buber, "What Is Man?," 153.

of our history have resurfaced), the church now finds itself on unfamiliar ground, struggling to take its bearings within the continuing story of the God of Jesus Christ.

Our sense of who and where we are is therefore defined in crucial respects by which story we tell of how we arrived here and now.[21] "Our past is sedimented in our present," states Charles Taylor, "and we are doomed to misidentify ourselves, as long as we can't do justice to where we come from."[22] An important task is therefore not simply to account for the world as it is presently configured, but also to say something about how it got this way. If we are to understand our time we must retrace the social and intellectual journey of our ancestors that brought us to our current situation. In such circumstances, and in light of the less than exemplary record of the church's witness in the last few centuries, the church can no longer claim the privileges it once enjoyed, but must recognize the presence of a deep justice in history.[23] Bonhoeffer offers both a keen sense of the ways that the status of Christian faith has changed in the wake of momentous political, economic, technological, and social changes, and perceptive insight into the ways it would continue to change. His descriptions and analyses provide us with both a point of departure and a direction to follow as we venture forth, at times boldly, at others more tentatively, into the complexities of the world where God has sent us.

I have not tried in this volume to provide a general introduction to, or a comprehensive survey of, Bonhoeffer's life and thought. It is instead an attempt to think faithfully and truthfully about this time after Christendom, with him as primary interlocutor. I seek to understand his descriptions, analyses, and insights in order to bring them to bear on the world given to us to attest to the works of God in the world. My hope is that we might take advantage of his wisdom but also learn from his occasional missteps as we work, think, and deliberate together about the claim of Jesus Christ on the world, the one to whom we bear witness through responsible action. To do this is not to ignore what his writings signified in their original settings, but to make good use of what he said and did in those circumstances, to continue down the path that he (together with many others) sets before us. It is to take up the theological trajectory he establishes in his writings (a contested task to be sure) and develop it further so that we might address

21. Among the possibilities is the story of modernity, which is the story "that you should have no story except the story you have chosen when you had no story. . . . The project of liberal societies is simply to make the freedom of choice a necessity." Hauerwas, *Dispatches*, 166–67. I shall return to this topic in chapter 3.

22. Taylor, *Secular Age*, 29.

23. *DBWE* 8:389.

the particulars of the time and place given to us by God, and then entrust both our genuine insights and unwitting errors to those who come after us.

Interpreting a text or series of texts by an author is a performative work in itself, taking what she has done, said, or written and adding to it, responding to what she gives us with descriptions, judgments, and insights we formulate for our own context. What we produce is addressed to those with whom we currently share this earth, in the hope of developing a common reading and a shared, or at least continuous, form of life together.[24] In this sense of the term, interpretation takes place within the context of shared or overlapping projects or traditions characterized by distinctive sets of goods, habits, practices, and goals. Traditions in good working order, Bonhoeffer suggests, consist of "a historical heritage that we must make our own, use in the present, and pass on to the future."[25]

As I go about this work I try to steer a course between two false paths. On the one hand, we should never treat Bonhoeffer as an oracle, such that if we could just decipher his intentions and meanings we would have a sufficient handle on our own time. As every honest appraisal of his work acknowledges, at times he gets matters wrong, and even his best insights need to be supplemented, revised, or reconfigured, if for no other reason than to account for the changed circumstances we face in our time and place, or to take advantage of historical hindsight. His thoughts are best served when seasoned with (and, when necessary, corrected by) insights, ideas, and images from his fellow laborers. Bonhoeffer cannot speak *for* us in our struggle to be faithful members of the body of Christ, nor should we want him to, but he still has quite a bit to say *to* us on the topic of what it means to be the church in the modern world.

On the other hand, I have no wish simply to "poach"[26] isolated statements, ideas, or images from his writings for my own purposes without regard for the integrity of his work, in effect turning what he has written into a blank wall on which to tag whatever graffiti I choose. Because his writings contain so many memorable lines (some of which are the result of less than stellar translations), they are ripe for this kind of exploitation. Though the most egregious examples came early on in connection with the intense but short-lived death of God debate in the 1960s,[27] there are others who more

24. R. D. Williams, "Suspicion of Suspicion," 40.

25. *DBWE* 6:128.

26. See Certeau, *Practice of Everyday Life*, 165–76.

27. According to Eberhard Bethge, one of the principal figures of that movement, William Hamilton, acknowledged that their references to Bonhoeffer represented a "creative misuse of Bonhoeffer." Bethge, *Bonhoeffer*, 24.

recently have deliberately engaged in this practice.[28] I suppose they should be commended for their honesty, if nothing else.

Another method of using an author's work in a constructive fashion is bricolage, which refers to the use of ideas and lines of thought without developing a more extensive continuity between one's own work and that of the other author.[29] Jeffrey Stout has argued that all great works of creative ethical thought, as well as some not so great ones, involve bricolage: "They start off by taking stock of problems that need solving and available conceptual resources for solving them. Then they proceed by taking apart, putting together, reordering, weighting, weeding out, and filling in." Stout names Thomas Aquinas as a *bricoleur*, working creatively with Jewish, Pauline, Platonic, Stoic, Augustinian, Islamic, and Aristotelian elements to form his masterwork, the *Summa Theologica*.[30] In this sense of the term, then, bricolage is a tried-and-tested method of argumentation in theological circles, making use, among other things, of what Augustine aptly refers to as Egyptian gold.[31]

What I am attempting to do with Bonhoeffer's thought, however, goes beyond bricolage. Though I do seek to go on and go further with regard to the questions he raises and the descriptions and analyses he puts forward, I nonetheless see my working in close alignment and continuity with what I take to be the main trajectories in his theology and in his life. Theology, when done well, is a microcosm of human life well lived, consisting of both recollection and nonidentical repetition. A good interpretation of an author's work may use images, ideas, and arguments in ways that he may never have anticipated, but to which (it is hoped) he would have responded favorably. This is the warrant for figural interpretations of the Old Testament in light of the coming of Christ, an approach to scripture that Bonhoeffer employs in his preaching and writing, to the consternation of biblical scholars of his day (and ours). Aristotle states that events in a good story "occur unexpectedly and at the same time in consequence of one another."[32] Given the dynamic nature of God's activity in Christ, in which the reality of God is united to the reality of the world, good theological interpretations exhibit the same character.

28. See, for example, Beaudoin, *Witness to Dispossession*, 103–22.

29. See, for example, several of the essays in Clark and Mawson, *Ontology and Ethics*.

30. Stout, *Ethics After Babel*, 75–76.

31. Augustine, *Confessions* VII.15; Augustine, *Teaching Christianity* II.60.

32. Aristotle, *Poetics* 1452a. Interpretive disagreements may therefore have more to do with the assumptions that the various participants bring to the conversation than with what is indicated or implied in a text.

Though my primary aim in this book is constructive and not exegetical, a comprehensive picture of Bonhoeffer's overall theological project does emerge, elements of which some will contest (and not always the same elements). One persistent line of interpretation that has taken hold in North America in particular—but which, I contend, does not do justice to Bonhoeffer—argues that during the war he abandons his earlier embrace of a peace ethic and adopts a more "realistic" ethic that converges with the Christian realism of Reinhold Niebuhr.[33] Renate Wind, for example, states that "it had become clear to him that his own ethical rigorism no longer worked; that it was too much bound up with his own personal search for perfection."[34]

By contrast, I count myself among those who see a substantial continuity between his earlier and later writings, though it is important to allow for development and change of emphasis as he matures and faces new and difficult challenges. I submit that reading him in this way not only makes better sense of what he writes, but it also makes for a more faithful and incisive theology in our time. Among other things, continuity means that, as Ernst Feil puts it, "Bonhoeffer differentiated between Christianity or Christian faith and religion, but he could not separate Christianity and church."[35] Moreover, to the extent that it even makes sense to talk about Bonhoeffer as proposing a "realism" of some sort, his understanding of what is real is not determined pragmatically by what will "work," but by what God has accomplished, continues to accomplish, and finally will achieve in Jesus Christ.

Attempts to make Bonhoeffer fit neatly into categories such as evangelical or mainline, conservative or progressive, are also bound to come up short.[36] The complexities and nuances of ecclesial and political life in Germany in the first half of the twentieth century do not map cleanly onto the intellectual and social landscape of the United States, a fact he documents in his reflections on Protestantism in America, "Protestantism Without Reformation."[37] Moreover, his understanding of human existence is from start to finish eschatological, which rules out assimilation to any political stance in a fallen world. No doubt he has affinities with certain currently dominant categories—for example, the notion of human rights, though even here his understanding, unlike classic liberal conceptions rooted in

33. See, for example, Marsh, *Strange Glory*, 315, 341–42; Kelly and Nelson, *Cost of Moral Leadership*, 108; and Gides, *Pacifism, Just War, and Tyrannicide*.

34. Wind, *Dietrich Bonhoeffer*, 144.

35. Feil, *Theology of Dietrich Bonhoeffer*, 175.

36. See, for example, Metaxas, *Bonhoeffer*, and Marsh, *Strange Glory*.

37. *DBWE* 15:438–62.

the philosophical tradition of John Locke, is inextricably connected with a determinate conception of the good in Christ.[38]

Though some have asserted that toward the end of life Bonhoeffer downplays the tight connection between his Christology and the church,[39] there is little evidence that he departs from his earlier assertion that it is only "because proclamation and the sacraments are carried out in the church" that we can "inquire about Christ."[40] If anything, a profound this-worldliness in a post-Christendom world calls for a renewed emphasis on ecclesiology. As he puts it at the end of *Ethics*, the church should be seen both as an instrument and a means to the end of effectively proclaiming Christ to the whole world, *and* as the goal and center of all that God is doing with the world, as "the place where the world fulfills its own destiny; the church-community is the 'new creation,' the 'new creature,' the goal of God's ways on earth." It is in this context that he invokes the crucial concept of *Stellvertretung* to define the connection between this double divine purpose, as the Christian community both bears witness to a fallen world, but also stands in the place in which that world should stand.[41]

The connection that Bonhoeffer draws between Christ and the church is not, however, restricted to what happens within either the material or the spiritual confines of the church, for the church communicates the unlimited message of Christ through its delimited resources, and the universality of that message summons believers back into the delimited domain of the church-community.[42] The church exists, in other words, to demonstrate to a world come of age that it is different just to the extent that God became human, lived among us, died and was raised from the dead; it exists to show the world that the boundaries of tribe and language, people and nation, no longer define what it means to be a human being; it exists so that the world is allowed to be the world, to be that which is loved, judged, and reconciled in Jesus Christ; it exists not for its own sake, but for the sake of the world, offering itself as a sacrament of union with God and unity among humans.

38. Bonhoeffer states that human beings have no rights before God (hence the notion of human rights as such has no ontological basis), but the gift of natural life does entail the notion of rights, though it cannot be rightly understood apart from the particularity of social and historical circumstances (*DBWE* 6:180).

39. See, for example, Pangritz, "Who Is Jesus Christ, for Us, Today?," 151.

40. *DBWE* 12:310.

41. *DBWE* 6:404–5 (*DBW* 6:408). The concept of *Stellvertretung* has no English cognate, and has been variously (though not happily) translated as "deputyship" and "vicarious representative action." Though from time to time I use the latter expression, for the most part I leave it untranslated or render it in an extended phrase such as Christ's suffering, or the church's action, on behalf of the world.

42. *DBWE* 6:405.

One of my assumptions in developing this portrait of Bonhoeffer is that he is a dogmatician and not an ethicist as that term is typically used. The discipline of ethics, as O'Donovan has argued, has no specific set of objects, no particular slice of reality, for which it can claim proprietary ownership. It is rather "the explication of the logic of practical reason that directs our conduct, individual and collective." Ethical reasoning terminates, not in a descriptive judgment about things in general or about some particular feature of the world, but in a practical judgment having to do with how we act in connection with this or that feature of the world. As such, practical judgment is dependent on some assumed set of descriptions about the world, which is another way of saying that it presupposes a social and cosmic imaginary. Practical reason is an extension of descriptive reason broadly conceived, building on these descriptions in order to indicate the path we should take through the world.[43]

Bonhoeffer's theological ethics, by contrast, explicitly and extensively engage in developing further the descriptive and referential work of dogmatics or systematic theology. He states in *Ethics* that the problem of Christian ethics "is God's reality revealed in Christ become real . . . among God's creatures, just as the subject matter of doctrinal theology is the truth of God's reality revealed in Christ."[44] This approach to Christian ethics leads him almost immediately to a consideration of the question of the good, which together with truth and beauty comprise the transcendentals, each of which is convertible with being. Theological inquiry can be carried out from the perspective of any one of the three, and Bonhoeffer increasingly operates from the good in his writings, but never in isolation from truth and, to a lesser extent, beauty.[45]

The importance of recognizing Bonhoeffer's writings as dogmatic in nature is in part to account for their poetic character. The ability to know how to go on and go further in the use of the expressions of a language, says Alasdair MacIntyre, constitutes that part of the ability of every language user that is poetic. Poets do not have an exclusive claim to this ability, but only develop it to a preeminent degree.[46] Bonhoeffer exhibits this ability

---

43. O'Donovan, *Church in Crisis*, 37–38.

44. *DBWE* 6:49.

45. Though he mentions beauty only in passing in *Ethics*, Bonhoeffer refers to it numerous times in his prison writings. That said, he does little to reverse what Natalie Carnes describes as the marginalization and exile of beauty "from her once-central location in theological thought and scholarly work" (*Beauty*, 1.) The work of Carnes and other theologians to restore beauty to a central place in theology suggests a way of distinguishing between approaches to dogmatics in terms of which transcendental takes the lead: doctrine (truth), ethics (goodness), or aesthetics (beauty).

46. MacIntyre, *Whose Justice? Which Rationality?*, 382.

as well, his works consisting of "beautiful iterations of doctrine, a sort of visionary orthodoxy."[47] His books, sermons, and essays are replete with descriptions that have captivated the imagination of countless readers for decades. But as Christian Gremmels cautions, Bonhoeffer's focus "is *not* the 'coming of age,' 'this-worldliness,' and 'religionlessness' of the modern world." Though these enigmatic expressions are winsome and compelling, they function only as auxiliary terms that derive their significance solely in relation to Bonhoeffer's primary concern, which is "the claim of Jesus Christ on the world that has come of age," and these other ideas are noteworthy only to the extent that they serve the theological task of witnessing to Jesus Christ in the present.[48]

The job of parsing these terms constitutes the grammatical work of theology, a task that Bonhoeffer takes seriously, as even a casual perusal of his Christology lectures demonstrates.[49] Grammar, writes Ludwig Wittgenstein, "tells what kind of object anything is,"[50] up to and including that object we call the world. Our ability to reason, to "'take in' as a unity, the whole and the universal in reality,"[51] presupposes a stable (though never static) grammatical structure to a language in use. As a form of critical inquiry, grammar attends to the ways a particular community uses language at a specific time and place, explicating what it makes sense to say about something for members of that community, what it is for talk about some *thing*, be it person, event, or object, to qualify *as* talk about that thing. It thus "articulates the terms in which that kind of thing can intelligibly be represented (truly or falsely)."[52]

The work of grammar is a vital component of the interpretive work of theology, for it is through the church's distinctive, even peculiar use of the languages that it has appropriated throughout the centuries that theology formulates its understanding of how women and men should live, move, and have their being in the world, and of the origin, essence, and goal of that life, that movement, that existence. The practices of intellectual, moral, and spiritual formation that take place in and through the church— baptism, Eucharist, catechetical and mystagogical instruction, confession, proclamation, scripture reading, prayer, reconciliation, the giving and receiving of counsel, and works of mercy and justice—presuppose a stable

47. Robinson, "Dietrich Bonhoeffer," 115.

48. *DBWE* 8:588–89, Gremmel's emphasis.

49. *DBWE* 12:299–360.

50. Wittgenstein, *Philosophical Investigations*, 116e.

51. *DBWE* 6:174.

52. Mulhall, "Wittgenstein on Faith," 200.

understanding of how we use language. Crafted slowly, sometimes painfully over many centuries in a cautious, approximate, and often negative mode, this ever-evolving grammar is foundational for reading scripture, but also for reading the "text" of the world and all it contains. A theological grammar in good working order is therefore a necessary condition for the body of Christ to worship, act, and think as a corporate body that exists to testify, by truthful proclamation and responsible action on behalf of the whole world, to the presence and power of the triune God.

Finally, given Bonhoeffer's repeated emphasis on the claim of Christ on the whole of life and on the whole person,[53] a profound this-worldliness is from beginning to end political, or as he puts it in *Discipleship*, "political."[54] The scare quotes are significant (as they always are in his writings), suggesting that the church is distinct from the type of polity represented by the state (which many simply assume to be the sole and thus paradigmatic form of political association), and yet it directly challenges the claim that the state makes on its inhabitants regarding the whole of life. Bonhoeffer struggles with the question of the relationship between politics and "politics," statecraft and churchcraft, his entire life, which is why his interpreters who have very different positions on this matter can find something to support their views in his writings. He initially posits a very close relationship between the church and the German people [*Volk*]: "Every people . . . has within itself a call from God to create its history, to enter into the struggle that is the life of the nations. This call must be heeded amid the growth and development so that it takes place before the face of God. God calls a people to diversity, to struggle, to victory."[55] Though he later moves away from this kind of cultural and racial nationalism to embrace the nascent ecumenism of the day and articulate a peace ethic rooted in the Sermon on the Mount, he never does come to a definitive conclusion, and thus I must go beyond what he explicitly offers.

The theological significance of Bonhoeffer's ecclesial focus needs to be considered in juxtaposition to a type of nostalgia for Christendom on the part of many theologians. This nostalgia is not for the forms that the *corpus christianum* took in the past, which he derides as the *salto mortale*, the death leap, back to the Middle Ages.[56] It is instead a kind of cosmopolitan aspiration that is often accompanied by a de-emphasis on the church. Such aspirations seldom stray far from imperialist aims, beginning with the

53   *DBWE* 6:97, 146–47; *DBWE* 8:395, 456–57.
54   *DBWE* 4:261–62.
55   *DBWE* 10:373.
56   *DBWE* 8:478.

Stoic writings of Marcus Aurelius, who hands on the fruit of a long history of speculation in antiquity about the links between the order of the physical world, the *cosmos*, exemplified in the motion of the stars and planets, and that of the human world, the *polis*.[57] Though all such global aspirations, whether Christian or Stoic in form, are predicated, as Gerald Schlabach puts it, on "a vision of *shalom*" in which "right relationship with God is rightly ordering and reintegrating every relationship and all of life," their chief failing is that they do not reckon with the Faustian bargain they must make with the technological powers that currently organize the world. In spite of their good intentions, all such efforts invariably represent "a premature effort to grasp through faithless violence at the fullness of life that is God's to give fully at the eschaton."[58] In Bonhoeffer's terms, the cosmopolitan impulse represents the compromise solution to what he calls the "lasting and irremovable tension" between the present age and the age to come, a move that absolutizes the essence of human beings as they presently are.[59]

The alternative to such premature and presumptuous hopes, grounded as they are on the conflation of an overly realized eschatology with the will to mastery that animates the social technologies that organize life in the modern world, is not a sectarian withdrawal of some sort on the part of the church. On the contrary, as Bonhoeffer puts it in the preface to *Discipleship*, "Today it seems so difficult to walk with certainty the narrow path of the church's decision and yet remain wide open to Christ's love for all people, and in God's patience, mercy and loving-kindness (Titus 3:4) for the weak and godless. Still, both must remain together, or else we will follow merely human paths." He repeats this position in *Ethics*, stating that any action in accord with reality as it exists in the uniting of God and the world in Christ must both acknowledge the status quo and protest against it: "Affirmation and contradiction come together in concrete action in the world."[60]

In other words, the church must maintain its distinctiveness, not over against humanity as a whole, but as Rowan Williams states, "from all communities and kinships whose limits fall short of the human race,"[61] and thus which comprise the merely human paths that prematurely seek to establish what is God's to achieve. The church, according to its distinctive "political" character, exists and acts to "'remember' the future" for all nations and peoples, and in remembering become for the world an imaginative

57. Marcus Aurelius, *Meditations* 3.11, 4.3.

58. Schlabach, "Deuteronomic or Constantinian," 456.

59. *DBWE* 6:104, 154.

60. *DBWE* 4:40; *DBWE* 6:223–24.

61. R. D. Williams, *On Christian Theology*, 233.

interpretation of the world "in terms of the presence to it of Christ, its future."[62] Through the interaction of memory (starting with scripture and liturgy) and imagination (the ability to create adequate representations of reality by combining elements provided by memory[63]) the body of Christ becomes the sacramental sign of what Bonhoeffer calls the polyphony of life.[64]

The emphasis on the church is dialectical and ironic. It is not the King-dom of God, and as history testifies, it too often reverts to what Bonhoeffer names the *sicut deus*, the fallen character of humankind that erupts from our idolatrous desire to be like God rather than participate in Christ's re-creation of the *imago Dei*.[65] The community and communion of Christ is implicated in virtually every onerous aspect of a world come of age, and we must live in a state of permanent dissatisfaction with it.[66] And yet in spite of its decadence, corruption, and "sheer silliness," writes Herbert McCabe, "there is nowhere else to go . . . here are the words of eternal life, here is the language, the human presence and contact of the future." The ironic and dialectical characterization of the church is not merely negative, how-ever, nor is it simply a warning not to confuse the church for the kingdom. Instead, it enables us to detect in our present language the presence of the language of the future, and thus the communication of that future to us.[67]

Structure of the Book

In the first three chapters I examine two concepts that Bonhoeffer devel-ops in *Letters and Papers from Prison*, one having to do with the central idea of the this-worldliness of Christianity, and the other, with the ironic myth of a world come of age. As I have already noted, Bonhoeffer asserts that Christianity has at its core a deep and abiding this-worldliness that is grounded in the apocalyptic witness of the New Testament to the uniting of the reality of God with the reality of the world in Jesus Christ. The notion of this-worldliness may be disconcerting for those whose understanding

62. McCabe, *Law, Love and Language*, 141, 143.

63. R. D. Williams, *Edge of Words*, 45.

64. *DBWE* 8:393–94.

65. *DBWE* 3:111–14.

66. Guardini, *Church and the Catholic*, 55.

67. McCabe, "Comment," 229; *God Matters*, 178. Joerg Rieger and Kwok Pui-lan suggest an alternative in their book *Occupy Religion*, pointing to the recent Occupy Movement protests as a possibility. But as Eugene McCarraher points out, this move-ment, and theologies tied to it and to all such movements, cannot deliver what they promise. McCarraher, "Love Covers a Multitude."

of Christian faith see it as concerned primarily about the next world, the so-called afterlife. Nevertheless, he argues that the gospel addresses human-kind in the midst of their lives now, not in a shallow or banal manner, but in a way that "shows discipline and includes the ever-present knowledge of death and resurrection."[68] As for the irony implicit in the notion of a world come of age, Bonhoeffer's main concern in proposing this idea has to do precisely with how best to confront the technological organization and governance of life in the modern world with the uniting of God and world in Christ.

The next three chapters critique the concepts of religion, culture, and race, all crucial terms in the lexicon and grammar of the modern world. Over the last five hundred years these notions have served as social technologies used by the governing powers of the age to describe, differentiate, classify, and control the alien, the stranger, the other. Bonhoeffer's critique of the concept of religion as a constructive theological category for interpreting Christian life and thought provides the initial basis for crucial insights into the ways a world come of age accounts for difference using these notions. Such a critique helps the church understand not only how the world got to this juncture but also how it was implicated in their parturition, in order that it may extricate itself from their influence and cultivate once again a profound this-worldliness.

There are other concepts that I could have included with religion, culture, and race in this study—for example, nature, a term that also has undergone a substantial and significant change in meaning.[69] Up until the thirteenth century it principally denoted the essential character of a thing in accordance with its specific end and function, and thus when it was a fully developed member of its species. Should one pose a question about nature, the question would come back, the nature of what? In other words, what is it that you are asking about? The nature of a seed, in this regard, is to become a fully developed plant. The nature of a human being is to be a fully rational man or woman (sadly, this understanding was denied to too many in antiquity). We still retain this sense of the concept when we say that it is the nature of a carnivorous animal, a wolf or tiger, to hunt and kill other animals for its food. We also use it, though less often, to speak about moral traits of human being (e.g., we say it is natural for parents to care for their offspring).

---

68. *DBWE* 8:485–86.

69. Other concepts not dealt with in this volume include gender and sexuality. Per-haps the most sustained treatment of these contested ideas from the perspective that I develop here is Coakley, *God, Sexuality, and the Self.*

In the thirteenth century a distinction was introduced between super-natural and natural activities and ends. The notion of the supernatural was correlated with the gift of divine grace, which opened up room to think about what was natural as a given rather than as a gift. As David Burrell rightly observes, "A conceptual device which was to prove immensely useful in opening traditional Augustinian theology to assimilate the analysis of Ar-istotle unwittingly augmented a tendency to 'naturalize' the created universe and so further obscured the theological import of the Christian profession of faith in the creator."[70] A conceptual instrument was now in hand to make a hard-and-fast separation between the human and nonhuman worlds so that the mastery of the latter by the former becomes imaginable. A series of criti-cal divisions followed: the separation of, and sovereignty of, history from nature, the distinction of *Naturwissenschaften* from *Geisteswissenschaften* and "fact" from "value" in nineteenth-century academic discourse, and so on. As "nature," the nonhuman aspects of creation are repositioned for our use as "natural resources" in pursuit of our self-selected values. Whereas it once designated an order of things that was independent of human thought and action, standing over against our ability to engage and shape the world of which we were inextricably a part, "nature" now refers to that which has value only to the extent that we confer it.[71] The current ecological crisis facing all humanity is the most evident consequence of this technological development.

I have not expanded the critique of "nature" into a separate chapter for several reasons, in part because it is not a focal concern for Bonhoeffer, but primarily because it is deserving of much greater explication and develop-ment than I am able to provide for it in this work. Its absence should not be interpreted therefore as a tacit assertion that it is a minor issue in relation to the other foci in this study. Global climate change could well be the prover-bial straw that collapses the entire technological organization that has been built over the last several centuries. If this turns out to be the case, it would constitute the ultimate irony associated with the myth of a world come of age, creating the instruments of its own demise.[72]

The next two chapters take a constructive turn, as I develop two of Bonhoeffer's more seminal insights into the character of Christian faith. The first chapter revolves around his contention that the church's life and witness have suffered because we have failed to read the New Testament in

---

70. Burrell, *Freedom and Creation*, 3–4.

71. Rouse, *Knowledge and Power*, 66.

72. For those who wish to pursue this most important question, I would suggest that they begin with Northcott, *A Political Theology of Climate Change*.

light of the Old. Implicit in his admonition, and especially in the selection of Old Testament texts he cites in his prison correspondence, is the basis of a serious challenge to the varieties of supersessionism that have fueled the distortions wrought within the body politic of the church by the technologies of religion, culture, and race. In the following chapter I extend Bonhoeffer's metaphor of the polyphony of life, developing it as a way of describing the ecclesial shape and apocalyptic character of profound worldliness in a world come of age.

The last chapter, in which I take up the question of Bonhoeffer's involvement in the conspiracy against Adolf Hitler during World War II, forms a kind of coda to the book. His decision to cast his lot with the conspirators quickly became the focus of the debate about what it means to act responsibly for others. I propose to refocus attention around the question of what we in our time and place should learn from his decision in comparison to that made by another group of Christians in France.

1

A Sacramental This-Worldliness

"Yes'm," The Misfit said as if he agreed. "Jesus thrown everything off balance."

—FLANNERY O'CONNOR, "A Good Man Is Hard to Find"

IN RICHARD STRAUSS'S OPERA *Ariadne auf Naxos*, the wealthiest man in Vienna hosts a grand banquet, to be followed by two performances—one a tragic grand opera based on the Ariadne legend, the other an example of Italian *commedia dell'arte*, featuring a cast of harlequins, nymphs, and buffoons. This is disconcerting to the young composer of the opera, given that the theme of his work is "the expression of ultimate solitude," a subject he thinks unsuitable for pairing with a vulgar comedy. Matters are only made worse when it is announced that the lord of the manor wishes that the two performances be staged simultaneously, in part to leave time for a fireworks display afterwards, but also because, after watching the rehearsals, he was also "most displeased that such a well-furnished establishment as his has been forced to accommodate a scene as miserable as a desert island." His plan was to liven up the somber character of the tragedy with characters from the comedy.

After an extended prologue in which the story and characters are introduced, the tragic production begins with the spotlight on Ariadne, who is grieving after being abandoned by her lover, Theseus. She declares that she will wait for Hermes, the messenger of death, to bring her suffering to an end by taking her to the underworld, the realm of death. Her lament is brusquely interrupted by the dance troupe, led by Zerbinetta, who is accomplished at improvisation, says the dance master, "as she always plays herself, you see. She can fit into any kind of *mise en scène*." Zerbinetta tells

Ariadne that what she actually desires is not death but a new lover. At that moment Bacchus comes onto the scene, whom Ariadne initially mistakes for Hermes. She is caught up in the advances of the deity of wine and eternal renewal, and turns her back on death. Bacchus speaks the last word: "Your pain has made me rich indeed; / my body is bathed in immortal desire / and Death will extinguish the stars in the heavens, / ere you perish in my embrace."[1]

The staging of two different performances in one space, at the same time, with the music, characters, and plot of one intruding on and interacting with those of the other, affords a superb illustration—or better yet, a splendid allegory—first for investigating what Dietrich Bonhoeffer describes as an essential feature of Christianity, and then for going on and going further with that description. From the time he returns from New York until his execution by the Gestapo, he contends against a conceptual framework that had entrenched itself in the Christian imagination in the modern era, which stipulates that faith occupies a sphere of operations utterly separate from the "worldly" concerns of politics, economics, and the like.[2] This framework assumes that there is one and only one public space created by the institution of the nation-state on which the grand theatre of the human is to be played out. The church is one of many voluntary associations that are permitted a limited role within this one performance, so long as it keeps to its proper place.[3] Bonhoeffer rejects this assumption in the strongest possible terms and contends instead for what he calls "the profound this-worldliness [die tiefe Diesseitigkeit] of Christianity."[4]

There are several aspects to this designation of what Bonhoeffer regards as central for Christian faith that need to be explicated at the outset, the first of which is that "world" is not a synonym for created reality as such. For human beings the world is both a material and a linguistic reality, and thus it can never be taken as simply a given, but always as something that we human beings fashion for ourselves. The various and conflicting ways we have configured our common life, the structures that divide us, mean that

1. Richard Strauss, *Ariadne auf Naxos*. I am deeply indebted to William Cavanaugh in *Migrations of the Holy*, not only for bringing Strauss's opera to my attention, but also for the way he uses it to relate Augustine's understanding of the two cities to the modern political setting, an interpretation that, *mutatis mutandis*, also applies to Bonhoeffer's understanding of this-worldliness.

2. *DBWE* 6:58. Though the concept of modernity can have a variety of meanings, in this volume I use it to designate the period that comes after the middle of the sixteenth century. This is not a hard and fast definition, as elements of what is now associated with the modern world can be traced to the twelfth or thirteenth centuries.

3. Cavanaugh, *Migrations of the Holy*, 64.

4. *DBWE* 8:485 (*DBW* 8:541).

"world" is an essentially contested concept. To borrow an expression from Sarah Coakley, "worldliness" is not natural, but always "performed." Which performance we take to be decisive therefore makes all the difference.[5]

Second, the meaning of profound worldliness is therefore not to be found in the production of sermons, biblical commentaries, systematic theologies, scholarly monographs, or works of fiction. The reading and writing of texts do play an important role, says Nicholas Lash, but the fundamental form of interpreting the wager of faith subsists in patterns of human action and passion: what was said, done, and suffered by those in biblical Israel, culminating with the life and passion of Jesus and the early church, and what is said, done, and suffered by those who are presently caught up in the counterpoint[6] of revelation that these people and events initiated. These patterns, says Lash, render the one "whose words and deeds, discourse and suffering, 'rendered' the truth of God in human history."[7]

Third, Bonhoeffer understands that if these patterns of worldliness are to be visible for all to see, the church needs its own space for its distinctive performance, as it were, on the world stage. He points out that a truth, doctrine, or religion does not need a space of its own, for as with all such things these notional entities are bodiless. They need only to be heard, learned, and understood. By contrast, the incarnate Son of God needs not just ears and hearts but actual, living human beings who are his followers, for he calls to himself a community that everyone can see: "Those who had been called could no longer remain hidden; they were the light which has to shine, the city on a hill which is bound to be seen." Standing over both Lord and followers in this visibility is the cross, and thus for the sake of their fellowship with Christ the disciples had to give up everything and take on suffering and persecution, all the while receiving back in visible form all that they had given up: brothers and sisters, fields and houses (Mark 10:28–31).[8]

---

5. Coakley, *Powers and Submissions*, 158. Though a profound worldliness is not "natural" it is also not "unnatural" in the sense that Bonhoeffer uses those terms, as that which is open or closed to the coming of Christ (*DBWE* 6:173).

6. "Counterpoint" refers to the technique used by composers to bring together independent melodic lines such that they form elaborate harmonies. Bonhoeffer speaks in several of his prison letters of the polyphony of life, in which our love for God establishes the cantus firmus—the lead melody in a polyphonic composition, to which the other melodies relate to form constantly unfolding harmonic patterns—to which our other loves are related (*DBWE* 8:393–94). I develop this image of the polyphony of life more fully in chapter 8, where it serves as the generative image for the form of worldliness to which the church is summoned.

7. Lash, *Theology on the Way to Emmaus*, 42, 40.

8. *DBWE* 4:226.

Finally and crucially, Bonhoeffer invariably juxtaposes the idea of profound this-worldliness, not just to conceptions of Christianity that are focused on otherworldly realms, but also to deficient and deceptive performances of what it means to be worldly. He thus sketches a very different picture of what it means to be "worldly" from that configured by the modern age. The world as such is the stage on which two distinct productions are being presented. The church performs what Bonhoeffer calls the polyphony of life in the midst of a world come of age, which is also a social performance that is orchestrated by "technological organization of all kinds,"[9] foremost among which are the nation-state and global capitalism. Both performances occupy the same stage and make use of the same goods, and both are concerned with the same questions: "What is the purpose of human life? How should human life be ordered to achieve that purpose?"[10] Like the intrusion of the comedy troupe into the young composer's tragic opera, the church intrudes on godless and banal conceptions of worldliness by participating in, and bearing witness to, the uniting of the reality of God and the reality of the world in Jesus Christ.

The performance of worldliness on the part of the Christian community presupposes an imaginative construal of the stage on which the members of that body "politic" live, move, and have their being. The key question is which construal forms the imaginary of the church. The fundamental motifs of Bonhoeffer's conception of profound this-worldliness derive from what Philip Ziegler identifies as the apocalyptic character of his theology.[11] There is a risk in describing his theology thus, for it is popularly associated with bizarre speculations about the imminent end of the physical universe and expectations regarding an otherworldly paradise, neither of which is of concern to Bonhoeffer. Ziegler's use of the term is predicated instead on recent studies by biblical scholars who use the term to name the imaginative format for the disclosure of God's action in Jesus Christ that sets the world to rights.

Every such construal at some point requires a metaphysical surmise to lay bare the contemplative and noninstrumental dimension to the shared existence projected by its performance.[12] The existence of this permanent

9. *DBWE* 8:393–94, 500.

10. Cavanaugh, *Migrations of the Holy*, 64.

11. Ziegler, "Dietrich Bonhoeffer."

12. See R. D. Williams, "Between Politics and Metaphysics," 6. Experienced readers of Bonhoeffer might object at this point, noting his rejection of "metaphysics," especially in *Letters and Papers from Prison* (*DBWE* 8:447–48). But as I argue in chapter 4, Bonhoeffer has a very specific and delimited sense of metaphysics in these passages that does not rule out a more general use of the term.

setting is seldom if ever self-evident, and it must be explicated time and again whenever interpretive doubts emerge about the nature of the performance, as they invariably do.[13] As we shall see, Bonhoeffer identifies several of the interpretive doubts that haunt theology in the modern age. In response to these doubts he coins a set of enigmatic terms—a world come of age, a nonreligious interpretation of scripture and Christianity, and above all this-worldliness—to serve, not as replacements for the Bible or the traditional language of dogmatics, but as the means for faithfully and truthfully interpreting the inheritance that had been handed down to his generation (and subsequently to us) over the last few centuries.

Bonhoeffer works diligently throughout his career to develop a theology that can assist the church as it bears truthful witness that the whole of reality "has already been drawn into and is held together in Christ,"[14] and to do so before a world that has undergone substantial and far-reaching changes and that prides itself on having come of age. The notion of this-worldliness, understood as a performative gesture, ties many of his proposals together in ways that are both insightful and in need of extension and elaboration.

Bonhoeffer on the Grammar of Worldliness

Christians are called not to religiosity but to a profound this-worldliness, says Bonhoeffer, which means to be human "in the same way that Jesus was a human being." He quickly adds that he does not mean "the shallow and banal this-worldliness of the enlightened, the bustling, the comfortable, or the lascivious." On the contrary, profound worldliness "shows discipline and includes the ever-present knowledge of death and resurrection." This type of worldliness only happens when we throw ourselves without reservation into the arms of God, "living fully in the midst of life's tasks, questions, successes and failures, experiences, and perplexities." Not our own suffering, but the suffering of God in the world becomes paramount. Faith means staying awake with Jesus in Gethsemane.[15]

The assertion that worldliness is a defining mark of Christian faith does not abruptly appear late in *Letters and Papers from Prison* but is a persistent emphasis in his writings. It first appears in embryonic form in a set of lectures on the nature of the church given at the University of Berlin during the summer 1932 term. In a lecture reconstructed from student notes,

13. Milbank, *Theology and Social Theory*, 385.

14. *DBWE* 6:58.

15. *DBWE* 8:485–86.

Bonhoeffer insists that God penetrates every aspect of everyday reality. The church must therefore see itself, not as removed from the world, but as embedded in its everydayness. The word it proclaims must stand in that everydayness, for it is not an "exceptional light" outside the profane realm. And in the penultimate lecture of the series, he explicitly links together the concept of worldliness (*Weltlichkeit*) and the Christian character (*Christlichkeit*) of the church, stating that the church exists in the world and thus "does not wish to give a picture of the church-community of saints; renunciation of [the] ideal of purity."[16]

In an essay on the petition in the Lord's Prayer for the kingdom of God to come, written that same year, Bonhoeffer contrasts the kind of worldliness that he later connects to the form of Christ taking form in the church with, on the one hand, an otherworldliness that grows out of a hatred of the earth, and on the other, a pious, "Christian" secularism, which sees believers as bound completely to the earth and fully involved in the confrontation of power with power. These secularists seek to build strong fortresses in which they can dwell safely and securely with God, and in their own strength secure the right of God to be in the world. For all the obvious differences, what connects the two groups is that they no longer believe in God's kingdom.[17]

It is a third group, the wanderers (*die Wanderers*), who neither seek to flee the earth nor hold hard and fast to it, that performs genuine this-worldliness. They love the earth that bears them because it is on the earth that they travel toward that foreign land, that city which is to come, which they love above all. Only the wanderers, who love both the earth and God in one, "can believe in God's kingdom."[18] A genuine love for both God and the earth, according to which our love for the earth finds its origin, essence, and goal in our love for God,[19] is possible only for those who, as Bonhoeffer puts it in *Creation and Fall*, live from the end, think from the end, act from the end, and thus live and speak "within the old world about the new world."[20]

16. *DBWE* 11:281, 328 (*DBW* 11:250–51, 299–300).

17. *DBWE* 12:285–88.

18. *DBWE* 12:286 (*DBW* 12:264–65). Though he does not emphasize the sense that we are wanderers on earth in his later writings, this is still his conviction in prison. In a letter to Bethge written at the end of 1943 he cites a line from the *Evangelisches Gesangbuch*: "that we may not forget / what one so readily forgets, / that this poor earth / is not our home," and then states that this "is indeed important but is nevertheless only the very last thing [*aber doch nur etwas Allerletztes*]. I believe we are so to love God in our *life* and in the good things God gives us and to lay hold of such trust in God that, when the time comes and is here—but truly only then!—we also go to God with love, trust, and joy" (*DBWE* 8:228).

19. *DBWE* 6:226; 8:394.

20. *DBWE* 3:21. *Creation and Fall* is based on lectures that Bonhoeffer was giving at the same time he writes "Thy Kingdom Come!"

It is these wanderers who truly can cultivate the profound this-worldliness that is Christian faith.

Those who love God's kingdom love it wholly as God's kingdom on earth: "The hour in which the church prays for the kingdom today forces the church, for better or worse, to identify completely with the fellowship of the children of the Earth and world. It binds the church by oaths of fealty to the Earth, to misery, to hunger, to death." Those who pray this prayer profess the most profound solidarity with the world (*tiefsten Zusammenstehens mit der Welt*).[21] Lurking in the background of this essay is Friedrich Nietzsche's critique of Christians as those who hate the earth.[22] Bonhoeffer draws a straight line from Friedrich Schleiermacher, who located religion in its own special province in the soul, to both Ludwig Feuerbach, "Schleiermacher's most consistent pupil," and Nietzsche, who insists that the human being is "not a transcendent being that only appears to exist, but is *ens realissimum* [the most real being]."[23] An otherworldly church has no problems attracting all the "weaklings" (*Schwächlichen*), "all those who are only too glad to be deceived, all the dreamers, all disloyal children of the Earth." Christian secularists, on the other hand, build fortresses to defend religion against the world. "How could it be otherwise?" Bonhoeffer writes. "The human being—including the religious person—enjoys a good fight and putting his strength to the test." Who could possibly object, save for the have-nots in their envy?[24]

In *Creation and Fall* he says that the blessing of God upon humankind at creation "affirms humankind wholly with the world of the living in which it is placed. It is humankind's whole empirical existence that is blessed here, its creatureliness, its worldliness, its earthliness." He states that the tree of life, which denotes humankind's boundary, stands at the center of human existence, not at the margin. The limit or constraint that humans seek at the margins is "the limit of the human condition, the limit of technology, the limit of what is possible for humanity," where, as he puts it in his prison correspondence, our human powers give out.[25] God, from whom and before

---

21. *DBWE* 12:288–89 (*DBW* 12:268–69).

22. "Christianity should not be beautified and embellished: it has waged deadly war against this higher type of man; it has placed all the basic instincts of this type under the ban. . . . Christianity has sided with all that is weak and base, with all failures; it has made an ideal of whatever *contradicts* the instinct of the strong life to preserve itself; it has corrupted the reason even of those strongest in spirit by teaching men to consider the supreme values of the spirit as something sinful, as something that leads into error—as temptations" (Nietzsche, *Antichrist*, 5).

23. *DBWE* 11:184–86 (*DBW* 11:147–48).

24. *DBWE* 12:286–87 (*DBW* 12:265–66).

25. *DBWE* 8:367.

whom humans have life, is by contrast both the boundary and center of human reality, of human existence as such.[26]

The next stage in the development of this idea comes in *Discipleship*, where Bonhoeffer first makes a decisive distinction between different conceptions of what constitutes genuine worldliness. It is imperative that Christians remain in the world, he writes, not because it possesses God-given goodness or because they are responsible for the course the world takes. They do so instead for the sake of the body of Christ who became incarnate, that is, for the sake of the church-community. They remain in the world to engage it "in a frontal assault [*Angriff*]." Disciples must, in other words, "'live out their vocation in this world' in order that their 'unworldliness' might become fully visible. The world must be contradicted within the world. That is the reason why Christ became a human being and died in the midst of his enemies."[27]

From both the context and his use of scare quotes it is clear that by unworldliness Bonhoeffer does not mean that Christians should see themselves disconnected from the day-to-day concerns of the world, and he clarifies his intention by an appeal to Luther's rationale for leaving the monastery and engaging in a secular vocation (*weltlichen Beruf*). It was not the "unworldliness" of monastic life that Luther attacked but the fact that within the confines of the cloister, this separation from the world in which most people lived, moved, and had their being, which in the early centuries of the church was a living protest against the first signs of cheap grace, had been transformed into a new spiritual conformity to it. True "unworldliness" always takes place in the midst of this world, and thus Luther, by calling Christians back into the world, calls them to become in the true sense of the word "unworldly."[28]

The most extended discussions of worldliness are located in *Ethics*, where Bonhoeffer states that Christians live in the world for the most part like everyone else. This is as it should be, he writes, for "the church is nothing but that piece of humanity where Christ really has taken form." Its primary concern is not at all with religion, "but with the existence in the world of whole human beings in all their relationships."[29] At the same time, he goes to great lengths to distinguish between the performance of worldliness he has in mind—the worldliness of faith and discipleship—and the justifica-

26. *DBWE* 3:68, 84–86.

27. *DBWE* 4:244 (*DBW* 4:260). Bonhoeffer also uses the image of a frontal assault to describe Luther's departure from the monastery, because "following Jesus now had to be lived out in the midst of the world" (*DBWE* 4:48; *DBW* 4:35).

28. *DBWE* 4:46–47, 244–45 (*DBW* 4:260–61).

29. *DBWE* 6:97.

tion of "the worldly as such" (*des Weltlichen an sich*). Only a distinction of this sort can at the same time allow the world to be the world, and show it to be world, that is, to be that which is loved, judged, and reconciled by God in Christ.[30]

Bonhoeffer carefully differentiates Christian worldliness from the world's own self-understanding and self-justification. He laments that in the seventeenth and eighteenth centuries Protestants embraced the whole the process of secularization, seeing in a misunderstanding of Luther's doctrine of the two kingdoms "a liberation and sanctification of the world and the natural order." Government, reason, economy, and culture claimed an autonomy that was at the same time said to be consistent with Christianity. The original impulse of the Reformation was forgotten and reinterpreted as the justification of the worldly as such. The ground in which rational and empirical science could bloom was thus prepared, and though the scientists were generally believers, "the disappearance of faith in God left behind only a rationalized and mechanized world."[31] The same emphasis is found in a section on the concept of vocation, which Bonhoeffer contends cannot be confused with a secular conception as a definite field of action, a definition he attributes to Max Weber, or with the kind of pseudo-Lutheranism that uses the term to sanction the worldly orders as such.[32]

In what was one of the first sections of *Ethics* to be drafted, "Christ, Reality, and Good," he introduces the idea of the worldly in connection with his insistence that there are not two realities, but only one, which is God's reality as revealed in Christ within the reality of the world: "Partaking in Christ, we stand at the same time in the reality of God and in the reality of the world." The world, which Christ embraces in his reality, has no reality of its own independent of God's revelation in Christ. As a result, he states that "it is a denial of God's revelation in Jesus Christ to wish to be 'Christian' without being 'worldly,' or [to] be worldly without seeing and recognizing the world in Christ." Once again his meticulous use of scare quotes alerts us to a nuanced understanding of worldliness.[33] There is but one world, but two different forms of worldliness.

One of Bonhoeffer's principal concerns is the division of reality into two distinct spheres, a notion that had entrenched itself in the working imaginary of Christian thought in the modern era, and for many continues to do so. There are not two realms, "but only *the one realm of the*

---

30. *DBWE* 6:114, 264 (*DBW* 6:104).
31. *DBWE* 6:114; cf. 289, 291.
32. *DBWE* 6:289, 290.
33. *DBWE* 6:58.

Christ-reality [Christuswirklichkeit], in which the reality of God and the reality of the world are united."[34] The paired concepts of worldly-Christian, natural-supernatural, profane-sacred, and rational-revelation do not refer to static opposites, with each occupying its "proper place,"[35] each prohibited from trespassing on its opposite. The world, the natural, the profane, and the rational do not exist in and for themselves, but by virtue of the incarnation are included in God from the outset. At the same time, however, though we should not separate these matters into discrete domains, we must also not confuse them. Their unity consists solely in their reconciliation in the life, death, and resurrection of Christ. Consequently, that which is Christian is not identical with what is worldly as such, nor is the natural identical with the supernatural or the rational with the revelational.[36] To borrow from Chalcedon, these matters can neither be confused nor separated.

We therefore err if we seek a principle to define either what is Christian or worldly independently of their reconciliation in Christ, a statement that reasserts a dogmatic axiom Bonhoeffer makes in his Christology lectures. In these lectures he rejects any reading of Chalcedon's formula that "speaks of the nature [Wesen] of God and human nature in the theoretical manner of an onlooker, as if these were two material things, normally distinguished from each other, which only come together in Jesus Christ."[37] In other words, the theological grammar regulating the concept of incarnation does not relate the two natures as two species of being, such that uniting them creates a hybrid, or as a zero-sum game, such that the more of one necessarily excludes to that same degree the other.

In like manner, what is Christian, if parsed in isolation from the world, becomes an abstract law that can then only be forced on the world as an alien principle. He cites the attempts to make the precepts of the Sermon on the Mount—abolition of military service, property, and the swearing of oaths—the law of action in the world, and when these attempts fail it gives rise to proposals making the worldly arena into a principle and according it rights of its own, "over against what is Christian," in the affairs of the world, "i.e., in all matters of political and historical action." In such matters all things Christian are thus declared to be out of their proper place: "This

34. Ibid.

35. Michel de Certeau argues that the modern world works systematically to establish a definitive and comprehensive knowledge and containment of persons, things, events, and groups by assigning these to their proper place within the social whole (*Practice of Everyday Life,* xix). I shall elaborate on this work of locating and confining Christianity at the margins of a world come of age in chapter 3.

36. *DBWE* 6:58–59.

37. *DBWE* 12:352; cf. DeJonge, *Bonhoeffer's Theological Formation,* 89–90.

whole arena is governed by the autonomous nature [*Eigengesetzlichkeit*] of the world. Things Christian belong to a special ecclesial, religious, or private domain in which alone they can be rightfully exercised."[38] These limits, by creating a proper place for "religious" matters, are clearly intended to confine and marginalize everything placed therein.

Bonhoeffer then contends, with a note of irony, that sectarianism or otherworldliness and secularism are united in their understanding of the worldly and the Christian as principles, because each construes these "independently of the fact of God's becoming human." As principles, what is Christian and what is worldly can only be seen as involved in an eternally insoluble conflict that all practical action cannot overcome. Christian existence becomes a tragic heroism, enduring "with the pathos of a very profound knowledge of reality," but a knowledge that is utterly alien to the sayings of Jesus and the total witness of the New Testament. Scripture does not commend Christian action in the world out of a bitter resignation over the rift between two autonomous realms, "but from the joy over the already accomplished reconciliation of the world with God, from the peace of the already accomplished work of salvation in Jesus Christ." As in Christ God and humanity become one, so also through Christ, and only through him, does what is Christian and what is worldly become one for the believer.[39]

Bonhoeffer is suspicious of all attempts to see what is authentically worldly as independent of the reality of God in Christ. In a short, unfinished essay titled "'Personal' and 'Objective' Ethics," probably written around the time that he was working on the *Ethics* manuscript, he states that the church does not abandon the world to itself (a theme that he repeats not only in *Ethics* but also in the prison correspondence[40]) but calls it to submit to the rule of Christ. The focus of this comment is the *primus usus*, the first use of the commandments, which have to do with the establishment of a just civil order. This use of the law, Bonhoeffer writes, is not concerned primarily with the action of Christians within the worldly orders, but with these orders as they exist within the will of God. Their purpose is not to Christianize them or to make them conform more closely to the church, which would entail an illicit abrogation of their "relative" autonomy, but to promote a genuine worldliness and "naturalness" in obedient response to the word of God. It is with respect to this genuine worldliness that worldly orders stand

---

38. *DBWE* 6:236–37 (*DBW* 6:235–36).

39. *DBWE* 6:237–38.

40. *DBWE* 8:373, 428, 431, 482.

under the dominion of Christ, and their relative autonomy consists not it their independence from the law of Christ, but from earthly heteronomies.[41]

Bonhoeffer returns to this notion of genuine worldliness in the last portion of the *Ethics* manuscript written, titled "The Concrete Command-ment and the Divine Mandates." It is noteworthy that he treats it, not simply in terms of God becoming flesh, but under the heading of Jesus Christ, the crucified Reconciler. The cross of Christ identifies worldliness as such, for "by its rejection of Jesus Christ the entire world has become godless, and . . . no effort on its part can lift this curse from it." Apart from the proclama-tion of the cross of Christ, and left to its own devices, the worldly always seeks to fulfill its unending thirst for its own deification, and ceases to be authentically worldly precisely at that point: "Consequently it is precisely this decidedly and exclusively worldly life that becomes trapped in a half-hearted pseudo-worldliness. It lacks the freedom and courage for a genuine and full-blown worldliness, that is, the freedom and courage to let the world be what it really is before God, a world that in its godlessness is reconciled with God."[42]

This same cross, however, is also the sign of the world's reconciliation with God, and thus it is the godless world that stands under this identifying mark of reconciliation. The cross sets us free to live in genuine worldliness before God in the middle of this godless world. This profound worldliness, which only exists because of the proclamation of the cross of Christ, liberates us from the delusion that is the self-deifying of the world precisely because it overcomes the tensions, conflicts, and divisions that exist between what is "Christian" and what is "worldly." The members of Christ's body are set free to a single-minded action and life in faith within the ambit of what God has already accomplished in the reconciliation made possible by the cross. It is from this standpoint that the godlessness and godforsakenness of the world are truthfully named. This recognition is crucial, because on its own the worldly will always seek to deify itself by establishing its own law over against the proclamation of Christ. When it does so it falls under its own spell, setting itself in God's place. When left to its own devices, the world is not satisfied with simply being worldly, but invariably, "it desperately and frantically seeks its own deification." This appetite for a decidedly and ex-clusively worldly life traps the world in its halfhearted pseudo-worldliness, and thus it lacks the freedom and courage to let a godless world be what God has made and reconciled it to be.[43]

41. *DBWE* 16:546; cf. *DBWE* 6:362.

42. *DBWE* 6:401.

43. *DBWE* 6:400–401.

The key distinction here is between what a godless world regards as worldly and what the church proclaims in the cross about worldliness. "A life of genuine worldliness," he writes, "is possible only through the proclamation of the crucified Christ." Genuine worldliness is a cruciform life, and thus it is not possible in contradiction to the proclamation of Christ, nor can it subsist alongside an essential autonomy of the worldly, which in the end is only a pseudo-worldliness. Indeed, says Bonhoeffer, it is precisely "in, with, and under" the proclamation of Christ's cross that the kind of worldliness he sees at the heart of Christianity is possible and real.[44] His use here of spatial imagery drawn from Lutheran sacramental theology gestures toward a specific way of looking at the church as a society[45] that exists not for itself but for God and, as example (*Vorbild*), for its neighbors:

> So the first task given to those who belong to the church of God is not to be something for themselves, for example, by creating a religious organization or leading a pious life, but to be witnesses of Jesus Christ to the world. For this the Holy Spirit equips those to whom the Spirit comes. Of course, it is presupposed that such a witness to the world can only happen in the right way when it comes out of sanctified life in God's church-community.[46]

The fullest development of a profound worldliness comes in Bonhoeffer's prison correspondence, first appearing in a letter to Bethge dated March 9, 1944, in which he expresses interest in a form of worldliness that in his estimation has its roots, not in the Renaissance or classical antiquity, but in the thirteenth century. This was a "Christian" worldliness, not an "emancipated" one (as always, he makes careful use of scare quotes), but he adds an important proviso: it was anticlerical in nature.[47] This negative assessment of clericalism, which occurs in four prison letters and is implied

44. *DBWE* 6:401.

45. As I discuss in more detail in chapter 3, using this term to describe the church challenges the assumption that there is one, unitary social space to which all those who live within the territorial boundaries of a state properly belong and in which they derive their fundamental identity. There are two societies, one that is coterminous with the state and the other gathered together in the church, and together they make up two performances of human life in a world come of age. See Cavanaugh, *Migrations of the Holy*, 18–33.

46. *DBWE* 6:64. These comments echo what Bonhoeffer says in his Christology lectures: "Only because proclamation and the sacraments are carried out in the church can we inquire about Christ" (*DBWE* 12:310).

47. *DBWE* 8:319–20. Clericalism is a consistent object of criticism in these letters. Bonhoeffer associates the term both with medieval heteronomy and with the cheap excuse of hiding behind "the faith of the church" rather than stating honestly what one believes (*DBWE* 8:478, 502).

in at least two others,[48] extends his critique of religion. What transpired in Jesus is not a religious happening but a cosmic event that radically changes the world, and it is this to which the church testifies. He does not elaborate on medieval worldliness in this letter, save to say that the fundamental concepts of humanism—humaneness, tolerance, leniency, and moderation—were already present.[49]

The next time Bonhoeffer mentions worldliness is in the letter of April 30, 1944. After a series of questions in which he questions the viability of the concept of religion as a basic term in the grammar of theology, he asks, "What does a church, a congregation, a sermon, a liturgy, a Christian life, mean in a religionless world?" He then wonders how to speak in a worldly way about God, how to go about living as "religionless-worldly" Christians, above all, how to see ourselves as ἐκ-κλησία, that is, as "those who are called out, without understanding ourselves religiously as privileged, but instead seeing ourselves as belonging wholly to the world?" These questions are central for him because they position the confession of Christ, not as the object of religion lingering at the margins of everyday life, but as truly lord of the world. Pressing the question further, he asks, "In a religionless situation, what do ritual [Kultus] and prayer mean? Is this where the 'arcane discipline' [Arkandisziplin], or the difference . . . between the penultimate and ultimate, have new significance?"[50]

In the conclusion to this letter Bonhoeffer distinguishes profound this-worldliness from the category of religion that expels God and faith to the boundaries of life, where anxiety and death are invoked to exploit human weakness and limitations. In a powerful summary of his position, he states that we should speak of God, not as a reality lurking at the boundaries of human existence, but in the center, not in weakness, death, and guilt, but in strength, life, and goodness. "That's the way it is in the Old Testament, and in this sense we don't read the New Testament nearly enough in light of the Old."[51]

Bonhoeffer frames this insistence that God and faith operate at the center of life with two important critiques of ways Christianity has typically been construed in the modern world, the first of which is that belief in the resurrection is the "solution" to the problem of death.[52] The proclamation

---

48. *DBWE* 8:172, 320, 427, 456, 478, 502.

49. *DBWE* 8:319–20.

50. *DBWE* 8:364–65.

51. *DBWE* 8:367. I shall return to the significance of his efforts to reclaim the Old Testament for Christian life and thought in chapter 7.

52. *DBWE* 8:366–67.

of Christ in the New Testament, like the way faith is spoken of in the Old Testament (but unlike the redemption myths of other traditions), does not have its sights set primarily on a reality beyond history and death: "The Christian hope of resurrection is different from the mythological in that it refers people to their life on earth in a wholly new way, and more sharply than the OT [Old Testament]. Unlike believers in the redemption myths, Christians do not have an ultimate escape route out of their earthly tasks and difficulties into eternity." They must drink this cup of earthly life to the dregs[53] as did Christ, "and only when they do this is the Crucified and Risen One with them, and they are crucified and resurrected with Christ." Both Old and New Testament are united on the affirmation that this-worldliness (*das Diesseits*) cannot be abolished ahead of time, for Christ takes hold of humankind in the midst of their lives.[54]

The second critique that Bonhoeffer makes in connection with the need to speak of God at the center of life has to do with the habit of both philosophy and theology to identify epistemic transcendence with the transcendence of God. He states emphatically that "God's 'beyond' is not what is beyond our cognition!"[55] He is drawing here on work that he develops initially in *Act and Being*, where he critiques attempts in nineteenth- and early twentieth-century theology to locate the reality of divine transcendence within the epistemic structures of the mind or spirit, thereby reducing the reality of revelation to a purely human possibility.[56] This critique and its implied reference to the contingent revelation of God in Christ's life, death, and resurrection take on added weight in connection with Bonhoeffer's description of genuine worldliness in *Ethics* and *Letters and Papers*, with their focus on our embodied existence within the world, fully caught up in the midst of its comings and goings, triumphs and tragedies.[57]

The essential character of worldliness continues to be consistently defined in the prison writings in terms of Christology. Being Christian means

---

53. A possible allusion to a statement by Ivan Karamazov to his brother Alyosha at the beginning of a conversation in which Ivan delivers his famous parable of the Grand Inquisitor. Dostoevsky, *Brothers Karamazov*, 230.

54. *DBWE* 8:447–48 (*DBW* 8:501).

55. *DBWE* 8:367.

56. *DBWE* 2:25–80. See DeJonge, *Bonhoeffer's Theological Formation*, 1–5, 12–14, 19–35.

57. With respect to the contingent nature of revelation, Bonhoeffer states in his Christology lectures that Christ is not timelessly and universally accessible as an idea, but "is heard as Word only there where he allows himself to be heard . . . only when and where it pleases the Father in heaven." Christ as the incarnate Word comprehends both the contingent nature of revelation and God's commitment to humankind (*DBWE* 12:317).

being human, and more specifically being the human being that Christ creates in us. Not the religious act, but participating in God's suffering in the world, makes one a Christian. "That," he writes, "is 'μετάνοια,' not thinking first of one's own needs, questions, sins, and fears but allowing oneself to be pulled into walking the path that Jesus walks, into the messianic event, in which Isa. 53 is now being fulfilled!" True humanity, the new human being created in and through Christ for us, exists fully in this world, though not in and for itself, but rather for the world's sake.[58]

Bonhoeffer's Apocalyptic Imagination

For Bonhoeffer, Christian worldliness refers to the mode of our participation in the reality of God revealed in Christ, and therefore in the whole of life and in the suffering of our fellow human beings. Given his emphasis on both the worldliness of faith and the centrality of divine revelation that comes to us from outside ourselves, and more precisely from the future, I need to specify the imaginative stage that is presupposed by his theology. We have already noted that he regards Christians as those who live in the world from the end, think about it from the end, and act in it from the end, and that only on this basis can a genuine and enduring love of both God and the earth be sustained. Eschatology is at the heart of a profound this-worldliness.

Few would question that an eschatological thread runs the length of Bonhoeffer's theology prior to the start of World War II. In *Sanctorum Communio* he insists that the logic of the primal state of humankind belongs wholly with eschatology.[59] Eschatological themes are especially prominent in *Discipleship*, in which he states that the Christian community is a colony of strangers and sojourners on earth, bearing witness in the midst of the world that its present form is passing away and that "all its hopes and dreams are set on the Lord's return."[60] This emphasis is continued in *Ethics*, where he locates true worldliness within the tensile relationship between last things (*die letzten Dinge*) and the things before the last (*die vorletzten Dinge*).[61]

Some have argued that near the end of his life he abandons or at least modifies his eschatological frame of reference in favor of a more "realistic"

58. *DBWE* 8:480.
59. *DBWE* 1:58.
60. *DBWE* 4:250.
61. *DBWE* 6:146–70; *DBWE* 8:213, 342, 365; cf. 373.

turn of mind,[62] but there is actually little in the prison writings to support such a substantial change of mind and heart. On the contrary, he goes out of his way to affirm continuity with what he had said and done in the past. In a note to Bethge written just prior to the crucial letter of April 30, 1944, he asserts that he had not changed a great deal, save for when he first became aware of his father's personality, and "at the time of my first impressions abroad," referring to the years 1928–31, when he served as an associate pastor in Spain and then spent a year in New York.[63] This observation is reaffirmed when, on the day after the failed attempt on Hitler's life, he writes that in spite of the dangers of misinterpretation inherent in it, he stands by what he wrote in *Discipleship*.[64]

The assumption made by many who downplay the significance of eschatology in Bonhoeffer's later theology is due no doubt to its association with otherworldliness and the neglect of life on this earth, which presupposes that eschatology and concern for living fully and completely in this world constitute a zero-sum game. Given the claims of popular speakers and authors who distort the primary sense and significance of biblical eschatology with bizarre speculations about "the end time," it is easy to understand why this assumption is made. Paul Lehmann notes that the extravagances of speculative eschatology confuse "large sections of the believing and the unbelieving American public."[65] Dubious readings of scripture, with their obsessions with timetables, numerology, and the like, should not prevent readers of Bonhoeffer from taking seriously the pervasive eschatological references in all of his writings, including his prison correspondence. Lehmann echoes Bonhoeffer's contention that "what is beyond this world is meant, in the gospel, to be there for this world"[66] when he states that

---

62. See, for example, Woelfel, *Bonhoeffer's Theology*, 251–52, and Feil, *Theology of Dietrich Bonhoeffer*, 152. The origin of the theory that Bonhoeffer downplays the centrality of the church after April 1944 is Müller, *Von der Kirche zur Welt*. Müller makes what I regard as a category error in the juxtaposition of church and world.

63. *DBWE* 8:357–58. In a 1942 letter to Max Diestel, Bonhoeffer states that these ventures "set my entire thinking on a track from which it has not yet deviated and never will" (*DBWE* 16:367).

64. *DBWE* 8:486. Florian Schmitz pinpoints the danger that could emerge from an improperly guided reading of *Discipleship*: "*the resolve to remain pure from guilt, no matter what evil is loose in the world and demands a decision on behalf of the oppressed.*" At the same time, Schmitz adds, if we fail to differentiate between Bonhoeffer's basic assumptions and the way these assumptions develop over time and circumstance, we shall miss the theological foundations of his work, "which have always been the same" ("Reading *Discipleship* and *Ethics* Together," 152–53).

65. Lehmann, "Evanston," 149.

66. *DBWE* 8:373.

"it makes no sense to talk about the 'last things' apart from what is going on here and now."[67] Eschatology, as Lehmann puts it, "has to do with the connection between the *course* and the *consummation* of human experience *in this world*."[68]

Another reason that interpreters of Bonhoeffer tend to downplay the eschatological dimensions of his work is that it competes with the eschatological thrust that a world come of age claims for itself. J. Kameron Carter charts the ways that "the West came to conceive of itself as an eschaton—the Utopian path and goal of progress for the world." In positing itself in this way it claimed that "Western Man [*sic*]" was "the stabilizing center . . . that rightly orders political and secular space."[69] The ersatz eschatology of a world come of age is what makes "ultimate" and "penultimate" problematic terms for translating the German *Letzten* and *Vorletzten* in Bonhoeffer. As John Macquarrie points out, these terms in English have connotations that do not always have the temporal-historical frame of reference that they can have in German, and which they have in Bonhoeffer's writings: "The 'last things' may be the things that come along at the end of a series, and here 'last' has primarily a temporal significance. Yet since it is what closes a series that gives to it any meaning or character it may have, the 'last things' may also be understood as what is final and ultimate, what is of most importance; and in some modern theologians (Bultmann and Tillich are examples) the eschatological is virtually voided of any temporal reference and is understood as the ultimate or decisive moment."[70] In a sense, these theologians were suggesting that humanity had reached the end of history long before Francis Fukuyama ever coined the concept.[71]

If there is an eschatological framework for Bonhoeffer's writings as a whole, should it be described as apocalyptic as well? Any answer again depends to a significant degree on how we define apocalyptic, a concept derived from the Greek ἀποκάλυψις and typically translated as "revelation," usually with reference to divine matters. The English transliteration of this word conjures up in the popular mind sensational depictions of cataclysmic upheavals of this world and millenarian visions of an otherworldly paradise that awaits the faithful, often with esoteric clues as to the time and means for the end of the world tossed into the mix. The awaited end to this world is total and absolute, as is the establishment of a new aeon or age. Christians

---

67. Lehmann, *Ethics in a Christian Context*, 118.

68. Lehmann, "Evanston," 149.

69. Carter, "Unlikely Convergence," 173.

70. Macquarrie, *Christian Hope*, 32.

71. Fukuyama, "The End of History?"

are those who live in the present age but who are citizens of the next, which gives rise to an ethic that consists solely of criticism of and resistance to the old world. For those working with this picture, any sense of responsibility to participate in this age, to help preserve it and to create structures of relative justice, is ruled out from the outset.[72]

Ziegler argues that Bonhoeffer's writings do in fact display a distinctly apocalyptic tone and trajectory. Larry Rasmussen first raises this as a possibility but then dismisses it because he believes that Bonhoeffer had been for all intents and purposes immunized by his confessional and academic training "against whatever 'elective affinities' . . . might have been drawn between the 'apocalyptic' character of his time and place and apocalyptic themes in Scripture."[73] But Bonhoeffer's appropriation of biblical apocalyptic extends far beyond a superficial resemblance between the tumult of life in Nazi Germany and the graphic apocalyptic imagery in the Bible.

Ziegler makes his case for the apocalyptic nature of Bonhoeffer's theology by appealing to recent studies by New Testament scholars, principally in the Pauline corpus[74] (though it also pervades the gospels[75]), that challenge this construal of apocalyptic thought. According to what in scholarly circles has been dubbed "the new perspective," the category of apocalyptic should not be restricted to a literary genre or a class of visionary imaginings that provide a timetable for calculating when and how the world will come to an end. As employed by the New Testament, it is first and foremost a conceptual format for interpreting Christ's life and passion as "the effective and definitive disclosure of God's rectifying action" in the world. What takes place in Christ, says Ziegler, "is the incursion of God's power into the world *with effect*. Revelation is 'no mere disclosure of previously hidden secrets, nor is it simply information about future events.'" It first and foremost *initiates* a new state of affairs in the world, simultaneously "a making way for" and "a making known" the way that God sets to rights the human condition as *new creation*.[76]

---

72. West, "Review of *Dietrich Bonhoeffer*," 471–72.

73. Rasmussen, *Dietrich Bonhoeffer*, 75.

74. Names that are commonly associated with this movement include J. Christiaan Beker, Martinus de Boer, James D. G. Dunn, Douglas Harink, Richard Hays, Bruce Longenecker, J. Louis Martyn, E. P. Sanders, David Scholer, and N. T. Wright. As Wright points out, however, there is no such thing as *the* new perspective on Paul, "only a disparate family of perspectives, some with more, some with less family likeness, and with fierce squabbles and sibling rivalries going on inside" (*Justification*, 28).

75. See in this regard Allison, *Historical Christ and the Theological Jesus* and *Constructing Jesus*; Dunn, *Jesus Remembered*; Gaventa and Hays, *Seeking the Identity of Jesus*.

76. Ziegler, "Dietrich Bonhoeffer," 581, Ziegler's emphasis.

A second hallmark of Paul's apocalyptic understanding of the gospel has to do with its construal of reality, and more specifically of what has taken place with God's incursion into the world, namely, the gift of the new creation. The logic of this gospel is not that of an idea or of a possibility, nor is it of an offer that can be realized only if humans accept it. Bonhoeffer regularly invokes imagery of God intruding on a sinful and corrupt world, at one point in *Discipleship* going so far as to say that the "visible church-community whose reality fully extends to all areas of life [*Lebensgemeinschaft*] invades the world and snatches its children."[77] As he puts it in *Ethics*, "the whole reality of the world has already been drawn into and is held together in Christ."[78] This is a consistent emphasis, for as he states some ten years earlier in an essay on the petition in the Lord's Prayer for God to send the kingdom, "It is not what *God* could do and what *we* could do that forms the basis of our prayer for the coming of the kingdom, but what God *does* for us and what God will do for us again and again."[79] Even in the form of promise, the emphasis rests on the reality and the decisiveness of God's redemptive work. In a passage in a sermon on Zechariah, in which the high priest Joshua is described as standing before God in dirty clothes, and God rebukes Satan's attempt to accuse him because God has taken away the high priest's sin, Bonhoeffer asserts, "*God* has done it, *God* has borne it, and we are free."[80]

Bonhoeffer recapitulates in these passages three messages that, according to J. Louis Martyn, are combined in Paul's understanding of apocalyptic: "'*God has done it!*' and 'You are to live it out!' and 'You are to live it out *because* God has done it *and* because God will do it!'" Indeed, says Martyn, due to the cross of Christ "God's war of liberation was commenced and decisively settled."[81] Reconciliation, established by God's gracious justification in Christ, establishes our true status in the world, without asking first for our permission.[82] Bonhoeffer describes this prevenient and decisive activity of God on our behalf with the Lutheran terminology of *iustitia passiva*, a passive justice. We live out what God has done in relationship to Christ, which is not in any sense an activation of a human potential or possibility or a structure of human existence, but "a given relation, a relation in which human beings are set."[83]

77. *DBWE* 4:233.

78. *DBWE* 6:58.

79. *DBWE* 12:291, Bonhoeffer's emphasis.

80. *DBWE* 14:859, Bonhoeffer's emphasis.

81. Martyn, *Galatians*, 103, 105, Martyn's emphasis.

82. Ziegler, "Dietrich Bonhoeffer," 582.

83. *DBWE* 3:65; cf. 2:134, 4:160; 14:418.

We should not summarily dismiss apocalyptic discourse as millenarian rhetoric or fantasy depictions of the hereafter, but understand it as "a mode of discourse fit to give voice to the radical ontological and epistemological consequences of the gospel." Ziegler concludes that the way that Bonhoeffer unpacks the doctrine of justification in *Discipleship* and *Ethics* is "freighted with the logic of Pauline apocalyptic."[84] In a letter written to Karl Barth in 1936, Bonhoeffer states that while working on these topics he had been engaged in an ongoing and silent conversation with Barth.[85] In his reply Barth says that he is eager to see the results of Bonhoeffer's work, but admits to some trepidation as well, because so many commentators on this subject slight its "original christological and eschatological approach in favor of (in fact, increasingly abstract!) actualizations in a specifically human sphere."[86] Bonhoeffer clearly takes Barth's concerns on this matter to heart.[87]

According to Ziegler, Bonhoeffer makes two claims in *Ethics* having to do with the connection in the Pauline correspondence between apocalyptic discourse and thought and the doctrine of justification, the first of which is that revelation is reconciliation. In Christ nothing less than the reality of God, that which is "beyond and in all that exists,"[88] has broken into the world, securing a victory over human unrighteousness on the cross and in the resurrection. As a result of the word of God that "bursts in" on men and women, the "labyrinth of their previous lives collapses."[89] This incursion of God's reality into the reality of the world unsettles long-standing moral schemes and gives rise to "wholly other" and "completely different questions" because the act of God tears humanity out of its insular reflection.[90] Due to "God's *breaking into* history through Christ,"[91] something is substantively different about the world. There is a radically different mode of existence that has invaded the world, a different performance of worldliness, which requires a break, beginning with baptism.[92]

Bonhoeffer anticipates this insight in a lecture given at Finkenwalde: "As that particular bit of world and humankind created anew out of God's

---

84. Ziegler, "Dietrich Bonhoeffer," 580, 583.

85. *DBWE* 14:252–53.

86. *DBWE* 14:267.

87. Ziegler, "Dietrich Bonhoeffer," 583.

88. *DBWE* 6:54.

89. *DBWE* 6:146. Bonhoeffer says in *Sanctorum Communio* that while death first constitutes history, the life that abides in love breaks its continuity, "not empirically, but objectively [*sachlich*]" (*DBWE* 1:146).

90. Ziegler, "Dietrich Bonhoeffer," 583–85.

91. *DBWE* 12:363, Bonhoeffer's emphasis.

92. *DBWE* 4:64, 297.

Spirit, the church asks about total obedience to the Spirit, which creates (both the religious and the secular) anew.[93] Because the church is concerned with God, the Holy Spirit, and the word, it is concerned not specifically with religion but rather with *obedience* to the word, with the *actions* of the Father, that is, with actually implementing this new creation from the Spirit."[94] Revelation is nothing less than the ongoing transformative act of God erupting within the human condition, the Father's self-communication of our true humanity to us in the Word become human through the power of the Spirit.[95]

The second claim Bonhoeffer makes in *Ethics* that presupposes the apocalyptic trajectory in his understanding of justification, says Ziegler, is that reality is constituted by the event of reconciliation in Christ. The good, Bonhoeffer writes in a comment that echoes Martyn's assertion about the three messages in Paul's gospel, "consists of nothing more than allowing our action to be determined by the knowledge that it is not us but indeed God alone who accomplishes good in history." The world is not just shown for what it always has been by the event of justification, but that event makes a difference ontologically. The world is no longer what it was:

> In Jesus Christ the reality of God has entered into the reality of this world. The place where the questions about the reality of God and about the reality of the world are answered at the same time is characterized solely by the name: Jesus Christ. God and the world are enclosed in this name. In Christ all things exist (Col. 1:17). From now on we cannot speak rightly of either God or the world without speaking of Jesus Christ.[96]

Bonhoeffer does not limit justification to the status of individual sinners standing alone *coram deo*, before God, as Luther had done,[97] nor is it merely a forensic declaration on God's part. Bonhoeffer first advances this understanding in *Sanctorum Communio*, where he states,

> Now human sin cannot be viewed by the true God "as if it did not exist"; it must truly be "undone," that is, it must be wiped out. This occurs not by reversing time, but through divine punishment and re-creating the will to do good. God does not

93. In his notes from this lecture Bethge wrote, "Jesus thus not the founder of a religion, but one who creates anew," and two of his classmates have in their notes: "Christ was not the founder of a religion but the καινός ἄνθρωπος" (*DBWE* 14:442 n. 49).

94. *DBWE* 14:442.

95. McCabe, *Law, Love, and Language*, 126.

96. *DBWE* 6:228, 67, 54.

97. Luther, *Freedom of a Christian*, 73.

"overlook" sin; that would mean not taking human beings seriously as personal beings in their very culpability; and that would mean no re-creation of the person, and therefore no re-creation of community.[98]

Justification has everything to do with the setting right of the whole creation, at the very heart of which is the apocalyptic language of "the new creation of the new human being."[99] The cosmic scope of Christ's reconciling and redemptive death and resurrection means that the world can no longer be thought of as an autonomous realm, for that would entail a rejection of the fact that in Christ the reality of the world has been grounded in revelational reality. For Bonhoeffer, God remakes the world as a whole in Christ.[100]

I would add to Ziegler's list a third defining mark of apocalyptic reasoning having to do with the tension that characterizes the historical relationship between the church and the present social order. The members of Christ's body live in continuous tension between being *for* the world and being *against* the world. If the church advocates sectarian withdrawal from the world, says J. Christiaan Beker, it creates a dualistic understanding of the gospel that "betrays the death and resurrection of Christ as God's redemptive plan for the world." On the other hand, if it lays stress only on participation in the world, "it threatens to become another 'worldly' phenomenon, accommodating itself to whatever the world will buy and so becoming part of the world."[101] Though it is simpler to think in terms of the two extremes, and easier to sustain on a daily basis, than is living in the tension created by the intrusion of God into a world whose basic patterns of relating are radically skewed, the church must, in the words of the author of Ecclesiastes, hold on to the one without letting go of the other (7:18).

Bonhoeffer states in *Ethics* that the concept of a historical heritage, and in particular the Western notion of history as such, is possible only when human thinking is determined by the intrusion of God into history at a particular time and place in the incarnation: "Here history becomes serious, without being sanctified." In the fact of God's becoming human in Jesus Christ, God's word of judgment and reconciliation, the divine No and Yes, introduces "a lasting and irremovable tension into every historical moment." History thus only becomes completely temporal for the first time due to the life and death of Jesus Christ, and only as such does God affirm it.[102]

---

98. *DBWE* 1:155.

99. *DBWE* 4:260.

100. Ziegler, "Dietrich Bonhoeffer," 585–86.

101. Beker, *Paul's Apocalyptic Gospel*, 41.

102. *DBWE* 6:104.

Sectarian withdrawal, which only acknowledges the last things and thus posits a radical break with this time before the last things, is therefore not an option for Bonhoeffer, for in the body of Christ "all humanity is accepted, included, and borne, and the church-community of believers is to make this known to the world by word and life," which happens not by "being separated from the world, but [by] calling the world into the community of the body of Christ to which the world in truth already belongs."[103] Accommodating the existing order, what he calls the way of compromise with human beings as they are currently, is equally objectionable. He laments the way that Luther's doctrine of grace unwittingly led Christians back to Constantine's alliance with the church, resulting in a minimal ethics that made the existence of the Christian indistinguishable from that of the average citizen. He acknowledges that this was of course not what Luther wanted, that he was looking for a full ethics for everyone, not just for those in religious orders. But the result is clear: the New Testament message is radically misunderstood and the possibility of a genuinely worldly life is reduced to an abstract principle.[104]

Bonhoeffer takes up again the ironic consequences of the Reformation in a prison letter to his parents, stating that Luther's actions had the exact opposite effect of what he intended. Luther wanted a genuine unity of the church and of the peoples of the West, but instead both church and Europe collapsed; he aspired to authentic Christian freedom, but instead saw complacency and degeneration; he argued for a worldly ordering of society without clerical domination, but in its place erupted the peasants' revolt, followed by the slow dissolution of the bonds and orders of a genuinely worldly life. "Already one hundred years ago Kierkegaard said that Luther today would say the opposite of what he said back then," writes Bonhoeffer in reluctant agreement: "I think that is true—*cum grano salis*."[105]

Mindful of the tension between what is and what is to come, says Ziegler, Bonhoeffer forswears both sectarian and *volkskirchliche* (the people's church) ecclesiologies: "Neither pietism ('a last effort to maintain Protestant Christianity as a religion') nor the civil religion of the established church as an 'institution of salvation' comport with *this* gospel."[106] These options do not truly embody the apocalyptic impulse of the gospel, suspended between the "Yes" and the "No" addressed to the fallen world by the word of God. The No signifies that the fallen life we now live can only become

---

103. *DBWE* 6:153, 67; cf. 98.

104. *DBWE* 14:432. Bethge reconstructed this portion of the lecture from his notes.

105. *DBWE* 8:172–73.

106. Ziegler, "Dietrich Bonhoeffer," 586.

the life that is Jesus if it is prefaced by its own end, annihilation, and death. "We now live stretched between the No and the Yes," he writes, the former word spoken over an existence that has fallen away from its origin, essence, and goal, which is only life in the sense that even in our rebellion we live from the life of Christ. The Yes is the gift of creation, reconciliation, and redemption that comes to us from outside us, which Bonhoeffer, following the sixteenth-century Reformers, refers to as an "'alien righteousness' ['*fremde Gerechtigkeit*'], a righteousness that comes from outside of us (*extra nos*)."[107] This gift is not, however, a distant and strange thing unrelated to daily life, for it constitutes our worldliness.[108]

This tension between church and world depicted by the apocalyptic imaginary of the New Testament determines the sense and significance of the present by what comes to us from the future, from Christ and the Holy Spirit. "The criterion of the authentic present," Bonhoeffer states in his lecture series on the interpretation of the New Testament at Finkenwalde, "resides outside the present itself, resides in the future, in Scripture and in the word of Christ attested there. And thus an orientation toward substance will consist in allowing that external element, that element before us, that 'future element' that comes toward us to come to expression as the present—the alien gospel, not the familiar gospel, will be the present or contemporary gospel."[109]

Bonhoeffer here is returning to a theme he first articulates in *Act and Being* and then again in his Christology lectures regarding the distinctive logic that governs the contingent character of divine revelation. Contingency, he writes, is a characteristic of the present; the past, as "having happened," is in principle ensconced in the past unless it is raised up into the present by a proclamation "coming to" us ("in the future"). In the contingency that comes to us from beyond ourselves, from the revelation of God in Christ, the future determines the significance of the present. In the various "systems" of modern philosophy that confer priority to the coherence of reason, by contrast, the present is determined by the past. "It may be said of Christian revelation," Bonhoeffer concludes, "that the proclamation of cross and resurrection, determined by eschatology and predestination, and the occurrence effective within that proclamation, lifts even the past into the present, or paradoxically, into something 'in the future.'"[110]

---

107. *DBWE* 5:31.
108. *DBWE* 6:251.
109. *DBWE* 14:418.
110. *DBWE* 2:111.

This line of reasoning recurs in his Christology lectures, where he states that the historical fact about Christ is not grammatically set for theology by the simple past tense, but by the present tense: "that which happens by chance is the absolute, that precisely the past is that which is present; that the historical is that which is simultaneously here and now." The claim that what is past is now present becomes a historical possibility "only through faith in the miracle that God accomplished in Jesus's resurrection" that released him from the confines of mortal existence.[111]

Bonhoeffer positions both profound and banal forms of worldliness in the tension between the present time and the last things. The apocalyptic imagination traverses the eschatological interval between the contingency of the present under divine judgment—its struggles, suffering, and death—and the uniting of all things in Christ, and takes form as responsible action, another crucial idea in his thought. Such action that sees the world thus shows rather than explains the connection between the course and consummation of God's labors, without forcing a Promethean resolution of the suffering of past and present in favor of the future, or a Sisyphean resignation to sin and death.[112] Our participation as members of Christ's body in this reality is therefore a gift that is also a task, which is to act responsibly in the immediate future of our lives.[113]

Not everyone is convinced that an apocalyptic storyline decisively shapes Bonhoeffer's theology. Charles West contends that Bonhoeffer's thought has no room for the historic and mythic scene of apocalyptic. What Bonhoeffer calls the ultimate is not really new, writes West, because grace is not new, having "accompanied the history of the world from the beginning." Apocalyptic images and ideas push theology "in the direction of a revolutionary eschatology and an Anabaptist ecclesiology," emphasizing criticism and resistance at the expense of participation, preservation, and building of structures of relative justice in this world, and these simply are not options for Bonhoeffer.[114]

West is right to observe that an apocalyptic storyline running throughout Bonhoeffer's theology has profound implications for ecclesiology. His conclusion, however, that apocalyptic requires an "Anabaptist ecclesiology," with an implication of sectarian withdrawal from the world, does not follow, and the claim that it would necessarily mandate a revolutionary eschatology is without merit as well. Most problematic is his assertion that grace is

---

111. *DBWE* 12:330.

112. See Moltmann, *Theology of Hope*, 24.

113. See O'Hanlon, "Theological Dramatics," 109.

114. West, "Review of *Dietrich Bonhoeffer*," 471–72.

not new but is evident throughout history, contradicting what Bonhoeffer explicitly says in *Ethics*: "Not all time is a time of grace; but now—precisely now and finally now—is the 'day of salvation' (2 Cor 6:2)."[115] As Martyn notes in connection with Paul's understanding of the apocalypse of God in Christ, "there are no through-trains from the scriptural, patriarchal traditions and their perceptive criteria to the gospel of God's Son."[116]

West's description of grace also pitches it at a very abstract level and disconnects it from the historical nature of the incarnation. As Bonhoeffer never tires of saying, "God did not become an idea, a principle, a program, a universally valid belief, or a law; God became human."[117] It follows that grace is also not an idea, a principle, a program, a universally valid belief, or a law. West's way of talking about grace also makes no allowance for the contingent act of God in revelation, reducing it to an unveiling of what has always been the case, such that what happens in the life, passion, and resurrection of Christ, for all intents and purposes, changes nothing, which is a position that runs counter to the pervasive sense in Bonhoeffer's writings that with Christ's life, death, and resurrection the world is no longer the same.

For Bonhoeffer the decisive content and term of reference for apocalyptic, as Alexander Schmemann so insightfully puts it, is "not the world but the Kingdom of God," and thus rather than being "anti-world" it is "pro-Kingdom." The eschatological reign of Israel's God, "announced, inaugurated and given by and in Christ," thus governs the church's distinctive relationship with this world, which has "condemned itself to die, to be the world whose form and image 'fade away' so that the Kingdom of God 'is not of this world.' This is the Christian *no* to the world and, from the first day, Christianity proclaimed the end of 'this world' and required from those who believe in Christ and want to partake of his Kingdom that they be 'dead with Christ' and their true life be 'hid with Christ in God.'" At the same time, writes Schmemann, this same creation in rebellion is redeemed and re-created in Christ, in whom all things find their true end: "This means that for those who believe in Christ and are united to Him, this very world—its time and matter, its life, and even death—have become the 'means' of communion with the Kingdom of God, the sacrament, i.e., the mode, of its coming and presence among men."[118]

---

115. *DBWE* 6:151.

116. Martyn, *Theological Issues*, 224.

117. *DBWE* 6:99.

118. Schmemann, *Church, World, Mission*, 29–30; cf. Harvey, *Another City*, 68–69.

The resemblance between the Lutheran Bonhoeffer and the Orthodox Schmemann on the relationship between the church and the world as such is neither accidental nor superficial, but arises from a shared interpretation of the apocalyptic message of the New Testament. The wanderers and sojourners that Bonhoeffer juxtaposes with both the otherworldly who hate the earth and the sectarians who try to possess it are those whose love for God entails a genuine love for this world. Only the wanderers truly "love the Earth that bears them," because "it is on it that they travel toward that foreign land that they love above all; otherwise they would not be wandering at all. Only wanderers of this kind, who love the Earth and God in one, can believe in God's kingdom."[119] There are significant differences between Bonhoeffer and the Orthodox on a range of topics, but on this question they share a common view of the relationship between the world and the church grounded in the apocalyptic testimony of the New Testament.[120]

Worldliness in the Twenty-First Century

There is a great deal in Bonhoeffer's discussion of worldliness that engages our own time and place directly, above all in his steadfast insistence that in Christ God has decisively changed the character and course of creation. God has done it, and we are called to participate in that reality because it is God who has done it, who continues to do it, and who will bring it to its fitting consummation. Other comments that he makes in connection to profound this-worldliness have the potential to move the conversation forward but require further development on our part. There is, for example, his openness to and investment in the ecumenical movement prior to the war, and especially his interest in Catholicism, the seeds of which had been planted as a teenager during his trip to Rome. As Ernst Feil observes, Bonhoeffer regards the differences between Protestants and Catholics as rooted in historical variations and therefore not permanent.[121] In a letter written to Bethge in 1940 he notes that the union between Lutherans and the Reformed was not the result of a theological solution, but rather the "'guidance' of God (Union, Confessing Church), and by the recognition of what is objectively given in the sacrament—Christ is more important than

---

119. *DBWE* 12:286, translation altered. The German phrase is "An das Reich Gottes glauben kann nur, wer so wanadert, wer die Erde und Gott in einem liebt" (*DBW* 265); cf. *DBWE* 4:251.

120. For one theologian's take on the family resemblances between Bonhoeffer and Orthodox theology, see Sopko, "Bonhoeffer," 81–88.

121. Feil, *Theology of Dietrich Bonhoeffer*, 25.

our thoughts about him and about his presence." He then asks, "Would not both of these things also be possible in relation to the Catholic Church: recognition of the 'guidance' of God in recent years and recognition of the objectivity of the presence of Christ (for traditional Lutherans, even easier with Catholics than with Calvinists!)."[122]

Feil also calls our attention to a comment Bonhoeffer makes in prison about reading the church fathers: "To some extent they are much more contemporaneous than the Reformers and simultaneously a basis for Protestant-Catholic conversation."[123] Feil concludes, "Perhaps Bonhoeffer's theology itself could become a basis for those talks."[124] Indeed, one of the points of convergence that could emerge from such talks might be the recovery of virtue ethics that has reshaped moral theology and philosophy over the last thirty years in both Catholic and Protestant circles, a recovery that Bonhoeffer himself, with his stress on the importance of formation, initiates. Some might protest at this point, noting that Bonhoeffer is critical of those who strive for a private virtuousness; who do not steal, murder, or commit adultery; and who do good insofar as it lies within their power, but who close their eyes to the injustice around them.[125] And yet, as Jennifer Moberly shows, he combines an ethics of formation with divine command, and therefore something like a virtue ethic is implied, particularly when, as he constantly emphasizes, responsible action can never be reduced to abstract principles.[126]

In his essay "What Does It Mean to Tell the Truth?," for example, Bonhoeffer gestures toward the need for an account of virtue when he says that telling the truth is a matter not only of intention but also of an accurate perception of reality, which is a skill—or better, a complex set of skills—that must be learned.[127] In addition, he often goes out of his way to praise one or more moral virtues. In the essay "After Ten Years" he praises the Aristotelian-Thomistic concept of wisdom, stating that wisdom and stupidity are not ethically indifferent: "In the fullness of the concrete situation and in the possibilities it offers, the wise person discerns the impassable limits that are imposed on every action by the abiding laws of human communal life. In this discernment that wise person acts well and the good person acts

---

122. *DBWE* 16:84.

123. *DBWE* 8:189.

124. Feil, *Theology of Dietrich Bonhoeffer*, 25.

125. *DBWE* 6:80; 8:40; cf. R. D. Williams, *Edge of Words*, 46–50.

126. Moberly, *Virtue of Bonhoeffer's Ethics*.

127. *DBWE* 16:603.

wisely."[128] He says much the same thing in *Ethics*, noting at one point that it is necessary in a given situation "to observe, weigh, evaluate, and decide, and to do all that with limited human understanding."[129]

Finally, there are several places in *Letters and Papers from Prison* where the role of virtue is implied. In the first stanza of his poem "Stations on the Way to Freedom" he states that it is imperative that one discipline one's soul and senses, "lest your desire / and then your limbs perchance should lead you now hither, now yon." And in the last chapter of "Outline for a Book" Bonhoeffer addresses the form of communal life the church should take in a world come of age. He states that it must participate in the day-to-day tasks of life, not as those in authority, but as those who help and serve: "It must tell people in every calling what a life with Christ is, what it means 'to be there for others.'" In particular, the church will have to confront the roots of evil: *hubris*, the adoration of power, envy and self-deception. To confront these vices Christians need a specific set of moral dispositions, among which he lists moderation, authenticity, trust, faithfulness, steadfastness, patience, discipline, humility, modesty, and contentment.[130]

What then keeps Bonhoeffer's harsh critique of private virtuousness and his constant appeals to particular virtues in the course of living responsibly from collapsing into a blatant contradiction? In part it has to do with the fact that, as we have just noted, deliberation is an inescapable aspect of responsible action, which entails being adequately formed in the requisite intellectual, moral, and theological virtues. The case is similar to that of ethical principles, in that while responsible action cannot be reduced to these abstractions, they can be useful tools in the hands of God.[131] As Bonhoeffer clearly states, the acquisition and exercise of the virtues is thus never the end of the moral life, but he also tacitly recognizes that they are valuable instruments through which we participate in the reality of the incarnation. The aim is never to justify one's self or one's actions, for that resides solely in God's hands.[132]

Another point of convergence that could emerge from a *rapprochement* between Catholics and Protestants has to do with the sacramental character of the church. What I have in mind here is the assertion made by the Second Vatican Council that "the Church, in Christ, is in the nature of

128. *DBWE* 8:45; cf. *DBWE* 6:81

129. *DBWE* 6:268.

130. *DBWE* 8:512, 503.

131. *DBWE* 6:82; cf. 270–73.

132. Implied here is an important distinction that Bonhoeffer shares with Karl Barth between responsibility as our basic stance and condition before God, and the need to deliberate on ends and appropriate means. Barth, *CD* II/2, 643.

a sacrament—a sign and instrument, that is, of communion with God and of unity among men."[133] An emphasis on the sacramental character of the church accords well with Bonhoeffer's understanding of the church as the form of Christ existing in the form of the church, for it is in the church that, in and through the power of the Holy Spirit, "Jesus makes his form real in the midst of the world."[134] It is, as he puts it, that particular bit of world and humankind that is created anew and that is concerned to testify to what the triune God is doing in the world.[135]

To see the church as sacrament, says Herbert McCabe, is to regard it as "a continuing creative interpretation of human life; revealing and realising the revolutionary future of the world." The sacramental practices of the church communicate to the world the real but dimly perceived apocalyptic depth of human life now in the light of the world to come. To partake of the sacraments, says McCabe, is to actually encounter the future reality that is at the heart of what it means to be human, and on that basis to take our actions in the present world seriously. Baptism and Eucharist thus function "as does the experience of literature and drama: providing us with an insight (but a uniquely authentic insight) into the nature and destiny of man."[136]

The advantage of using the notion of sacrament to describe the church's practice of a profound worldliness is that, first, it underscores the fact that, as Bonhoeffer puts it, Christians are not responsible for turning the world into the kingdom of God, for it is God alone who accomplishes the good in history. Our responsibility as members of Christ's body—to take the next step that corresponds to the fact of God's becoming human—constitutes a concrete sign to the world that it is no longer the same, that its reality is grounded and sustained by the reality of God being united to the reality of the world in Christ.[137] The sacramental task that falls to the church is to live as an effective sign of that divine activity, "bearing witness to his presence and his work of reconciling all things without either arrogating his functions to ourselves or putting up any kind of smokescreen in front of them, and yet actually representing them."[138] Testifying to God's works does not consist principally in talk, for the sacramental mission of the church is to

---

133. *Lumen Gentium* 1.

134. *DBWE* 6:135; cf. 1:145–208.

135. *DBWE* 14:442.

136. McCabe, *Law, Love and Language*, 145–46. Together with Bonhoeffer I would add music to this list.

137. *DBWE* 6:224–25.

138. Marlé, *Bonhoeffer*, 141.

reveal and to realize "again and again,"[139] in prayer and just action among our fellow creatures,[140] the revolutionary future of the world. And as Bonhoeffer notes, "such a witness can only happen in the right way when it comes out of sanctified life in God's church-community."[141]

Those who wish to argue that Bonhoeffer moves away from this view at the end of his life need to indicate in some detail how such a witness could develop and sustain itself over time apart from a historically extended, socially embodied, and geographically located society: "Only to the extent that what happens to the church truly concerns all humanity is the concept of formation—indirectly—meaningful for all human beings." This is not the claim that the church functions simply as a model for the world, but that Christians can only perceive and talk about the formation of the world when we address humanity in the light of the world's true form in Christ, "which belongs to it, which it has already received, but which it has not grasped and accepted." In the form of Christ taking form in the church, "humanity is—so to speak, proleptically—drawn into the church. It is still the case that, even where one talks about the formation of the world, only the form of Jesus Christ is meant."[142]

To speak of the church as sacrament naturally leads one to ask about the sacraments in relation to a profound worldliness. Here we must move beyond Bonhoeffer, who does not write about the church as a sacrament. He does, however, affirm the importance of the sacraments themselves. In his Christology lectures he states that after the fall the self, people, history, and the church are no longer the same, for the continuity between the Word and creature has been lost. As a result, "the natural world is no longer a transparent world," for its meaning has been obscured by sin and death. Sacrament only exists where God has hallowed an element in the midst of the world of creatures, setting up in an enslaved creation a sign of its liberation, "set free from their dumb condition, from their interpretation by humankind. These elements themselves speak and say what they are."[143] It is a small step from

139. *DBWE* 6:59.

140. *DBWE* 8:388.

141. *DBWE* 6:64.

142. *DBWE* 6:97–98; cf. 4:217. In this regard Bonhoeffer sounds very much like the founders of the Catholic Worker Movement, Dorothy Day and Peter Maurin, who regularly speak of all humanity as potentially members of Christ's mystical body. See in this regard Werntz, *Bodies of War and Peace.*

143. *DBWE* 12:318–19, 327. In a sermon he preaches in May 1933 in Berlin, he speaks of the Eucharist as a time of joy as the congregation gathers together in the midst of an evil world with its Lord, and also the joy of communion among brethren. He then locates the joy of this sacrament in an eschatological setting: "Joy in the sacraments— that is the joy of the heart full of longing and desire for its God whom it has found; that

the sacraments interpreting the true significance of the world to the reality of the church, in which the whole Christ is present and active *nunc et hic*,[144] as a continuing interpretation of human life.

Bonhoeffer does, however, provide openings at several points for describing the church as a sacramental sign of what God has done, is doing and will do in and for the world in Jesus Christ. At the end of *Discipleship* he states that the life of Jesus Christ continues to live in the lives of his followers, and thus we should not speak about our Christian life "but about the true life of Jesus Christ in us." The incarnate, crucified, and transfigured Christ has entered into every Christian and takes form (*Gestalt*) in each one because every Christian is a member of Christ's body, the church, which is, "first of all, Christ's image." Within Christ's body we are now "like Christ [*wie Christus*]." The summons to be like Christ in the New Testament therefore denotes more than simply following a moral example, "because we have already been shaped into the image of Christ. Only because we bear Christ's image [*Bild*] already can Christ be the 'example' [*Vorbild*] whom we follow."[145]

A second place where Bonhoeffer makes room for the sacramental character of the church's life and witness is in *Ethics*, where he emphasizes the need to prepare the way of the Lord. The entry of grace into the world is the last reality (*das Einzug der Gnade ist das Letzte*), but we must first speak of preparing the way of the Lord and of the things before the last. There must be a concrete intervention if people are to be made ready to receive Jesus Christ. This intervention cannot be simply a matter of developing programs of social reform but must involve visible deeds of humility and repentance, "the concrete changing of one's ways." Though it must be as concrete and visible as hunger and nourishment, "everything depends on this action being a *spiritual reality*, since what is finally at stake is not the reform of worldly conditions but the coming of Christ."[146]

The potential of the notion of sacrament for thinking about the nature of Christian worldliness is heightened by Bonhoeffer's frequent invocation of the concept of participation, beginning in *Sanctorum Communio*, to describe the relationship Christians have to the life and suffering of Christ in this world.[147] Early on in the dissertation he raises the question of the

---

is the anticipation of the strangers, the homeless, as they look forward to their eternal home and pray that it may come" (*DBWE* 12:470).

144. *DBWE* 12:310.

145. *DBWE* 4:286–87 (*DBW* 4:303).

146. *DBWE* 6:163–65 (*DBW* 6:155–56), my emphasis.

147. Bonhoeffer is thoroughly consistent with the view of the Apostle Paul here. The view of his contemporaries, that Paul's use of participatory language signals merely

"metaphysical possibility" of "an individual collective person in which the individual participates [teilhaben]." A few pages later he states that our participation (die Teilnahme) in the ethical nature of humanity in response to the call of Jesus Christ "is demonstrated in every act of repentance and recognition of culpability. Wherever individuals recognize themselves both as individuals and as the human race, and submit to the demand of God, there beats the heart of the collective person."[148]

In *Discipleship* Bonhoeffer asserts, in terms virtually identical to Aquinas's discussion of the divine attributes in *Summa Theologica*,[149] that Jesus does not just have righteousness, but by virtue of his complete, true, and personal communion with God, "he *is* righteousness personified."[150] And in his call to the disciples and in their community with him, Jesus grants them participation in himself (*hat teilgegeben an sich selbst*), and as a result they participate (*teihaftig*) in his own righteousness. Simply put, says Bonhoeffer, "He is the disciples' righteousness." Their righteousness "really is righteousness, because they themselves now truly do the will of God and fulfill the law."[151] One would be hard-pressed to put such comments into a strictly forensic or contractual frame of reference, but they accommodate a sacramental understanding quite easily.

The notion of participation also appears multiple times in *Ethics*.[152] The first references come, not surprisingly, in "Christ, Reality, and Good." He states that the question of the good cannot be answered in the abstract, but is grounded in *"God's reality revealed in Christ becoming real [Wirklichwerden] among God's creatures."* The question of the good is thus "the question of participating [teilhaben] in God's reality revealed in Christ."

---

a change in self-understanding, can no longer be sustained. See Dunn, *Theology of Paul the Apostle*, 392–412, and Sanders, *Paul and Palestinian Judaism*, 453–72; cf. Gorman, *Inhabiting the Cruciform God*.

148. *DBWE* 1:77–78, 120–21 (*DBW* 1:48, 75–76). The concept of collective person will be explored in more detail in chapter 8.

149. "Boethius says . . . that all things but God are good by participation. Therefore they are not good essentially. God alone is good essentially." Aquinas, *Summa Theologica* 1a.6.3. Bonhoeffer's assertion in *Ethics* that only God does good in history, and thus "human historical action is good only insofar as God draws it into God's own action and as the human agent completely surrenders to God's action without claiming any other justification," strongly echoes both Boethius and Aquinas (*DBWE* 6:227).

150. *DBWE* 4:119, Bonhoeffer's emphasis

151. *DBWE* 4:119–20 (*DBW* 4:121).

152. There are at least fourteen distinct references to participation in God or Christ in *Ethics*, using several related German terms (*Teilnehmen, Teilhaben*, the adjective *teilhaftig*, and the verb *teilbekommen*), but neither the Dietrich Bonhoeffer Werke nor the Dietrich Bonhoeffer Works includes the concept in their indices.

Only by participating in this ultimate reality do we find the true meaning of the question concerning the good: "In Christ we are invited to participate [*teil zu bekommen*] in the reality of God and the reality of the world at the same time, the one not without the other." For Christians there are not two realities, but one, and thus participating in Christ we stand at the same time in the reality of God and the reality of the world.[153] A second series of references to participation occurs in "Guilt, Justification, Renewal," where Bonhoeffer asserts that "only the person who participates [*teilhaftige*] in the resurrection of Christ is the renewed human being." The justification of both church and believer "consists in their becoming participants in the form of Christ [*teilbekommen an der Gestalt Christi*]." The form of Christ is that which has been judged in Christ, handed over to the death of the sinner, and then resurrected to new life. It is this form that stands before God in truth.[154]

The use of participation language takes on a new intensity in the prison writings. Echoing his insistence in *Ethics* that Christians are to participate fully in the reality of the world at the same time they participate in the reality of God, Bonhoeffer states in the baptismal meditation for his grandnephew that Christians demonstrate their worthiness to survive by participating (*Teilnahme*) in a complete, generous, and selfless way in the suffering of their neighbors as an implication of a life with Christ, an assertion that he repeats in "Outline for a Book."[155] It is in the July 19, 1944 letter and in "Outline," however, that he offers the most poignant use of the idea of participation, stating that our lives must be worldly so that we can participate in God's suffering in Christ: "Being a Christian does not mean being religious in a certain way, making oneself into something or other. . . . Instead it means being human, not a certain type of human being, but the human being Christ creates in us. It is not a religious act that makes someone a Christian, but sharing [*Teilnehmen*] in God's suffering in the worldly life." Only in this way, through participation in the being of Jesus (*das Teilnehmen an diesem Sein Jesu*), which *is* faith, do we attain to true worldliness, which at the same time is existence for others.[156]

The grammar of participation refers to a two-way, asymmetrical relation between a participant or participants and a "participated." Those who participate receive of, or take part in, the participated. That which is participated in gives part of itself to the participants. Participants thus take or

---

153. *DBWE* 6:50–51, 55, 58 (*DBW* 6:34–35, 40–41, 43).

154. *DBWE* 6:134, 142 (*DBW* 6:125, 133).

155. *DBWE* 8:389, 503 (*DBW* 8:435).

156. *DBWE* 8:480–82, 501, 503 (*DBW* 8:535–37, 558, 560).

receive from this relation; the participated in gives or grants this property to the participants. Those who wish to play a sport must become participants in a game, and from that game receive their identity and purpose as players. With respect to the relation between creator and creature, participation is not a competitive, zero-sum game, as the relation diminishes neither party, and participants actually gain by it. The baseline of participation in this relationship is that of being, for anything and everything that exists does so owing to its participation in God,[157] which, as Bonhoeffer puts it, preserves creation for its destiny in the new creation in Christ.[158]

In the sense that Bonhoeffer uses it, participation names the intimate yet asymmetrical relationship of faith that exists between ourselves as participants in God's messianic suffering, and Christ as the one in whom we participate, in whom the triune God unites the divine reality with the reality of the world. In *Ethics* Bonhoeffer uses the idea of form to elaborate on the shape of our participation in Christ, on what is given and what is received in this relationship. In the incarnation the form of humanity is created anew, and does so precisely that this form, the form of Christ, can take form among and in us here and now. This form is not something that the believer accomplishes by applying the teachings of Christ or so-called Christian principles, for it "occurs only by being drawn into the form of Jesus, by *being conformed to the unique form of the one who became human, was crucified, and is risen.*" We do not imitate Christ, striving by dint of our own efforts to become like him, but the form of Christ himself so works on us in the church that our form is conformed to that of Christ.[159]

Bonhoeffer's recovery of the grammar of participation is significant since Protestants have for the most part shied away from such language until recently, opting instead for covenantal language that at times is difficult to distinguish from modern notions of contract (though participation and covenant are not necessarily antithetical terms). This retrieval moreover opens the door to a rapprochement with the patristic and medieval traditions, a move that Bonhoeffer had already suggested in a previous letter, stating that the church fathers are more contemporaneous than the Reformers.[160] The church fathers insist that all human beings are summed up in the incarnation and that it is through the sacraments, preeminently baptism

157. Griffiths, *Intellectual Appetite*, 78.

158. *DBWE* 3:140.

159. *DBWE* 6:93–97; cf. *DBWE* 8:475.

160. *DBWE* 8:189.

and Eucharist, that we enter into and participate in the new humanity inaugurated by Christ.[161]

Bonhoeffer's emphasis on being caught up in the form of Christ places his understanding of participation squarely within the orbit of the patristic doctrine of theosis. Unfortunately, as seen, for example, in his Christology lectures, he mistakenly associates it with monophysitism, which held that Christ's human nature is swallowed up by the divine. In *Ethics*, however, he inches closer to the ancient formulas, stating that owing to the incarnation the form of human nature is created anew: "Human beings become human because God became human." The editors contend Bonhoeffer reverses the ancient dictum that God became human so that humans might become divine, but I contend this is not the case, appearances to the contrary notwithstanding.[162] Though he never wavers from his assertion that human beings are not transformed into an alien form, the form of God, but into the form that belongs to them as God's human creatures, his contention is not with patristic thought but with those who misinterpret the theological grammar of the fathers, who never asserted that human beings are transformed into an alien form, be it that of God or of anything else. John Meyendorff writes that Christ's humanity is "a *deified* humanity, which, however, does not in any way lose its human characteristics. Quite to the contrary. These characteristics become even more real and authentic by contact with the divine model according to which they were created. In this defied humanity of Christ's man is called to participate, and to share in its deification."[163]

With the language of theotic participation Bonhoeffer links the tensions of profound this-worldliness to the contrapuntal progressions of God's revelation in Christ and through the Spirit. As Rowan Williams observes, "revelation is bound up with memory and yet not simply specified by reference to a sealed-off past occurrence." Past occurrences initiate the process of revelation, to be sure, but it also includes the process by which that past is taken into (or rather draws into itself) human life and understanding.[164] The fundamental aim of revelation, and thus the ground of profound this-worldliness, is the ongoing work of God uniting the reality of the world with the divine reality in and through this Jesus Christ. It is not to convey information of the way things have always been, reminding us of an event that is essentially over and done with, nor is it to awaken the interior motions of the soul, its feelings and self-understanding, in an effort to find that

---

161. See Zimmermann, *Incarnational Humanism*, 196.

162. *DBWE* 6:6, 96 and n. 86; *DBWE* 12:340–52.

163. Meyendorff, *Byzantine Theology*, 163–64.

164. R. D. Williams, *On Christian Theology*, 135.

which a world come of age labors diligently to shunt to the boundaries of life. It is instead to draw women and men into the apocalyptic counterpoint of Christ's death and resurrection, to bring to naught the way things "have always been" and "always will be," and to fashion time and again within this time before the last signs of a new creation, of a new set of relations between God and humanity and between humans. Because this "comedy" plays out in the middle of the fallen circumstances of human existence in the here and now, the only way to participate in this new creation, says Bonhoeffer, is to be caught up into the messianic suffering of God.

It is in connection with our participation in Christ and the contrapuntal movements of the Spirit that the concepts of *Stellvertretung* and "being for others" occupy a central place in Bonhoeffer's theology. In Christ the reality of the new humanity has been established, and thus "he represents the whole history of humanity in his historical life." In Christ "humanity has been brought once and for all—this is essential to *real* vicarious representative action [Stellvertretung]—into community with God." It is from our participation in this reality that our service to the other springs; we now "live *one* life, with each other and for each other." We are thus summoned and empowered to act on behalf of the neighbor in day-to-day life, giving up "possessions, honor, even our whole lives."[165]

This link between Christ's life and sacrifice on our behalf and our sharing in that action recurs in *Ethics*. As the one who acts solely out of selfless love for real human beings, Jesus does not desire to be thought of as the only perfect or guiltless one, or to acquit himself of our guilt that leads to death: "A love that would abandon human beings to their guilt would not be a love for real human beings. As one who acts responsibly within the historical existence of human beings, Jesus becomes guilty." All that Jesus did and suffered he did and suffered on our behalf before God and on God's behalf for us: "In Christ we see humanity as a humanity that is accepted, borne, loved, and reconciled with God. In Christ we see God in the form of the poorest of our brothers and sisters." Christ takes human guilt upon himself for our sakes, thus linking in his person sinlessness and the bearing of guilt. Here also is the origin of action on our part for others. Springing as it does from the selfless love for the real brother or sister, such action cannot seek to withdraw from the community of human guilt.[166]

What profound worldliness looks like at a given time and place must take the distinctiveness of that time and place into account. The worldliness

---

165. *DBWE* 1:145–46, 183–84, Bonhoeffer's emphases.

166. *DBWE* 6:275, 258, 253. I return to this question of sharing in the guilt of others in the last chapter, where I take up the question of Bonhoeffer's participation in the conspiracy against Hitler and, at least in some sense, in the effort to assassinate him.

that Bonhoeffer advocates, and to which we are also called by Christ, must engage a world that prides itself on achieving a level of intellectual and moral maturity to which previous generations only aspired. Though some have argued that he takes the world's claim that it has come of age at face value, there is good reason to question that interpretation, for to do so would fly in the face of Bonhoeffer's assertion that it must be understood better than it understands itself.[167] As I shall argue in the next two chapters, a more fitting description would be that of an ironic myth that ultimately promotes an illusion.

---

167. *DBWE* 8:428, 431. In *Act and Being* Bonhoeffer critiques the epistemology of Immanuel Kant, stating that new attempts need to be made to understand the famed philosopher better than he understood himself (*DBWE* 2:38 n. 6).

2

The Ironic Myth of a World Come of Age

An enlightened trust in the sovereignty of human reason can be every bit as magical as the exploits of Merlin, and a faith in our capacity for limitless self-improvement just as much a wide-eyed superstition as a faith in leprechauns. There is even a sense in which humanism, looking around our world, seems at times almost as implausible as papal infallibility. Can a world incapable of feeding so many of its inhabitants really be described as mature?

—TERRY EAGLETON, *Reason, Faith, and Revolution*

ONE SEPTEMBER EVENING IN 1931, as he took a stroll around the grounds of Magdalen College with J. R. R. Tolkien and Hugo Dyson, C. S. Lewis exclaimed to his colleagues that myths "are lies and therefore worthless, even though breathed through silver."[1] Though he eventually repented of this view, Lewis gave apt expression that evening to what many believe about the imaginative discourse of myth. Of course, not everyone speaks so contemptuously, adopting instead a more conciliatory tone (or is it condescending?). "We" now know that myths are childlike attempts on the part of primitive societies to explain the world and themselves, a kind of prescientific form of rationality. But now, given that "we" have achieved a stage of intellectual and moral maturity unmatched by previous civilizations, with the various forms of critical rationality aligned with modern science in hand, they may safely be relegated to the realm of children's stories and Hollywood blockbusters, where they offer entertaining diversions but little else.[2] If they have

---

1. Carpenter, *Inklings*, 43.

2. See, for example, Freud, *Future of an Illusion*, 19–25, and Bultmann, *Jesus Christ and Mythology*, 15–17.

any residual value, it is as regulative ideas, conferring a practical orientation to life "as if" the stories were true (which if course we know they are not).

Characterizing the claim that the world has reached a level of maturity heretofore unrealized as an ironic myth will doubtlessly strike some as odd. Dietrich Bonhoeffer, who bequeaths to us the phrase "a world come of age," does not describe it as such, though he does regard myth as an inextricable feature of scripture, asserting that "anthropomorphism in thinking of God, or blatant mythology, is no more irrelevant or unsuitable as an expression for God's being than is the abstract use of the generic term 'deity.'"[3] And in a prison letter he criticizes Rudolf Bultmann for excising the "mythological" elements in an attempt to reduce Christianity to its "essence." "My view," he writes, "is that the full content, including the 'mythological' concepts, must remain—the New Testament is not a mythological dressing up of a universal truth, but this mythology (resurrection and so forth) is the thing itself!"[4]

Bonhoeffer thus acknowledges that describing a way of seeing the world as mythic thus does not summarily dismiss it either as deceptive or as an archaic and feeble attempt at doing "science." Indeed, a truthful description of the world and especially of human existence ultimately requires mythic form.[5] The tales that women and men have fashioned and passed down through the centuries to discern the overall sense and significance of their existence are "never just 'lies,'" says Tolkien, as "there is always something of the truth in them."[6] Even the postmodern claim that "metanarratives" have come to an end is itself such a myth, as are the new atheism's tales about selfish genes and cultural memes.[7] And while we academics squabble among ourselves about such minutiae, global capitalism has been busy establishing its credentials "as perhaps the most rapacious grand narrative" in human history.[8]

The goal of the next two chapters is to examine the particularities of the times and places given to us by God to be for the world a sacrament and foretaste of joyful fellowship with God and with one another in God in the

---

3. *DBWE* 3:75; cf. 82.

4. *DBWE* 8:430. Again note Bonhoeffer's use of scare quotes. Andreas Pangritz observes that though Bonhoeffer welcomes the "breath of air" that characterizes free discussion and sympathizes with Bultmann's "intellectual integrity," he does not want to be read as agreeing with what Bultmann says. Pangritz, *Karl Barth*, 81.

5. See Tolkien, preface to *Silmarillion*, xv. Plato is perhaps to be credited with formulating a conception of myth that does not exclude its capacity to speak truthfully. See Smith, "Plato's Myths," 24–42.

6. As cited by Carpenter, *Inklings*, 43.

7. See Dawkins, *Selfish Gene*.

8. Coakley, *Powers and Submissions*, xiv.

age to come. It is to that end that Bonhoeffer has much to offer us on the subject of deciphering the ironic myth of a world come of age. In particular, it is his critique of the wager that the modern world has placed on the capacity of social technologies such as the nation-state and the marketplace to cultivate the kind of human flourishing consistent with a genuine worldliness that reveals that the self-described maturity of the modern world is anything but that.

Myth and Imagination

Human beings only act in the world that we see, and we only perceive the world in terms of the tropes, analogies, and concepts we have been taught to use as our instruments for describing it.[9] The ability to use signs and also to use things as signs in order to organize a world that we share with other human beings and with the rest of creation constitutes to a great extent our freedom as human beings. But it is also the case that the particular languages we use place constraints on our freedom, for the received meanings that our stories, metaphors, and similes create, while they liberate us from the sensual life that governs other creatures, also dispose us to think and act in certain ways and not in others.[10]

Seeing is never simply an autonomic reaction to sensory stimuli impinging on our eyes. The sense and significance of the things we attend to as we make our way in and through this world, the relationships we foster with our neighbors, and the institutions that sustain the practices in which these relationships are configured, are not self-evident (though they can seem that way if one has never entertained alternative ways of talking about the world). As Bonhoeffer puts it with respect to human reason, we only take in and interact with the people, places, things, and events around us *as* a world, *as* an intelligible whole, because of the languages we speak, the stories we tell, the comparisons and contrasts we invoke as we make our way in our daily lives.[11] In other words, our reason is formed to a significant degree by imagination. *Which* myth we tell makes all the difference in the world, or rather, it makes all the difference *of* the world.

With respect to the ironic character of the modern age, though again Bonhoeffer does not call it that in his prison writings, we can easily discern it in several of his comments, particularly in the baptismal meditation for his godson and in "Outline for a Book." There is in any case more than

9. Hauerwas, "Abortion, Theologically Understood," 611.

10. McCabe, *God Matters*, 170; *Law, Love and Language*, 72.

11. *DBWE* 6:174.

sufficient reason to describe the myth of a world come of age as ironic. Can we really regard as mature a world that is unable to muster the resources to feed a sizable number of its inhabitants? Can a society that condones torture and turns a blind eye to the effects of an economic system that treats people and the environment merely as means to its own avaricious ends honestly speak about itself as intellectually and morally advanced with a straight face? The widespread belief in humanity's coming of age, "magnificently expressed in the liberalism of Immanuel Kant," is in actuality inseparable from "a certain infantile anxiety."[12] We live, says Paul Lehmann, not in the age of maturity, but in an age of anxiety more akin to adolescence.[13] Nicholas Lash agrees, contending that it is "the Cartesian anxiety, the terror of self-importance (twin faces of egotism) which leads us to suppose that we can only find identity, security, and peace in the measure that we establish ourselves as the explaining center of a world whose center of explanation we so anxiously seek."[14] Irony is a fitting description for what can only be described as the self-deifying claim, both chauvinistic and childish, that the civilization in which God has placed us is more advanced, more rational (and by implication less "religious"), and more humane than any other in human history.

Sarah Coakley eloquently captures the true nature of a world come of age: "The original Enlightenment resistance to 'submission' has ultimately spawned, it seems, an economic system that ironically guarantees the continuation of multiple forms of oppression."[15] She puts an interesting spin on the German title of the prison correspondence—*Widerstand und Ergebung*, "Resistance and Submission"—highlighting the fact that the long-desired autonomy from the guardianship of "God" turns out to be little more than an exchange of one tutelary power for a new, more omnivorous Leviathan. If casting off religion was meant to free us and give to us our full dignity as persons, we now find ourselves handed over to new, more callous experts, rulers, and authorities.[16]

Credit for the ironic character of our times can be liberally shared. As Bonhoeffer recognizes, the Protestant Reformation made its own contributions to this situation, such that the existence of the Christian is not only indistinguishable from that of the average citizen, but also parasitic on what counts as moral formation within a particular people or nation. In a

12. Eagleton, *Reason, Faith, and Revolution*, 89, 82.

13. Lehmann, *Ethics*, 96.

14. Lash, *Easter in Ordinary*, 225.

15. Coakley, *Powers and Submissions*, xiv.

16. Taylor, *Secular Age*, 620.

similar manner, the celebrated architects of modernity—Descartes, Hobbes, Locke, Hume, Rousseau, Smith, Kant—were for the most part conservative men, particularly in terms of ethics, eager to save moral appearances while replacing the ground beneath them. It took Friedrich Nietzsche to point out the ironic self-deception that pervaded the rise of the modern world. As Terry Eagleton has put it, while it may not follow that goodness, justice, and wisdom are chimeras because the existence of God has been shown to be one, it does not follow either that "we can dispense with divine authority and continue to conduct our moral business as usual."[17]

The protagonist of the modern myth is "the Man of Reason"[18]—free, self-possessing, and self-realizing, autonomous, responsible, invulnerable and disengaged. These godlike traits that are said to be the deliverances of Reason (uppercase R),[19] surely a fundamentalist doctrine if there ever has been one, the proof of which is the way it has called its own nemesis into being in the form of religious fundamentalism.[20] True believers in either track of the fundamentalist saga consistently fail to recognize the adolescent anxiety embedded in their lust for mastery. "Knowing without loving," writes Bonhoeffer, "is childish, childish reasoning, a childish attempt to become master of the world in a sneaking way. Proud knowledge without love is like the bragging of a stupid youngster who does not deserve to be taken seriously, at which a mature adult can only smile."[21] And like children who loudly boast to their parents that they are unafraid of the dark but then plead with them to leave the hall light on, our efforts to gain control over a world that is seen as threatening and alien betrays a fundamental angst.

These observations by Bonhoeffer reflect insights he develops in *Creation and Fall* and *Ethics*. In our disunion with our origin, center, and limit in God, we have become self-reflective. As those who have sought and who continue to seek to be like God, *sicut deus*, life now consists, first, of understanding ourselves from the springs of our own life and being, and then of understanding everything else in relation to ourselves. "All knowing is now based on self-knowledge," he writes. "The original comprehending [Begreifen] of God, human beings, and things has now become a sacrilegious grasping [Sichvergreifen] of God, human beings and things. Knowing now means establishing the relation to oneself, recognizing oneself in everything

17. Eagleton, *Culture and the Death of God*, 156.

18. Coakley, *Powers and Submissions*, 89–94.

19. With both Eagleton and Charles Taylor I applaud reason, progress, freedom, and decency, but have little patience for or interest in Reason, Progress, Freedom, and Decency (Eagleton, *Reason, Faith, and Revolution*, 84; Taylor, *Secular Age*, 716).

20. Seligman, *Modernity's Wager*, 12.

21. *DBWE* 13:390.

and everything in oneself."[22] For our knowledge of God in particular we renounce the word of God that comes to us again and again from the beyond that is both the center and the boundary of our life, and in so doing we renounce the life that comes in and through this word and seek in vain to grab it for ourselves out of the center that we have made of ourselves.[23] In the renunciation our own ego blocks the way both to God and to the other.[24]

The effort to disengage from the nonhuman world in order to secure our independence from it, grounded in the technological organization and representation of reality that is at the heart of our world, brings with it a solitude that now haunts us. "Our discarnate freedom has no place in the universe," writes William Poteat, "our visible form recapitulates no cosmos, no breath of God shines in our faces."[25] Any assertion of "values" on our part is accompanied by a sense of arbitrariness that grows ever more acute as time goes on. In the words of Eagleton, "What is the point of extracting from the world with one hand values which the other hand has just put in?"[26] Bonhoeffer eloquently sums up the irony implicit in a world come of age: "The human being is thrown back on his own resources. He has learned to cope with everything except himself. He can insure himself against everything but other human beings. In the end it all comes down to the human being."[27]

The meaning of the myths we tell is both presupposed and explicated by the social idioms of the group or groups to which we belong, and the grammar that informs these idioms must continually be passed down, discovered and rediscovered, teased out, suffered, explicated, reconceived, corrupted, and too often lost sight of and then reclaimed. The desire of the modern world to live without myth and without mystery means that we today take "the world seriously only to the extent to which it can be calculated and exploited, never looking for what is behind the world of calculation and of gain."[28] Hence the irony entailed in Bonhoeffer's description of the world

---

22. *DBWE* 6:308. Paul Griffiths labels these two postures as curiosity and studiousness respectively. Both are orderings of the affections governing the intellect. The former desires a reflexive intimacy with the objects of its knowledge in order to control, dominate, or possess them; the latter strives to participate lovingly with the object of its knowing, to respond to it "as gift rather than as potential possession." Griffiths, *Intellectual Appetite*, 20–21.

23. *DBWE* 3:116–17.

24. *DBWE* 5:33.

25. Poteat, *Polanyian Meditations*, 5.

26. Eagleton, *Reason, Faith, and Revolution*, 82–83.

27. *DBWE* 8:500.

28. *DBWE* 13:360.

as having come of age, for the claim that the world has come of age and thus advanced beyond the need for myths cannot help taking mythic form.

Bonhoeffer on a World Come of Age in the Prison Letters

Most analyses of Bonhoeffer on the topic of a world come of age point to his April 30, 1944 letter to Eberhard Bethge as the pivotal text where his most provocative and enigmatic insights first come to light. Though this letter does in many respects form the proper point of departure, care needs to be exercised when starting with it. If we read this letter and what follows out of their context in the prison correspondence in particular, and in his entire body of work more generally, we can be caught up in the erroneous conclusion made by many that he makes a sudden shift away from virtually all that he had previously affirmed and written about God, Christ, and the church. On the contrary, he had already called into question in earlier works most of the key elements of what he connects with the notion of a world come of age in these letters.

Bonhoeffer prefaces his inquiry into the nature of a world come of age by asking, "Who is Christ actually for us today?"[29] The form of this question is significant in two respects. First, as Bonhoeffer insists in both his lectures on Christology and in *Creation and Fall*, the only access human beings have to the transcendent stage on which we play our roles in life is in connection to this question of who: "The question of 'who' is the question about transcendence." It is this question, asked in connection with the person of Jesus Christ, that interrogates us about the limits of our own being.[30] Second, he contends in *Ethics* that this question of who Christ is cannot be posed in the abstract but must be asked in the form of "how Christ may take form among us today and here."[31] Though the form of Christ is one and the same in every time and place, it is not possible to determine for all times and places the manner in which this interrogation takes place. Instead, we ask this question, or more precisely we submit to its interrogation of us, in connection with what is at stake in the time and the place given to us as the domain of our decisions and our encounters.[32]

---

29. *DBWE* 8:362.

30. *DBWE* 12:302–3; *DBWE* 3:28–29.

31. *DBWE* 6:100. Bonhoeffer first raises the question of how the human exists in *Act and Being*, stating that in both the form of Adam and the form of Christ, created being (*Dasein*, there-being) is intrinsically related to how-being (*Wiesein*). *DBWE* 2:137–38, 161.

32. *DBWE* 6:100–101.

The questions of who Christ is today and how he takes form in us here and now have become particularly urgent, says Bonhoeffer, because the world is approaching a completely religionless age, one in which people simply cannot be religious anymore. He worries in particular about what these changes portend for the church, given that the "entire nineteen hundred years of Christian preaching and theology are built on the 'religious a priori' in human beings." What happens if it becomes obvious that this "a priori" does not exist? What does a religionless world mean for a church, a congregation, a sermon, a liturgy, a Christian life as such? How can Christ become Lord of the religionless? How do ritual and prayer function in a religionless situation? What significance does the ancient practice of the arcane discipline and the distinction between the last things and the things before the last have in this situation?[33]

Beyond the demise of religion (the details of which I shall examine in chapter 4), Bonhoeffer does not give specifics about the constitutive features of a world come of age in this letter. It is important to note, however, that he speaks about a number of Christian practices, virtually all of which are connected in some way with worship, as distinct from "religion." It would seem that whatever else these ecclesial activities are, they are not intrinsically "religious." He also refers to the eschatological distinction between the last things and the things before the last, and suggests that it will play an expanded role in the future.

The eschatological motif and the practice of the arcane discipline reappear in the next letter that Bonhoeffer writes to Bethge. He rejects any attempt to tie Christianity to an otherworldly or individualistic frame of reference, asking rhetorically where in the Old Testament does the question of saving one's soul ever come up. The righteousness and kingdom of God are reaffirmed as the center of everything, and thus what matters "is not the beyond but this world, how it is created and preserved, is given laws, reconciled, and renewed." He then adds that the question of what is beyond, that is, the question of transcendence, is understood in the gospel only in relation to this world and on behalf of this world, "not in the anthropocentric sense of liberal, mystical, pietistic, ethical theology, but in the biblical sense of the creation and the incarnation, crucifixion, and resurrection of Jesus Christ." He credits Karl Barth with being the first to address these questions, but then says that Barth put in place of religion a positivist doctrine of revelation that "says, in effect, 'like it or lump it.'" The problem is that every doctrine—be it the virgin birth or the Trinity—"must be swallowed whole or not at all," and that's not the biblical path. Instead Bonhoeffer states that

33. *DBWE* 8:362–65.

an arcane discipline must be reestablished, a practice that formerly sheltered the mysteries of the Christian faith from profanation but that now would also allow for the recognition that there are "degrees of cognition and degrees of significance."[34]

Bonhoeffer returns briefly to the topic of a world come of age in a letter dated May 29, 1944. His comments take an epistemic turn, noting the profound changes in the perception of reality that have taken place since the Middle Ages. He asserts that we should not use God as a stopgap for the incompleteness of our knowledge, and we must refrain from doing so for God's sake, "because then—as is objectively inevitable—when the boundaries of knowledge are pushed ever further, God too is pushed away and thus ever on the retreat." Christians should seek God in what we know and not in the unsolved questions, and this applies not only to the relation between God and scientific knowledge, but also in connection to the universal questions of death, suffering, and guilt. We should also not avoid the fact that there are answers to these universal questions that completely disregard God, and that these answers have been around throughout the ages. "As for the idea of a 'solution,' we would have to say that the Christian answers are just as uncompelling (or just as compelling) as other possible solutions."[35] In other words, Christianity should not be seen as yet another anxious attempt to find an ultimate explanation for the world that underwrites our efforts to gain a measure of autonomous agency over the sense and significance of things. To speak of God as a cog in our explanatory systems reduces the divine reality to but one feature of the world that we construct for ourselves.

The first time that Bonhoeffer actually uses the expression *die mündig gewordenen Welt*[36] to refer to the specific character of the modern world is in his next letter to Bethge, dated June 8, 1944. Though context is obviously important, these terms routinely signify only that a man or woman has reached chronological and physical adulthood, and not necessarily intellectual or moral maturity.[37] It is also interesting to note that in a sermon that he delivers in 1934 he uses a different form of expression, *der reife Mann* and *das reife Mannesalter*, to talk about the kind of insight and knowledge exhibited by a well-formed, mature adult.[38] Bonhoeffer does on occasion use *mündig* in earlier writings, but without the degree of emphasis he would

---

34. *DBWE* 8:372–73.

35. *DBWE* 8:405–6.

36. Variations include *mündige Welt*, "mature world," and *Mündigkeit*, *Mündigwerden*, "maturity."

37. Kelly, *Liberating Faith*, 184 n. 80.

38. *DBW* 13:397.

give to it in his prison writings. The closest he comes to the sense he assigns to it in his prison writings is in *Ethics*, where in the course of a description of the French Revolution he states that "the people found that they were mature enough to take their affairs into their own hands, in both domestic and foreign matters."[39]

There is little doubt that the appearance of these terms at this point in the prison correspondence is due to a significant degree to Wilhelm Dilthey's book *Weltanschauung und Analyse des Menschen seit Renaissance und Reformation*. We know from an earlier letter that Bonhoeffer had been reading it in the weeks leading up to this letter, and we also know that he continued to read it late into his imprisonment. Dilthey states that in the seventeenth century there appeared a science come of age (*eine mündig gewordene Wissenschaft*) that would provide the general principles for the conduct of life and governance of society (*allgemeingültige Prinzipien für die Führung des Lebens und die Leitung der Gesellschaft*).[40] The key question is, does Bonhoeffer adopt Dilthey's overall outlook on the modern world, which would mean among other things that he must reverse course with regard to the normative status of abstract principles, or does he as the consummate *bricoleur* adapt Dilthey's terminology for his own distinctive purposes, as he routinely does with other authors? Ralf Wüstenberg, for example, posits a rather sharp contrast between Bonhoeffer's view of the modern world in *Ethics* and that found in his prison correspondence: "Whereas in a manuscript from the *Ethics* the world, which is in the process of 'coming of age,' was regarded negatively in terms of 'nihilism,' in the prison letters Bonhoeffer reflects positively on the autonomy of the world, humanity, and life." What caused this change? "Between the *Ethics* and these positive statements in the *Letters and Papers from Prison*," writes Wüstenberg, "Bonhoeffer had read Wilhelm Dilthey."[41]

When we look more closely at these two texts, however, the claim that a decisive break exists between *Ethics* and the prison correspondence on the question of how Bonhoeffer assesses the moral state of the world as it is presently ordered is not compelling. Though it is true that in the prison writings he does not use the idea of *das Nichts*, the nothing, as he does in *Ethics*,[42] this is an argument from silence, which never makes for a strong case, and in this instance, given the occasional nature of letters, it is even weaker. Moreover, in both texts he refers to the world as godless, a term that

---

39. *DBWE* 6:120; cf. *DBWE* 12:120, 398, *DBWE* 16:494.
40. Dilthey, *Weltanschauung und Analyse*, 90.
41. Wüstenberg, "Philosophical Influences," 147–48.
42. *DBWE* 6:127–31, 179.

he does not use lightly, and which he uses in conjunction with the nothing.[43] He also speaks of a promising godlessness in *Ethics* that "protests against pious godlessness insofar as that has spoiled the churches,"[44] which both recalls his rejection of pious Christian secularism in "Thy Kingdom Come!" and anticipates the famous assertion in a later letter that "the world is more god-less and perhaps just because of that closer to God than the world not yet come of age."[45]

It also fails to take into account Bonhoeffer's introduction of the concept in *Creation and Fall*. He contrasts philosophical thinking on the question of nothingness, which he describes as the ultimate attempt at an explanation of the beginning, with its theological meaning: "This nothingness is therefore not a primal possibility or a ground of God; it 'is' absolutely nothing." *Das Nichts* happens only in relation to God's action as what has already happened and negated. He thus calls it the obedient nothing, the nothing that waits on God, whose glory and whose existence resides only in God's action.[46] When he says in *Ethics* that the West, having lost its unity in the form of Jesus Christ, has fallen victim to the nothing,[47] it is less a note of pessimism or despair than a recognition that our aspiration to be like God, *sicut deus*, throws us once again back on our own inadequate resources and abilities. As he puts it in "Outline for a Book," a humanity come of age has learned to cope with everything except itself.[48]

Though Bonhoeffer does indeed acknowledge the claim to autonomy on the part of a world come of age, he neither endorses or affirms it nor makes it the starting point for a properly theological assessment of the present order of things, stating on multiple occasions in the prison writings that it cannot be left to its own self-understanding, but must be understood from the gospel and from Christ.[49] Dilthey, by contrast, espouses a thoroughly religious conception of Christianity and thus a turn to inwardness in connection with his assertions of the maturity of the modern world, stances that Bonhoeffer explicitly rejects, not just in these late prison letters but throughout his career. It is also difficult to imagine that he would embrace the stoicism that Dilthey associates with the moral and scientific systems

---

43. *DBWE* 8:480, 482; *DBWE* 6:127–28.

44. *DBWE* 6:124.

45. *DBWE* 8:482.

46. *DBWE* 3:33–34.

47. *DBWE* 6:128.

48. *DBWE* 8:500.

49. *DBWE* 8:373, 428, 431, 482.

of modernity.[50] In a stinging indictment, Daniel Hardy and David Ford describe the religiosity that Bonhoeffer finds so problematic as "stoicism with Christian influence," and observe that the modern nation-state "is delighted to welcome a religion that is so timid and orderly, leaving the passions free for economics, war and collective sport."[51] Jacob Phillips's contention that Bonhoeffer both subverts Dilthey's approach and reconfigures elements of it for his own purposes is a more accurate assessment.[52]

Bonhoeffer's assertion in *Ethics*, that the church must continue to reckon with the worldliness of the world, but always in connection with God's rule over it—which means that affirmation and negation, judgment and reconciliation come together in concrete action in the world[53]—is not negated but updated[54] and amplified in the prison correspondence to better account for the ever-evolving character of a world come of age. He thus finds in Dilthey a conceptual framework in terms of which to narrate the peculiarities of the times, and more specifically to describe more precisely the performance of a world come of age, but not the basis for a radical reformulation of what Christianity is all about.

The June 8 letter also provides more information about what Bonhoeffer associates with the modern age. He states that the historical movement toward human autonomy in matters of science, society and government, art, ethics, and religion, the origins of which he locates in the thirteenth century, has reached a stage of completeness in the present. As a result, humans have learned how to handle all the important issues of life by themselves without having recourse to the "working hypothesis" of "God."[55] This self-confidence and independence is clearly the case in science, art, and ethics, he writes, but it is becoming increasingly the case in religious matters as well. It is becoming evident, he writes, "that everything gets along without 'God' and does so just as well as before." In human affairs generally, and not just in the scientific realm, "God" is being pushed further and further out of life.[56] Once again we see Bonhoeffer acknowledging the shift in the perception of reality as one of the hallmarks of a world come of age.

50. Feil, *Theology of Dietrich Bonhoeffer*, 181–83, 236 n. 195; cf. Dilthey, *Weltanschauung und Analyse*, 153–61, 260–67, 285–96.

51. Hardy and Ford, *Praising and Knowing God*, 144.

52. Phillips, "Dispossessed Science, Dispossessed Self," 65.

53. *DBWE* 6:224.

54. Schmitz, "Reading *Discipleship* and *Ethics* Together," 152.

55. When Napoleon complained to Pierre Laplace that he allowed no place for God in his book on physics, Laplace reportedly responded, "Sire, I have no need of that hypothesis." Cited by Hahn, "Laplace and the Mechanistic Universe," 256.

56. *DBWE* 8:425–26; cf. 319–20.

The world has become conscious of itself and the laws of its existence, and in the process is now very sure of itself, exuding a confidence that nothing, no failure, not even a cataclysmic war, can shake. Catholics and Protestants see these developments as the "great falling-away" from God and from Christ, "and the more they lay claim to God and Christ in opposing this, and play them off against it, the more this development considers itself anti-Christian." But this does not deter Christian apologetics from striking at this worldly self-confidence: "It is trying to persuade this world that has come of age that it cannot live without 'God' as its guardian. Even after we have capitulated on all worldly matters, there still remain the so-called ultimate questions—death, guilt—which only 'God' can answer, and for which people need God and the church and the pastor. . . . But what happens if some day they no longer exist as such, or if they are being answered 'without God'?"[57]

There are several items of interest to be noted in this letter. First, Bonhoeffer's assertion that the historical movement toward human autonomy has reached a state of completeness in the present, with the result that the world has become conscious of itself and the laws of its existence, implicitly acknowledges that modernity has achieved an explicitly mythic stage in its development. Second, he once again rejects any attempt to treat God as an element in a stand-alone explanatory scheme, whether in reference to the history or makeup of the physical world, or to systems of moral thought and action. As he notes in *Ethics*, the roots of cultural Protestantism are found here.[58]

But perhaps most importantly, he reiterates in this letter as well as in the letter of May 27 an understanding of the gospel that he had formulated more than ten years earlier in response to Nietzsche's contention that Christianity is a slave religion that grows out of *ressentiment*, that is, the response of those for whom the will to power has been thwarted by the noble or master class, and who invert the healthy values of the powerful into their opposites, manifesting in the sentiments of hatred, revenge, jealousy, and envy.[59] This construal of Christianity comes through most clearly in his essay "Thy Kingdom Come!," in which he critiques an understanding of the gospel that dares to exploit the weakness and suffering of humankind in service of an otherworldly or secular faith.[60] Bonhoeffer refuses to accept the consignment of faith to the margins in an attempt to reserve space for

57. *DBWE* 8:426–27.
58. *DBWE* 6:59–60.
59. Nietzsche, *Antichrist*, 20, 22, 24.
60. *DBWE* 12:285–87.

God in the so-called ultimate questions of death, guilt, and suffering. As he puts it in a later letter, God meets us in the midst of our lives, and thus the church stands at the center of the village, not at its periphery.[61]

We should note the meticulous care that Bonhoeffer takes in these letters in the use of scare quotes for his descriptions of a world come of age. When he employs them around "God" he clearly refers to generic conceptions of deity that are elements in some kind of independent cosmological or moral schema. When he does not use them, the word is invariably rendered in close conjunction with Christ and the church. This use of scare quotes with reference to God also appears in "Outline for a Book," where he states that "'God' as working hypothesis, as stopgap for our embarrassments, has become superfluous."[62] He uses them to make precisely this distinction in a seminar paper that he gave several years earlier at Union Seminary: "The attempt of cosmology, that is of a genetical [sic] interpretation of the world on the basis of natural science, can never reach beyond the limits of human thinking. Cosmology may come to the assumption of a last ground of the world and may call that 'God,' all we can say in the name of christian theology is that this God is not the God of revelation and not the creator."[63]

Like Barth, Bonhoeffer associates all attempts of natural reason to speak about the beginning and end of the world with nineteenth-century Protestant efforts to bypass or downplay the contingency of historical revelation, and therefore gives no credence to the possibility that an idea of the divine developed on the basis of natural reason (for example, the five ways of Thomas Aquinas) may in fact bear a "natural"[64] relationship to the understanding of the triune God in the Christian tradition. Though Bonhoeffer is right to reject an understanding of God that sets the terms for God's revelation in Christ, it is also clear that we cannot make sense of talk about Jesus as the Son of God without some prior understanding of and use for "God" developed apart from revelation.[65]

---

61. *DBWE* 8:406, 427, 367. Again we find continuity with his earliest work, for as he states in *Sanctorum Communio*, one enters into the state of reality as the whole person is confronted and addressed by another person in the midst of time. *DBWE* 1:48.

62. *DBWE* 8:500. As noted in chapter 1, he also uses scare quotes in his descriptions of what constitutes a true worldliness.

63. *DBWE* 10:475; cf. *DBWE* 8:501.

64. Bonhoeffer seeks to recover in *Ethics* the idea of the natural for Protestant theology, employing it to refer to those aspects of a fallen world that remain open to the coming of Christ, among which he includes reason as the ability to perceive as a unity the whole and the universal in reality. *DBWE* 6:174.

65. McCabe, *God Matters*, 42. Rowan Williams rightly observes that "when Hebrew Scripture says that YHWH (the enigmatic and unpronounceable designation of Israel's Lord and Saviour) is God, *elohim*, or that YHWH *elohim* does or says this or that, there

In his next letter, written on the last day of June 1944, Bonhoeffer returns to epistemic matters, stating once again that in recent years God has been pushed out of the realm of knowledge and life, and relegated to the ground "beyond the world of experience," singling out Kant as a key player in this development.[66] In response theologians have taken one of two paths, both of which he declines to take, and both of which are still heard in recent debates about the religious foundations of Western civilization.[67] On one side are those who engage in a type of apologetics, in vain taking up arms against "Darwinism" and related matters. On the other side are theologians who resign themselves to the expulsion of God from the field of knowledge, allowing God to function as a deus ex machina, literally, "the god from the machine,"[68] swooping in as the solution to the so-called ultimate questions. Those who seemingly have no such questions or who refuse to admit to such must therefore be closed off from talking about God. They must be shown that they are deceived about such matters, that their happiness is in fact disastrous, their health sickness, and their vitality an object of despair, tasks that existential philosophy and psychotherapy are ready to perform. If they are still unconvinced, then theologians are at their wits' end.[69]

It is this antipathy toward those who are no longer religious or look to the church for succor and reassurance in times of crisis that Bonhoeffer finds so troubling. "When Jesus made sinners whole," he writes, "they were real sinners, but Jesus didn't begin by making every person into a sinner. He called people from their sin, not into it." To be sure, the encounter with Jesus turns all human values upside down, as with the conversion of Paul on the Damascus Road, but it is the encounter that acts as the catalyst for the recognition of sin. Jesus never called into question a person's health, strength, or fortune, or dismissed them as rotten fruit; "otherwise why would he have made sick people well or given strength back to the weak?" The claim of

---

is a presupposition that we already know something of what *elohim* means. . . . An implicit grammar is at work." R. D. Williams, *Edge of Words*, 6.

66. Bonhoeffer does not use scare quotes in this letter when speaking of God being pushed out of a world come of age. Nevertheless, he states that he is picking up where he left off in the letter of June 8, and gives no indication that the distinction that he so carefully set forth previously is no longer in force.

67. See Hunter, *Culture Wars*.

68. Cf. *DBWE* 8:366, 405–7, 425–26, 500. Deus ex machina refers to a mechanical device that was used in Greek and Roman theater to introduce a divine figure into the action who would resolve whatever dilemma the plot had conjured up. In an interesting turn of phrase Bonhoeffer also rejects the notion of diaboli ex machina, devils from the machine, as a way to explain the fall in *Creation and Fall* (*DBWE* 3:104).

69. *DBWE* 8:450.

God in Christ is over all human life, in all of its manifestations, most especially in its health and strength.[70]

As with other facets of the prison correspondence, Bonhoeffer's insistence that God meets the world, most especially a world come of age, in the center of life, in its full vigor and health, not in weakness and guilt, draws on points made in earlier writings. In "Thy Kingdom Come!" he states that both otherworldliness and secularity are rejections of the reign of God. Otherworldliness means that we are hostile to the earth because we seek to be better than it, and secularity signifies hostility to God because God takes away the earth from us. "Otherworldliness . . . makes it easy to preach and speak words of comfort. An otherworldly church can be sure that it will in no time at all attract all the weaklings, all those who are only too glad to be deceived and deluded, all the dreamers, all disloyal children of the Earth." Christ, on the other hand, does not want these weaknesses, but looks to make the weak human being strong: "Christ does not lead him into the otherworldliness of religious escapism. Rather, Christ returns him to the Earth as its true son."[71]

Bonhoeffer provides his most extensive genealogy of a world come of age in the July 16, 1944 letter to Bethge, identifying developmental landmarks in religion, politics, philosophy, and natural science that left many asking what room is left in the world for the working hypothesis of God. Anyone familiar with this history will recognize the names in his brief survey of how we arrived at this point in time: Lord Herbert of Cherbury, Michel de Montaigne, Jean Bodin, Nicholas of Cusa, Girodano Bruno, Niccolò Machiavelli, Hugo Grotius, René Descartes, Baruch Spinoza, Immanuel Kant, Johann Gottlieb Fichte, and of course Georg Wilhelm Friedrich Hegel.[72] He rejects those who condemn wholesale what this history has brought about as well as those who propose the *salto mortale*, the heteronomous death-leap back into the clericalism of the Middle Ages, a feat that he regards not only as a counsel of despair, but as something that could only be attempted at the cost of intellectual honesty. It is a matter of basic intellectual integrity that the working hypothesis be dropped in scientific matters, or at the very least eliminated as much as possible—an edifying scientist or physician is a hybrid, he states.[73]

At the same time, however, Bonhoeffer gives little aid and comfort to those who would argue that a world come of age is in some sense a necessary

70. *DBWE* 8:450–51.
71. *DBWE* 12:285–86.
72. *DBWE* 8:475–77.
73. *DBWE* 8:478.

outworking of reality. This is clearly stated in his grave doubts about bio-
logically inspired interpretations of history which, on the assumption that
ontogenesis (the maturation pattern of a person) recapitulates phylogenesis
(the development of a species), portray it as a steady progress of human
maturation from ancient through medieval to modern. He refuses to turn
what can be a heuristic analogy, that of the human person maturing from
infancy through adolescence to adulthood, into "a Procrustean bed . . . into
which, willy-nilly, the evidence is to be pressed."[74] He attributes this dubious
concept that sees the whole course of history culminating in "modernity" to
Hegel, who then identified with his own philosophical system (though he
was far from the only one to make this move).[75]

Bonhoeffer then returns to the question of the identity of God and his
relation to the world in what is perhaps the most often cited passage, and
certainly the most enigmatic, from *Letters and Papers from Prison*:

> And we cannot be honest unless we recognize that we have to
> live in the world—"etsi deus non daretur." And this is precisely
> what we do recognize—before God! God himself compels us to
> recognize it. Thus our coming of age leads us to a truer recogni-
> tion of our situation before God. God would have us know that
> we must live as those who manage their lives without God. The
> same God who is with us is the God who forsakes us (Mark
> 15:34!). The same God who makes us to live in the world with-
> out the working hypothesis of God is the God before whom we
> stand continually. Before God, and with God, we live without
> God.[76]

He concludes this portion of the letter with the telling comment that the
development toward the world's coming of age has eliminated a false conception of God, thereby freeing us to recognize the God of the Bible as one
who wins power and space in the world through being powerless.

These comments were taken up in a short-lived but intense debate in
the mid-twentieth century about the "death of God." Whatever we might
want to make of that controversy, the sense and significance of this passage
remain contested. Assuming that what Bonhoeffer says here is consistent
with what he had written previously, and taking into consideration the
many references to the working hypothesis of God, his constant rejections
of false notions of God, the careful use of scare quotes in previous letters
when distinguishing between incommensurate and incompatible uses of

74. Lash, *Easter in Ordinary*, 155.

75. *DBWE* 8:321.

76. *DBWE* 8:478–79.

the term, and the repeated insistence that we cannot be content with the self-understanding of a world come of age, the conclusion of some that he is positing a new understanding of God's absence as a mode of the divine presence is unpersuasive, to say the least.[77] Unless someone wants to suggest that he is indulging in a blatant contradiction, Bonhoeffer is deliberately and provocatively using "God" in equivocal senses in this passage. The question is, therefore, to what end?

Part of the answer is found, as it often is, in his earlier writings. In *Creation and Fall* Bonhoeffer describes what humankind has lost as a result of the fall. By virtue of its desire to be *sicut deus*, like God, humankind no longer receives life as divine gift but as a command, which brings with it death, for it "obliges me to live out of myself, out of my own resources, and I am unable to do that." We now live in a vicious circle, live out of our own resources, and thus we are alone, deprived of God's gift. And yet we cannot live, for living out of our own resources "just is [our] death." Thrown back on ourselves, back on our knowledge of good and evil, we recognize that "death consists in having to live before God without the life that comes from God."[78] In light of this observation, the statement in the prison letter that in a world come of age we must now live before God without God takes on a very different ontological sense and reference from what has often been attributed to it.

With respect to the ontological status of this passage, Bonhoeffer's seemingly contradictory assertions can be read as a creative recovery of a type of dialectical inquiry that was common in patristic theology and the High Middle Ages having to do with what can and cannot be truthfully said about the nature of God, but which dropped out of favor in later medieval, Renaissance, and Enlightenment thought. The attempt to refer intelligibly to what is beyond expression—the essence of God—was done in one of two ways. One method takes the form of an ascending dialectic of affirmation and negation, in which we simultaneously affirm and deny all things to God: "By, as it were in one breath, both affirming what God is and denying . . . 'that there is any kind of thing that God is,' we step off the very boundary of language itself, beyond every assertion and every denial, into the 'negation of the negation' and the 'brilliant darkness' of God."[79] The *via negativa*, the way of negation, does not however stand alone, as though negations are somehow more adequate to the reality of God than are affirmations. They

77. See, for example, *DBWE* 8:479 n. 38. A recent article that presupposes this dubious reading of living before God without God is Miller, "Reframing the Faith-Learning Relationship."

78. *DBWE* 3:91, 142; cf. *DBWE* 6:400, *DBWE* 4:282.

79. Turner, *Faith, Reason and the Existence of God*, 156.

are instead folded dialectically into an ascending hierarchy that culminates with the negation of negation. Pseudo-Dionysius offers a series of negations juxtaposed with affirmations of the names that may be used of God, asserting in conclusion that "we make both assertions and denials of what is next to it, but never of it, for it is both beyond every assertion, being the perfect and unique cause of all things, and, by virtue of its preeminently simple and absolute nature, free of every limitation, beyond every limitation; it is also beyond every denial."[80]

A second way of apprehending what is beyond comprehension is found in the writings of Augustine, Bonaventure, and Julian of Norwich. As Denys Turner observes, the limitations of the human mind with respect to the divine are brought to light by the coincidence of opposites, that is, a profusion of affirmations that conflict and thus negate each other, leading to a recognition of their collective deficiency.[81] Early in *Confessions*, for example, Augustine offers this imaginative description of the divine nature:

> never new, never old, renewing all things yet wearing down the proud though they know it not; ever active, ever at rest, gathering while knowing no need . . . seeking although you lack nothing. You love without frenzy, you are jealous yet secure, you regret without sadness, you grow angry yet remain tranquil . . . you take back what you find although you never lost it; you are never in need yet you rejoice in your gains, never avaricious yet you demand profits. You allow us to pay you more than you demand, and so you become our debtor, yet which of us possesses anything that does not already belong to you? You owe us nothing, yet you pay your debts; you write off our debts to you, yet you lose nothing thereby.[82]

In *The Journey of the Mind to God*, Bonaventure employs the coincidence of opposites to gesture to the simplicity and thus the incomprehensibility of God, who is both first and last, eternal and most present, simple and yet the greatest, most actual and most changeless, most perfect and immense, supremely one yet pervading all things.[83] And finally Julian, in her description of Christ's labors on our behalf, uses a similar strategy to correct misconceptions about God and gender: "In our Mother, Christ, we profit and grow, and in mercy he reforms and restores us, through the power of his

---

80. Pseudo-Dionysius, "The Mystical Theology," I.1.V; cf. Turner, *Darkness of God*, 33–34.

81. Turner, *Darkness of God*, 29–34.

82. Augustine, *Confessions* I.4,4.

83. Bonaventure, *Journey of the Mind*, V.7.

Passion and his death and rising again, he unites us to our essential being. This is how our Mother mercifully acts to all his children who are submissive and obedient to him."[84]

Bonhoeffer does something very similar in the letter of July 16, only in this case it has to do with the nature of God's presence in the world rather than with our understanding of the divine nature itself. With this letter he definitively renounces every attempt to reinstitute a "Christian worldview," as he puts it in a sermon delivered some twelve years earlier in Berlin, shortly after Chancellor Franz von Papen had issued a proclamation in which he reintroduced the custom of invoking the name of God at the opening of parliament. This sermon, based on the passage from Colossians that states that our lives have been raised and hidden in Christ, anticipates many of the themes that he raises in his prison letters. Bonhoeffer observes that Paul's words seem incomprehensible to us, with little sense of how they relate to our personal or pubic lives, and it makes little difference whether one is talking about Christianity in America, where churches are filled to overflowing, or in Germany, where they are nearly empty. The church takes refuge in religious busyness and talk, all the while refusing to be told that God is dangerous, that God will not be mocked, and that we must lose our life if we really want to have anything to do with the living God.[85]

When Bonhoeffer states in *Letters and Papers* that Christians must now live as those do who manage their lives without God and that God compels us to live without God, he is speaking not about the absence of God *simpliciter*, but instead about a life lived with and before the God of Jesus Christ that does not require the church to find or fashion a space reserved for the stopgap God, the working hypothesis God, or the *ex machina* God. Theologians should no longer seek to supply "principles of social and political order"[86] derived from an abstract or generic idea of the divine that is unconnected to the God of the crucified and resurrected Christ, in a futile attempt to ground the explanatory schemes that human beings have devised to make sense of their day-to-day existence. That God—or rather, "God"—is no longer necessary or even desirable. Indeed, such schemes get in the way of helping a world come of age see that it is in fact godless, poised pre-

---

84. Julian of Norwich, *Revelations*, 58. See also Coakley, *Powers and Submissions*, 109–29.

85. *DBWE* 11:450–57.

86. *DBWE* 15:451; cf. 11:223–24. The felt need to offer principles of social and political order to the earthly city, such as one finds in Charles Mathewes's contention that churches should articulate to the whole community, "in richly theological terms, a comprehensive civic vision," is a vestige of the impulse of Christendom. Mathewes, *Theology of Public Life*, 203.

cariously in the wrathful hands of the God who reigns in and through the figure of a suffering messiah. They serve instead as ways of claiming that the present social order should be seen as a given, to which we therefore have a nonfunctional, "contemplative" relation, with theological understanding penetrating "into the essential structure in the mind and will of God."[87] Such conceptions treat revelation as chiefly a cognitive affair, inviting men and women simply "to consider the world differently"[88] and not as actually different. In other words, the relationships and identities formed within a world come of age—nation-states, capitalist markets, nuclear families, and the like—are not seen as contingent realities that arose in interaction with the social and material conditions of their times, but as substantially the way that God had originally designed them to fit human beings together.[89]

The last comment we have from the prison letters that bears directly on the nature of a world come of age, found in the letter to Bethge dated August 14, 1944, confirms Bonhoeffer's earlier estimations of it as less than ideal. He states that God allows women and men to serve him in all that is human and that everything else is a manifestation of hubris. He then qualifies that sentiment in an instructive way: "To be sure, an excessive cultivation of human relationships and of meaning something to one another . . . can also lead to a cult of the human that is disproportionate to reality."[90] Once again this statement has precedents in what he had written previously, beginning in *Sanctorum Communio*, in which he asserts that the human person as such is not holy; what is holy about the other is that, as the creation and thus the image of God, the other is that through which the divine You becomes visible.[91] This emphasis pervades the entire corpus, as seen in *Ethics*, where he states that affirming the essential goodness of humanity results in the deification of humanity, which is "the proclamation of nihilism," and at the beginning of the section "Natural Life," he says that life which makes itself absolute and posits itself as its own goal destroys itself: "It is a

---

87. R. D. Williams, *On Christian Theology*, 228.

88. Ziegler, "Dietrich Bonhoeffer," 581.

89. Karl Marx and Frederick Engels pinpoint the presumption in this position by observing that every ruling class in every age makes the same assertion, transforming "into eternal laws of nature and of reason the social forms springing from [their] present mode of production and form of property—historical relations that rise and disappear in the progress of production." Marx and Engels, *Communist Manifesto*, 226.

90. *DBWE* 8:509.

91. *DBWE* 1:55.

movement without end, without goal, movement into nothingness."[92] For Bonhoeffer it is possible to be "all too human."[93]

The Technological Regime of a World Come of Age

Though the prison letters to Bethge are central to our efforts to understand what Bonhoeffer intends by this notion of a world come of age, the best clues are found in two non-epistolary documents that come from the same period of time. The letters are occasional writings in which he engages in thought experiments offered to his friend for his consideration, not as conclusions that follow directly from premises but as attempts to explore the implications of what he has observed over the course of his lifetime. By contrast, the baptismal meditation and the book outline show evidence of having been reworked and revised.[94]

Bonhoeffer pens the meditation in Tegel prison for the baptism of his grandnephew and godson, Dietrich Wilhelm Rüdiger Bethge. In it he laments the dismantling of long-established practices and institutions in recent decades, especially those of the upper-class German household, in which young people were formed with an awareness of being called to public service, intellectual achievement and leadership, and the obligation to be guardians of a great historical heritage and intellectual tradition. And he anticipates that there would be a great migration out of European cities that would complete the alteration of rural life begun by the contrivances of modern technology—radios, cars, and the telephone—and the organizing of virtually every aspect of life. He thus commends living in rural areas with a plot of land underfoot, affording the opportunity for "a new, simpler, more natural and contented life of daily work and evening leisure." He then cites an intriguing passage from the book of Jeremiah: "Flee from the midst of Babylon . . . she could not be healed. Forsake her, and let each of us go to our own country (Jer 51:61ff.)."[95]

92. DBWE 6:123, 178. J. Kameron Carter refers to this process of deifying humanity as the creation of "the Imperial God-Man." Carter, "Unlikely Convergence," 172.

93. Nietzsche, Human, All Too Human.

94. According to an editorial note in the critical edition, the book outline was written in Latin script (DBWE 8:499 n. 1). Though it would be unwise to make too much of this fact, it is worth noting that Bonhoeffer twice mentions in letters that he typically used German script when roughing out a first draft (374, 518). The use of the Latin script here suggests that, unlike the letters to which scholars usually turn when investigating his concept of a world come of age, Bonhoeffer had taken the time to rework to some extent the ideas in the outline.

95. DBWE 8:385–86.

Among the differences that Bonhoeffer sees between the world that previous generations had known and the world his grandnephew would inherit is that his parents and grandparents believed that one could and should plan, develop, and shape one's own life, decide on a lifework and then pursue it with all one's might. In contrast, "from our own experience we have learned that we cannot even plan for the next day, that what we have built up is destroyed overnight. Our lives, unlike our parents' lives, have become formless or even fragmentary." He then declares that he and his generation recognize more clearly than in previous times that the world rests, not in our power, but in the wrathful and gracious hands of God.[96]

This is not the first time Bonhoeffer reflects on the increasingly fragmented nature of life in the modern world while in prison. In earlier letters he contrasts the fate of his generation to that of his parents, stating that in personal matters he and his contemporaries could not depend on having whole and balanced lives. He says that this constitutes the greatest renunciation that has been imposed "on us younger folk and is required of us. Probably that is why we feel especially strongly how unfinished and fragmentary our lives are."[97] The sense of fragmentation is not limited, however, just to personal life. Bonhoeffer adds that if the end of the eighteenth century marked the demise of "universal scholarship," the nineteenth century signaled the rise of intensive study that brought to an end extensive inquiry. Now everyone is a "specialist" or "technician," even in the arts. "Our intellectual existence," he laments, "remains but a torso."[98]

Once again drawing on Jeremiah to frame his thoughts, Bonhoeffer says that given these developments, the task is not to seek great things but "to save and preserve our souls out of the chaos, and to realize that this is the only thing we can carry as 'booty' out of the burning house." He and his contemporaries "shall have to bear our lives more than to shape them, to hope more than to plan, to hold out more than to stride ahead," in the hope that they will preserve what is necessary for his godson's generation, so that they might plan, build up, and shape a new and better life. In particular, his generation spent too much time cultivating a style of reasoning that assumes that rational individuals, from the privileged standpoint of "onlookers," could weigh the possibilities of action and then execute the desired action. For his generation, and for those who follow, the readiness to take responsibility would be the mainspring of action.[99]

96. *DBWE* 8:387.
97. *DBWE* 8:301.
98. *DBWE* 8:305–6.
99. *DBWE* 8:387.

Bonhoeffer then makes a telling comment about two of the most cherished values of the modern age: "We believed we could make our way in life with reason and justice [*Vernunft und Recht*], and when both failed us, we no longer saw any way forward. We have also overestimated, time and again, the importance of reasonableness and justice in influencing the course of history." He concludes by saying that this world "is ruled by forces against which reason can do nothing."[100] This comment is especially significant for unpacking all that Bonhoeffer associates with the notion of a world come of age, since he prefaces it by saying that his nephew would live in such a world, thus indicating that he is not limiting these observations to wartime or its immediate aftermath.

Bonhoeffer's insights into the performative character of a world come of age culminate in "Outline for a Book," one of the last documents that Bethge received from him. He begins this sketch by describing humanity's coming of age [*das Mündigwerden*] as consisting in the safeguarding of human life against "accidents" and "blows of fate." The aim of these efforts is to make human life independent of the menace of nature. This menace had formerly been overcome by the spiritual powers of soul, but for us it is "conquered through technological organization [*technische Organisation*] of all kinds." As a consequence of seeking to create a buffer between ourselves and the earth, our immediate environment is no longer nature but technologies of all sorts.[101]

Bonhoeffer turns on its head the standard explanation for religious belief offered by the leading lights of the modern age. Sigmund Freud, for example, simply states as a self-evident truth that primitive human beings, under assault from the forces of nature—earthquakes, floods, storms, disease, and death—personified them so that they might employ methods routinely used to deal with those in human society: "to adjure them, to appease them, to bribe them, and by so influencing them [to] rob them of a part of their power."[102] John Dewey says much the same thing, asserting as a matter of fact that fear of natural forces in the face of which primitive humanity was impotent created the gods, and thus our ancestors fabricated rites of expiation, propitiation, and communion to deal with these personified forces.[103] Both Freud and Dewey add, in virtually identical terms, that science is the only sure road to knowledge of the world.[104] Bonhoeffer, by

---

100. *DBWE* 8:388 (*DBW* 8:433).

101. *DBWE* 8:500.

102. Freud, *Future of an Illusion*, 21–22.

103. Dewey, *Common Faith*, 24.

104. Freud writes, "But scientific work is the only road which can lead us to a

contrast, states that in view of the threats made to our well-being by nature, modern humans seek through technological organization to become like God (*sicut deus*).

Bonhoeffer then attends to the ironic effects that the technological reconfiguration of space and time have had in the modern world. With this protection from the menace of nature, "a new threat to life is created in turn, namely, through organization itself. Now the power of the soul is lacking!" Due to the thoroughgoing reorganization of space and knowledge, men and women no longer possess the spiritual means to cope with this peculiarly modern menace. The question that plagues us is, "What will protect us from the menace of organization?" We are thrown back on our own resources. We can insure ourselves against everything but other human beings. When all is said and done, "It all comes down to the human being."[105]

In the final chapter of the book Bonhoeffer plans to discuss the form of communal life the church should take in a world come of age. He states that it must participate in the day-to-day tasks of life, not dominating, as those in authority do, but rather helping and serving: "It must tell people in every calling what a life with Christ is, what it means 'to be there for others.'"[106] In particular, our church will have to confront the roots of evil: *hubris*, the adoration of power, envy and self-deception, a list of vices that reveals the basic character of a world come of age. Christians will need a very special set of moral dispositions, among which he lists moderation, authenticity, trust, faithfulness, steadfastness, patience, discipline, humility, modesty, and contentment, traits that are not typically valued in the technological regime of a world come of age that organizes it with ruthless and all too often brutal efficiency.[107]

The irony that Bonhoeffer clearly and decisively associates with the leading role that technological organization plays in our lives recalls his observations about the desire to master nature by means of technology in earlier works. In *Creation and Fall* he contends that human freedom and the divine mandate to rule creation in Genesis 1 do not signify that we are free

---

knowledge of reality outside ourselves" (*Future of an Illusion*, 40); Dewey: "There is but one sure road of access to truth—the road of patient, cooperative inquiry operating by means of observation, experiment, record and controlled reflection" (*Common Faith*, 32).

105. *DBWE* 8:500.

106. *DBWE* 8:503; cf. Bonhoeffer and Franz Hildebrand's draft for a catechism: "The true church . . . is where the community of the Spirit exists in service and not in domination . . . where one exists for the other in prayer, tells him all and forgives him all, and the promise that here one may become 'a Christ to the other person' (Luther)" (*DBWE* 11:265–66).

107. *DBWE* 8:503.

from nature: "On the contrary, this freedom to rule includes being bound to the creatures who are ruled. The ground and the animals over which I am lord constitute the world in which I live, without which I cease to be." With the fall this connection to the earth is lost, and with it our mandate to rule. We do not rule, we are ruled, and technology is, again ironically, the power that renders our dominion an illusion, the power by which the earth seizes hold of humanity and achieves a mastery over it.[108]

The modern reliance on technology and technological organization, says Bonhoeffer, is an outgrowth of the desire to master nature by means of "*Technik*," a term whose connotations we miss if we restrict its primary reference to the sophisticated machines we have created in our struggle with a cosmos under the dominion of sin and violence. Bonhoeffer notes that *Technik* once comprised a type of handicraft, serving religion, royalty, artistry, and the daily needs of all people. But in the modern West (*neuzeitlichen Abendlandes*) it has freed itself from every kind of service, so that now its essence is mastery over nature: "A wholly new spirit has produced it, the spirit of violent subjection of nature to thinking and experimenting human beings." Technology has become an end in itself, possessing its own soul. The instruments we have fashioned are its symbols, not its essence.[109]

The moral effect of the lust for mastery is not limited to the nonhuman world, for our relationships with each other are also subject to this desire. The hope placed in technology and technological organization for a "world-wide society of free and equal people"[110] never came about. The irony here is acute, for in place of free and equal individuals, mass society was created: "Although technology produces the masses and the masses in turn demand increased technology, technology itself is an affair of strong, intellectually superior personalities."[111] Bonhoeffer cites the function of engineers and entrepreneurs in this regard, and in other venues he refers to experts in politics, economics, and the health and education professions.[112]

One other indication of the significance that Bonhoeffer attributes to the technological organization of modern life can be seen in the way he distances the gospel from the notion of solution (*Lösung*), which is a term that in a world come of age is closely wedded, perhaps inextricably so, to the instrumentalist world of technology. In *Ethics* this notion appears

---

108. *DBWE* 3:66–67. The prospect of dramatic climate change in the twenty-first century comes to mind here.

109. *DBWE* 6:116–17.

110. Grant, *Technology and Justice*, 15.

111. *DBWE* 6:121.

112. *DBWE* 11:453.

prominently in his critique of the extremes of radicalism and compromise: "To advocates of the radical solution it must be said that Christ is not radical in their sense; to followers of the compromise solution it must likewise be said that Christ does not make compromises." Later he calls into question the notion that the task of the church is to offer the world solutions for its problems, and doubts whether there even are "Christian" solutions, noting that this assumption is particularly characteristic of Anglo-Saxon thought. Jesus is rarely concerned with solving the world's problems, for his word is not a solution but redemption (*Erlösung*). Bonhoeffer also questions whether all the world's problems can be solved and concludes that the kind of thinking that begins with human problems and then looks for solutions is unbiblical, stating that "the essence of the gospel does not consist in solving worldly problems . . . this cannot be the essential task of the church." This is not to say that the church does not have any legitimate involvement in such matters, but that it cannot be the starting point.[113]

Bonhoeffer's suspicion of the technologically charged notion of solution is, if anything, more pronounced in the later prison letters. He states that the longing for solutions is part and parcel of the deus ex machina, which is only invoked "to solve insoluble problems or to provide strength when human powers fail." God desires to be acknowledged by us in what is known, in what has been solved. There is no reason to assume that Christian "solutions" to crises are any more compelling than any other, and to think so again attempts to conceive of God as a stopgap to what we do not know. Most importantly, the resurrection is not the "solution" to the problem of death.[114]

Bonhoeffer's understanding of technology anticipates that of Martin Heidegger, who states in writings published after the war that modern technology is incomparably different from earlier forms, in that *technē* is no longer a poetic bringing-forth but a desire for reflexive immediacy with a creature: "Everywhere everything is ordered to stand by, to be immediately on hand, indeed to stand there just so that it may be on call for a further ordering."[115] This concept does not primarily signify a making or producing, says Heidegger, but "that knowledge which supports and conducts every human irruption into the midst of beings." It thus refers to the knowledge that, apart from the mediation of Christ, shapes and directs what Heidegger refers to as our "confrontation with and mastery over beings . . . the disclosing of beings as such, in the manner of a knowing guidance of

---

113. *DBWE* 6:152–54, 355–56.
114. *DBWE* 8:366–67, 406, 450.
115. Heidegger, "Question Concerning Technology," 294, 298.

bringing-forth."[116] Technology thus entails a distinctive mode of inhabiting the world and of representing it, which causes things, places, and people (including ourselves) to show themselves in specified ways, assigning to them (and to us) their (our) proper place in obedience to our lust for mastery.[117] In Augustinian terms, things—inanimate objects, places, material and social processes, events, and persons—become signs of the technological regime that comprises a world come of age.[118]

There is little in his prison writings to suggest that Bonhoeffer has left behind the sober vision of the fallen world in his previous writings in order to bring Christianity closer in line with modernity. He instead describes it in a straightforward manner as a technological edifice that human beings have both imagined and constructed in an effort to secure their independence from the ravages of fate and the harshness of nature, but with deeply ironic results. As he often does in his prison writings, he recalls ideas and arguments from previous writings to portray what we have labeled the technological character and tendencies of a world come of age. Four in particular are of interest in this regard, the first being a contrast that Bonhoeffer draws in *Creation and Fall* between the mythical and magical images (*die Bilder der Magie*) and world (*die magische Welt*) depicted in the second chapter of Genesis and our technological world (*die technische Welt*). Each world uses a different set of images (*die Bilder*), and he describes the images that prevail in our time as technological and abstract (*unsere technisierende Begriffsbilder*).[119]

The second text is an unpublished essay on Christianity in America, "Protestantism Without Reformation," written in 1939. Bonhoeffer refers to the modern state as a technological organization and administrative apparatus (*technische Organisation und Verwaltungsapparat*) that strives only to implement whatever principles and policies have been deemed to be desirable. As such, the dignity of the divine office of just governance has been lost sight of.[120] The state is not a humane institution that has as its mandate the care and preservation of the moral character of its citizens, but a technological apparatus that exists to implement whatever modes of "worldly" conduct are in favor at a given time, which for a world come of age revolves around the acquisition and consumption of material goods and services.

---

116. Heidegger, *Nietzsche*, 1:81–82; cf. Inwood, *Heidegger Dictionary*, 209–12.

117. For Heidegger the mechanization of time exemplifies *Technik* as much more than simply a matter of handling objects with tools. Heidegger, *Being and Time*, 466–72; cf. Bock, *Christian Ethics*, 39–41.

118. Augustine, *Teaching Christianity* I.2.

119. *DBWE* 3:82–83.

120. *DBWE* 15:451–52.

The third text is a sermon that he preaches in 1932 in Berlin, in which he reckons with the fact that the modern world no longer takes seriously the church's proclamation of the gospel. As noted earlier, for most of us Paul's contention that our lives are hidden with Christ in God has little or no bearing on our relationships to family, friends, or coworkers. There may have been a time when people believed such things, but now the conviction that we have been raised with Christ has no relation to the important matters of politics, economics, education, or marriage. Men and women seek their salvation instead in the ideal form of the state or the well-oiled market, the stable monetary system or the newest education method, the newest psychological technique or the latest diet or infallible cure that will guarantee their health. "Isn't it true that for a large segment of our people, salvation is expected from nothing other than these things?" he asks. "And the more this longed-for salvation eludes us, the more our plans come to nothing again and again, and the more our life falls from cliff to cliff and from crisis to crisis, the more we cry out for specialists, for experts. *They* must know it. *They* must be able to do it."[121] We see here the same affirmation of faith in the ability of these institutions to deliver us from blows of fate and the menace of nature that is expressed in the first chapter of the "Outline."

Finally, his contention in the "Outline" that with its dependence on an evolving and expanding technological regime human beings are thrown back on their own resources, with the result that they can cope with everything except themselves, draws directly on his theological commentary on the fall in *Creation and Fall*. The passage in question occurs in the context of his discussion of tob and ra, good and evil, the tree of life and the tree of knowledge. When humans are divided between good and evil they experience the pain and pleasure with which they die, for "a human being who knows about tob and ra, knows immediately about death. Knowing about tob and ra itself constitutes death." Death in this sense means having life not as a gift but as a divine command, a decree from which no one can escape, a terrible form of bondage: "*To be dead means to-have-to-live.*"[122]

The commandment to live, which replaces life as a gift from God, demands of humanity something that we are not able to accomplish, either individually or collectively. It obliges us to live out of ourselves, out of our own resources, and we are unable to do that. We manage for a time, but only by living out of our inner split, living with our own good that comes out of evil and by our own evil that comes out of good. As a result, humankind lives in a circle: "It *lives* out of its own resources; it is alone. Yet it *cannot live*, because

---

121. *DBWE* 11:453.
122. *DBWE* 3:90–91.

in fact it does not live but in this life is dead, because it *must* live, that is, it *must* accomplish life out of its own resources and just that is its death (as the basis at once of its knowledge and of its existence!)." The upshot of all this, says Bonhoeffer, is that humankind "whom God's commandment confronts with a demand is thrown back upon itself and now has to live in this way. Humankind now lives only out of its own resources, by its knowledge of good and evil, and thus is dead."[123] In spite of the rhetoric that might at first seem to extol the maturity of the modern world, the intellectual and moral progress our species has supposedly made, upon closer inspection Bonhoeffer states that human beings, once again having been thrown back on our own resources, this time by our faith in *Technik*, find ourselves where we started: expelled from the garden.

Viewed as a whole, Bonhoeffer's description of the world as having come of age should not be read as either a summary affirmation or rejection of the current state of our shared existence, or as an abandonment either of the church as the intellectual and ethical context of Christian life and thought or of the eschatological distinction between the last things and the things before the last. He is attempting to specify more precisely and in a sober and clear-sighted manner its contingent features at a particular point in time, and in so doing its ironic character comes into focus. He affirms living fully and unreservedly in this world, but this does not constitute in any sense an unqualified endorsement of the relationships and institutions of modernity, nor does it commend a contemplative relation to the ontology projected by it. Above all, he seeks to disabuse people of their hope that the clock might be turned back and the church's traditional guardianship over society restored.[124]

A world come of age is the world we inhabit, and the world to which we are sent to witness to what God has done, is doing, and will do in Christ, and we need to attend to it truthfully and faithfully. In addition, to say as he does that we should not make the coming of age of the world the subject for either polemics or apologetics strongly suggests that he is not interested in either condemning or confirming its basic features. Instead, as he says explicitly, it is a call for a better interpretation of those features than it supplies for itself, namely, from the standpoint of the gospel and of Christ.[125] It is to that task of interpretation for our own time that I now turn.

123. *DBWE* 3:91; cf. 66–67.

124. See Correll, *Shepherds of the Empire.*

125. *DBWE* 8:431; cf. *DBWE* 6:270.

3

The Future of a Technological Illusion

Modern technology is not simply an extension of human making through the power of a perfected science, but is a new account of what it is to know and to make in which both activities are changed by their co-penetration.

—GEORGE GRANT, *Technology and Justice*

DIETRICH BONHOEFFER'S CRITIQUE OF a world come of age, scattered across a handful of documents from prison, offers keen insight into the time in which we live and the place where we have been sent to testify to God's work of judgment and reconciliation in Christ. He brings to light the irony in modernity's claim to have reached a stage of intellectual and moral maturity, enabling us to see that for all of its knowledge, expertise, and technological success, the age is as godless and without resource as previous generations. But he also draws our attention to the distinctive and substantial effects these changes have had on the warp and woof of a worldly existence, and insists that the Christian community must take them into consideration if it is to live and act responsibly before God and for the sake of its neighbors.

The story of these changes is long and complex, and cannot be reduced to what Charles Taylor calls subtraction stories that narrate the rise of secular modernity as a process of liberation from earlier "mythological" accounts of the world and the discovery of alternatives in science. These changes are instead the outcome of an extended and contingent set of developments that took hundreds of years and involved a wide range of ideas, movements, and societal transformations.[1] It is beyond the scope of this book to provide

1. Taylor, *Secular Age*, 22, 26.

an historical account of the emergence of the modern world such as those found in John Milbank's *Theology and Social Theory*, Michael Gillespie's *The Theological Origins of Modernity*, Brad Gregory's *The Unintended Reformation*, or Taylor's magisterial *A Secular Age*. Some such examination is ultimately necessary, however, particularly if one contends, as Bonhoeffer does, that the emergence of the modern world was in no way inevitable or necessary, and thus our relationship to it is not "contemplative." The present needs to be seen in part as the contingent product of the past, and we shall misidentify both the basic character of a world come of age and the summons to participate in the messianic suffering of God in Christ in its midst if we do not have a coherent and cogent account of what has brought us to this place and time.

What follows is a brief attempt to take up and take further some of Bonhoeffer's descriptions and assessments of modernity, the most significant of which is that of technological organization of all kinds. The fact that he chooses this concept as the principal frame of reference for his proposed inquiry into the foundations of a world come of age cannot be underestimated, for in so doing he picks up on the distinctive character of modern civilization that too often goes unnoticed. In this regard, writes George Grant, speakers of American English are in a better position to attend to the novelty of our age. The neologism of "technology" helpfully puts together the Greek word for art or craft, *technē*, with the term for a systematic study, *lógos*, similar to that of biology, life (*bíos*) and study. This conjunction brings to our attention the new and unique co-penetration of knowing and making that distinguishes a world come of age from all previous civilizations.[2] As Michel de Certeau puts it, "Power is the precondition of this knowledge and not merely its effect or its attribute. It makes this knowledge possible and at the same time determines its characteristics. It produces itself in and through this knowledge."[3]

It is a serious mistake, says Grant, to assume that the difference between what we call *technē* and that of previous generations is simply that we have developed an efficiency of making that the ancients and medievals lacked because they had not yet happened upon the path of pure reason, for if they had they would have pursued the same will to mastery that we have. (The same supposition informs the modern misperceptions of myth as primitive attempts at doing science.) There is more to the distinctiveness of modern technology than simply the advances we have made over the last few centuries in the invention of instruments that permit us to act on the

2. Grant, *Technology and Justice*, 11–13.

3. Certeau, *Practice of Everyday Life*, 36.

world with an unprecedented level of efficiency. The illusion is that "technology" is but a name for the whole apparatus of machines at our disposal, and not the pervasive mode of being in our political and social lives, an ethos or habitus, which profoundly alters both our self-understanding and our perception of the world.[4]

There is novelty even in how we conceive novelty itself: "To put the matter crudely, when we represent technology to ourselves through its own common sense we think of ourselves as picking and choosing in a supermarket, rather than within the analogy of the package deal."[5] In other words, the technological organization of the world has reconfigured how we see ourselves in relation to one another and to the earth. We now function as knowing, willing, and feeling subjects within a new and distinct "picture" of how we are situated in the world. Women and men now imagine the world and themselves very differently from the ways our ancestors did.

The irony of our age is that, though we think of ourselves as picking and choosing as though we were in a supermarket, we have actually wagered our entire existence on a package deal of far greater novelty than we realize, catching us up into a destiny "which enfolds us in its own conceptions of instrumentality, neutrality and purposiveness." Not only is technology the dominant ethos of the age, it has become the decisive ontology as well: "Western peoples (and perhaps soon all peoples) take themselves as subjects confronting otherness as objects—objects lying as raw material at the disposal of knowing and making subjects." As a result, when we reflect on our times our judgments act like a mirror that reflects back "the very metaphysic of the technology which we are supposed to be deliberating about in detail."[6] Though every exercise of practical reasoning is dependent on some assumed set of descriptions about the world, and thus there is always a certain amount of circularity in any interpretation of the world and of our place in it, it would be hard to imagine a more vicious one than this.

Bonhoeffer grasps the novelty of our situation in the much the same way Grant does, observing in *Ethics* that technology was once a matter of handicraft (*der Handwerk*), serving religion, royalty, artistry, and the daily needs of all people. But something fundamentally new arose in history, the "liberation of reason for dominance over creation," which when taken as a working hypothesis and heuristic principle led to "the incomparable rise of technology." This new form of technology renounced its former role as servant and took instead as its essence and goal the mastery over nature: "A

4. Grant, *Technology and Justice*, 17–19.

5. Ibid., 32.

6. Ibid., 32–33.

wholly new spirit has produced it, the spirit of violent subjection of nature to thinking and experimenting human beings." The nature of technology has changed, becoming an end in itself, possessing its own soul, and in the process has given rise to what we now take to be the quintessential human task: the mastery of ourselves.[7] A new destiny—conceived in Europe, realized in North America, and now extended to every corner of the earth by means of the global market—has been imposed on all humankind.

Theologians too often fail to follow Bonhoeffer's lead in this regard, assuming that the modern world's self-understanding of its technological constitution, an interpretation that is deeply embedded in that establishment, is adequate for the work of theological reflection.[8] He states on multiple occasions in *Letters and Papers from Prison* that a world come of age needs to be understood better than it understands itself, from the gospel and from Christ.[9] This better understanding must grapple with the profound effects it has on human existence, and in particular, with the technological restructuring of the context in which our thoughts, actions, and communications are located, to make both time and space subject to our will to mastery.

The purpose of the critique of the technological contours of a world come of age is not to urge that Christians attempt the *salto mortale*, the death-defying leap into what some falsely imagine was a pre-technological utopia, for such efforts are indeed symptomatic of a profound despair and a troubling lack of intellectual integrity. "The technological age is a true heritage of our Western history," Bonhoeffer says, "with which we must grapple, and which we cannot reverse."[10] We should also acknowledge that the advent of a world come of age was motivated from the outset by the belief that the mastery of nature would eventually overcome hunger and labor, disease and war, on a scale that would enable all humans to live in a world of free and equal people. "Let none of us who live in the well-cushioned west," says Grant, "speak with an aesthetic tiredness about our 'worldliness.'"[11] It is doubtful that many of us would want to do without antibiotics, computers, or contemporary modes of transportation.

Nevertheless, believing that the technological organization of life will ultimately lead to these noble and well-intentioned ends is, as Sigmund

7. *DBWE* 6:116–17 (*DBW* 6:106).

8. Grant, *Technology and Justice*, 12–13.

9. *DBWE* 8:373, 428, 431, 482.

10. *DBWE* 8:478; 6:117.

11. Grant, *Technology and Justice*, 15.

Freud once described religion, an illusion,[12] which, as he pointed out, is not the same thing as an error. Illusions derive from human wishes, and though the fulfillment of those wishes may well be improbable, they need not be in contradiction to reality. One of the principal tasks of the church in a world come of age, writes Bonhoeffer, is to confront the vice of illusionism, together with hubris, the worship of power, and envy, as the root of all evil.[13] My purpose in engaging in this critique of the technological organization that is at the heart of a world come of age, then, is to cultivate a mode of worldliness in which the polyphonic form of Christ can be heard and repeated in its midst.

Life in the Technological Cocoon

Though he does not have the opportunity after his arrest to develop a detailed account of the changes that gave birth to a world come of age, Bonhoeffer is aware, above all from his reading of Dilthey, that there is a history that needs to be told about its parturition. He states that its origins could be traced as far back as the thirteenth century, and later mentions many of the figures that played key roles in its growth and development. Moreover, he does not flinch from including Martin Luther and the Protestant Reformation in the birthing process. Bonhoeffer also draws attention to the unwitting contributions that the sixteenth-century reformers, and Luther in particular, made to the modern flirtation with idolatry: "The Reformation biblical faith in God had radically desacralized [entgöttert] the world. Thus the ground was prepared in which rational and empirical science could blossom; and even though the natural scientists of the seventeenth and eighteenth centuries were believing Christians, the disappearance of faith in God left behind only a rationalized and mechanized world."[14] A few pages later he states that Luther's discovery of the freedom of the Christian, when combined with what he calls the "Catholic heresy" of humankind's essential goodness,[15] "resulted in deifying humanity. But deifying humanity

---

12. Freud, *Future of an Illusion*, 39.

13. *DBWE* 8:503.

14. *DBWE* 6:114.

15. Though Bonhoeffer routinely defends the Protestant side in these age-old debates with Catholic theology, the harshness of this description is not typical of his understanding of Catholicism. Catholic teaching on the question of humanity's essential goodness has also taken some interesting turns since his death at the hands of the Gestapo in connection with the emergence within Catholic circles of the debate about "pure nature." See in this regard A. N. Williams, "Future of the Past," 347–61.

is, properly understood, the proclamation of nihilism."[16] Such comments reinforce his later observations about the technological organization of the modern era throwing humanity back upon itself and its own resources.

Bonhoeffer's decision to begin his examination of a world come of age in the "Outline for a Book" with a critique of technological organizations of all kinds affords us an insightful point of departure for our own investigations into the character of our times. This starting point does not devalue intellectual virtues and theological convictions, or posit a vulgar base-superstructure relationship between social practices and institutions, on the one hand, and ideas on the other. It functions instead to make us aware that the life of the mind does not exist in a vacuum but is woven into the whole fabric of our lives. Like threads in a finely woven garment, if convictions are removed from that cloth they lose their distinct patterns.

The conviction that is at the heart of the technological organization known as the liberal nation-state, says Jeffrey Stout, is the idea of a body of citizens who take the time to give and ask for reasons about the ethical issues that divide them.[17] Stout thus places the burden for sustaining a coherent and integrated society on "reason." Among the many problems with putting the weight on our human capacity to reason together across our differences is that the radically pluralist societies of Europe and North America (the "West") have largely withdrawn from making moral judgments about their shared form of life that might give substance to Stout's hopes. What these societies have now are technological organizations that see their job as securing "a pragmatic minimum of peaceful coexistence between groups" through the exercise of managerial skills and economic inducements.[18]

A world come of age no longer attempts to form those habits of intellectual and moral character that create the conditions for a genuinely mature world but defines its sole task as "management and manipulation [rather than] the communal shaping of a common life."[19] The global regime in which most of the world now lives, moves, and has its being neither has nor desires a shared vision of the common good. The coherence and stability it does possess, says Bryan Turner, is achieved instead by a set of interlocking factors:

> (1) an extensive regulatory apparatus which has various legal, political and repressive elements; (2) the difficulty of maintaining

16. *DBWE* 6:123. The reference Bonhoeffer makes to the cult of the human in the letter of August 14, 1944, bears a striking similarity to this comment. *DBWE* 8:509.

17. Stout, *Democracy and Tradition*, 6, 279.

18. R. D. Williams, *On Christian Theology*, 34; cf. MacIntyre, *After Virtue*, 30.

19. Eagleton, *Meaning of Life*, 22.

political opposition; (3) welfare inducements which are pragmatically accepted; (4) passive political participation; and (5)
the "dull compulsion" of economic relations which creates social
dependency, despite a general decline in the demand for labour
which technological change produces in advanced capitalist
enterprises.[20]

This list reminds us that instead of the dignity of the mandates for society
that Bonhoeffer sets forth in *Ethics*, the technological regime of a world
come of age represents a new and more elusive Leviathan, whose modes of
governance over us are both anonymous and indirect, but for this reason all
the more pervasive and total.[21]

In place of a society that could make it possible for its members to
give and ask for ethical reasons, a society that attempts to make it easier
for women and men to be good,[22] the technological organization of life has
given birth to a new social reality, which Anthony Giddens has labeled a risk
culture. He is not suggesting that life in the modern world is intrinsically
more dangerous now than it was in the past. It is instead that the concepts of
risk, risk calculation, and lifestyle choice have displaced traditional notions
of providence, fortune, destiny, and fate in the grammar that governs our
perception of daily existence. The exchange of the concept of risk for that
of fortune or providence "represents an alteration in the perception of determination and contingency, such that human moral imperatives, natural
causes, and chance reign in place of religious cosmologies."[23]

This shift in the way we view the world and ourselves has thrown us
back on ourselves yet again, handing us over to a new (but still godless)
destiny. Our actions and perceptions are set within a world that shows itself
to us in ways determined by the social technologies that humankind has
developed to protect it from the menaces of nature and the vicissitudes of
fortune; these include systems of organizing production and distribution of
material goods, and electronic modes of communication, such as television,
the Internet, and motion pictures. Giddens refers to these technologies as
"knowledge environments" that form a "protective cocoon" surrounding

---

20. Turner, *Religion and Social Theory*, 197–98.

21. "[Thomas] Hobbes was simply more clear-sighted than later apparently more
'liberal' thinkers like [John] Locke in realizing that a liberal peace requires a single
undisputed power, but not necessarily a continued majority consensus, which may not
be forthcoming." Milbank, *Theology and Social Theory*, 14.

22. Day, *Long Loneliness*, 181, 280.

23. Giddens, *Consequences of Modernity*, 34; Giddens, *Modernity and Self-Identity*,
3; cf. Harvey, *Another City*, 124–26. On the role of risk and risk-taking in the method-
ologies of the social sciences, see Douglas, *Risk Acceptability*.

the self in its dealings with everyday reality. This enclosure "'brackets out' potential occurrences which, were the individual seriously to contemplate them, would produce a paralysis of the will, or feelings of engulfment." Not only is the world of nature compelled to reveal itself to us in specific ways, but our sense of self has also been fabricated by these technologies. Were this cocoon to be stripped away, the "outside world" would puncture the carefully cultivated sense that our human resources are sufficient to the task of protecting us from nature and fortune.[24]

That this cocoon is an artifact formed by the knowledge environments of our technological regime is seen in the double irony that accompanies the fact that everyone must choose her or his own values. It deprives these values, no matter what they are, of any substantial sense of authority over the self, since we who initially posited them can just as easily unposit them if they, for whatever reason, fail to suit us.[25] In addition, these values, safely sequestered within the cocoon of the individual and thus a private matter, are therefore "free" precisely to the extent that they are free from relevance, displaced from the public media of organizing the world where "factories are working, wages are being paid, goods are being distributed."[26]

As a result of these changes in the ways we organize the world and ourselves, argues Giddens, "individuals are forced to negotiate lifestyle choices among a diversity of options."[27] In other words, freedom of choice is now a necessity. We have indeed been thrown back on ourselves by powers of our own making, each of us compelled to choose her or his own values, forced to live out of ourselves, out of our own resources, and according to Bonhoeffer, we are unable to do this.[28] This state of affairs is no accident in a world that seeks to fashion every person around the only socially meaningful identities in such a society, those of producer and consumer. The irony of a world come of age once again shows itself, as we are unwitting (if not unwilling) participants in this momentous wager.

Taylor elaborates on the notion that men and women perceive the world and themselves from within a protective cocoon by contrasting the way we see our relationship to the world, and the way our medieval ancestors saw it. Within this technological cocoon, "meaning" becomes a property that exists solely and safely in "the mind," a ghostly entity that is confined to a body. Exterior realities thus have significance solely to the

---

24. Giddens, *Modernity and Self-Identity*, 3, 126–33.
25. Dreyfus, "Knowledge and Human Values," 512.
26. McCabe, *Law, Love and Language*, 158, 26.
27. Giddens, *Consequences of Modernity*, 5.
28. *DBWE* 3:91.

extent they evoke a certain response in the mind. This "inner space" of the mind is an artifact created by a new kind of reflexivity, generated by the adoption of a first-person epistemic standpoint and by the belief that this standpoint, once adequately theorized, would provide intellectual resources sufficient for individuals to generate truths for themselves *qua* individuals, and with these truths a "sense of freedom, control, invulnerability, and hence dignity."[29] The activity of knowing is thus reconfigured as an epic engineering project, the goal of which is to construct a reliable bridge across the gap that separates the inner space of the mind from the external environment of objects, persons, and events that in themselves are devoid of intrinsic meaning. (This picture mimics the way that Christians traditionally describe God's relationship to a world created *ex nihilo*, out of nothing.) These objects, persons, and events that exist in time and space are simply external stimuli, matters whose only significance is that which individuals assign to them.

The significance of living in a world come of age thus revolves around this distinctively modern perception of a self that is surrounded by a "buffer" separating it from everyone and everything else. This buffer forms the illusory ambition of disengaging from the world of things and other people, and ultimately from the earth itself. "My ultimate purposes," writes Taylor, "are those which arise within me, the crucial meanings of things are those defined in my responses to them." These self-selected purposes and meanings are influenced by external reality, but the self can counter these with its own actions, such as avoiding distressing or tempting experiences. The self, existing in its imagined isolation, is formed by a world come of age to interpret its own significance and destiny as a self-initiated, rationally calculated venture.[30] Men and women have no choice but to choose to be "venture capitalists."

This picture of what it means to be a human person constitutes the unencumbered individual of modernity, its basic identity existing independently of nonvoluntary relations with others, and fully divested of inherited convictions and even language, yet somehow in full possession of the procedures that enable it to reason and choose. This is precisely the illusion of independence that a world come of age wishes to cultivate in us, and thus the irony once again comes to the fore.[31] Separating our sense of self from social entanglements does not liberate us; rather, it makes us completely dependent on the technological regime we have fashioned for ourselves,

29. Taylor, *Secular Age*, 30, 285; cf., Taylor, *Sources of the Self*, 130.

30. Taylor, *Secular Age*, 29–30, 38.

31. Poteat, *Polanyian Meditations*, 12.

but that now holds us within its grasp. As Bonhoeffer says in *Creation and Fall*, "Humankind is a prisoner, a slave, of the world, and its dominion is an illusion. Technology is the power with which the earth seizes hold of humankind and masters it."[32]

Finally, the fictional buffer between the inner realm of meaning, including any residual sense of morality it might retain, and all that is exterior to it goes hand in hand with the interpretation of the material world as a domain of exceptionless natural law, which was the working hypothesis of the mechanistic understanding of science that emerged in the seventeenth century. The proper end of science was no longer to contemplate the beauty and order of a cosmos that is a reflection of its creator, but to compel the physical world to stand by as the object of prediction and control. Taylor says of the origins of the modern scientific age among the Puritans that "our grasp of this [new] order was referred to by the term '*technologia*,' and the unity of God's order was seen not as a structure to be contemplated but as an interlocking set of things calling for actions which formed a harmonious whole. The harmony between its parts . . . was more a matter of the coherence of the occasions for action than of the mutual reflection of things in an order of signs."[33] This shift was necessary if we were to create the epistemic buffer that would protect us from "blows of fate" by making us independent of what is now called "nature," the material world.

In the "enchanted"[34] world of the late Middle Ages, by contrast, men and women saw themselves as living in a world of objects inhabited by good and bad spirits that possessed their own meanings independently of the human mind and could impose these meanings on the self, either directly (through being possessed) or by bringing it into the field of force belonging to these spirits.[35] Meaning did not subsist in the inner space of mind but in the things themselves (*res*) understood as signs (*signa*),[36] and thus in the created matrix formed by the providentially governed interactions between persons, things, and God. The self who lived in this world was vulnerable to spirits, demons, and cosmic forces of all kinds that could influence it in an almost infinite number of ways, both negatively (demons) and positively

32. *DBWE* 3:67; cf. *DBWE* 12:271.

33. Taylor, *Sources of the Self*, 232–33.

34. Taylor is not particularly happy with the notion of enchantment for describing a world "not yet" come of age, evoking as it often does images of light and fairies, but given the fact that Max Weber's description of modernity as disenchanted is well established in the grammar of social discourse he uses it as the most appropriate antonym. Taylor, *Secular Age*, 25–26.

35. Ibid., 29–33.

36. Augustine, *Teaching Christianity* I.2.

(angels and other good spirits).[37] As Bonhoeffer notes in "Outline for a Book," this self had to contend more directly (though perhaps more honestly) with certain fears that could overwhelm it at times, but it also had access to spiritual resources for dealing with these powers and principalities. By contrast, the buffered self has no resource other than its own powers of imagination and volition, and thus when reality breaks through its protective cocoon it is overtaken by the anxiety and despair so characteristic of the age.

Life in the world of our forebears was also inherently and explicitly social. Spiritual forces were intuitively understood to impinge not only on women and men personally, but on the whole community, and thus it also had to be protected and defended by the shared spiritual means of that community. The commonweal of late medieval life was sustained by collective rites, devotions, and allegiances as the various societies that made up the shared existence of human life in the sixteenth century stood before God, and thus a man or woman's divergent beliefs and actions were never just the business of an individual, but potentially introduced disorder that could easily incur divine wrath.[38]

Our "premodern" ancestors thus saw so-called natural events as actions, sometimes of evil spirits, and sometimes of angels, saints, and God. The term "act of God" (still used today by the insurance carriers) thus referred to what were seen as real agents. Taylor uses the terms "cosmos" and "universe" to distinguish between the two ways of seeing the physical world. The former term signifies the ancient idea of the totality of existence as an ordered whole that was in its complex operations humanly meaningful. The principle of that order, at least for sixteenth-century Christians, was God, who stood at its apex and center, around which all created things were related hierarchically. Modern humans, by contrast, live in a universe that is also ordered, but the principles that order it are neutral with respect to human meaning.[39]

---

37. Taylor, *Secular Age*, 38.

38. Ibid., 42–43. Taylor notes that this sense of the solidarity of society did not die completely with the rise of an "enlightened" age, as even John Locke believed that atheists could not serve in public office, for their oaths of allegiance would have no effect on them. In our own time most people believe that fidelity to some sense of proper order is necessary for the well-being of society, be it civil religion, the principles of liberal democracy, or the rule of the free market. There is still no place for those labeled fanatic or intolerant.

39. Ibid., 40–41, 59–61.

Conquering Time and Space

The alteration in the conception of determination and contingency that characterizes the world's coming of age profoundly changes the ways we perceive not just individual objects, events, or persons but time and space as such. We no longer envision the temporal and spatial stage of our lives as the occasion and the means of our participation in God's created order and redemptive design, but as opportunities to be possessed and targets to be conquered. We wagered our existence on technological organization to protect us from nature and fortune, and in the process handed ourselves over to a novel destiny that deceives us with the illusion of control and mastery.

In his doctoral dissertation, Bonhoeffer ties the question of time to the ethical encounter with the other. When one is addressed by the other we enter into the state of responsibility in the midst of time. Over against Kant's contention that continuously advancing time is a pure form of the mind's intuition, which depicts thinking as essentially timeless, Bonhoeffer argues that in the state of responsibility we exist in the value-related (not value-filled) moment. Our perception of time and its value-relatedness are co-posited in this idea of moment, yielding concrete time, that is, time related to God: "Only in concrete time is the real claim of ethics effectual; and only when I am responsible am I fully conscious of being bound to time." Persons thus exist in the rising and passing away of time, re-fashioned again and again in the perpetual flux of life.[40]

The modern triumph over this flux has its origins in part in the invention of the mechanical clock, the derivation of Greenwich Mean Time, and the rapid diffusion of these technologies to virtually every corner of the globe. They separated the reckoning of time from the distinctive features of particular locales (e.g., topography and climate), allowing it to be quantified into uniform and therefore empty units. Time now shows itself to us as a sequence of identical moments flowing through an empty container, what Walter Benjamin calls homogeneous, empty time.[41] As such the passing of time now shows itself as indifferent to what it "contains."[42] The uniform measurement of time in turn permits, and in a sense demands, a homogeneity in the social organization of time, exemplified in the worldwide standardization of time zones and calendars.[43]

---

40. *DBWE* 1:47–48.

41. Benjamin, *Illuminations*, 262. Though contemporary physics has called this Newtonian view of time into question, for social life it still is in force.

42. Taylor, *Secular Age*, 58.

43. Giddens, *Consequences of Modernity*, 14, 16–18; B. Anderson, *Imagined Communities*, 24; Harvey, "Wound of History," 78–83.

The perception of time in premodern societies, by contrast, was organically linked to local places and practices, typically in ways that were concrete, imprecise, and variable. In sixteenth-century Europe, for example, time was a complex reality, divided between ordinary time—in which people earn a living, raise their children, bury their loved ones, suffer through tyranny, and pay their taxes and tributes—and higher times, during which the divine gathers and re-orders ordinary time. For example, on feast days the eternal comes closer to ordinary time, hallowing it, and thus, as Shakespeare's Marcellus observes, ghosts and goblins do not dare to walk the earth on Christmas Eve. But the time can also be "out of joint," as Hamlet puts it, meaning that things are not fitting together as they do when they are drawn closer to the ordering paradigm of God.[44]

The sense of time produced by the modern technological imagination divides it into sequential periods that create what moderns call "history," in terms of which the significance of the past and future may be effectively managed in relation to the present. Past events and future prospects are extracted from settings that traditionally were connected with particular locales and with stories told about them, in order to assimilate them into a unitary and consolidated present. The mastery of time enables the self, in its new identity as a buffered, world-constituting subject, to seek to capitalize on acquired advantages, prepare for future expansions, and secure a certain independence over against the variability of circumstances.[45]

The reorganization of time works in conjunction with other social technologies—rationalized relations of production, consumption, and accumulation, mechanical printing, the ascendency of vernacular languages and the resulting spread of literacy among the general population—to create the state, a polity that is delimited in space but that exercises unfettered sovereignty within it. This political artifact is seen as moving "calendrically" through time, says Benedict Anderson, constituting the semblance of "a solid community moving steadily down (or up) history." Depicting the state thusly generates a strong sense of social identity and bonds of comradeship, which "makes it possible, over the past two centuries, for so many millions of people, not so much to kill, as willingly to die for such limited imaginings."[46] The seeds of the idolatry of nationalism are inconceivable apart from the contrived image of the state.[47]

44. Taylor, *Secular Age*, 54–58; Shakespeare, *Hamlet*, I.1.140–42; I.5.196.

45. Certeau, *Practice of Everyday Life*, xix–xxiv, 35–36.

46. B. Anderson, *Imagined Communities*, 7, 26.

47. *DBWE* 6:119–21.

Within this new form of political community another social artifact is imagined: "society." Though this word has been in the English language since the late Middle Ages,[48] within the technological organization of modernity it has acquired new significance. At times it refers, as it has for centuries, to a generic sense of social association—for example, a professional society—but more often it designates what a world come of age sees as the overarching system of social relations within which all other systems are located. In this sense of the term, "society" is the creation of the nation-state, which replaced the overlapping *societates* of the Middle Ages, a complex space composed of church, guild, family and clan, religious orders, and various ranks of nobility, with a single and simplified social order "bounded by borders and ruled by one sovereign to whom allegiance is owed in a way that trumps all other allegiances."[49] In short, says Giddens, "'societies' are plainly *nation-states*."[50] Stout, for example, simply assumes that the term designates the comprehensive social order fashioned around the institutions of the liberal democratic nation-state, and everyone who lives within the geographical and regulative boundaries of that state owe their primary identity and allegiance to it. Those who suggest that the church is the determinative social association for Christians are summarily accused of advocating "withdrawal" into "enclaves."[51]

The social technologies of a world come of age thus create simple, abstract, unitary space—in musical terms, monophonic space. In the polyphonic world of premodern societies, space and place are inextricable from the complexities of communal identity, such that "the spatial dimensions of social life are, for most of the population, and in most respects, dominated by 'presence'—by localised activities."[52] Premodern peoples regularly speak of a kinship between themselves and the land, flora and fauna, and watershed of specific places, creating a reciprocal aesthetic tied to particular geographic locations.[53] Technological reorganization displaces these specific corners of the earth as the determiners of identity, initially in the "Old World" through a variety of political and economic innovations, beginning with so-called original or primitive accumulation,[54] and then through

48. R. Williams, *Keywords*, 291.

49. Cavanaugh, *Migrations of the Holy*, 19.

50. Giddens, *Consequences of Modernity*, 13, Giddens' emphasis.

51. Stout, *Democracy and Tradition*, 112–15.

52. Giddens, *Consequences of Modernity*, 14–19. These activities are misunderstood if they are viewed solely as anticipations of modern forms of social interaction and economic exchange.

53. Martin, *Way of the Human Being*, 33, 69.

54. See Smith, *Wealth of Nations*, I.2.276–78.

colonization in the "New World." Space is represented as identical units, allowing for spatial interactions between persons over vast distances. Once perception of time and space is displaced from local ecologies, they can be endlessly recombined in order to allow for a more precise "time-space 'zoning' of social life"—for example, the five days of the standard workweek that is essential to organization of a society ordered around the requirements of state and market[55] but that bears little relation to the local rhythms of an agrarian people.

The sundering of the connection between place and identity, first in Europe, and then in Africa, Asia, and the Americas, is critical to the conversion of the earth from a world to which people, animals, objects, and events organically belong to a global repository of raw material standing by for our disposal. Creation is reconfigured as "a system of potentialities, a mass of undeveloped, underdeveloped, unused, underutilized, misunderstood, not fully understood potentialities. Everything—from peoples and their bodies to plants and animals, from the ground and the sky—was subject to change, subjects for change, subjected to change.... The earth itself was barred from being a constant signifier of identity." Indigenous locales are transformed into commodity and consumerist spaces.[56]

The organization of space into identical units allows it to be mapped, both actually and virtually, in ways that are predicated on Euclidean and descriptive geometry. These maps plot what was heterogeneous space on a uniform grid, thereby establishing a definitive and comprehensive mastery of diverse locales. The result is "a formal ensemble of abstract places" in terms of which elements of varying origin and significance come to exist within a precise representation of space, a synchronized "tableau of a 'state' of geographical knowledge." Space, once deprived of its former significance and subdivided into identical units, can be assigned to what Certeau calls "proper places," each unit carefully situated side by side as on a map, with no two occupying the same space.[57]

Proper places need not be simply locations in physical space but extend to the spiritual self-consciousness of a nation. Jonathan Sheehan chronicles the manner in which textual translation of scripture performs a technological function. He refers to the way Luther's translation of the Bible became the basis for the emergence of the national culture of Germany: "The appearance of a great translation fixes the face of a foreign literature into place, ripping it from its original soil and planting it firmly in the soil

55. Giddens, *Consequences of Modernity*, 14–19.

56. Jennings, *Christian Imagination*, 43, 200.

57. Certeau, *Practice of Everyday Life*, 119–21.

of its new possessor." When Germans in the nineteenth century read their Luther Bibles, what they read was not a translation of the ancient languages of Hebrew, Aramaic, and Greek, but "an originally German book." Translation serves as a "technique of deracination" designed to buttress the self-consciousness, political as well as spiritual, of the nation, which is then fused with the state to form a unitary space.[58]

Language itself, together with the various media it finds for dissemination (e.g., newspapers, radio, international press services, motion picture newsreels, television, cable television, the Internet), becomes a technology for creating unified simple space and proper places. Alasdair MacIntyre points out that there never has been such a thing as English as such, Hebrew as such, Spanish as such, or even classical Greek or Old English. There is rather Greek as written and spoken at the time of the Apostle Paul, and English as written and spoken at the time of Julian of Norwich.[59] According to E. J. Hobsbawm, at the start of the French Revolution only 50 percent of the citizens of France spoke French, and far fewer than that spoke it "correctly." When the state of Italy was created in 1860, only 2.5 percent used Italian for everyday purposes. The standardization of language within a nation-state by new media technologies, beginning with mass-produced newspapers, plays a crucial role in this process.[60]

In premodern societies, says Ernest Gellner, different activities—the hunt, harvest, rites of worship, council meetings, kitchen, and harem—employed distinct and context-specific languages. Any effort to "conjoin statements drawn from these various disparate fields, to probe for inconsistencies between them, to try to unify them all, this would be a social solecism or worse, probably blasphemy or impiety, and the very endeavour would be unintelligible." In the modern world, by contrast, it is assumed that these different vocabularies and grammars all refer to one coherent world, and thus can be reduced to a unitary idiom within a unified society.[61]

Fashioning simple space and proper places involves what Certeau labels a strategic logic of action, which is the predominant form of rationality in a risk culture. This logic requires the designation of a "subject with will and power"[62] as the proper locus of choice and action, for as Bonhoeffer observes of fallen humankind, "Knowing now means establishing the relation

58. Sheehan, *Enlightenment Bible*, 225–27; Cavanaugh, *Migrations of the Holy*, 30.
59. MacIntyre, *Whose Justice? Which Rationality*, 373.
60. Hobsbawm, *Nations and Nationalism since 1780*, 60–61.
61. Gellner, *Nations and Nationalisms*, 21.
62. Certeau, *Practice of Everyday Life*, 35–36.

to oneself, recognizing oneself in everything and everything in oneself."[63] This subject need not refer only to a buffered self, but may also refer to businesses, scientific laboratories, armies, and governments (as Bonhoeffer states, modern technology has its own soul, animating and constraining those who exist within its reach).[64] The subject, once its place is identified as the locus of action, serves "as the base from which relations with an *exteriority* composed of targets or threats . . . can be managed. As in management, every 'strategic' rationalization seeks first of all to distinguish its 'own' place, that is, the place of its own power and will, from an 'environment.'" This logic of action is the working rationality of modern science, politics, and military strategy,[65] and thus it forms the basis—the *radical*—of conceptions of technological reasoning in service to the will to mastery.

Three important effects emerge from the strategic identification of a proper subject and its coordination with proper places. The first is the triumph of the place of the subject over time, which is the ability to capitalize on what the subject has previously acquired, to prepare for future expeditions, and to secure independence over against the variability of circumstances, to protect against *fortuna*. The particularity and contingency, the irreducibility and irreversibility, of *history* are reconceived as the manageable pluralism of *historicity*.[66] This strategic mode of perceiving time, which depends upon technological interventions that were unknown and unavailable to previous societies, comprises what Zygmunt Bauman labels chronopolitics. The principal aim of chronopolitics is to project the differentiation of life into discrete action frames of reference back on the past, so that premodern societies may be seen as "'allochronic'—belonging to a different time, and surviving into the present on false pretenses, while being merely relics doomed to extinction." Chronopolitics inserts the particularity and contingency, irreducibility and heterogeneity of local settings into manageable space, such that all other forms of life are "*temporalized* in a way characteristic of the idea of progress: time stood for hierarchy—'later' being identical with 'better,' and 'ill' with the 'outdated,' or 'not-yet-properly-developed.'"[67] If there is

---

63. *DBWE* 6:308. In his copy of Josef Pieper's *Reality and the Good*, Bonhoeffer underlines and puts an exclamation point in the margin next to the following statement: "Kant makes the practical reason entirely independent of the theoretical," and in so doing "sees . . . nothing less than 'the conquest of the metaphysics of being, the transfer of the center of gravity from the object to the subject'" (*DBWE* 6:175 n. 16; Pieper, *Reality and the Good*, 142).

64. *DBWE* 6:116.

65. Certeau, *Practice of Everyday Life*, xix, 35–37.

66. Ibid., 36.

67. Bauman, *Postmodern Ethics*, 38–39.

anything of value in the past, it must justify itself in the forum of the present; it must be a vehicle, as it were, bearing "knowledge, norms, universal truths already given in the present."[68]

These technological mechanisms of time-space displacement and replacement, predicated on the strategic break between the buffered, world-constituting subject that creates for itself its own meaning of things and its "environment," make possible the *colonization of the future*. A territory in time is carved out in order for it to be colonized. As a result, "the future is continually drawn into the present by means of the reflexive organisation of knowledge environments," where it "becomes a new terrain—a territory of counterfactual possibility. Once thus established, that terrain lends itself to colonial invasion through counterfactual thought and risk calculation."[69] The future is no longer the unknown but lies open to our grasp as subjects with will and power.

A second effect connected to the strategic identification of the proper subject and the creation of proper places has to do with the role that "vision" plays in the technological organization of a world come of age. The establishment of a break between the place appropriated as one's own and that of its other enables a mastery of places through a distinctive way of seeing the world. "The division of space makes possible," writes Certeau, "a *panoptic practice* proceeding from a place whence the eye can transform foreign forces into objects that can be observed and measured, and thus control and 'include' them within its scope of vision. To be able to see (far into the distance) is also to be able to predict, to run ahead of time by reading a space."[70] Seeing the world around us as places and objects for our control, use, and enjoyment, and not as gifts and signs that serve as the means of our participation in the messianic suffering of God, is only possible on this basis.

The third effect emerging from the asymmetric relation between proper subject and proper place is a specific type of knowledge, "one sustained and determined by the power to provide oneself with one's own place." A certain form of power, consisting in the ability to make, creates the preconditions of this knowledge, making it possible and determining its defining traits. This form of power produces itself in and through this knowledge.[71] The form of power that constitutes the precondition of knowledge in this regard is, once again, a characteristic of the co-penetration of knowing and

---

68. *DBWE* 14:420.

69. Giddens, *Modernity and Self-Identity*, 3, 111.

70. Certeau, *Practice of Everyday Life*, 36.

71. Ibid.

making that is the technological organization of life. The age-old desire to be like God, *sicut deus*, has reached a level previously unimaginable.

The Gearing Mechanisms of a World Come of Age

The displacement of time and space from local settings and their re-placement in empty and interchangeable units create the conditions for what Giddens calls the gearing mechanisms that connect the local and the global in ways that would have previously been unimaginable. These connections are achieved through the disembedding of social relations by means of social technologies that lift them out of local contexts (where they are subject to the constraints and restrictions of "restrictive" activities and institutions) and redistribute them across indefinite spans of time-space, such that global ties, which are less apparent but more pervasive, govern their sense and significance. As a result, says Giddens, local settings are increasingly *phantasmagoric*, "thoroughly penetrated by and shaped in terms of social influences quite distant from them. What structures the locale is not simply that which is present on the scene; the 'visible form' of the locale conceals the distanciated relations which determine its nature."[72]

Two types of disembedding mechanisms characterize a world come of age, one of which is symbolic tokens, "media of interchange which can be 'passed around' without regard to the specific characteristics of individuals or groups that handle them at any particular juncture." Money is perhaps the most recognizable token in an age in which currency is so readily convertible. According to Giddens, money is less a medium of circulation that flows in time than a means of reconfiguring time and space so as to lift transactions out of local contexts of exchange where they are subject to the "irrational" limitations of traditional practices and institutions such as religion. In short, "money is a means of time-space distanciation." This omnipresent token couples instantaneity and deferral, presence and absence.[73] It is also the great social leveler, since "cash from a prince is no better than cash from a pastry cook."[74]

Another such mechanism is the proliferation of expert systems that continuously organize ever-larger areas of the material and social environments in which we live today. Like symbolic tokens, expert systems displace social relations from the social webs of local contexts. Most of us know little or nothing about the codes and techniques used by architects, engineers,

---

72. Giddens, *Consequences of Modernity*, 18–19, 21.

73. Ibid., 22, 24; Harvey, *Another City*, 121–23.

74. Boyle, *Who Are We Now?*, 156.

and economists, and yet every day in countless ways we place our faith in what they do. Simply by riding in a car or buying a house, for example, we involve ourselves in a series of such systems—and we seemingly have no choice but to place our trust in them.[75] As the "helping professions" have increasingly taken over our day-to-day lives, we no longer trust our inherited assumptions concerning happiness, fulfillment, and childrearing.[76] When combined with the collapse of local standards and the disappearance of social ties beyond the expediencies of voluntary associations and lifestyle enclaves, the vaunted goal of autonomy has led, in perhaps the most ironic fashion conceivable, to a form of life that fits perfectly into the instrumental, technologically organized world over against which it supposedly stands.

Bonhoeffer notes the increasing prevalence of these expert systems—the ideal state, the efficient market, the stable monetary system, the perfect educational method, the best practices of hygiene and health, or the infallible cure—and criticizes the faith we vest in them. He questions the belief that the key to wisdom for all areas of life is to be found in them and observes that though faith in these experts is unrequited time and again, and in spite of the fact that our lives continue to be suspended between escalating crises, we nonetheless look to them for our redemption: "*They* must know; *they* must be able to do it. After all, the most exact science must be able to bring us to our goal, must bring order in our chaos."[77]

MacIntyre, who contends that the moral nature of a society may be specified through its central characters, isolates the significance of these expert systems for a world come of age. Certain characters enact "a very special type of social role which places a certain kind of moral constraint on the personality of those who inhabit them in a way in which many other social roles do not." They must therefore not be confused with social roles in general, for understanding their distinctive roles allows one to interpret the behavior not only of the actors who play these parts but also that of other social actors who define themselves with reference to these central characters. The requirements of a character are "imposed from the outside, from the way in which others regard and use characters to understand and to evaluate themselves." Consequently, differences between cultures may largely be specified with reference to which stock of social roles are characters. In previous eras, for example, the priest or shaman, the person of noble birth, and the warrior were the important social characters.[78]

75. Giddens, *Consequences of Modernity*, 27–28.

76. Taylor, *Sources of the Self*, 508.

77. *DBWE* 11:453.

78. MacIntyre, *After Virtue*, 26, 28.

MacIntyre identifies the rich aesthete, the manager, and the therapist as the pivotal characters for a world come of age. The latter two enact in the social and personal sphere respectively the eclipse of tradition, the demise of teleology, and belief in technique: "The manager treats ends as given, as outside his scope; his concern is with technique, with effectiveness in transforming raw materials into final products, unskilled labour into skilled labour, investment into profits. The therapist also treats ends as given, as outside his scope; his concern is also with technique, with effectiveness in transforming neurotic symptoms into directed energy, maladjusted individuals into well-adjusted ones." The outlook of the rich aesthete in turn serves to foster a consumerist conception of the social world as "nothing but a meeting place for individual wills, each with its own set of attitudes and preferences and who understand that world solely as an arena for the achievement of their own satisfaction, who interpret reality as a series of opportunities for their enjoyment and for whom the last enemy is boredom." The three social roles of rich aesthete, manager, and therapist make up the central characters of modernity, MacIntyre concludes, because they embody the obliteration of the distinction between manipulative and non-manipulative social relations.[79]

Though he does not develop the concept of character as an analytical instrument to the extent that MacIntyre does, Bonhoeffer is critical of the role that experts play in modern society. He states that technology, mass movements, and nationalism are closely bound together in the heritage of the West, and points to the engineer and the entrepreneur in particular as pivotal figures in this legacy: "Although technology produces the masses and the masses in turn demand increased technology, technology itself is an affair of strong, intellectually superior personalities. The engineer and the entrepreneur do not belong to the masses." He contends that technology and the masses have risen together in connection with nationalism, but that they also display "an irresistible tendency" to overcome national boundaries. He then concludes by asserting that the masses and nationalism are the enemies of reason; technology and the masses are antinationalistic; and nationalism and technology are enemies of the masses.[80]

Some may question Bonhoeffer's contention that the masses are antinationalistic, but in light of the large-scale migrations of labor throughout the world, with tens of millions moving from violent and impoverished areas of the globe to Europe and North America in particular, his assertions have merit. To be sure, the masses are often rallied in support of nationalistic

79. Ibid., 24, 29.
80. *DBWE* 6:121.

aims, particularly when these aims are identified with a state, but since the end of World War II the world has witnessed the emergence of political organizations with no connection to a state but with organic ties to an ethnic group. The allegiance that modernity has assumed belongs exclusively to duly constituted states is no longer a given. Moreover, movements and coalitions have emerged within countries such as the United States that seek to push democracy beyond its present state-based forms.[81]

Bonhoeffer's related assertion that technology is an affair of strong, intellectually superior personalities and thus the enemy of the masses is significant, because he contends in *Ethics* that the celebrated freedom of a world come of age brings about a new form of human enslavement, as human beings become things under the power of another and thus as only means to another person's ends.[82] Ernst Jünger makes a similar observation, noting that

> The individual no longer stands in society like a tree in a forest; instead he resembles a passenger on a fast-moving vehicle, which could be called Titanic, or also Leviathan. While the weather holds and the outlook remains pleasant, he will hardly perceive the state of reduced freedom that he has fallen into. On the contrary, an optimism arises, a sense of power produced by the high speed. All this will change when the fire-spitting islands and icebergs loom on the horizon. Then, not only does technology step over from the field of comfort into very different domains, but the lack of freedom simultaneously becomes apparent—be it in the triumph of elemental powers, or in the fact that any individuals who have remained strong command an absolute authority.[83]

Once again our attention is directed to the distinctive effects that the technological organization of modern society, in particular its *re-placement* of space, time, and knowledge in relation to those who occupy the position of the proper subjects, has on human existence.

It is the demise of traditional goods and virtues that occurs as these experts assume control over virtually every aspect of our lives, and the faith we habitually place in their technologies, that underwrites the abdication of the need in a world come of age to make substantive moral judgments. The triumph of these expert systems in the modern regime may be seen in the ways the idioms of engineering, entrepreneurial, therapeutic, and

81. See, for example, Coles, *Beyond Gated Politics*.
82. *DBWE* 6:215; cf. 6:121 n. 87.
83. Jünger, *Forest Passage*, 27–28.

managerial expertise increasingly colonize the realms of politics, education, religion, and even law enforcement. The social role of the rich aesthete, for its part, exemplifies the modern transformation of life into lifestyle, a process that is not limited to the more affluent classes but now encompasses even the excluded and marginalized sectors of our society.[84]

The reduction of the past to an allochronic "prehistory," the development of strategies to colonize the future on the part of the proper subject, the emergence of these gearing mechanisms, and the social authority exercised by expert systems offer prime examples of why a world come of age cannot be left to its own devices and self-understanding. The social technologies that reorganize time operate in stark contrast to the way that divine revelation orders it within the communion of the body of Christ. Revelation is not limited to a record of something that "has happened," but through proclamation and sacrament it breaks into the present and the future. Through the agency of the Holy Spirit, the divine apocalypse intrudes on the present because the "once-and-for-all occurrence . . . is always something 'of the future.'" The church thus rightly perceives revelation in the form of the present Christ, "Christ existing as community." Acting in and through the church, Christ is the proper subject who determines the significance of both past and present. In the contrapuntal movements of revelation that come to us from outside ourselves and catch us up in it, the future determines the significance of both past and present. Proclamation and sacrament thus bridge the temporal caesura or interval between past and present, and between present and future.[85]

Bonhoeffer's concern for the space of the church takes on additional significance in light of the technological organization of life in a world come of age. Among the proper places imposed by these social technologies is that of "religion," which attempts to confine and manage the potentially disruptive practices of the church (and other traditions and practices that predate modernity) from interfering with their sovereignty. Only by refusing its putative proper place and claiming its own space (and organization of that space) is the church able to bear witness to a world come of age about the technological illusion it has embraced.

Radical Reflexivity and a World Come of Age

Finally, there is the role played by radical reflexivity in the technological organization of a world come of age. In one sense, says Giddens, there is

84. Giddens, *Modernity and Self-Identity*, 5–6.
85. *DBWE* 2:111; *DBWE* 12:330; *DBWE* 6:40–50.

nothing new here; all human beings have, to one degree or another, "kept in touch" with the grounds of what they believe and do as integral elements of belief and action.[86] It is this "feedback capacity," as Rowan Williams calls it, that enables humans to "stand apart from the material causal nexus to the extent that it can represent itself—including its location in the material causal nexus."[87] Bonhoeffer, beginning in *Act and Being*, acknowledges this fact in a distinction between *actus directus*, direct consciousness, and *actus reflexus*, the consciousness of reflection. The former is consciousness that is directed toward Christ, while in the latter consciousness "has the power to become its own object of attention." He derives this distinction from an earlier dogmatic distinction between *fides directa*, which is "the act of faith, which, even though completed within a person's consciousness, could not be reflected in it," and *fides reflexa*, or faith mediated by reflection. Both forms have a place in Christian life, though they should never be confused. Faith is at bottom *actus directus*, which means that it is "no longer a reflection upon the I. Rather, it expresses the personality in relation, which, even in the position of intentionality, remains a personality in relation."[88]

Bonhoeffer returns to this distinction time and again throughout his work. As he puts it in a circular Christmas letter in 1939, for example, *theologia sacra*, sacred theology, "originates in prayerful kneeling before the mystery of the divine child in the stable." In its reflection, reason must be "captive to obedience to Jesus Christ," and therefore whenever theology sees its task as decoding the mystery, it succumbs to foolishness.[89] *Fides directa* is the acceptance of the gift of freedom and obedience, while *fides reflexa* is the way that gift of grace is made explicit to our understanding.[90] In *Discipleship* he states that "the only required reflection for disciples is to be completely oblivious, completely unreflective in obedience, in discipleship, in love."[91] And in one of his last letters from prison he links the notion of *fides directa* to the possibilities for a "natural piety" and an "unconscious Christianity."[92]

Though some might dismiss Bonhoeffer with respect to the relationship he draws between *actus directa* and *actus reflexa* as a return to a kind of literalism or fundamentalism, something quite different and profound is being put forward. Paul Ricoeur, for example, speaks of "second naiveté"

---

86. Giddens, *Consequences of Modernity*, 36.

87. R. D. Williams, *Edge of Words*, 61.

88. *DBWE* 2:158.

89. *DBWE* 15:529. See Feil, *Theology of Dietrich Bonhoeffer*, 10–11, 28–30, 189.

90. *DBWE* 12:221; cf. *DBWE* 14:736; *DBWE* 16:562.

91. *DBWE* 4:150.

92. *DBWE* 8:489.

to refer to the passage from an original or first naiveté, through the stage of criticism, which he describes as a desert, to the sense of once again having been called. Ricoeur points us in the right direction, though his construal of the notion of second naiveté, which he names "the full responsibility of autonomous thought," does not completely shed the connection with *actus reflexus*.[93] Friedrich von Hügel provides a more nuanced description in a paper on the three elements of religion. There is, first, the historical-institutional dimension, which confronts the self as "a Fact and Thing": "The five senses then, perhaps that of touch first, and certainly that of sight most; the picturing and associative powers of the imagination; and the retentiveness of memory, are the side of human nature specially called forth." This aspect—Scripture, liturgies, prayers, ecclesiastical authorities—is most in evidence in children, who believe what they see and are told, "equally, as so much fact, as something to build on."[94]

Hügel names the second element the critical-speculative, "the reasoning, argumentative, abstractive side of human nature that begins to come into play." This dimension is particularly strong during adolescence, which is a time of questioning, both of others and of oneself: "The old impressions get now more and more consciously sought out, and selected from among other conflicting ones; the facts seem to clamour for reasons to back them, against the other hostile facts and appearances, or at least against those men in books, if not in life, who dare to question or reject them."[95]

By themselves, these first two elements are incomplete, each trapped in a form of one-sidedness to which individuals and communities are ever vulnerable.[96] Without the critical and speculative aspect, the historical and institutional dimension is blind; without the historical and institutional element, the critical and speculative side is empty. Hügel identifies a third dimension that he associates with mature adulthood, called the mystical-operative, which "is action and power, rather than either external fact or intellectual verification."[97] Neither "fact" nor "reason" forms the beginning and end of faith, nor are they progressively transcended and left behind as ontogeny recapitulates modernity's phylogenic myth (as James Fowler contends in *Stages of Faith* and Bonhoeffer repudiates in *Letters and Papers*

93. Ricoeur, *Symbolism of Evil*, 349–52.
94. Hügel, *Mystical Element of Religion*, 1:51.
95. Ibid., 52.
96. Lash, *Easter in Ordinary*, 154.
97. Hügel, *Mystical Element of Religion*, 2:393–94.

from Prison[98]), but are "set to the service of action and decision undertaken as the expression of personal responsibility."[99]

In a world come of age, however, a substantially different form of reflexivity is installed as a result of the wager on a new locus of sacrality made at the outset of the modern age. As a result, writes Bonhoeffer, "reflection signifies refusal" of what is "yet to come," as the direct relation to Christ is replaced by "a reflection upon the I."[100] Radical reflexivity has it roots in the philosophy of Descartes, for whom rationality requires "disengagement from world and body and the assumption of an instrumental stance toward them. It is of the essence of reason, both speculative and practical, that it push us to disengage." Reason is no longer construed substantially, as Plato saw it, in terms of how we relate to an ontic order of Ideas (or as Bonhoeffer sees it, in terms of our participation in the life, death, and resurrection of Christ), but procedurally, in terms of the standards by which the buffered self creates for itself intra-mental orders of meaning. "For Plato," writes Taylor, "to be rational we have to be right about the order of things. For Descartes rationality means thinking according to certain canons. The judgement now turns on properties of the activity of thinking rather than on the substantive beliefs which emerge from it."[101] Bonhoeffer puts the matter succinctly: "Epistemology is the attempt of the I to understand itself. I reflect on my myself; I and myself move apart and come together again. . . . And in this attitude of reflection the self-understanding of the I is, in one way or another, closed within itself."[102]

An inherited reserve of moral and ontological convictions about the world and humankind provided for a time the moral and social infrastructure underwriting the canons of the modern wager. But as these beliefs were extracted from their historic source in an explicit set of practices and exposed to the erosive effects of radical reflexivity, they gradually began to wither away, somewhat slowly at the beginning, and then with increasing velocity as the eighteenth and nineteenth centuries progressed. While the first causality was "religion," scientists, philosophers, and social and literary theorists alike have discovered that the modern wager that sought to ground the notions of reason, knowledge, and interpretation in a set of procedures can neither establish its own validity nor re-establish the validity of the convictions of traditions that had been discarded or had fallen by the wayside.

98. Fowler, *Stages of Faith*; DBWE 8:321.

99. Lash, *Easter in Ordinary*, 155.

100. *DBWE* 2:157, 158.

101. Taylor, *Sources of the Self*, 155–56.

102. *DBWE* 2:33.

Reflexivity now resides in the social technologies that constitute the epistemic cocoon around each individual, comprising the very basis of everyday life "such that thought and action are constantly refracted back upon one another." The risk culture women and men are compelled to inhabit, and in terms of which they now interpret themselves and the world about them, is thus fashioned in and through the reflexive organization of these knowledge environments. Though the classic Cartesian principle of radical doubt may have few defenders in academic circles, it has been thoroughly institutionalized within the technological organizations of the modern age, as seen in the insistence that every claim to knowledge must take the form of a hypothesis, which may be true but is always in principle open to revision and which may at some point have to be abandoned.[103]

Radical reflexivity works in concert with the gearing mechanisms of money and expert systems to pry social relations away from the particularities of local contexts of presence so that they may be redistributed across indefinite spans of time-space. Men and women are caught up in a world where "the formation of knowledge and the increase of power regularly reinforce one another in a circular process." There is, says Michel Foucault, a double process at work in the co-penetration of knowing and doing: on the one hand, "an epistemological 'thaw' through a refinement of power relations," and on the other, "a multiplication of the effects of power through the formation and accumulation of new forms of knowledge."[104] It is modernity's distinctive form of reflexivity, "the regularised use of knowledge about circumstances of social life as a constitutive element in organisation and transformation"—that is, technological organization—that finally distinguishes a world come of age from "premodern" social orders.[105]

The construction of self-identity through these knowledge environments did not result in the general increase of freedom and human flourishing. Our increasing dependence on expert systems, coupled with modernity's unswerving (and for that reason uncritical) faith in technological organization of all kinds, has had the opposite effect. The hopes we vested in technology to master nature and fortune turned out to be, as Bonhoeffer labels them, illusory: "Technology is the power with which the earth seizes hold of humankind and masters it."[106] As he is quick to point out, the fault here lies not in the instruments we have devised but in us, in our boundless desire and unrelenting efforts to make ourselves lords and

---

103. Giddens, *Consequences of Modernity*, 36–39.
104. Foucault, *Discipline and Punish*, 224.
105. Giddens, *Modernity and Self-Identity*, 20.
106. *DBWE* 3:67.

masters of our existence. We have been thrown back on ourselves, without the spiritual resources to direct our desires and constrain our fears. The instruments that we have devised to gain mastery over our destiny, to be like God, *sicut deus*, have become the means of our enslavement.

We who are the result of this thoroughgoing reconfiguration of life and divinization of ourselves are the unwitting products of criticism, revolution, and self-inflicted amnesia.[107] Only in retrospect are we discovering that we have come to dominate a world in which there is no sign that we still exist, save for the overriding concern to maintain the powers of our sovereignty.[108] Our activities and achievements, our doings and our knowings, have been focused by the will to mastery, "a continual striving for increased control and more precise determination of ourselves and the world, that is *never* subordinated to any other concern."[109]

To complicate matters further, every attempt on the part of modernity to get a fix on who we are and what is at issue in our practices has only perpetuated the endless expansion of strategic rationality and the social technologies that are its bearers, resulting in the continuing and unwitting subjection of ourselves, our neighbors, and our world to more precise manipulations and control. In short, the will to mastery inevitably undermines any stable field of significance that might provide direction and coherence to our lives.[110] William Poteat notes that even our "'humanism' is very often the despairing offspring of this impiety. Our discarnate freedom has no place in the universe, our visible form recapitulates no cosmos, no breath of God shines in our faces." He continues, "There is a strain of self-hatred in our Western protests against dehumanization, a bad faith that shows itself more the more mordant and shrill the protest, as if we have to still with the sound of our own voices the deeper doubt that there is anything genuinely and intrinsically human to be defended." In the end, he observes ironically, "Our humanism keeps a mistress whose name is Nihilism."[111]

If the rise of modernity is associated with the disenchantment of the world, then the recently fashionable "disenchantment with disenchantment"[112] is that ambiguous phenomenon called postmodernism. It is ambiguous because postmodernism has no story of its own, save for its endless demonstrations that the modern wager on the ability of radical

107. Poteat, *Polanyian Meditations*, 4.

108. Polanyi, *Personal Knowledge*, 380; Levinas, "Ethics as First Philosophy," 78.

109. Rouse, *Knowledge and Power*, 261.

110. Ibid., 262; cf. Harvey, "Post-Critical Approach," 40–41.

111. Poteat, *Polanyian Meditations*, 5.

112. See Surin, "*Contemptus mundi* and the Disenchantment of the World," 192.

reflexivity to give rise to an untrammeled freedom in human affairs has led humankind (and the rest of creation with us) to "an impasse, if not actual shipwreck." Postmodernism is thus "the rhetorical frenzy of the latest attempt of the self-contradictory nature of Enlightenment to enforce itself as a solution to its own incoherence."[113]

The postmodern reaction to the myth of a world come of age thus reveals much about a social order that prides itself on its ostensive maturity, showing, first and foremost, that it is not the realization of latent universal tendencies that had gestated in the womb of civilization for centuries, but "the result of the contingent emergence of imposed interpretations."[114] In other words, a world come of age is not "natural," realized in accordance with some divine or metaphysical blueprint.[115] It is a historically determinate series of practices, social roles, disciplinary techniques, material forces, institutions, and political configurations that, in its efficient anonymity, is both the instrument *and* effect of human intelligence and activity. The modern world has been shown to be a contingent array of practices, institutions, and social relations, orchestrated by a *mythos* disguised as the necessary laws of the natural and human sciences. It is therefore not a given that only needs to be unveiled by a better science, but more like "the temporary partitions used to subdivide the interior space of a building, so that more efficient containment, surveillance and supervision of what goes on within it might be achieved."[116]

Consistent with Bonhoeffer's expressed aim to understand the world better than it understands itself, postmodernism is a potential ally in exposing a world come of age to an unexpected light that shows that it is indeed godless, thereby bringing it closer to divine judgment and grace. By depriving its technological regime of legitimacy, shattering its claims to certainty, stability, and security, and undermining attempts to assign the status of the given to its contingent impositions, this movement helps us understand a world come of age better than it has understood itself. In particular, it demonstrates that the particulars of our time and place are not *facts*, that is, givens, but *artifacts*.[117]

Postmodern thought also reinforces something that Bonhoeffer emphasizes throughout his career, beginning with *Sanctorum Communio*,

---

113. Rosen, *Hermeneutics as Politics*, 11, 49.

114. Dreyfus and Rabinow, *Michel Foucault*, 108.

115. See Taylor, *Secular Age*, 126.

116. Harvey, "Body Politic of Christ," 324.

117. It is interesting to note at this point that the English words "fact" and "artifact" are both derived from the Latin *factum*, signifying a deed, act, event, or accomplishment.

which is that who we are as persons is not something that we are inwardly and privately, which is the presumption of radical reflexivity. Who we are as individual persons is caught up in the complex of power relations and interactions with others. Human beings, he writes, "do not exist 'unmediated' qua spirit in and of themselves, but only in responsibility vis-à-vis an 'other' . . . One cannot even speak of the individual without at the same time necessarily thinking of the 'other' who moves the individual into the ethical sphere."[118] In other words, says Nicholas Lash, "the whole complex, conflictual, unstable process of human history is a matter of the production and destruction of the 'personal.'"[119] The question is, therefore, what kinds of persons have we been producing within the technological organizations of modernity?

As Bonhoeffer expresses it in his prison poem "Who Am I?"[120] our identities as human beings are not constituted by what we are inwardly and privately, either isolated or under threat from the "external" world. The buffered self, created and trained to see itself as self-determining by what Foucault calls the modern technologies of the self,[121] is ultimately an ironic illusion. The self is at any given moment a made self (not to be confused with the mistaken notion that each of us is, in the end, self-made), "whose present range of responses is part of a developing story."[122] There is no safe haven of meaning, no substantial "self" immune from the particularities of history and its contingent networks of power, no transcendental or idealist *a priori* that supplies a foundational identity and purpose to our contingent existence or to what we do and achieve. To the extent that each of us is some *body*, therefore, we are, both individually and corporately, the products of our common history, scripted by stories and crafted by practices, social roles, institutions, and goals that in a sense possess us. Paradoxically, it is this narrative framework that also enables us to be intentional, purposeful beings. The question thus becomes, *which imaginary* shapes us as human beings and actors, and therefore forms the basis of our interpretive wager regarding the beginning and end of human life?

A world come of age thus names a contingent form of life, one that for most of us, most of the time, simply "has" us. It is a particular and concrete mode of existence that determines the range of alternative responses among

118. *DBWE* 1:50. He adds that it is chiefly language that renders reciprocal interaction with other minds in self-conscious thinking and willing possible and meaningful. *DBWE* 1:68–69.

119. Lash, *Theology on the Way to Emmaus*, 153.

120. *DBWE* 8:459–60.

121. Foucault, *Technologies of the Self*, 18.

122. R. D. Williams, *Resurrection*, 29.

which we are "free" to choose, but virtually every exercise of this freedom extends and consolidates its hold over us. The relations of knowing and doing that sustain this way of life lead to an ambiguous sense of ourselves as both quasi-divine subjects and the pliable objects of power. We see ourselves as constructing our lives, both individually and communally, and yet we recognize in retrospect that the form and coherence of our existence is caught up within a web of powers we helped create yet over which we have no control. In the end, it is *we* who have been compelled to produce signs of our presence and behavior.[123]

The primary object and target of these relations of *techne/logos* is the human body, which has been manipulated, supervised, transformed, and used; in a word, the body has been masterfully "subjected." The body's integrity, motility, sentience, and intentionality have been carefully formed by these technologies so that they can be reinvested in their proper place, that is, in a social economy that governs its range of possibilities. Through this process of formation the body is involved in a complex web of relations, for as Foucault notes, "it is largely as a force of production that the body is invested with relations of power and domination. . . . Its constitution as labour power is possible only if it is caught up in a system of subjection. . . . The body becomes a useful force only if it is both a productive body and a subjected body."[124]

This connection between capitalist relations of production and social hegemony is not a new insight. James Stewart (sometimes spelled Steuart) argued over against Adam Smith that wage-labor was a mode of *discipline*, not freedom. He denounced the Catholic practice of distributing surplus public wealth to the needy. This practice is like the miracle of manna from heaven, not the regular and predictable management needed by society: "'The regulation of need,' and not charity, is a more reliable means of social control and increasing the population."[125] For Stewart, says S. R. Sen, both the size of the population and the size of the classes need to be carefully controlled.[126]

A Space of Its Own

Given these dynamics, Bonhoeffer's contention that the church needs its own space becomes more pertinent than ever. Just as God claims space in

123. Rouse, *Knowledge and Power*, 247.
124. Foucault, *Discipline and Punish*, 25; cf. Harvey, "Post-Critical Approach," 43.
125. Stewart, *Works*, 1:118, cited by Milbank, *Theology and Social Theory*, 31.
126. Sen, *Economics of Sir James Steuart*, 135.

the world in Jesus Christ, "even space in a stable because 'there was no other place in the inn,'" God makes the same claim for the church of Jesus Christ as the place (*Ort*) and space (*Raum*) where Christ's reign over the whole world continues to be demonstrated and proclaimed.[127] The church needs its own space, organized according to the form of Christ, so that it can fulfill its sacramental mission, which is to seek the good of all through participation in Christ.

Some may fear that by emphasizing the church's need for its own space the communion of Christ is thinking only of its own self-preservation, and though this is a legitimate concern, it can easily be overstated. In the last section of the *Ethics* manuscript to be composed prior to his arrest, Bonhoeffer contends that though the church does not exist just for itself, it is a community (*Gemeinwesen*) that bears a double purpose, and it must do justice to that double purpose, "namely, being oriented toward the world, and, in this very act, simultaneously being oriented toward itself as the place [*Stätte*] where Jesus Christ is present." The church thus serves the world in the first instance as participant in the vicarious representative action of Christ, living, moving, and existing for the sake of the world, and in the second as the place where the world comes to its own destiny: "the church-community is the 'new creation,' the 'new creature,' the goal of God's ways on earth." The church therefore does exist for itself precisely in its being-for-the-world (*die gerade in ihrem Sein für die Welt besteht*),[128] so that it might "testify to the world that it is still the world, namely, the world that is loved and reconciled by God." The church does not need to claim authority over all earthly spaces, but it does need its own space to serve as sacramental witness to God's reconciling work through Jesus Christ.[129] There is a need within the church, in other words, for what Bonhoeffer calls selfless self-assertion and even selfless self-love, the latter an expression he borrows from Josef Pieper.[130]

Of course the church does not exist in a social vacuum. It would be foolish to deny that there are sorts of belonging—for example, national citizenship or familial ties—that Christians do not and cannot choose. But too often, says Rowan Williams, theologians move with disturbing quickness from this rather banal observation to the assertion that "our relation

127. *DBWE* 6:63.

128. *DBWE* 6:404–7 (*DBW* 6:408–9).

129. *DBWE* 6:63–64. Bonhoeffer's statements about the importance of the arcane discipline in several prison letters strongly suggest that he does not abandon this position. *DBWE* 8:365, 372–73.

130. *DBWE* 6:254; *DBWE* 8:375; *DBWE* 16:78; cf. Pieper, *Four Cardinal Virtues*, 149; Pieper, *Faith, Hope, Love*, 142–43.

to these contexts is basically 'contemplative,' a penetration by theological understanding into the essential structure in the mind and will of God."[131] A contemplative frame of reference invariably treats the divine act of revelation as chiefly a cognitive affair, inviting men and women simply to consider the present state of the world differently, which, as Karl Barth observes, makes God's self-disclosure merely a modification of our self-consciousness.[132] In other words, the relationships and identities formed within a world come of age—nation-states, capitalist markets, expert systems, disembedding mechanisms, and the like—are not regarded as contingent realities that came about in interaction with the historical and material conditions of their times, but as representing the way that God had originally designed them to fit human beings together. The inevitable result of this vision of the world is a sanctioning of all existing orders and a romantic conservatism.[133]

Closely related to his concern to claim space for the church is Bonhoeffer's rejection of the concept of movement (*Bewegung*) to describe the body of Christ. In a circular letter to the members of the Bruderhaus sent on November 29, 1935, Bonhoeffer warns his students to be prepared for state action against the Confessing Church, and also to be ready to support their church leadership. He then adds, "Under no circumstances allow yourselves to be led astray by assertions that we are a 'movement' rather than a church," emphasizing that to do so would be to abandon everything that was confessed at Barmen and Dahlem, and to place themselves alongside the German Christian movement. Later in a lecture he states again that the church is not a "movement," that those who are moved tend toward groups such as the Communists, National Socialists, and German Christians. The danger is that one ends in the flesh.[134]

Bonhoeffer circles back to this theme of refusing a "movement" designation for the church-community in *Ethics*, stating that the church must defend its own space by struggling not for space as such but for the salvation of the world; otherwise "the church becomes a 'religious society' [*Religionsgesellschaft*] that fights in its own interest and thus has ceased to be the church of God in the world." The end and goal of the church claiming space in the world is therefore not to create something for itself, a religious organization or pious life, but to be witnesses to Jesus Christ in the world.

131. R. D. Williams, *On Christian Theology*, 228. Williams's use of "contemplative" harkens back to Aristotle's distinction between what cannot be otherwise (and thus our relation to it is contemplative) and what can be otherwise (to which we have a practical relation).

132. Barth, *Theology of Schleiermacher*, 235.

133. *DBWE* 6:389.

134. *DBWE* 14:124, 523 (*DBW* 14:120, 516–17); cf. *DBWE* 3:45.

At the same time, such a witness can only happen in the right way when it comes from the sanctified life in the church-community: "True sanctified life in the church-community of God is distinguished from any pious imitation by the fact that it leads the believer at the same time into witness to the world."[135] Accepting the designation of "movement" or "religious society" to identify the nature of the church-community, by contrast, would mean conceding its proper place within the ordering of space by a world come of age.

In his discussion of the importance of space, he neither identifies the church with any configuration of order and power nor instructs it to withdraw into some illusory sphere of private purity. Instead, he states that the apocalyptic action of God in Christ establishes "a lasting and irremovable tension"[136] between the form of the church and those structures—family, language, state, people, culture, nation, and civilization—that the technological organization of life would have us simply regard as givens. At certain times and in certain places the tension between the two will be generative rather than oppositional, and opportunities for collaboration in pursuit of the goods of human existence will be numerous and substantial. In such circumstances the church is able to act in concert with the current regime. At other times and places, most clearly in the situation faced by Bonhoeffer during the Nazi era, the tension becomes increasingly antagonistic, and the community is summoned by its participation in Christ to act instead over against the current configuration. At no time, however, should the church see this time and place before the last as exhibiting a perfect or near-perfect fit with the last things (a topic I shall return to in chapter 8).

The church-community's need for its own space puts on the table for discussion the question of politics, understood first and foremost as having to do with the structures that fashion the basic relationships within which human beings live with one another and before God. It is the seal of the Holy Spirit, says Bonhoeffer in *Discipleship*, that sets the church off from the world. It is by virtue of this seal and the line that is thereby drawn between itself and the world that the church insists on God's claim to the whole world. The church is therefore "the city on the hill, the 'polis' (Matt. 5:14)," established with its own "political" character as "an inseparable aspect of its sanctification," the goal of which "is that the world be world and community be community, and that nevertheless, God's word goes out from the church-community to all the world, as the proclamation that the earth and all it contains is the Lord's."[137]

135. *DBWE* 6:64 (*DBW* 6:49–50).

136. *DBWE* 6:104.

137. *DBWE* 4:261–62. The question of a political ethic comes up again in *Ethics* in connection with the question of the validity of the Sermon on the Mount. *DBWE* 6:244.

Once again we see Bonhoeffer using scare quotes to great effect, gesturing in this case to a key difference between that which is "political" and that which is simply political. By putting the matter thusly he uses these concepts analogically.[138] This is a crucial move on his part, particularly in our social context, in which politics is a univocal term that is completely subsumed by the state. Politics has become simply those activities and institutions having exclusively to do with statecraft, the maintenance and operation of the mechanisms of the modern nation-state. This presumptive definition confers on the state virtually unlimited sovereignty over a geographically defined space, thus privileging it as the fulcrum of all meaningful social identity.[139]

Bonhoeffer recognizes that whenever the body of Christ fails to cultivate its own "political" character in the form of churchcraft, with its own distinctive habits, rites, and institutions, and above all its distinctive uses of material goods, it is invariably absorbed into the ways, means, and ends of the technological organizations that govern the present age, which in turn causes us Christians to lose sight of its character as the time before the last. When, on the other hand, the church seriously develops its own performance of worldliness, it is better able to serve as an "antidote to the overwhelming inertia of the status quo," enabling all who take the time to look to see that the way things are is not the way they always have been, have to be or will be.[140]

By refusing to be confined to its "proper place" in the technological ordering of a world come of age, the church is in the position to recognize that the present situation always has a context, a history that is made and therefore is not immutable.[141] At stake, then, is the ability to recognize that every regime—in our case, a liberal capitalist society—is not a given but a contingent performance of practices, institutions, modes of knowing, and social relations that should never be understood solely or finally on its own terms. This knowledge makes it possible for the "citizens" of Christ's body "politic" to avoid both a servile attitude toward the status quo and a facile protest against it based on some imagined ideal.[142] They are instead free, in and through the power of the Holy Spirit, to engage in an alternative performance that both foreshadows the future life for which God created and reconciled the world in Christ,[143] and provides the time and the space in the

138. Harvey, "Path of the Church's Decision," 94.
139. Skinner, *Age of Reformation*, 353.
140. Bell, *Economy of Desire*, 25.
141. R. D. Williams, *Resurrection*, 30.
142. *DBWE* 6:223.
143. McCabe, *New Creation*, xii.

present to prepare for responsible action. (The importance of preparation will be taken up in chapter 9.)

Comments about the "political" character of the church might make more than a few readers of *Discipleship* very nervous, and thus tempt them to adopt interpretive strategies of his work that posit a substantial shift in his thinking between his tenure as head of the seminary in Finkenwalde and during the war. When his discussion of the church's sanctification, for example, is read in isolation from the overall trajectory of his work, it is easy to see why he says in one of his later prison letters that he clearly sees dangers in the book, but immediately adds, "I still stand by it."[144] Florian Schmitz correctly pinpoints the danger that could emerge from an improperly guided reading of *Discipleship*: "*the resolve to remain pure from guilt, no matter what evil is loose in the world and demands a decision on behalf of the oppressed.*" At the same, if we fail to differentiate between Bonhoeffer's basic assumptions and the way these assumptions develop over time and circumstance we shall miss the theological foundations of his work, which, as Schmitz says, "have always been the same."[145]

Our genealogy of a world come of age is not yet finished, however, for we must first examine in more concrete detail some of the ways its technological organizations have taken form in us to produce the kinds of persons they need. Unless we undertake this examination, any effort on our part to recover what it might look like for the form of Christ to take form in us in our present circumstances will be short-circuited. The first of the technological relations of knowing and doing that constrain us, govern our conduct, and invest our lives in a political field has to do with a familiar notion: religion.

144. *DBWE* 8:486.

145. Schmitz, "Reading *Discipleship* and *Ethics* Together," 152–53 (emphasis in original). See also Schmitz, *Nachfolge*.

4

The End(s) of "Religion"

In the Bible to bless God is not a "religious" or a "cultic" act,
but the very *way of life*.

—ALEXANDER SCHMEMANN, *For the Life of the World*

ROWAN WILLIAMS IGNITED A heated debate in 2008 when he proposed in
a lecture that Muslim construals of *sharia* (together with Orthodox Jewish
practice) might be allowed to have a role in the conduct of public affairs,
primarily in civil matters, in a religiously and culturally diverse England.
He notes that social identities are not established by only one set of relations
or mode of belonging, and to insist that they should be thus established
is dangerous. The menace arises, Williams writes, "not only when there is
an assumption on the religious side that membership of the community
(belonging to the *umma* or the Church or whatever) is the only significant
category, so that participation in other kinds of socio-political arrangement
is a kind of betrayal. It also occurs when secular government assumes a monopoly in terms of defining public and political identity." Room should be
made, not for parallel and therefore competing legal systems, but for overlapping, "supplementary" jurisdictions that would allow the convictions of
minority groups to play a role in resolving internal disputes and regulating
transactions.[1]

Reaction to the talk in the British press was swift and contentious, with
many accusing Williams, then archbishop of Canterbury, of advocating the

---

1. R. D. Williams, "Civil and Religious Law," 102.

establishment of parallel legal systems.[2] A blogger who goes by the pseud-
onym Gracchi, who expresses his admiration for the political theory of
Thomas Hobbes, states very plainly that "the law is the instrument by which
we maintain peace and mark out civil goods and bads [sic: it delineates
that which the country considers private and inoffensive and that which the
country considers public and dangerous."[3] Many other responses invoked
the same distinction between what is public, to which the law belongs, and
what is private, which is the domain to which religion belongs. Few of them
made any attempt to address the problems and tensions that the assumption
of a monopoly on public identity by the nation-state raises.

In the Middle Ages, when overlapping authorities and multiple modes
of belonging were the norm, Williams's proposal would have been redun-
dant. The social world of the period was comprised of intersecting associations—principalities and republics, parishes, clerical and religious orders,
guilds, clans, and town councils. The duties, immunities, and entitlements
that men and women owed to and expected from each other were neither
delineated nor conferred by a centralized state—an institution that effectively disconnects persons from local encumbrances in order to establish a
direct relationship to the sovereign center of power—but were the working
assumptions of these overlapping associations. Each person and association
was a whole that in turn constituted parts of a larger whole, generating a
complex conception of social space that was conceived on the Pauline theology of the body of Christ.[4]

The question is, what has happened in the meantime that makes
Williams's proposal so controversial? In raising this question I am not calling for a return to the Middle Ages, which would be, as Dietrich Bonhoeffer
says, a counsel of despair that could only be made at the cost of intellectual
integrity. We would do well, however, to heed whatever lessons our medieval
forebears have to teach us, beginning with an accurate accounting of what
actually was the norm then (the many misconceptions about this period

2. See, for example, Cranmer, "Archbishop and Sharia," 4–5.

3. The full text by this author may be found in Gracchi [pseud.], "Civil and Religious Law in England: Contra Canterbury!" Similar reactions to the use of sharia in
the United States have made their way into state legislatures; cf. Vischer, "Dangers of
Anti-Sharia Laws," 26–28.

4. Milbank, *Word Made Strange*, 268–92; Gierke, *Associations and Law*, 143–60;
Cavanaugh, *Theopolitical Imagination*, 99–100. Elements of this tradition are reflected
in Bonhoeffer's understanding of the difference between Anglo-Saxon and German
conceptions of human rights, contending that the language of rights must be set in a
social framework that recognizes the fact that one's existence as an individual and one's
membership in various social groupings are constitutively bound to each other. *DBWE*
16:528–33.

notwithstanding). Neither do I want to rule on the viability of Williams's suggestion, though it is worthy of serious consideration not just in England but elsewhere as well. My goal in the next three chapters is to describe, with Bonhoeffer's assistance, the way the technologies of a world come of age locate significant differences in human life within a political order that excludes or marginalizes other kinds of communal existence. I seek to amplify Bonhoeffer's contention that the church need not see itself according to the social grammar of a world come of age, or conduct its affairs within the constraints which that world would have us believe are simply givens to be accepted. Though each of us has multiple affiliations, affections, and attachments, the call of Christ requires that we subject all those ties to critical scrutiny under Christ's lordship.

These next chapters will focus on the concepts of religion, culture, and race, which are crucial terms in the working lexicon that organizes the world in which virtually every woman, man, and child must live and work. Over the last five hundred years these notions have increasingly served as categories in terms of which a world come of age has described, differentiated, and classified the other. These social technologies have served to "subject" the stranger, the alien, the non-neighbor, and the other, transforming them into docile and productive agents of reason and will, that is, into interchangeable "individuals" who can be "industrious, disciplined, do useful work, and above all can be relied upon. They have 'settled courses', and are thus mutually predictable."[5] Bonhoeffer's critique of the concept of religion as a constructive theological category for interpreting Christian life and thought provides a suitable starting point for investigating the ways a world come of age accounts for difference. Such a critique helps the church understand not only how the world arrived at this juncture but also how it may faithfully and truthfully cultivate in its midst a profound this-worldliness that engages difference very differently.

In what follows, I offer, in conversation with other scholars, an interpretation of Bonhoeffer on the question of religion. Moreover, when we extend his generative critiques of religion to the concepts of culture and race in subsequent chapters, we discover that these notions, far from being unrelated features of modern society, are actually complementary mechanisms, "born of a mix of Christian disputes about truth, European colonial exploits, and the formation of nation-states."[6] As elements of the technological organization of a world come of age, these artifacts sequester potentially disruptive persons, practices, and traditions in their proper place.

5. Taylor, *Secular Age*, 106.

6. Nongbri, *Before Religion*, 154.

They help weave every aspect of creation, above all human existence, into the risk culture of the modern world.

As with other aspects of his theology, Bonhoeffer's observations about the nature and fate of religion in a world come of age are at best incomplete, and at times they appear to miss the mark; thus they must not only be corrected and expanded, but in certain respects radicalized. Most obviously, reports of religion's demise, which he seems to accept at face value, have been greatly exaggerated. Though its distinctive features have been modified somewhat, what is typically regarded as religion has not disappeared from the human landscape—indeed, far from it. But we must proceed cautiously with respect to these assertions about a religionless age, for his primary concern has to do with the *theological role* this concept had played in the waning years of Christendom. Due to these social technologies, Christian ideas and images are no longer embodied in the habits and practices that form our day-to-day existence, but continue to be sequestered in carefully delimited realms.

The fact that, save for the nations of Western Europe, the predicted waning of what is still thought of as religious belief and practice has not materialized does not negate the primary force of Bonhoeffer's critique of religion or call for a religionless Christianity. Now, more than ever, the church needs to unseat this concept from its privileged place in the working grammar of Christian theology. The fact that in the decades since his execution we have not witnessed the advent of a completely nonreligious age does, however, require that we reformulate his thoughts on this question.

Bonhoeffer's insights into the social and theological functions of the concept of religion also need to be resituated within a more comprehensive theological critique of difference. This does not represent a significant departure from the basic trajectory he establishes in *Letters and Papers from Prison*, for as Eberhard Bethge observes with respect to Bonhoeffer's thinking on this subject, "Religion has become essentially a way of distinguishing people."[7] Religion is but one of several instruments in the toolbox that governs difference in a world come of age. As I have already suggested, the notions of culture and race need to be factored into this critique.

Bonhoeffer on the Concept of Religion

"Don't be alarmed," Bonhoeffer writes to Bethge in his prison letter of November 21, 1943, "I will definitely not come out of here as a 'homo religiosus'!" Indeed, he adds, his suspicion and fear of religiosity (*Religiosität*) have

7. Bethge, *Dietrich Bonhoeffer*, 876–77.

become greater than ever. Eight months later, on the day after the assassination attempt on Hitler had failed, he reiterates this position, stating that the Christian is not a *homo religiosus* but simply a human being.[8] His concern with religion as a theological concept does not suddenly appear out of thin air in the late prison letters, however, but had been gestating from the beginning of his professional career. Already as a university student he discerns a troubling separation between everyday life and religion. On holiday with his brother Klaus in North Africa following his first year at university, he notes "an immense similarity between Islam and the lifestyle and piety recorded in the Old Testament. In Islam, everyday life and religion are not separated at all." In his native Prussian Protestantism, by contrast, "one just goes to church. When one returns a completely different life begins."[9]

In his doctoral dissertation he wrestles with the place of the concept of religion within the grammar of theology, and it is not surprising that we see at this early date an unresolved ambivalence. At times he treats the concept sympathetically, stating at one point that though the general concept of religion has no intrinsic social implications, "the solitude of the soul with God" does tend to have communal expression, and thus we are directed "back from the general concept of religion to the concrete form of religion, which for us means the concept of the church."[10] Bonhoeffer here comes close to the influential definition of religion offered by the American philosopher and psychologist William James, who defines it as *"the feelings, acts, and experiences of individual men in their solitude, so far as they apprehend themselves to stand in relation to whatever they may consider the divine."*[11]

In the very next sentence, however, Bonhoeffer pulls back from this stance, contrasting the concept of religion to that of revelation, stating emphatically that *"only the concept of revelation can lead to the Christian concept of the church."*[12] This is not the only time he waffles on this matter. For example, to the question of whether Jesus was the founder of a religion or religious community he gives an unequivocal "no," or at least he seems to do so. The credit for establishing the church as a religious community, he writes, belongs to the apostles: "God established the reality of the church, of humanity pardoned in Jesus Christ—not religion, but revelation, *not religious community, but church.*" But in the very next sentence he states that there is in fact a necessary connection between revelation and religion,

---

8. *DBWE* 8:189, 485 (*DBW* 8:197).

9. *DBWE* 9:118.

10. *DBWE* 1:133.

11. James, *Varieties of Religious Experience*, 42 (James's emphasis).

12. *DBWE* 1:134, Bonhoeffer's emphasis.

between religious community and the church, a fact, he adds, that is often overlooked.[13] And in another part of the book he states that there are two ways to misunderstand the church, "*one historicizing and the other religious; the former confuses the church with the religious community, the latter with the Realm of God.*"[14] Bonhoeffer is obviously straining to make room for a relationship of the church-community with what he at this point regards as the dominant reality of religion in theological circles, but in a way that does not determine the nature of revelation.

As for the idea of religion itself, in a section of the thesis that he omitted in the published version he defines it as "the touching of the human will by the divine will, and as the overcoming of the former by the latter to enable free action," a definition that he attributes to his doctoral advisor at the University of Berlin, Reinhold Seeberg. This impulse, he adds, typically though not necessarily finds specific content in a religious community of some sort. In a footnote he qualifies this definition, stating that religion properly so-called requires some kind of deity, and thus Buddhism did not qualify until the Buddha was deified.[15] In the published version he simply says that the general concept of religion or idea of the holy becomes actual "in the solitude of the soul with God."[16]

The way that Bonhoeffer qualifies the notion of religion in his dissertation privileges Christianity and the other Abrahamic traditions, and does so under the guise of "objective" criteria. He is reflecting what has been in fact a long-standing debate within the academic community over the question of whether or not Buddhism is a religion. Martin Southwold, for example, argues that, save for not having a deity, "Buddhism markedly resembles religions, and especially the religion prototypical for our conception, i.e., Christianity. If we declare that Buddhism is not a religion, we take on the daunting task of explaining how a non-religion can come so uncannily to resemble religions."[17] There are two related problems with Southwold's argument. First, as William Cavanaugh points out, the purported fact that Buddhism in every respect but one "resembles religions" begs the question of what a religion is. Second, it is increasingly recognized in scholarly circles that "Buddhism, by 1860, had come to exist, not in the Orient, but in the Oriental libraries and institutions of the West."[18] Tomoko Masuzawa

13. *DBWE* 1:152–53, Bonhoeffer's emphasis.

14. *DBWE* 1:125, Bonhoeffer's emphasis.

15. *DBWE* 1:131 n. 23.

16. *DBWE* 1:133.

17. Southwold, "Buddhism and the Definition of Religion," 367.

18. Cavanaugh, *Myth of Religious Violence*, 93.

writes, "Until that time [the nineteenth century], neither European observers nor, for the most part, native 'practitioners' of those various devotional, contemplative, divinatory, funeral, and other ordinary and extraordinary cults that are now roundly called Buddhist had thought of these divergent rites and widely scattered institutions as constituting a single religion."[19]

The impulse to so define it therefore comes from an external source, rightly identified as the technological obsession of nineteenth-century Europeans and North Americans to classify and codify the other. The world witnessed a boom in scientific taxonomy and other forms of classification, says Jason Josephson, ranging from "lists of animal species to 'races' of mankind." Western categories of "scientific" taxonomy show up in Japan starting in the 1850s, where they transformed or superseded previous modes of describing reality. As this took place, Josephson observes, local ways of thinking about the coherence and cogency of existence fell prey to newly imported categories, including "religion."[20]

The ambivalence that we encountered in *Sanctorum Communio* is largely absent in Bonhoeffer's qualifying thesis, *Act and Being*, as he firmly declares that faith is of a different essence from religion. In his examination of Seeberg's treatment of the relationship between the concepts of religion and revelation, Bonhoeffer states that the notion of a religious a priori, which purportedly has no content but nevertheless enables one to receive revelation, already entails too much. Though he acknowledges that with this idea Seeberg works hard to avoid the identification of God and the self that Bonhoeffer links to idealism, it is nevertheless the case that when approached in this manner "revelation must become religion; that is its essence. Revelation is religion." The natural human being is curved in on itself, and thus religion, as a component of the natural, does not escape the flesh. Revelation, on the other hand, does not partake of a religious a priori, he writes, but depends solely on "God's contingent action on human beings." There is no specialized ability to hear it prior to the hearing itself.[21]

Of the many influences that we can discern in Bonhoeffer's early theology, two in particular are important for his early take on the concept of religion. The first is that of Seeberg, his doctoral advisor at the University of Berlin, who defines the religious a priori as "a purely formal, primeval endowment of the created spirit or ego that renders it capable of, and in need

19. Masuzawa, *Invention of World Religions*, 122; cf. Nongbri, *Before Religion*, 2, 124–29.

20. Josephson, *Invention of Religion in Japan*, 74.

21. *DBWE* 2:57–58.

of, the direct awareness of the absolute Spirit."[22] The other significant figure is, of course, Karl Barth, particularly his early writings on the subject.[23] The influence of Barth's doctrine of revelation in particular can already be seen in Bonhoeffer's effort in *Sanctorum Communio* and *Act and Being* to qualify the role that religion should play in forming the reality of the church. It is in *Act and Being*, however, that Barth's revolutionary critique of the concept of religion as the enemy of faith comes most clearly to the fore.

In his fully evolved critique in *Letters and Papers*, Bonhoeffer credits Barth for initiating this way of construing religion theologically: "Barth was the first to recognize the error of all these attempts (which were basically all still sailing in the wake of liberal theology, without intending to do so) in that they all aim to save some room for religion in the world or over against the world. He led the God of Jesus Christ forward to battle against religion, πνεῦμα against σάρξ." However, Bethge argues that Bonhoeffer's concluding reflections on religion differ substantially from those of his elder colleague, who continues to find a role for true religion as the form revelation assumes in the justified believer.[24] In Bonhoeffer's view Barth's efforts ultimately falter because they fail to give concrete guidance in either dogmatics or ethics, and settle instead for a positivism of revelation.[25]

The trajectory that he establishes in *Sanctorum Communio* and *Act and Being* continues throughout the major writings of the 1930s. In *Creation and Fall* he makes a passing reference to the conversation between the serpent and Eve in Genesis 3 as the first religious, theological conversation,

22. Reinhold Seeberg, *Christliche Dogmatik*, 1:103; cited in *DBWE* 8:362 n. 11. Seeberg's definition reappears in *Act and Being*: "the absolute, to use Seeberg's terminology, enters again into 'immediate' contact, into union with the I; my will is subjected to the primal will and God's will is active in me" (*DBWE* 2:58).

23. The extent of the debt that Bonhoeffer owes to Barth's account of religion in *Church Dogmatics* is a disputed question. Tom Greggs contends that there is more continuity between the two than what has been attributed (*Theology Against Religion*, 54–55). Feil, on the other hand, states that Barth's discussion of religion in *Church Dogmatics* had no obvious impact on Bonhoeffer (*Theology of Dietrich Bonhoeffer*, 171).

24. Bethge, *Dietrich Bonhoeffer*, 872; cf. Feil, *Theology of Dietrich Bonhoeffer*, 164–72; Greggs, *Theology Against Religion*, 28–35.

25. *DBWE* 8:428–29. The phrase "positivism of revelation" is not a happy one, particularly used in connection with Barth's theology. Bonhoeffer would seem to be troubled by what James McClendon calls a view of theological convictions like "so many 'propositions' to be catalogued or juggled like truth-functions in a computer," without a sense of how they relate to the concrete matter of who Jesus Christ is for us today. McClendon, *Biography as Theology*, 37. This is a legitimate concern, but whether Barth is guilty of doing this is a matter of some dispute. What Bonhoeffer calls revelational positivism may more accurately be described, says Hans Frei, as Barth's effort to re-create "a universe of theological discourse grown stagnant from miscontrual and neglect." Frei, *Types of Christian Theology*, 159.

and then a few pages later he depicts God speaking to Adam, admonishing him not to lose himself in religious despair. Bonhoeffer also uses the idea of piety, *fromme*, several times, and not always consistently. In the first chapter he states that God testifies to us of God by the word of a book, "the word of a pious human being . . . [which] is wholly a word that comes from the middle and not from the beginning." But later he will use the term in a negative sense, describing the questioning of the serpent in the garden as pious in character.[26]

In his Christology lectures, written around the same time, he makes two comments that are telling. Near the beginning he states that "everything depends on knowing whether Jesus Christ was the idealistic founder of a religion or the very Son of God. This is no less than a matter of life or death for a human being." If Jesus is but a founder of a religion my sins are still with me, but if his works are God's own works, "I have found the God of mercy."[27] And in a section titled "Christ as the Center of History" he states categorically that any attempt to justify philosophically the notion that Christ is the center, limit, or end of all religion must be rejected. Such attempts presuppose a prior conception of the absolute, to which Jesus, along with all other so-called religious phenomena, is then evaluated.[28]

Perhaps the most telling clues to Bonhoeffer's evolving understanding of the concept of religion are in the lecture series he gives at the University of Berlin in the winter semester of 1931–32 on the history of twentieth-century systematic theology, reconstructed from student notes. Though we should be cautious about drawing firm conclusions from such sources, we can with some confidence identify the central topics, interlocutors, and overall tenor and trajectory of the lectures. The fact that they culminate with a prolonged engagement with Barth's theology is particularly significant. Bonhoeffer is becoming ever more critical of religion as a constructive theological concept. We encounter themes in his treatment of Barth in these lectures that will reappear in the prison correspondence: the partiality of religion that illegitimately restricts God to one area of life, God as a possession of human beings, and religion tied to the concept of culture (*Kulturprotestantismus*).[29]

The critique of religion as a constructive concept is also in evidence in the writings leading up to the prison correspondence. In *Ethics* he states that the first concern of the church "is not with the so-called religious functions of human beings, but with the existence in the world of whole human beings

---

26. *DBWE* 3:111, 129, 30, 106–7.
27. *DBWE* 12:309.
28. *DBWE* 12:325.
29. *DBWE* 12:218–29.

in all their relationships. The church's concern is not religion, but the form of Christ and its taking form among a band of people." And in a key section of his first draft of "History and the Good" he states unequivocally that genuine Christian responsibility takes in all human activity in the world and cannot under any circumstances be confined to an isolated religious sphere.[30]

Turning now to the prison correspondence, Bonhoeffer does not formally define religion as such in *Letters and Papers*, and thus we must piece one together from the characteristics he mentions in connection with the term. As with the features of a world come of age, his first statement about religion[31] is in the crucial letter of April 30, 1944. He states that the time when Christians could answer the question of who Christ is for us today with words is past, as is the age of inwardness and conscience, "and that means the age of religion altogether. We are approaching a completely religionless age."[32] Though he does it in passing (as with most every topic he covers in these late letters), Bonhoeffer here provides us with a preliminary account of religion as an impulse or predisposition, located in the private, inner life of every individual.

With respect to the connection between religion and inwardness Bonhoeffer makes two qualifications, one that is historically ambiguous and thus tends to perpetuate past conceptions, the other which is quite perceptive. He says first that the religious a priori had grounded Christian preaching and theology for its entire history, and that "'Christianity' has always been a form (perhaps the true form) of 'religion.'" The claim that religion had been part and parcel of Christianity since the days of the apostles is ambiguous, but it is one that Bonhoeffer had embraced from the start of his career. His concession that at one time it may well have been the true form of religion would appear to be a passing nod to Barth's dialectical treatment of revelation as the *Aufhebung* of religion in *Church Dogmatics*.[33] But as Feil observes, Barth, unlike Bonhoeffer, is not in favor of religionlessness because "religion . . . is the antithesis of revelation and is given with revelation itself as the human medium of accepting revelation."[34]

---

30. *DBWE* 6:97, 239; cf. *DBWE* 8:475.

31. Bonhoeffer does make a passing reference to religion in an earlier letter, where he dismisses the notion that the Old Testament is a preliminary stage of religion, but gives no specifics (*DBWE* 8:214). On the idea of the Old Testament as containing a preliminary stage of religion, a claim posited by Bonhoeffer's mentor Reinhold Seeberg, see Kuske, *Old Testament as the Book of Christ*, 10–11.

32. *DBWE* 8:362.

33. *CD* I/2, 325–61.

34. Feil, *Theology of Dietrich Bonhoeffer*, 166; cf. Pangritz, *Karl Barth*, 93–94.

Bonhoeffer then makes an observation that very much points us in the right direction, taking us beyond anything Barth had imagined: "Yet if it becomes obvious one day that this 'a priori' doesn't exist, that it has been a historically conditioned and transitory form of human expression, then people really will become radically religionless—and I believe that this is already more or less the case (why, for example, doesn't this war provoke a 'religious' reaction like all the previous ones?)—what does that then mean for 'Christianity'?"[35] By describing this "a priori" as a historically conditioned and transitory form of human expression he corrects his mistake, implicitly at least, by classifying religion, as that term is typically used in a world come of age, not as a timeless aspect of human being as such, but as a social artifact of determinate design to serve a specific purpose.

Bonhoeffer continues this line of thought by characterizing religion as simply the garb in which Christianity has been clothed, which serves us as a segue for asking, what then is religionless Christianity? The editors of the critical edition liken this metaphor for religion to Adolf von Harnack's famous trope of kernel and husk, which Harnack uses to distinguish the enduring essence of Christianity from the many forms it has taken on since the time of Jesus and the first apostles: "There are only two possibilities here: either the gospel is in all respects identical with its earliest form, in which case it came with its time and has departed with it; or else it contains something which, under different historical forms, is of permanent validity." The attempt at a comparison here is strained, however, for Harnack identifies the religious quality of Christianity as the kernel that endures through all the husk-like changes: "It is to *man* that religion pertains, to man, as one who in the midst of all change and progress himself never changes. Christian apologetics must recognise, then, that it is with religion in its simple nature and its simple strength that it has to do."[36] Bonhoeffer, on the other hand, connects religion to the historical and thus ever-changing garb or husk, not the essence or kernel.[37]

The critique of religion as inwardness and otherworldliness reappears in the June 27 letter, in which he contends that faith in the Old Testament is not tied to a religion of redemption. To the objection that the theme of redemption is prominent in the exodus from Egypt and later from captivity in Babylon he replies that "this is redemption *within* history, that is, *this side of* the bounds of death, whereas everywhere else the aim of all the other myths of redemption is precisely to overcome death's boundary." The redemptions

---

35. *DBWE* 8:362–63.

36. Harnack, *What Is Christianity?*, 13–14, 8, Harnack's emphasis.

37. *DBWE* 8:363.

described in the Old Testament allow Israel to live before God, as God's people on earth. It is both erroneous and dangerous, says Bonhoeffer, to see in the Christian proclamation of the resurrection the epitome of a genuine religion of redemption, with an emphasis on being delivered from sorrow, death, guilt, anxieties, and longings, and to that which lies beyond death's boundary. On the contrary, the "Christian hope of resurrection is different from the mythological in that it refers people to their life on earth in a wholly new way, and more sharply than the OT [Old Testament]." Unlike those who embrace these redemption myths, Christians do not have an escape route secured that will lead them out of earthly tasks and sorrows into eternity; like Christ they are given the cup of earthly life, which they are to drink to the last drop, "and only when they do this is the Crucified and Risen One with them, and they are crucified and resurrected with Christ."[38] Old and New Testaments are united in the conviction that this-worldliness should not be abolished prematurely on this side of the eschaton.[39]

Bonhoeffer also links religion with what he refers to as the "temporally conditioned presuppositions of metaphysics." The association of metaphysics with religion has generated considerable discussion in scholarly circles. Some have suggested that Bonhoeffer is rejecting metaphysics as such, perhaps in the tradition of Immanuel Kant or in anticipation of postmodern thought.[40] Upon closer examination, however, it is clear that he is working with a carefully stipulated conception of the term, using it to critique any attempt to locate God and faith at the boundaries of human life and not at its center, where faith is lived in community and in this world. To be sure, Bonhoeffer rejects all conceptions of metaphysics that confine faith to what is otherworldly and thus over and done with, which he takes to be one of the leading marks of religion, which is its partiality, while biblical faith deals with the whole of life.[41] In its attempt to preserve a space for God, the creation of the otherworldly sphere of religion leaves the day-to-day world to forces, powers, and habits that regulate both human and nonhuman life.

---

38. N. T. Wright states that, in contrast to "the humans that speak of Jesus's resurrection in terms of our own assurance of a safe and happy rest in heaven . . . Jesus's resurrection summons us to dangerous and difficult tasks on earth" (*Surprised by Hope*, 241).

39. *DBWE* 8:447–48.

40. James Woelfel, for example, states that "Bonhoeffer rejected the metaphysical completely for the social and ethical . . ." (*Bonhoeffer's Theology*, 121).

41. *DBWE* 8:482. Paul Tillich rightly notes that ontology and metaphysics originally had the same aim—to ask about reality as a whole, the structure of being. Unfortunately, "the preposition *meta* now has the irremediable connotation of pointing to a duplication of this world by a transcendent realm of beings" (*Systematic Theology*, 1:20).

For Bonhoeffer, writes Heinrich Ott, "'Metaphysical' . . . means that behind the 'here' is concealed a 'beyond,' behind this world another world, that the existence of a God beyond is asserted and that man is directed away from the 'here' to this 'beyond,' that therefore we begin to speak of God as something metaphysical, belonging to the beyond, just at that point where man reaches his 'boundaries.'" Nevertheless, writes Ott, "*the question of the knowledge of the reality of the real, into which he flung himself so wholeheartedly, is in a wider sense 'metaphysical' or 'ontological'* . . . Indeed, the question, 'What is reality?' could be called the peculiar theme of all his theological thinking." In his understanding of reality, says Ott, Bonhoeffer shares a deep kinship with Thomas Aquinas.[42]

It is doubtful whether it is even possible to make a coherent argument that excludes every possible attempt to speak generally about the real or actual, or whether the notion of an ontology without metaphysics is finally intelligible.[43] A metaphysical surmise of some kind is ultimately unavoidable in every interpretive venture, for as Ott notes, every attempt at an unbroken immanence of thought is itself a metaphysical statement.[44] And as I noted previously, the technological organization of life in a world come of age, in so far as it orders difference and otherness, *is* the ontology, the metaphysics of the present age. To refuse all metaphysical questions will result in either "an impossible schizophrenia of *logos* and *mythos*, or else a faith-content reduced to a set of fideistic assertions beyond all logical discussion or development, even within their own terms."[45] Bonhoeffer is not interested in either of those options.

Williams agrees with Ott on this point, stating that the question of how we construe difference is irreducibly metaphysical, and cannot be settled by reference to a tangible state of affairs or to a matter of taste and private judgment. Moreover, to refuse the question altogether is to make otherness unthinkable, for it aspires to a solitary career of self-determination characterized by a nonhistorical freedom. Such an aspiration imagines "a situation in which there are few or no issues about power arising in the context of discourse: the exchanges envisaged are not what I have called negotiations, but simply the co-existence of (at best) mutually tangential projects—what Roy Bhaskar has called 'a succession of poems, all marginally different; and a succession of paradigm shifts, for which no overarching

---

42. Ott, *Reality and Faith*, 45–46, 153, 162 n. 27, 325, Ott's emphasis.

43. See in this regard Dumas, *Dietrich Bonhoeffer*, 112–17; cf. McCormack, *Orthodox and Modern*, 133.

44. Ott, *Reality and Faith*, 44–45.

45. Milbank, *Theology and Social Theory*, 297.

or commensurating criteria can be given."[46] The modern refusal of a meta-physical surmise is little more than an ideological justification for a leisured elite living in a situation of plenty.

Bethge concurs with Ott and Williams, stating that Bonhoeffer is not engaging in a sweeping rejection of metaphysics as such, but with a version that imprisons biblical faith within an unbiblical conception of reality, in which God is imagined as the *deus ex machina* swooping in at the end of the drama to save humankind when their own resources fail. The concept of religion confines God to "a point where human knowledge is at an end . . . or when human strength fails."[47] In his critique, writes Bethge, Bonhoeffer is actually attempting to regain a genuine sense of transcendence and thus of the real that flows from an engagement with history, one that is not remote from the earth and everyday life: "The metaphysically organized Christian religion provided the world with the kind of transcendence it longed for. God became necessary as the superstructure of being, and religious longing found its goal in a heavenly domain." Metaphysics thus construed "seduces the Christian religion into thinking statically in terms of two spheres, and forces it to give its redemptive nature a one-sided emphasis."[48] In place of this narrowly "metaphysical" sense of transcendence Bonhoeffer concludes this important letter with the contention that "God is the beyond in the midst of our lives," or as I would put it, a metaphysics of this-worldliness. He reiterates this claim in his next letter to Bethge: "What is beyond this world is meant, in the gospel, to be there *for* this world—not in the anthropocentric sense of liberal, mystical, pietistic, ethical theology, but in the biblical sense of the creation and the incarnation, crucifixion, and resurrection of Jesus Christ."[49]

With respect to the metaphysical understanding of "God" as *deus ex machina*, Bonhoeffer's poem "Christians and Heathens" provides us a vivid depiction of the concept: "People go to God when they're in need, / plead for help, pray for blessing and bread, / for rescue from their sickness, guilt, and death. / So do they all, all of them, Christians and heathens."[50] According to Bethge, all religion depends on the *deus ex machina*: "There must be a supreme being ('omnipotence, omniscience, omnipresence') so that we can be rescued from dangers, have our mysteries solved, and hear our questions answered." This way of thinking makes Christianity into "a spiritual

---

46. R. D. Williams, "Between Politics and Metaphysics," 5, 4.

47. *DBWE* 8:366.

48. Bethge, *Dietrich Bonhoeffer*, 873.

49. *DBWE* 8:367, 373, Bonhoeffer's emphasis.

50. *DBWE* 8:460.

pharmacy." Religiosity and pietism thus conspire to conceal the world's true godlessness by providing an escape from real life.[51] "It is wrong to say that God fills the emptiness," Bonhoeffer concludes. "God in no way fills it but rather keeps it empty and thus helps us preserve—even if in pain—our authentic communion."[52]

Another crucial mark of religion has to do with its privileged character. He asks in his April 30 letter to Bethge, "How do we go about being 'religionless-worldly' Christians, how can we be ἐκ-κλησία, those who are called out, without understanding ourselves religiously as privileged, but instead seeing ourselves as belonging wholly to the world?" Christians should give up their privileges in recognition of the justice of history.[53] According to Bethge, this may be the single most important characteristic of religion as Bonhoeffer describes it. Christianity has historically understood itself as a gift to especially favored people, with implications in every aspect of individual and social life: materially, financially, and legally. Faith became a possession that is either deserved or not, and thrust upon people in the form of a positivism of revelation. Religion ties Christian practice to conventions that make it a luxury of certain social classes, and thus it functions as the guarantor of the assurance and continuation of the existing order.[54]

Closely related to the notion of privilege is that of guardianship. In the letter of June 8, 1944, he once again rejects the notion that a space should be reserved for "God" (and thus for the church and the pastor) by preying on the so-called questions of death and guilt. He states that the efforts of Christian apologetics to undermine the world's autonomy from the guardianship of "God" (and by implication the church) is pointless, because it attempts to force the world back into a stage of adolescence; ignoble, because it attempts to exploit people's weaknesses for ends to which they have not given their consent; and unchristian, "because it confuses Christ with a particular stage of human religiousness, namely, with a human law."[55] This last comment is particularly important, says Bethge, because as a law, similar to the way that some Christians in the first century wanted to make circumcision a condition of faith, religion is essentially a way of making distinctions between people.[56]

51. Bethge, *Dietrich Bonhoeffer*, 876.

52. *DBWE* 8:238.

53. *DBWE* 8:364, 389.

54. Bethge, *Dietrich Bonhoeffer*, 876. The connection to a kind of Stoicism that was discussed in chapter 2 becomes evident here.

55. *DBWE* 8:427.

56. Bethge, *Dietrich Bonhoeffer*, 876–77; cf. *DBWE* 8:366, 430.

Bonhoeffer connects the notions of Christian privilege and the world's purported need for the guardianship of "God" (again note the scare quotes) to clericalism, which he associates with the medieval principle of heteronomy. He contends, for example, that what Luther wanted was to establish an authentically worldly ordering of society "without clerical domination."[57] In our time clericalism takes the form of *Seelsorge*, care for the soul (the body having been handed over to the technological powers of the state and market), making the "private," "inner," and "personal" life of the individual the hunting ground of pastors in their efforts to hold to a measure of public authority. Bonhoeffer labels any attempt to reinstate clerical guardianship over a world come of age, especially in the modern form of psychotherapy, as a counsel of despair that can be made only at the cost of intellectual integrity.[58]

"Religion" and Difference

Though insightful, Bonhoeffer's critique of the concept of religion is at several points in need of correction, clarification, and development. It also needs to be incorporated into a more comprehensive analysis of the social constructions of difference in a world come of age. To assert this is not to denigrate his work but simply to recognize that we must now build upon the foundation that he lays. The most obvious place where Bonhoeffer's comments miss the mark is in his contention that the world is quickly moving toward a completely religionless age. However one interprets this concept, Europe has thus far proved to be the exception regarding the prevalence of religious beliefs and affections. To be sure, what counts as religion has changed in some significant ways since his time, but in no wise can it be truthfully said that the world has entered, or is about to enter, a completely religionless time.[59]

One important sociological study, for example, that indicates that religion, in the sense that Bonhoeffer talks about it in *Letters and Papers from Prison*, is alive and well is found in a book titled *Soul Searching: The Religious and Spiritual Lives of American Teenagers*, written by Christian Smith, director of the Center for the Study of Religion and Society at the University of Notre Dame, and Melinda Denton. According to Smith and Denton, young people in America tend to be deeply religious, and their spirituality has virtually all of the vestiges of religion as described by Bonhoeffer,

57. *DBWE* 8:172.

58. *DBWE* 8:455–56, 478; cf. 502.

59. See, for example, *American Piety in the 21st Century*.

most especially inwardness. They also find a *deus ex machina* conception of the divine, that "God does not need to be particularly involved in one's life except when he is needed to resolve a problem," to be an especially attractive and comforting belief.[60] Given the popularity of the so-called prosperity gospel in Asia, Latin America, and Africa,[61] we can safely say that these tendencies are not limited to North America.

As I noted previously, there is an ambiguity in Bonhoeffer on the question of the nature of religion. He claims on the one hand that the religious a priori of humankind had constituted the Western form of Christianity for its entire nineteen-hundred-year history, and that "Christianity" has since the time of the apostles been a form, perhaps even the true form, of "religion" (again the use of scare quotes is significant). This is a position he originally sets forth in *Sanctorum Communio*, stating that Christ was not the founder of either a religion or a religious community: "The credit for both of these belongs to the earliest church, i.e., to the apostles."[62] Bonhoeffer sounds very much like his teacher Harnack, who declares in his famous lectures on the essence of Christianity that Jesus did not found a community organized for worship, that the credit for that feat goes to his band of disciples, which "at once underwent this transformation [and] became the ground upon which all subsequent developments rested."[63]

At the same time Bonhoeffer emphasizes the constructed nature of religion as an interpretive concept of recent intellectual pedigree, "that it has been a historically conditioned and transitory form of human expression." That makes religiousness into what he later calls a form of human law, and thus it would be unchristian to confuse any such law with Christ.[64] This second opinion is also found in lectures he gave during the winter semester of 1931–32, on the history of systematic theology in the twentieth century, where he observes that in a post-Copernican world "*religio*" replaces "faith" as the defining substance of theology.[65] Finally, with his observation that the movement toward human autonomy that has come to define a world come of age can be traced to the thirteenth century, Bonhoeffer notes the crucial shift in the historical relationship of church practices and theology within European society.[66]

60. Smith and Denton, *Soul Searching*, 162–63.

61. See, for example, Wiegele, *Investing in Miracles*, and Jenkins, *Next Christendom*.

62. Bonhoeffer goes on to say that this is why the question of whether Jesus founded a church is so ambiguous. *DBWE* 1:152–53.

63. Harnack, *What Is Christianity?*, 152.

64. *DBWE* 8:363, 427.

65. *DBWE* 11:183.

66. *DBWE* 8:425.

Bonhoeffer thus vacillates between Barth's dialectical relationship between revelation and religion ("Christianity" as the true form of "religion"), and an incisive analysis of the concept as a contingent artifact of Western intellectual history (and thus the religious a priori does not exist as a permanent feature of human life and thought, but is a historically conditioned and transitory form of human expression). As he goes on and goes further from Barth on the question of religion in important ways, so must we, both in terms of its genealogy and of its social function. Far from being a feature of the church since the time of the apostles, the concept of religion, as a name for a transhistorical and transcultural feature of human existence sequestered from other, more mundane areas of life, makes its first appearance in the fifteenth century, just in time, as it turns out, to support European colonial expansion. Careful historical, sociological, and philosophical examination reveals that prior to that time there is no evidence that such a faculty was recognized in this sense. These studies also show that the invention of this concept was not initially for the purpose of preserving a space for "God," but as a technology for coming to terms with human difference (both theoretically and practically).

In *The Myth of Religious Violence*, William Cavanaugh provides an exhaustive and detailed theological account on the subject of religion as an organizing institution of modernity. Drawing on a host of scholars from across the ideological and disciplinary spectrum, he demonstrates that there is no transhistorical or transcultural essence of religion. No one has to date provided a convincing definition of what is distinctively "religious" that can withstand objections and counterexamples. Many who still use the concept do not even try any longer, offering instead a vague assertion that says something along the lines of "everyone knows what we mean when we say 'religion.'" When academics resort to such rhetoric, it is clear that something has gone very wrong with their arguments.[67]

Cavanaugh also shows that the positing of a transhistorical or transcultural phenomenon under the category of religion has a history with clear political functions. Unknown prior to the fifteenth century, it first begins to assume its familiar shape at that time. What counts as religion, therefore, depends entirely on who or what has the power and authority to say what belongs to this category and what does not. As a constructive concept for schematizing social life, "religion" is one of the inventions of the modern social order, together with other well-known dichotomies: private-public, religion-politics, and church-state. What Bonhoeffer aptly calls a "historically conditioned and transitory form of human expression" is part and

---

67. Cavanaugh, *Myth of Religious Violence*, 16.

parcel of the technological regime of the modern state as it developed first in Europe and extended its grasp to Asia, Africa, and the Americas. This concept is now so firmly entrenched in the grammar of modernity that even some accomplished Bonhoeffer scholars find it difficult to talk about ecclesial practices such as prayer and worship as finally anything other than a form of religious expression, though nowhere does he connect these practices to the concept of religion.[68]

Cavanaugh is not alone is arriving at these conclusions. In his recent book, *Before Religion*, Brent Nongbri notes that when we look prior to the sixteenth century we discover that the modern understanding of religion simply does not exist. To be sure, ancient peoples had a variety of terms to denote proper reverence of the gods, but they were not what we typically think of as "religious" concepts. They were part of a vocabulary of social relations that was not limited to the divine, but designated "hierarchical social protocols of all sorts." He argues that there was a historical context in which the institutions of religion and the secular state first began to take shape, and humankind began to be conceptually carved up into different religions: "What is modern about the ideas of 'religions' and 'being religious' is the isolation and naming of some things as 'religious' and others as 'not religious.'"[69]

The invention of the modern notion of religion as an organizing concept serves two very important theological functions in the basic grammar of modern social thought and practice. First, it confines one's fundamental loyalty to God within a strictly private and interior realm, where it cannot interfere with the allegiance that is owed to the "secular" state[70] in which one resides, to which is assigned all matters public and social. It is this operation that effectively creates the two realms against which Bonhoeffer struggles virtually his entire career. As John Milbank puts it, "The new, secular *dominium* could not, according to the totalizing logic of willful occupation which now mediated transcendence in the public realm, really tolerate a 'political' Church as a cohabitant. Hence it was first necessary . . . to produce

---

68. According to Ralf Wüstenberg, for example, Bonhoeffer believes that "religious practices such as worship and prayer . . . should not be given up but should be performed secretly, in terms of the *disciplina arcana* (discipline of the secret)." Wüstenberg, "Philosophical Influences," 139. Tom Greggs also perpetuates this mode of thinking, stating that it would be misleading to read Bonhoeffer's concept of religionless Christianity as a way of translating from religious to equivalent secular terms, because he "continues to use terminology (in both German and Greek) such as church, baptism, sacrament and repentance." Greggs, *Theology Against Religion*, 40.

69. Nongbri, *Before Religion*, 4.

70. Talal Asad refers to the concept of the secular as religion's "Siamese twin" ("Reading a Modern Classic," 221).

the paradox of a purely 'suasive' Church which must yet involve external state coercion for its self-government."[71] Religion is the organizational instrument by which a world come of age segregates what is for the gospel the inextricably public and social relationship between last things and the things before the last.

Second, the idea of religion was one of the social technologies used by the colonialist powers for differentiating and ranking the peoples they encountered on their expeditions. This is a key element in what Willie Jennings calls the comparativist hermeneutic of colonialism that drew immediate historical comparisons between Christianity and other modes of orienting human life in the world. In its initial forms this hermeneutic was conducted as part of an explicitly theological operation, but it soon took on a more recognizably ethnographic character that bound together religious consciousness, race, and claims to land on a hierarchical scale.[72] The historical center of gravity thus shifts away from theology *per se* (though not completely) and toward an understanding of difference that could be understood *etsi deus non daretur*.

The Invention of "Religion"

One looks in vain for anything like the modern concept of religion in the working vocabularies of virtually every ancient civilization—Greek, Egyptian, Aztec, Indian, Chinese, and Japanese.[73] Though these societies engaged in a variety of activities that a technologically organized civilization classifies under the category of religion, they did not see practices associated with political institutions, family and tribal groupings, and civic obligations as "secular" in contrast with specifically "religious" actions. Of course, the fact that these societies lacked the concept does not in itself disprove the existence of a religious realm, separate from the public and political sphere, as its "proper" action frame of reference.

Philology also does not help establish a distinct domain of religion. For example, one of the candidates in Greek for the concept of religion, *eusebeia*, typically translated as "piety," is invoked by Plato to refer to what is owed to both the gods and parents.[74] The Roman Dionysius of Halicarnassus, who lived in the century before Christ, speaks highly of *eusebeia* as the

71. Milbank, *Theology and Social Theory*, 19.

72. Jennings, *Christian Imagination*, 102, 133–34.

73. Smith, *Meaning and End of Religion*, 54–55.

74. Plato, *Republic* 615c, 321. Other Greek terms—for example, *threskeia*—also have a long history of varying senses. See Nongbri, *Before Religion*, 4, 34–38.

proper attitude toward the bonds of kinship.[75] The English word "religion" derives from the Latin word *religio*, which was used in ancient Rome to denote any number of social acts that a person might be obligated to perform, from cultic observances (every shrine had a distinct *religio*) to civic oaths and family rituals. It was even possible for a "religious" person to be indifferent about the existence of the gods, even to doubt their existence, because *religio* "was primarily about the customs and traditions that provided the glue for the Roman social order." What moderns differentiate as civic duties, devotion to the divine, and family obligations were for the Romans interwoven elements in a complex web of social relations and activities.[76]

When we turn our attention to the early church we discover that *religio* was at best a minor concept in the working vocabulary of the first Christians. There is no term or set of terms that resemble it in the Old Testament (a point that Bonhoeffer emphatically makes[77]), and anything remotely resembling it in the Greek New Testament is extremely rare. Jerome in his Latin New Testament uses the term six times to translate several different Greek terms, and the Authorized Version (King James) uses "religion" only five times, and then not always for the same Greek words that Jerome translated as *religio*. It appears occasionally in the early Latin fathers with a variety of meanings, including clerical practice, clerical office, worship and piety, and the subjective disposition of one toward the divine.[78]

Some have disputed the claim that the present category of religion is a product of contingent circumstances that emerge only with the modern world. Daniel Boyarin, for example, claims that Eusebius clearly describes Judaism, Hellenism, and Christianity as religions.[79] But as Nongbri shows, Eusebius links these three methods of worship to ethnicities, as belonging to distinct peoples or races. Eusebius's motive is to refute the charge that Christians constitute a new and strange race of people, not a new religion. He accomplishes this, says Nongbri, by claiming the ancient Hebrews as the ancestors of the Christians, going so far as to argue that they were in fact the first Christians.[80]

The only church father who actually writes a treatise around the idea of religion, says Cavanaugh, is Augustine in *De vera religione*, in which he develops the distinction between true and false *religio* previously posited by

75. Dionysius of Halicarnassus, *Roman Antiquities* 8.44.
76. Cavanaugh, *Myth of Religious Violence*, 62.
77. DBWE 8:213–14.
78. Cavanaugh, *Myth of Religious Violence*, 62, 64.
79. Boyarin, *Border Lines*, 205; cf. Nongbri, *Before Religion*, 54.
80. Nongbri, *Before Religion*, 54–57.

Lactantius. In this tract Augustine typically uses the term to refer to worship, and more specifically the act of rendering praise. He does acknowledge that there is an impulse in all humans that, among other things, leads them to worship the creator, but he does not restrict this impulse to a specifically "religious" action frame, stating that any human pursuit can be the subject of *religio*.[81] In Book X of the *City of God* he declares that *religio, cultus*, and *pietas* are inadequate to express the worship of God alone, noting for example that the normal range of meaning for *religio* includes devotion to family and friends. But he has to use some word to talk about it, and so he uses it. There is thus no realm of belief, feeling, or practice for Augustine that is separate from mundane, "secular" obligations: the familial and civic oaths that bind the multiple levels of a society together. What moderns routinely separate into discrete and autonomous domains—family, civic participation, politics, economics, culture, and religion—Augustine, like his Roman contemporaries, understood to be threads that together constitute one complex fabric of social relations.[82]

Religio rarely occurs in medieval writings, and prior to the sixteenth century no one writes a book specifically on the topic of religion. When the term does appear it seldom retains its ancient meaning of duty or reverence, and most often refers to the rule or discipline of monastic life. "With very few exceptions," writes John Bossy, "the word was only used to describe different sorts of monastic or similar rule, and the way of life pursued under them."[83] This usage passed into English around 1200 and was gradually extended to include members of mendicant orders such as the Franciscans and Dominicans. This extension explains the medieval distinction between "religious" and "secular" clergy, the latter not being members of such an order. By 1400 references to the plural "religions" appear as a way of referring to the various orders.[84]

The ancient sense of duty or reverence associated with *religio* is recovered to an extent by Thomas Aquinas, who defines it as an acquired virtue similar to that of sanctity and linked to the cardinal virtue of justice. It is a moral and not a theological habit, because it pertains to rites and practices as its object, not to God. In concert with the other virtues connected to justice, this habit directs the faithful to render what is due to God, that is, to

81. Augustine, *Of True Religion*, 107–10; cf. Cavanaugh, *Myth of Religious Violence*, 62–63.

82. Augustine, *City of God* 10.1.392; cf. Cavanaugh, *Myth of Religious Violence*, 63–64.

83. Bossy, "Some Elementary Forms," 4; cf. Southern, *Western Society*, 214; Asad, *Genealogies of Religion*, 39 n. 22.

84. Cavanaugh, *Myth of Religious Violence*, 64.

know and love God: "the activity by which man gives the proper reverence to God through actions which specifically pertain to divine worship, such as sacrifice, oblations, and the like."[85] It does not name a universal genus of which Christianity, Islam, Buddhism, etc., are species, nor does it refer to a freestanding system of beliefs about reality. Aquinas does use *religio* to describe pagan worship, but like Augustine, he classifies it as false. The concept does not refer to an inner impulse of the human ego or spirit that renders one capable of, and in need of, the direct awareness of the absolute Spirit, and it does not refer to an institutional structure that is separable from other, "nonreligious" institutions. Medieval Christendom was a "theopolitical whole," writes Cavanaugh,[86] a trait that Bonhoeffer finds praiseworthy.[87]

In either sense of the term, then, the pre-fifteenth-century sense of *religio* and its derivatives culminates with Aquinas. It presupposes a context of practices embodied in the communal life of the church. As Cavanaugh puts it, "Virtuous actions do not proceed from rational principles separable from the agent's particular history; virtuous persons instead are embedded in communal practices of habituation of body and soul that give their lives direction to the good."[88] Prior to the Renaissance, the notion that there is a transhistorical and transcultural essence "waiting to be separated from the secular like a precious metal from its ore" finds no historical traction.[89] It had virtually little or no role to play in scripture or the early church fathers. During the Middle Ages *religio* functioned in a variety of ways as constituted by the configurations of power relations, practices and authorities peculiar to that age, principally as a way of distinguishing clerics who belonged to orders from those affiliated with dioceses, or as a virtue that functioned within a complex of practices and habits within the church.

With the birth of a world come of age in the Renaissance, however, new conceptualizations begin to emerge that would eventually confine Christian identity (along with every other tradition that predates a world come of age) to a new and restricted sphere of operation. "The appearance of 'religion' as a natural object," writes Peter Harrison, "coincided with the development of a *Religionswissenschaft* which both defined its object and explicated it. In other words, the intellectual construct 'religion' is to a large measure constituted by the methods which are supposed to elucidate it."[90]

85. Aquinas, *Summa Theologica* 2a.2ae.81.2.

86. Cavanaugh, *Myth of Religious Violence*, 65–68.

87. *DBWE* 8:319–20.

88. Cavanaugh, *Theopolitical Imagination*, 32.

89. Cavanaugh, *Myth of Religious Violence*, 69.

90. Harrison, *"Religion" and the Religions*, 5, 14.

These novel inventions fabricate the existence of a timeless and universal genus for which the various positive religions are but species, an essence that would eventually be separated from the secular domain that houses the activities and institutions of politics and economics. The *differentia* of these species is identified with the diverse and arbitrary systems of beliefs and activities one finds within them, while the genus itself is defined as an interior, purely private impulse within each individual that exists prior to thought and community. In Europe and North America these stipulations come to confine faith within the interior life of the individual and thus to keep it from direct access to the "worldly" projects of economics and political life, and in concert with the concept of the secular "gradually remove the practice of the Christian *religio* from a central place in the social order of the West."[91]

Cavanaugh contends that the invention of religion as a means of assigning the other to her or his proper place begins in the fifteenth century with two Christian Platonists. The first of these, Nicholas of Cusa, uses *religio* to categorize the different ways humans worship God. In itself that definition is not new, but what is innovative is his assertion that rites and related practices are not essential to it, that informing them is a universal, interior impulse shared by all human beings. Driving this novelty is a desire to find a principle of concord that would unite the peoples of the earth. To this end he posits the existence of "*una religio*," a transhistorical, transcultural *res* which is the wisdom that God teaches to all nations, but through different customs and languages, similar to the natural law tradition according to which the divine law is refracted in the various human laws. Over time and under the influence of sin, says Cusa, these customs harden into immutable truths, obscuring the fact that "there is, in spite of many varieties of rites, but one religion." According to Cusa, what is needed to make this concord a social reality is for each person "to walk according to his interior rather than his exterior nature," that is, to rely on supersensible reason: "all who use their reason have one religion and cult which is at the bottom of all the diversity of rites."[92]

It is clear that Cusa is not using the notion of religion here in the modern sense, but neither is he using it either in the conventional sense

---

91. Cavanaugh, *Myth of Religious Violence*, 69–70. Evidence for the assumed status of this separation irrupted in the media when Pope Francis included a short but incisive critique of capitalism in his first apostolic exhortation, *Evangelii Gaudium* 53–60. See Deneen, "Would Someone Just Shut That Pope Up?"

92. Cusa, *De pace fidei*, 197–99, 203; Cavanaugh, *Myth of Religious Violence*, 70; Harrison, *"Religion" and the Religions*, 11–12. Regarding Cusa's efforts to articulate a stable basis for concord between disputing parties, see Radner, *Brutal Unity*, 278–83.

of membership in a religious order of some type, or to denote an acquired virtue. Instead, says Harrison, "he seeks to promote the view that diverse religious customs (the accidents of 'religion,' if you will) conceal a true or ideal 'religion.' This 'una religo' is the unattainable truth about God—the Platonic ideal of which all existing belief systems are but shadowy expressions. The faithful of all nations and creeds should persevere in their particular expressions of piety in the firm belief that the one true 'religion' is the basis of them all."[93] Just as Bonhoeffer is willing to concede that Christianity might have been the true form of religion, Cusa identifies this universal impulse with Christianity in its revealed form, preeminently in Christ, who as the divine word is both source and mediator of the one wisdom of God. "Nevertheless," says Cavanaugh, "Cusa's position is a precursor to the hitherto unknown idea that there is a single genus of human activity called religion, of which Christianity, Islam, Buddhism, Sikhism, etc., are the various species."[94]

The second figure from the Renaissance who plays a crucial role in the development of the modern understanding of religion is Marsilio Ficino, who builds on Cusa's Platonic speculations in his 1474 book *De Christiana Religione*. According to Wilfred Cantwell Smith, *religio* for Ficino names a human impulse or propensity common to all women and men, "the fundamental distinguishing human characteristic, innate, natural, and primary."[95] The various historical manifestations of this predisposition, the varieties of rites that we now call religions, are all just more or less true approximations of the Platonic ideal of the one true *religio* divinely implanted in the human heart.[96] However, unlike Cusa, the multiplicity of rites is not due to human ignorance or sin but is ordained by God to lend beauty to the world. Also unlike Cusa, Ficino does not see Christ as the source and content of true religion. The true Christian is the one who worships as Christ did, thus making him into an exemplar of the universal impulse of religion.[97] That which directs us to know and love God is thus extricated from the realm of acquired moral virtue and for the first time is mapped onto what would become its proper place, an interiorized and naturalized trait orienting individuals toward the transcendent, but essentially unrelated to any particular communal context.[98]

93. Harrison, *"Religion" and the Religions*, 12; Harvey, *Can These Bones Live?*, 111.

94. Cavanaugh, *Myth of Religious Violence*, 71.

95. Smith, *Meaning and End of Religion*, 33.

96. Harrison, *"Religion" and the Religions*, 12–13; Smith, *Meaning and End of Religion*, 32–34; cf. Harvey, *Can These Bones Live?*, 111–12.

97. Cavanaugh, *Myth of Religious Violence*, 71.

98. Cavanaugh, *Theopolitical Imagination*, 33.

European colonialism made effective use of the invention of the modern concept of religion. "The need to explain unforeseen, exotic peoples," writes Jennings, invoked "new ways of creating knowledge." An interpretive schema emerged in the fifteenth century that directly compared Christianity with the native religions, with the latter typically being judged as inferior, demonic, and thus idolatrous. By the time we get to the nineteenth century, a modified schema takes over, one that is motivated by modern Protestant thought, but still tied to racial and cultural (i.e., ethnographic) categories. This new way of viewing non-European rites and beliefs sets them within a positive theological vision, but one that continues to operate within the ideological use of the concept of religion and of indigenous religious consciousness displaced from their connections to specific times and places.[99]

This movement to relocate and redefine the concept of religion picks up momentum in the sixteenth and seventeenth centuries, as the various exemplifications of this universal impulse come to be tied principally to beliefs rather than communal practices, thus adding yet another novelty to the list. Religion thus comes to denote systems of belief, sets of propositions that can be affirmed or denied by individuals about what is ultimately true and important in their lives, but without the need to participate in the worship and witness of the church. According to Cavanaugh, Guillaume Postel, again in an attempt to secure religious concord and liberty, states in *De orbis terrae concordia* that Christianity, Islam, etc., are species of religion, sets of demonstrable moral truths, rather than theological claims conjoined to a complex social regime such as the church. Christian truth, which Postel identifies as the true religion, is based on universal axioms that underlie all particular expressions of belief, and he is confident that they commend themselves to all rational women and men, even the infidel, once they learn of them.[100]

Postel, writes Cavanaugh, also makes what would become a crucial distinction between "external" and "internal" church, identifying the worship of the former as "narrow," while the internal, mystical church includes all the world's people. "Postel does not thereby dismiss the external church, with its rites and disciplines of the body, as unnecessary," says Cavanaugh, for "he believes that the external church is the primary instrument to unite the human race. But the external church has become merely instrumental to the pursuit of agreement on the common propositions of true religion."[101]

99. Jennings, *Christian Imagination*, 94–99, 135–37.

100. Cavanaugh, *Myth of Religious Violence*, 72; cf. Skinner, *Age of Reformation*, 244–46; cf. Harvey, *Can These Bones Live?*, 112.

101. Cavanaugh, *Myth of Religious Violence*, 72.

The dichotomy of internal and external is thus both a catalyst for and a response to changes that are taking place in the way the natural world is perceived. Increasingly the medium of external religion, the material world, is no longer seen as spoken by God, but in the hands of the new science come of age has become opaque, inert, and silent.[102] Matter is thus divorced from what properly belongs to the religious sphere, and by default becomes the sole provenance of the secular domain.

Harrison and Cavanaugh argue that the transformation of *religio* into a state of mind shifted into high gear with John Calvin and his successors. Initially the object of belief is God's will, namely, the assurance that one is among the elect and thus saved, but over time this saving knowledge comes to be tied to a set of objective truths to which one needs to give explicit assent. They trace this emphasis to Calvin's rejection of the medieval doctrine of implicit faith,[103] the notion that simpler and less-educated Christians do not need to understand the more difficult doctrines such as the Trinity but simply have to believe that the teaching office of the church had basically gotten it right. "The Reformation's democratization of the church," writes Cavanaugh, "meant less emphasis on mystery and more emphasis on the perspicuity of the faith."[104]

The Arminian controversy within the Reformed tradition serves to exacerbate this tendency to equate religion with mental assent to true propositions. Though he believes with all other Protestants that salvation could never be earned (and thus no moral act or work could be a part of the process), Jacobius Arminius, who is worried that a particular doctrine of election undermined all sense of human freedom, wants to reserve a role for the human agent to play in their salvation. He holds that faith is at bottom the assent of an individual to the central Christian doctrines. Arminius' patron is Hugo Grotius, of *etsi deus non daretur* fame, who asserts that Christianity *is* the true religion, that it *teaches* (rather than *being*) the correct worship of God.[105]

It is out of the fluid context created by the Reformation and then Counter-Reformation that the idea of religions in the plural begins to emerge in the seventeenth century, first within the Christian world, and then across

---

102. Certeau, *Mystic Fable*, 1:188; Ward, *True Religion*, 22.

103. Calvin, *Institutes*, 3.2.3; cf. Aquinas, *Summa Theologica* 2a.2ae.2.5. Bonhoeffer's advocacy of *actus directa* and the arcane discipline suggests an openness to this doctrine.

104. Harrison, *"Religion" and the Religions*, 19–23; Cavanaugh, *Myth of Religious Violence*, 73.

105. Harrison, *"Religion" and the Religions*, 23; Cavanaugh, *Myth of Religious Violence*, 73.

time and space to take in other traditions. As the century unfolds, it becomes possible to refer to religion in general, though it is more common to speak of "the Christian religion." This latter expression is typically used to refer to the various confessions within a fractured Christendom that are regarded as more or less adequate forms of an abstract essence of Christianity. Christianity is eventually identified as one species of the genus religion, and in the process an important threshold is crossed: the idea of Christianity, which once designated a body of people, is becoming an "ism," that is, a body of beliefs.[106]

It is important to emphasize this is not simply a phenomenon limited to Christianity. Modern Jewish thought has largely been a series of attempts to define Judaism as yet another species of the genus religion. David Sorkin, for example, states that the noted Jewish scholar Moses Mendelssohn sought with his non-theological translation of the Psalms to show to readers of all faiths that "this book was a model of the 'sublime'" and thus demonstrate that the ancient Hebrews had in fact achieved a high level of enlightenment.[107] Sheehan, who argues that the category of the sublime is a double-edged sword in these matters, contends that if Mendelssohn thought that his efforts in this regard would effectively make the case for the enlightened nature of the Jewish people, he seriously misjudged the age in which he lived: "It may have helped to regenerate interest in *Hebrew* poetry but it did nothing to recuperate the *Jews*."[108]

What is particularly striking in such efforts by Jewish authors in the modern era is the fact that, according to Leora Batnitzky, they arrive at virtually the same conclusions that the non-Jewish authors do. In the case of Judaism, writes Batnitzky, "the category of religion, defined as a sphere of life separate from other spheres (such as politics, morality, and science, just to name a few), simply does not quite fit."[109] In like fashion Lila Corwin Berman traces the ways that many Jewish intellectuals in America tried to create a public identity around the notion that to be Jewish was fundamentally to belong to an ethnic group. In the end, however, this attempt could not say what was at stake in remaining Jewish.[110]

What becomes apparent in these developments is the way that the domains of "religion" and the "secular" are complementary artifacts that operate in concert to help weave the various threads of creation into the

---

106. Cavanaugh, *Myth of Religious Violence*, 74; Bossy, *Christianity in the West*, 171.

107. Sorkin, *Moses Mendelssohn*, 47.

108. Sheehan, *Enlightenment Bible*, 178, Sheehan's emphasis.

109. Batnitzky, *How Judaism Became a Religion*, 190.

110. Berman, *Speaking of Jews*.

technological fabric of modern society. They are artifacts, because there was no necessity in the world being ordered along these lines; complementary, because they work hand in glove to assign every aspect of life to its proper place. A predictable pattern has emerged in which there are three distinct layers.[111] "Religion" as a universal and timeless feature of human existence is first located at the level of private experience, and refers to a perennial dimension of human existence, interpreted by its advocates as an inherent capacity for the transcendent, by its antagonists as wish fulfillment (just to mention two possibilities).

At a second stratum, that of "society" as a whole, religion also has a designated function, which Bonhoeffer refers to as cultural Protestantism (*Kulturprotestantismus*).[112] It is to help provide social capital, a stock of relations and shared values, without which no temporal social order could endure for long. Religion's function at this layer is to legitimate (often in terms borrowed from the church's vocabulary of sanctification and sacrifice) the various subsystems of society as well as their interrelations, and to help maintain a healthy equilibrium between them. (This is a function to which even some atheists give their assent.[113]) Keeping the global market at optimum flexibility, for example, exacts a high price in human terms. Corporations and states alike are interested in the potential of the church and other established religious institutions to ameliorate these costs, provided that their rituals and beliefs are supportive of their goals and work to deepen the loyalty and productivity of their citizens and employees.[114]

These first two strata designate the universal scope of the genus "religion," while sandwiched in between them are the different "religions" with their particular symbolic fields that express in diverse and thus arbitrary ways the prelinguistic and universal sublimity of private experience. The effect of this metaphysical sandwich is to render the differences between these species as "*merely* different,"[115] and thus not to be taken seriously. So long as the various religions stay within the proper place set for them by the technological organization of a world come of age, there is no difference between them that ultimately should make a difference. These individual religions serve the earthly city as independent repositories of beliefs, from among which individuals may pick and choose according to their predetermined

---

111. I am indebted to Milbank, *Theology and Social Theory*, 108–9, for the basic outlines of this pattern.

112. Cf. *DBWE* 6:57, 290.

113. Wright, *Evolution of God*.

114. Budde and Brimlow, *Christianity Incorporated*, 27–54.

115. McGrane, *Beyond Anthropology*, ix–x.

tastes and prejudices to fashion private worldviews, and as vendors of spiritual goods and services.

As significant as religion is in the classification and management of difference in a world come of age, it does not function by itself. The same individuals who crafted the constructive role for this notion also developed other forms of naming and organizing the other to serve the needs of the social regime that was evolving around the technologies of state and market. In particular, the idea of culture acquired an important function in close coordination with religion.

5

Culture, or Accounting for the Merely Different

"Order," they knew, "is Nature's first law," and they made it their own, for they were in harmony with Nature. They organized, they systematized, they classified, they codified, and all Nature, the universe itself, fell into order at their bidding....

—HENRY STEELE COMMAGER, *The Empire of Reason*

THERE ARE NO VILLAINS in the epic tale of capitalism, only accountants.[1] The division of material goods in a commonwealth, says Thomas Aquinas, "is not according to the natural law, but arose rather from human agreement which belongs to positive law. . . . The ownership of possessions is not contrary to the natural law, but an addition thereto devised by human reason."[2] Max Weber locates the wellspring of the forces that organize capitalist markets, not in some mysterious natural or historical necessity—class conflict, for example—but in bookkeeping, a contingent operation of human intellect. Capitalism only becomes a reality when procedures of accounting define capital as something distinct from income, thus making possible its distinctive regime of accumulation.[3] Capital is not a property that lay dormant in human nature for millennia,[4] but an artifact that, in coordination with other social technologies such as the state, orchestrates relationships between human beings, and also between human beings and

1. Boyle, *Who Are We Now?*, 66.
2. Aquinas, *Summa Theologica* 2a.2ae.66.2.
3. Weber, *Protestant Ethic*, 21–22, 67; cf. Boyle, *Who Are We Now?*, 66.
4. A position argued for by Ardrey, *Territorial Imperative*.

the earth itself, around the activities of production, consumption, accumulation, and exchange.

Though talk about accounting practices and the wellsprings of capital may seem an odd way to introduce the concept of culture in the context of a theological inquiry into the technological organization of a world come of age, there is a reason for it. Far from simply naming universal and timeless features of human existence, this concept represents a significant change in "bookkeeping procedures" that account for human difference in a world come of age. These procedures are part and parcel of the social regime that women and men have virtually no choice but to depend on to cope with the world they inhabit. "Culture" is a historically conditioned and transitory form of human expression that was first imagined at the dawn of the modern era in Europe to deal with a host of developments: the diversity of human life, revolution, and class struggle. It was also employed with increasing precision in connection with Europe's colonial enterprises, and it continues its operations with the spread of global capitalism. It helps push to the margins any and all activities, habits, and institutions that might impede "the otherwise free flow of the market and of government directions."[5]

How a world come of age accounts for difference is a crucial matter for study, for the ways human beings learn to see themselves in relation to the different peoples, places, and things they routinely encounter as they go about their daily lives determine to a significant extent the form of worldliness they perform. Indeed, men and women inhabit a world *as* world, that is, *as* some kind of ordered, intelligible whole, through the use of language. This work of description, which always presupposes some type of social lexicon and grammar, is as necessary for twenty-first-century urban commuters as it was for our hunting-and-gathering forebears. Dominant regimes in particular take upon themselves the task of constructing a world that purports to encompass all human beings, and invariably they do so in ways that make their forms of life normative. The ancient Greeks referred to non-Greek speakers as barbarians, as those who said nothing but "bar-bar-bar" (and thus obviously uncivilized). The poet Virgil in like fashion claimed that Rome's destiny was to "rule with all your power / the peoples of the earth—these will be your arts; / to put your stamp on the works and ways of peace, / to spare the defeated, break the proud in war."[6] A few centuries

---

5. Boyle, *Who Are We Now?*, 29.

6. Virgil, *Aeneid* VI.850–53. Augustine's contention that the earthly city is governed by the *libido dominandi*, the lust to mastery, thus applies with equal force to a world come of age. Augustine, *City of God* 1.Pref., 3.

later the emperor Marcus Aurelius envisioned the whole world as one city, a *cosmopolis*, with Rome of course as its organizing principle.[7]

The gospel reminds us that throughout history those who find themselves on the short end of history also formulate ways to account for the other, with their own rules of inclusion and exclusion. Jesus, in typical Jewish fashion, refers to non-Jews as Gentiles, telling his followers on the night before his crucifixion that Gentile rulers lord it over their subjects, and claim that they do so for their benefit (Luke 22:25). That someone and something should perform this work of describing and weighing differences within and between peoples should not be controversial, and a world come of age is no exception. What is significant in this otherwise mundane act is the particular way the modern world accounts for difference, and to what ends.

I should note at the outset that there is not a precise one-to-one correspondence between religion and culture as social technologies related to the ways the modern world positions difference in its proper place. It may not be particularly helpful to say that the church needs a noncultural interpretation of Christianity in exactly the same way it needs a nonreligious interpretation. It is relatively harmless, for example, to use "culture" to refer to the habits, practices, institutions, customs, rites, artifacts, and mores that comprise every society and that constitute the sense and coherence of its way of life and convey it to its members. As Bonhoeffer puts it in a working note for *Ethics*, culture (*Bildung*) is the working of reality as a whole into the mind and spirit.[8] Both a world come of age and the church, as distinct performances of worldly human existence, *have* a culture in the sense that each has a distinctive set of activities, structures, convictions, and dispositions that shapes the way it copes with the world.

The problems arise when one says that the church *is* a culture, or worse, that it *belongs* to culture. Such assertions only make sense when, within a world come of age, the habits, practices, institutions, customs, rites, artifacts, and mores of the church are displaced from the performative context where they originated and where they served as the basis for its worldly witness in word and deed, and relocated within the technological repertoire of the modern social regime, where they are used as instruments for classifying and ranking otherness to serve the world's organizing aims. The practices and institutions of the church are thereby domesticated to serve a form of worldliness in tension with the kind of worldliness envisioned by Bonhoeffer.

---

7. Marcus Aurelius, *Meditations*, 3.11, 4.3.

8. Bonhoeffer, *Zettelnotizen*, 76; cf. *DBWE* 6:217 n. 159.

Though Bonhoeffer's critique of religion offers us crucial insight into the social grammar of a world come of age, it needs not only to be developed further but supplemented as well by analyses of other social technologies by means of which modernity accounts for difference. In this regard the notion of culture has played a key role in a social project that has had as its goal for more than three centuries now the construction and reconstruction of a particular form of worldliness. In much the same way that the concept of society is implicitly identified with nation-states in the grammar of modernity, "culture" is implicated with the social regime of the state. Culture is "politics in non-political guise."[9]

The Road Not Taken: Bonhoeffer and "Culture"

Unlike Paul Tillich, who claims that religion "is the substance of culture, culture is the form of religion,"[10] Bonhoeffer does not as a rule invoke either *Bildung* or *Kultur* as a constructive theological concept, either by itself or in conjunction with religion, in his theological formulations. The one exception to this is when on occasion he uses *Kultur* as a synonym for the divine mandate of "work" (*Arbeit*) in connection with the notion of estates—economic, political, ecclesiastical—which of course is a holdover from feudalism, though he wants to move away from static conceptions of social being that prevailed in feudalism and toward the language of task.[11] He does not have a well-developed theory of the concept, and there is certainly little or nothing at stake theologically for him in it. Indeed, given the size of the corpus and the prevalence of the term in his historical and social context, it is intriguing to note how seldom the various cognates for culture in German actually appear in his writings.

This is not to say that he is unfamiliar with its multiple definitions, including its more aristocratic connotations, which at times he does espouse—for example, when he laments the fact that spiritual life (*geistige Existenz*) has become fragmented, a torso, that everyone is just a technician, even in music and the other arts.[12] According to Paul Lehmann, Bonhoeffer was thoroughly "German in his passion for perfection, whether of manners, or performance, or all that is connotated [*sic*] by the word *Kultur*. Here, in short, was an aristocracy of the spirit at its best."[13] Bonhoeffer can also

---

9. Eagleton, *Culture and the Death of God*, 123.

10. Tillich, *Theology of Culture*, 42.

11. *DBWE* 6:388 (*DBW* 6:392).

12. *DBWE* 8:306 (*DBW* 8:336).

13. Cited by Bethge, *Dietrich Bonhoeffer*, 155.

be highly critical of these associations, stating that a culture (*Bildung*) that breaks down in the face of danger is no culture.[14] At other times he uses these terms in a generic sense, as seen in his discussion of the mandates, employing it as a synonym for labor, or in connection with the notions of reason, freedom, humanity, and tolerance.[15] He has nothing of significance invested in the term, and nothing is at stake theologically for him in it.

Nevertheless, there is something noteworthy in the road not taken, particularly when that highway is so heavily travelled by his fellow intellectuals in Germany. Though nothing conclusive can be reliably inferred from the fact that Bonhoeffer does not make extensive use of the concept, it does suggest that he is working, at least implicitly, at cross purposes with important segments of the German society of his time. Nobel Prize laureate Thomas Mann, speaking to a group of republican students in 1923, addresses what he sees as the reluctance of middle-class Germans to be involved in politics in relation to the notion of culture:

> The inwardness, the culture ["Bildung"] of a German implies introspectiveness; an individualistic cultural conscience; consideration for the careful tending, the shaping, deepening and perfecting of one's own personality or, in religious terms, for the salvation and justification of one's own life; subjectivism in the things of the mind, therefore, a type of culture that might be called pietistic, given to autobiographical confession and deeply personal, one in which the world of the *objective*, the political world, is felt to be profane and is thrust aside with indifference "because," as Luther says, "this external order is of no consequence." What I mean by all this is that the idea of a republic meets with resistance in Germany chiefly because the ordinary middle-class man here, if he ever thought about culture, never considered politics to be part of it, and still does not do so today. To ask him to transfer his allegiance from inwardness to the objective, to politics, to what the peoples of Europe call *freedom*, would seem to him to amount to a demand that he should do violence to his own nature, and in fact give up his sense of national identity.[16]

According to W. H. Bruford, Mann believes that middle-class Germans of the time were relatively indifferent to politics because they were devoted

---

14. *DBWE* 8:267–69 (*DBW* 8:290–92).

15. *DBWE* 6:388, 340–42.

16. Thomas Mann, "Von deutscher Republik," cited by Bruford, *German Tradition of Self-Cultivation*, vii.

to the inner cultivation of the mind, "and this devotion to culture is good because it tends to make [them] humane."[17]

This connection between, on the one hand, inwardness and introspectiveness, which as we have seen is at the forefront of the critique of liberal theology in the prison correspondence, and on the other the concepts of culture and religion in German society, is not lost on Bonhoeffer. In a sermon preached in Barcelona in 1928, he states that in its desire to chart its own path to the eternal, the soul in its restlessness, its grandiose and gentle efforts at self-transcendence, produces great works of philosophy and art: "The systems of Plato and Hegel, the Adam of Michelangelo, the quartets and symphonies of Beethoven, the cathedrals of the Gothic period, the paintings of Rembrandt, or the Faust and Prometheus of Goethe." In addition there are the great preachers of morality, including Plato and Kant. But these are to no avail, because "God is God, and grace is grace. Here is the source of the great disturbance of our illusions and of our confidence in culture, the great disruption, which God brings about and which the ancient myth of the Tower of Babel illustrates." In the end, he writes, "Culture and religion [*Kultur wie Religion*] both stand under divine judgment."[18] He returns to this theme in a sermon given later that year in Madrid: "Not a cultivation of the soul, not human culture [*Nicht Seelenbildung, nicht Menschenkultur*], not moral polishing, but surrender of the soul to an other; not the soul as the center of the world but rather that to which the soul sacrifices itself."[19]

By refusing to privilege the concept of culture in either a constructive or polemical manner in his theology, as Tillich does, Bonhoeffer departs from the path established by Friedrich Schleiermacher for German theology beginning in the nineteenth century and extending well into the twentieth. Schleiermacher extracts faith from scripture (which he describes in *On Religion* as a mausoleum for true piety) and the church (with its "caved-in walls of their Jewish Zion and its Gothic pillars"), and substitutes a prethematic form of awareness or feeling as the basis of religion. This feeling is a diamond, but it is encased in a shell of metaphysics and morals that must be cracked open.[20] Karl Barth observes that in "the very places where

---

17. Bruford, *German Tradition of Self-Cultivation*, 228. Richard Evans disputes the notion that Germans were indifferent to politics, noting that participation in political activities—voting, parties, heated discussion and debates in pubs and bars—in the early years of the twentieth century was very high. Nevertheless, as Evans himself observes, much of the political foment had to do with the German "'struggle for culture' in its ideological ferocity." Evans, *Coming of the Third Reich*, 16–19. See also Lepenies, *Seduction of Culture in German History*.

18. *DBWE* 10:482–83 (*DBW* 10:456–58).

19. *DBWE* 10:533 (*DBW* 10:519).

20. Schleiermacher, *On Religion*, 4, 50, 22.

the theology of the Reformation had said 'the Gospel' or 'the Word of God' or 'Christ' Schleiermacher, three hundred years after the Reformation, now says, religion or piety."[21]

Schleiermacher not only separates the essence of religion from any substantial connection to Christian convictions, practices, and institutions, says Jonathan Sheehan, he reassigns it to a new proper place, the realm of culture, a concept that in nineteenth-century Germany quickly subsumes humankind's "entire spiritual, political, artistic, historical, and scholarly heritage." Initially its range of reference extended to all humanity, but this cosmopolitan spirit was rather quickly translated into German particularity.[22] (The breakdown of cosmopolitan aspirations into some sort of particularity is inevitable in any case, since "humankind" as a single society does not exist. Appeals to the "human community" are either "a glorification and reification of what are our *existing* contingent social practices and forms of life *or* a pious and vacuous generality."[23]) What Schleiermacher ultimately invents, then, is a theological foundation for cultural Protestantism (*Kulturprotestantismus*), the reconfiguration of the sense of scripture and tradition to underwrite societal conditions that exist in a nation or people at a given time.[24]

Bonhoeffer reserves some of his harshest criticism for this phenomenon. In a series of lectures he gives at the University of Berlin during the winter semester of 1931–32 on the history of twentieth-century systematic theology, he calls into question the synthesis of Christianity and culture that was a given to many theologians in his day. He states that Wilhelm Hermann secures a synthesis with culture through a reappropriation of Kant's categorical imperative. The essential function of Christianity is said to be to provide the overarching framework (*die Klammer*, literally "the clamp") that holds together "the cultural function of the age" (*der geistigen Besitz der Zeit*). When this sort of synthesis is presupposed as the goal of theology, writes Bonhoeffer in connection to the culture of personality advanced by Adolf von Harnack and Ernst Troeltsch, "Jesus is only the deepening and the justification of the modern ideal."[25]

Though the phrase "cultural Protestantism" itself does not appear in "Thy Kingdom Come!," which he writes at approximately the same time he

---

21. Barth, *From Rousseau to Ritschl*, 339.

22. Sheehan, *Enlightenment Bible*, 223.

23. Bernstein, "What Is the Difference That Makes a Difference?," 80.

24. Sheehan, *Enlightenment Bible*, 228–29.

25. *DBWE* 11:223–24 (*DBW* 11:223); cf. *DBWE* 6:346 n. 30. Here is the premise and precursor to Charles Mathewes' contention that churches should formulate a comprehensive civic vision. Mathewes, *Theology of Public Life*, 203.

delivers these lectures, it finds a cognate in what he calls "pious, Christian secularism," where faith hardens "into religious convention and morality, and the church into an organization of action for religious-moral reconstruction." In our pride we place limits on God, stating that he cannot come to us, and thus we must create the kingdom of God "in the strengthening of the church, in the Christianizing of culture and politics and upbringing, and in a renewal of Christian moral convention." But it is not what we and God could do that forms the basis of our prayer that God's kingdom might come, but what God has in fact done for us, and what God continues to do for us time and again.[26]

Bonhoeffer's suspicions about the idea of culture resurface at Finkenwalde. In a lecture in which he discusses the contemporizing of New Testament texts, Bonhoeffer groups together several ideas that have "shaped theology all the way to the theology of the G[erman] C[hristians]." He begins with rationalism, "the emancipation of autonomous reason," which he describes as the eruption of the claim, latent in humankind since our expulsion from Eden, that women and men should shape their lives free from the forces of the given world. Those autonomous human beings who wish to retain a Christian confession therefore demand that the Christian message justify itself before the forum of their own authority: "If this succeeds, then they call themselves *Christians*; if it does not succeed, they call themselves *pagans*." He then links the concept of culture with this effort:

> It makes not the slightest difference whether the forum before which the biblical message is to justify itself is called "reason" in the eighteenth century, "culture" [*Kultur*] in the nineteenth century, or "*Volkstum*" in the twentieth century or in the year 1933, along with everything that entails; it is *exactly the same question*: Can Christianity become contemporary for us as we simply—thank God!—are now?[27]

Bonhoeffer picks up the critique of cultural Protestantism in *Ethics*, where he explicitly connects the modern division of life into two realms with the secular or profane world that ostensibly exists over against the sacred domain, represented by monasticism. Whereas monasticism fashioned a form of spiritual existence that came to take no part in worldly existence, cultural Protestantism makes this-worldliness independent of Christ. This division of reality loses touch with the original Reformation message, which is that the proper place of human holiness (*eine Heiligkeit des Menschen*) is neither the sacred nor the profane as such, but only in God's gracious,

26. *DBWE* 12:291.
27. *DBWE* 14:414 (*DBW* 14:400).

sin-forgiving word. The Reformation came to be celebrated as the liberation of human conscience, reason and culture (*Kultur*), culminating in the justification of the worldly as such, all the while laying the groundwork for the emergence of a rationalized and mechanized world. The "disastrous misunderstanding" of cultural Protestantism creates the impression that people fulfill the responsibility given to them by God by faithfully performing their earthly vocational obligations as citizens, workers, and parents instead of hearing the call of Jesus Christ. That call does in fact lead them into earthly obligations but is never synonymous with it, for that would entail a false sanctioning of the worldly orders as such.[28]

Perhaps the most intriguing reference to cultural Protestantism comes in a lecture Bonhoeffer gives at Finkenwalde on pastoral care. He describes three different sorts of people: (1) those who consider themselves Christian but are fully occupied with family, work, and children, and thus believe they do not need or have time for the church; (2) the cultured or educated (*die Gebildeten*), who see themselves at a distance from the church, and thus everything, including the pastor, has its proper place; (3) those who are obstinate, disappointed, enlightened, or hostile to the church. Bonhoeffer takes special care when talking about the best ways to approach the educated, cautioning against trying to engage them in a philosophical or quasi-religious conversation. He concludes by saying that the cultured, in their opposition to the church, are victims of cultural Protestantism, "perhaps not unlike the tax collectors and prostitutes in the New Testament."[29]

The Invention of "Culture" as an Accounting Instrument for Difference

The absence of culture as a constructive concept in Bonhoeffer's thought notwithstanding, a substantial connection currently exists between it and the concept of religion that demands closer scrutiny. Indeed, in recent decades culture has taken the lead over religion in the lexicon and grammar by which a world come of age accounts for difference. In George Lindbeck's influential book *The Nature of Doctrine*, for example, "religion" is functionally

28. *DBWE* 6:57–60, 114, 290–91 (*DBW* 6:104).

29. *DBWE* 14:582 (*DBW* 14:578). In the *Ethics* manuscript Bonhoeffer notes that the modern concepts of reason, culture, humanity, tolerance, and autonomy, "which until recently had served as battle cries against the church, against Christianity, even against Jesus Christ, now surprisingly found themselves in very close proximity to the Christian domain." As the editors to the volume note, this is an allusion to the Confessing Church and its confessional stance as expressed in the Barmen Declaration. *DBWE* 6:340 and n. 8.

defined in the context of what makes for a culture.[30] More recently, Kathryn Tanner takes up and reformulates Lindbeck's thesis in a book appropriately titled *Theories of Culture: A New Agenda for Theology*, in which she argues for a more fluid and dynamic conception of culture as the groundwork for faith, as opposed to revelation.[31]

Lindbeck and Tanner are heirs to the work of H. Richard Niebuhr in his influential work *Christ and Culture*. Niebuhr defines culture as "the 'artificial, secondary environment' which man superimposes on the natural."[32] Included in this abstract description of culture is a group of traits, some of which are rather mundane: culture is social and involves human achievement. Much more significant is his contention that culture has principally to do with "values," a neo-Kantian concept that designates all that which does not belong to the empirical world of "facts," which have to do with the perception of causal relations in the natural and social worlds. Values have instead to do with the feelings of pleasure and pain, moral approbation and disapproval felt by the buffered self, which are brought about by our sense impressions.[33]

Once again we see the technological reconfiguration of the world, both human and nonhuman, compelling everything it encounters to produce specific signs of its presence and behavior, and like the concept of religion, the proper place for these signs is the inner life of the individual. The neat division between facts and values delimits a sphere separate from the world of politics and economics, a domain that in a carefully regulated sense is "free." It is free precisely because, in the words of Herbert McCabe, it "is free from relevance, and because it is irrelevant is not worth controlling. Philosophers, scientists, novelists and theologians need feel no responsibility to the community in what they say because nobody takes them seriously." McCabe adds that the project of modernity breaks down from time to time, and thus "the liberal society becomes subject to fits of illiberalism."[34]

Niebuhr also identifies the sphere of culture as the realm of pluralism, such that the society that takes form around the nation-state is "always involved in a more or less laborious effort to hold together in tolerable conflict the many efforts of many men in many groups to achieve and conserve many goods," or as Raymond Williams puts it, "The working-out of the idea

30. Lindbeck, *Nature of Doctrine*, 33.
31. Tanner, *Theories of Culture*.
32. Niebuhr, *Christ and Culture*, 32.
33. See, for example, Ritschl, *Christian Doctrine of Justification*, 3:204–5.
34. McCabe, *Law, Love and Language*, 158.

of culture is a slow reach again for control."[35] Niebuhr classifies the kingdom of God, for example, as a human value, "though scarcely as the one pearl of great price. Jesus Christ and God the Father, the gospel, the church, and eternal life may find places in the cultural complex, but only as elements in the great pluralism."[36] Very much in the manner first posited by Schleiermacher, human differences for Niebuhr have their "proper place" within culture, that is, in the pluralistic and altogether private domain of values, for which there need be no binding social agreement.

That the concept of culture performs this vital social function is not surprising, says Bernard McGrane: "We think under the hegemony of the ethnological response to the alienness of the Other; we are, today, *contained* within an anthropological concept of the Other. Anthropology has become our modern way of seeing the Other as, fundamentally and merely, *culturally* different."[37] This response to the other can never really take seriously the particularity of difference, because it stipulates that their core convictions and practices be regarded *merely* "as icing on a basically homogeneous cake."[38]

The pivotal role played by the concept of culture in theology is not limited to Protestant theology. In his book *The Naked Public Square*, Catholic theologian Richard John Neuhaus makes common cause with Tillich, Niebuhr, and others, linking together the ideas of politics, religion, and culture with that of the nation-state. According to Neuhaus, at the heart of culture is religion, which is not limited to ideas, activities, and attitudes normally connected to this term, but includes "all the ways we think and act and interact with respect to what we believe is ultimately true and important." The state, with its coercive role, cannot be the source of the network of binding obligations (derived from the Latin *religare*) that constitute society. These obligations, as expressed in law, derive their legitimacy from "what people believe to be their collective destiny or ultimate meaning." The only enduring foundations are the operative values of the American people, which "are overwhelmingly grounded in religious belief."[39]

---

35. R. Williams, *Culture and Society*, 295.

36. Niebuhr, *Christ and Culture*, 38–39.

37. McGrane, *Beyond Anthropology*, x, my emphases.

38. Fish, "Boutique Multiculturalism," 382, my emphasis.

39. Neuhaus, *Naked Public Square*, 27, 37; cf. Cavanaugh, *Theopolitical Imagination*, 58–59.

To justify their claim that religion is "the ground or the depth-level of culture,"[40] both Lindbeck[41] and Neuhaus defer to Clifford Geertz's sociological conception of culture as an interlocked system of signs forming a context within which people, events, institutions, behaviors, and processes can be intelligibly described.[42] Neuhaus, to his credit, acknowledges this level of dependence on sociology might be disconcerting for some, but quickly assures them that while Geertz's is "a very 'human' definition of religion,"[43] they should not be worried, for theological and sociological accounts are not mutually exclusive. Neuhaus is certainly correct in asserting that the two accounts may well be compatible, but it is also necessarily true that the grammar of one establishes the sense of the other, and it is Geertz's account, with the implicit assumption that the nation-state constitutes the normative paradigm for society, that is grammatically prior to theology.

Just as we did with the concept of religion, then, we need some sense of how we got to this point in the description and classification of the other by means of "culture." McGrane provides a point of departure for our inquiry when he states that "Westerners" have historically used four paradigms to describe and interpret non-European peoples. Up to the sixteenth century, the setting was Christianity, and the other was a pagan, a characterization that tended to demonize her or him, given that the only space of salvation was in the Christian church. During the Enlightenment, the medieval paradigm was superseded by a conception that envisioned otherness in epistemological terms, employing ideas such as ignorance, error, and superstition to mark the difference between Europeans (who were rational, civilized, *cultured*) and non-Europeans. The Enlightenment paradigm eventually gave way in the nineteenth century to an account of history that privileged the new technological organizing of time as the "proper" and "scientific" arbiter of difference, arranging the relationship between peoples in terms of stages of development: primitive and advanced.[44] Gotthold Ephraim Lessing inaugurated this new paradigm when in 1780 he published *Education of the Human Race,* in which he divides the history of the human race by comparing it to the maturation process of an individual, starting with childhood (exemplified by the Old Testament), progressing into adolescence (the New Testament), and culminating with the mature humanity of an enlightened

40. Neuhaus, *Naked Public Square,* 132.

41. Lindbeck, *Nature of Doctrine,* 115.

42. Geertz, *Interpretation of Cultures,* 14, 17, 26.

43. Neuhaus, *Naked Public Square,* 132.

44. McGrane, *Beyond Anthropology,* ix–x.

age and its promise of "a new eternal gospel."[45] Bonhoeffer distances himself from stadial accounts of this sort when he rejects the widespread notion that the Old Testament represents an earlier, "preliminary" stage of religion.[46]

In our time, says McGrane, difference is typically no longer demonized as pagan, or described derisively as primitive and superstitious, or relegated to an earlier period in the process of social evolution, surviving into the present on false pretenses and ultimately doomed to extinction. The dominant paradigm is now the ethnological concept of culture,[47] and it continues to be one of the principal instruments for containment of difference in a world come of age. It "democratizes" difference, such that the other is no longer a relic of another time and place; she or he belongs, but precisely in "our" time and in her or his proper place. The radical democratization of difference by means of culture authorizes "us," that is, members of the dominant society, to insert the other into "our" present, to transform her or him into "our" contemporary, always of course on "our" terms. "The non-European 'other' is still 'different' of course," says Kenneth Surin, "but now (s)he is *merely* 'different.'"[48] To put the matter in terms developed in chapter 4, the European, the proper subject of choice and action, has located the non-European other in her or his "proper place."

As with many of the seminal ideas of the Renaissance and Enlightenment, the inspiration for the modern concept of culture originated in antiquity, where its etymological Latin forerunner, *cultura*, was used to refer to what people of the soil typically did—tend natural growth. Human beings cultivated crops and animals, but not themselves, though a few authors did compare the intellectual, moral, and spiritual formation of persons to what the farmer and herder did. In his *Tusculan Disputations*, for example, Cicero says that

> just as a field, however good, cannot be productive without cultivation, so the soul cannot be productive without teaching. So true it is that the one without the other is ineffective. Now the cultivation of the soul is philosophy [*cultura autem animi philosophia est*]; this pulls out vices by the roots and makes souls fit for the reception of seed, and commits to the soul and, as we may say, sows in it seed of a kind to bear the richest fruit when fully grown.[49]

45. Sheehan, *Enlightenment Bible*, 131.

46. *DBWE* 5:53; *DBWE* 8:214.

47. McGrane, *Beyond Anthropology*, x; cf. Bauman, *Postmodern Ethics*, 39.

48. Surin, "Certain 'Politics of Speech,'" 74, Surin's emphasis.

49. Cicero, *Tusculan Disputations* II.v.13.

The ancients thus did not use this term as an independent noun or posit an aspect of life distinct from that of the *polis* as such, but as a way of describing the formative processes that would enable a genuine human life to flourish.

Beginning in the sixteenth and seventeenth centuries, writes Raymond Williams, "two crucial changes occurred: first, a degree of habituation to the metaphor, which made the sense of human tending direct; second, an extension of particular processes to a general process, which the word could abstractly carry." From this metaphorical habituation arose the first modern use of the abstract noun "culture" in both French and English to fashion, first, a process or program of intellectual, spiritual, and aesthetic development and refinement.[50] For example, Francis Bacon, with reference to Cicero, writes in 1605 that just as the proper cultivation of seeds and young plants is crucial to their thriving, "the culture and manurance of minds in Youth hath such a forcible (though vnseen) operacion, as hardly any length of time or contention of labour can counteruaile it afterwords."[51]

As one might expect, an aristocratic sense of what counts as the proper cultivation of the mind or soul attaches itself quite early to this concept, with unmistakable class and colonial connotations. The terms "colonize" and "culture" are both derived from the same Latin root, the implications of which are noted at the end of the eighteenth century by Johann Gottfried von Herder, who argues that "nothing is more indeterminate than this word [culture], and nothing more deceptive than its application to all nations and periods."[52] To be counted among the cultured, particularly in Britain and France (and extending eventually to America in the West and Russia in the East), came to be associated with conceptions of enlightened civilization, a sign that one had been formed in the manner of Europe's new social elites, who would efficiently and humanely manage society from a universal, "cosmopolitan" perspective. The man or woman of culture "possessed through habituation a refined, educated soul with a claim to distinctive social status by virtue of his intellectual training and aesthetic sensibilities."[53]

As Herder's comments suggest, the relationship between the ideas of culture and civilization was configured differently in Germany due to the influence of two different impulses. As noted above, there tended to be a more nationalistic character to the related notions of *Bildung* and *Kultur*, as German intellectuals resisted French and English claims to the universality

---

50. R. Williams, *Keywords*, 87.

51. Bacon, *Oxford Francis Bacon*, 4:132, original spelling.

52. Herder, *Ideas on the Philosophy of the History of Mankind*, cited by R. Williams, *Keywords*, 89.

53. Tanner, *Theories of Culture*, 4; R. Williams, *Keywords*, 87–88.

of their notion of a movable Enlightenment. In *On Religion*, Schleiermacher wastes no time in distinguishing the spiritual accomplishments of the German people over against the vulgarities of the English and French. The former care for nothing other than profit and enjoyment of material goods; the latter are incapable of holy awe and true adoration.[54]

Figures such as Schleiermacher singled out intellectual, artistic, and spiritual endeavors as the nation's bulwark against French- and English-dominated internationalism, in part because they thought that these feats constituted a higher form of achievement than any set of practices imposed from outside, but especially because they manifested a spirit that was distinctively German. Herder objects in particular to the suggestion that there is a single and universal process of human development subsisting in Europe, and he insists instead that we speak instead of "cultures."[55] "The distinctively German character of its *Kultur*," writes Tanner, "interrupted the uniformity of Enlightenment civilization" as the cosmopolitan ideal for all peoples.[56]

The emerging concept of *Kultur* in nineteenth-century Germany embodies the Romantic critique of the notion of a single, enlightened rational order to which all peoples should be conformed.[57] The notion of "civilization" that was held in such esteem in Britain and France was frequently regarded in nineteenth-century Germany as artificial in comparison with "Nature." Natural human needs and impulses were seen as more basic to life and therefore to be elevated above the artificial manners of politeness and elegance. There developed an interest in folk cultures, which were held to be closer to nature and thus offered an alternative to civilization, which was regarded as mechanical, the product of an abstract rationalism and the inhumanity of the Industrial Revolution. The emphasis of the culture-concept thus shifted from the rational cultivation of an enlightened intellect to the activities and achievements of literary and artistic endeavor: literature, music, dance, food, clothing, and the like. The concept of civilization was reserved for political and economic practices and institutions, which

54. Schleiermacher, *On Religion*, 9–10.

55. R. Williams, *Keywords*, 89–90.

56. Tanner, *Theories of Culture*, 9–10. Michael DeJonge notes that this distinction can be detected in Bonhoeffer's *Ethics*, where he uses the adjective *westlich* (western) to the exclusion of Germany: "Thus Bonhoeffer uses the term *westliche Völker* to refer to Germany's western neighbors, such as Holland, England, and especially France." When he wishes to refer to a European political-cultural unity that embraces both western people and Germany, he uses *Abendland*. DeJonge, "Bonhoeffer's Concept of the West," 40.

57. The preeminent forerunner of this position was Jean-Jacques Rousseau, articulated masterfully in his *Discourse on the Origin of Inequality*.

were seen as human artifacts, whereas *Kultur* was reserved for referring to the highest intellectual and artistic achievements in German society.[58] The range of the culture-concept was therefore extended once again, this time to name that which stood between human beings and the machines that had been invented to dominate "Nature" but that increasingly had imprisoned men and women within the iron cage of instrumental rationality.[59]

As the nineteenth century progressed, the Romantic meaning of culture in German society, which in the meantime had migrated to England,[60] increasingly became intransitive and self-contained, much like Aristotle's concept of *praxis*. This had the effect of privatizing everything that was classified under the concept as a matter of personal taste instead of public fact. The aim of culture was no longer to accomplish some end but simply to do something well, namely, to cultivate certain standards of thought and feeling, or as Matthew Arnold puts it, "inward spiritual activity,"[61] emphasizing "levels of excellence in fine art, literature, music and individual personal perfection."[62] The homology with the concept of religion, and in particular its confinement to its own private realm, becomes more apparent than ever.

The plural "cultures" initially posited by Herder made possible the anthropological sense of the concept, specifying a particular way of life practiced by a nation or people. Taylor expresses this sense of the term when he says of these developments that "the people as 'nation' is often seen as the bearer of a certain language or culture. The world is lived and sung in a way which is special to our nation and its language."[63] It is in this use that the concept comes to play a central role in the ethnological discourses of a world come of age in response to the unparalleled social change brought about by a number of interrelated factors: the demise of Christendom, the advent of colonialism, the rise of modern science and technology, the emergence and expansion of the political institutions of the modern nation-state, and the development of capitalist modes of accumulation and consumption. All of these developments (and others could be specified) led to the widespread encounters between, and massive displacements of, whole populations.

In the face of such rapid and radical diversification in the nineteenth and early twentieth centuries, says Raymond Williams, the development of

58. The fluidity of language allowed some authors to reverse this relationship, "culture" being used to talk about material development and "civilization" the spiritual. R. Williams, *Keywords*, 89–90.

59. See Weber, *Protestant Ethic*, 181.

60. Sheehan, *Enlightenment Bible*, 220–21.

61. Arnold, *Culture and Anarchy*, 44.

62. Jenks, *Culture*, 9.

63. Taylor, *Secular Age*, 579.

the idea of culture in European countries such as Great Britain was a general reaction to a general and major change in the conditions of common life, the result of the Industrial Revolution and rise of democratic polities. The concept itself is both an abstraction and absolute that emerges in response to, first, a recognition that certain moral and intellectual activities had become separated from the impulses of a new kind of society, and second, the need to offer a mitigating and rallying alternative over against the processes of social practical judgment as a court of human appeal: "We can now see that a result of the changes in society at the time of the Industrial Revolution, cultivation could not be taken for granted as a process, but had to be stated as an absolute, an agreed centre for defence. Against mechanism, the amassing of fortunes and the proposition of utility as the source of value, it offered a different and a superior social idea."[64]

The basic element of this concept of culture was an effort at total qualitative assessment and social control. Unlike the particular changes that every society must deal with on a regular basis, changes that modify only specific habitual actions, the kind of radical change experienced by Great Britain in the nineteenth century drove this people back to look at general designs as a whole. Changes in the whole form of a common life of the nation necessarily focused attention on it, and thus there was a need to reconstruct it on what was considered to be a rational basis.[65] Though it was posited as an alternative to the mechanisms of the state and the imposition of wage labor, among other media, for the protection of what is truly human, the creation of culture is nonetheless co-constitutive of the technological organization of life in a world come of age.

Nowhere is this perceived need for discipline and control more explicit than in the writings of Arnold, who states that modern society, characterized by its industrialized, mechanical framework and fragmented nature, is threatened by anarchy and a pervasive sense of moral malaise. According to Arnold, "as feudalism, which with its ideas and habits of subordination was for many centuries silently behind the British Constitution, dies out, and we are left with nothing but our system of checks, and our notion of its being the great right and happiness of an Englishman to do as far as possible what he likes, we are in danger of drifting towards anarchy."[66] The loss of a sense of transcendence and the fact of social fragmentation, together with the growing value placed by modernity on the mechanical and the material, combined to create an atomistic and potentially barbarous society. The solution, writes Arnold, is "culture," by which he means

64. R. Williams, *Culture and Society*, xviii, 63.

65. Ibid., 295.

66. Arnold, *Culture and Anarchy*, 50.

a pursuit of our total perfection by means of getting to know, on all the matters which most concern us, the best which has been thought and said in the world, and, through this knowledge, turning a stream of fresh and free thought upon our stock notions and habits, which we now follow staunchly but mechanically, vainly imagining that there is a virtue in following them staunchly which makes up for the mischief of following them mechanically.[67]

Culture, in this sense of the term, would replace religion as the spiritual and moral framework of modern civilization.

The technological innovation of culture plays a somewhat different role in the workings of the British Empire. Talal Asad notes that the "problem of culture" was applied strictly to the nonwhite populations of the empire, having to do with "practices of controlled reconstruction." When the social habits, political order and other customs of "a dominant stock" (the proper subject) come into contact with a "native culture" (assigned by colonialist rule to its proper place), the question of mixture and co-ordination arises, and thus everything depends on the rational coordination of the participants: "The fact of imperial rule thus renders 'the problem of culture' into the British obligation to identify, study, and normalize the culture of its subject peoples (whence the importance of the 'rise of sociology and anthropology')." The aim of these ethnological disciplines was to help integrate them into modern (i.e., Western) civilization by way of "amalgamation" and "persuasion." Imperial talk of "amalgam," says Asad, presupposes the idea of original, "pure" cultures coming into contact with each other, creating a new, emergent, and more progressive historical identity.[68]

The social grammar of the culture-concept also permeates recent discussions about pluralism and multiculturalism, writes Asad, concepts that have essentially to do with the proper theoretical and practical coordination of dominant (i.e., European and North American) and subaltern ("native") peoples. There is to be equal respect and tolerance for all, but the "realities" of political and economic power require the subordinate cultures, which are less "progressive," to accommodate themselves to the dominant and more progressive heritage and ethos.[69] Bronisław Malinowski thus states that "there are cultural elements which are not allowed to continue because they are repugnant to the Whites." He cites in particular cannibalism, intertribal warfare, mutilation, headhunting, witchcraft, and slavery as examples

---

67. Arnold, *Culture and Anarchy*, 5; cf. Taylor, *Secular Age*, 380–88, 402, 405.

68. Asad, *Genealogies of Religion*, 249–51.

69. Ibid., 253.

of practices that are offensive to white sensibilities.[70] This indictment is revealing not only because he puts the conflict of cultures in racial terms but also because these "repugnant cultural elements" were previously cited as justification by the Spanish for the enslavement of the Andeans in South America and by the British of the Zulu in Natal.[71] (More recently the suggestion in both academia and the popular press that Islam needs its own "Renaissance"—European history once again implicitly serving as the norm for what constitutes genuinely civilized development—is only the latest example of how a world come of age accounts for difference.)

Once traditional activities and institutions are classified as cultural, and no longer part of the constitutive—which is to say, *political*—practice of a people or nation (hence the visceral reaction to Rowan Williams's proposal that *sharia* be allowed to have a role in the public square), then artistic expression and taste (broadly conceived as including literature, music, dance, food, and clothing) remain the only markers to identify the social way of life of the other. In particular, the significance of what is now labeled as "art" (a category, as Taylor points out, that also did not exist prior to the fifteenth century[72]) is safely privatized around the cultivation of individual sensibility (a form of "inward spiritual activity"), or contained within "cultural enclaves."[73] The ways of the other are assigned to their proper place, and those formed by them are rendered useful, reliable, productive, and consuming subjects, in both the political and economic sense of the term.[74] The same processes were employed by the colonial powers of Europe to prepare indigenous peoples to live and serve as proper colonial subjects: scrubbed and well-dressed, living in a square house, trained in the ethos of individualism, hard work, and the Bible, the man of the house at his cubicle or assembly line earning an honest living, the wife faithfully at home raising

---

70. Malinowski, "Introductory Essay," xxviii.

71. See Hanke, *All Mankind Is One*, cited by Jennings, *Christian Imagination*, 100; cf. 122–23.

72. The separation of "art" from the category of making, *technē* or *ars*, is traceable to the rise of the peculiarly modern sense of technology. Whereas music, poetry, mosaics, and the like were once understood ontically, as a kind of activity that allows women and men to participate in the overarching order of things (praying, praising heroes who established our way of life), now they are lumped together in "aesthetic" categories that emphasize the way our emotions are moved by them. Taylor, *Secular Age*, 354–55.

73. Clifford Geertz, for example, identifies religion as a cultural system, which assigns to it an essentially cognitive function, having to do with what he calls reality maintenance. Geertz, *Interpretation of Cultures*, 182.

74. Lentricchia, *Criticism and Social Change*, 1–2.

their children to reinforce and repeat the process, and above all spending their income in order to perpetuate the social order well into the future.[75]

The democratization of difference by way of the normalizing project of culture, particularly as it pertains to the sequestration of "art" as a separate activity, is a necessary condition for categorizing and commodifying the customs, convictions, rites, and habits of the world's peoples and traditions, turning them into raw materials for what Theodor Adorno and Max Horkheimer appropriately label the "culture industries": movies, television, and popular music, distribution systems (cable and satellite systems, telecommunications firms, and the Internet), data processing networks such as computer software and hardware interests, marketing and advertising firms, and educational institutions.[76] These means of mass communication account for the majority of the world's output of shared images, stories, information, news, entertainment, and the like, which are the stock-in-trade of the formative practices that constitute the ethos of every society. They exert an inordinate influence on the grammar of social interaction, that is, on the ways people relate not only to the processes and products of political and economic activity, but also to each other, both the neighbor with a face (increasingly unknown to many of us) and the anonymous producer of goods who lives quite literally on the other side of the globe.

Consider the way that, for example, television, with its titillating combination of sight and sound, its evocative appeals to the emotions rather than to the intellect, and its never-ending stream of images and ideas, dominates the social grammar of capitalism. As the cornerstone of the expansion of global culture industries (together with the Internet), it intrudes into nearly every space of everyday life, crowding out other formative influences in the lives of young people, including the practices of the church. Television has an unparalleled ability to captivate our attention for extended periods of time via powerful images and deceptively subtle messages that take very little effort to understand. Images, ideas, and personalities are extricated from their conventional referents in a process. These fragments are then recombined and reshuffled to confer novel meanings to products and consumption opportunities. Commercial television programming, which takes features of a past or contemporary "exotic" culture (music, dance, dress, language, stories, images) and recycles them with those extracted from other peoples to form disjointed images and impressions with no purpose other than to entice viewers and sell products, is so prevalent in our society

---

75. Jennings, *Christian Imagination*, 132; Guy, *Heretic*, 81.

76. Horkheimer and Adorno, "Culture Industry," 94–136. See also Budde, *(Magic) Kingdom of God*, 28–52, and Harvey, *Can These Bones Live?*, 149.

that our perceptions and dispositions have been profoundly affected. The dream of the Idealists and Romantics to gain sway over the imagination of the masses via mythology, writes Terry Eagleton, "was finally to arrive in the shape of cinema, television, advertising and the popular press."[77]

Slavoj Žižek points to a related use of the concept of culture, which is to name beliefs and practices that we have disowned, that is, "all those things we practice without really believing in them, without 'taking them seriously.'" In matters of religion, for example, most people no longer "really believe," though they may still follow (some) traditional rituals and mores to show respect for the "lifestyle" of the community to which they belong: "'I don't really believe in it, it's just part of my culture' effectively seems to be the predominant mode of the disavowed or displaced belief characteristic of our times." What *is* a "cultural lifestyle," writes Žižek, "if not the fact that, although we don't believe in Santa Claus, there is a Christmas tree in every house, and even in public places, every December?"[78]

If such claims seem overstated, Žižek asks, why then do most people not include science within the ambit of culture? Is it not because it is all too real, something we cannot hold at arm's length, and thus it is not "cultural"? Is this not why those of us who pride ourselves on being cultured derisively dismiss fundamentalist believers as barbarians, as anti-cultural, as a threat to culture, because "they dare to *take their beliefs seriously*?" Those who lack cognitive or interpretive distance from their beliefs, who live them immediately, we perceive as a threat to culture:

> Recall the outrage when . . . the Taliban forces in Afghanistan destroyed the ancient Buddhist statutes at Bamiyan: although none of us enlightened Westerners believe in the divinity of the Buddha, we were outraged because the Taliban Muslims did not show the appropriate respect for the "cultural heritage" of their own country and the entire world. Instead of believing through the other, like all people of culture, they really believed in their own religion, and thus had no great sensitivity toward the cultural value of the monuments of other religions—to them, the Buddha statues were just fake idols, not "cultural treasures."[79]

The risk that Žižek runs in making this point, of course, is that some might hear him trying to justify the actions of the Taliban, which is not his aim. He is attempting instead to bring to light the dilemmas that attend attempts to account for difference by means of the concept of culture.

77. Eagleton, *Culture and the Death of God*, 120; cf. 56.
78. Žižek, *Puppet and the Dwarf*, 7–8.
79. Ibid.

What we get are two versions of what is now called multiculturalism, the difference between which is only a matter of degree. I too risk being misunderstood at this point, for there are few concepts more widely celebrated or politically axiomatic in our time than those of pluralism and multiculturalism, particularly among intellectuals and in such culture industries as the mass media and entertainment providers. For one even to raise a question about them is to be regarded by some as *prima facie* evidence that he or she is prejudiced, biased, blind, and hateful, the enemy of difference and tolerance, of humanity itself. And yet it is a risk that I must make, precisely for the sake of advocating for a sense of difference that makes a difference.

According to Stanley Fish, one version is what one social critic calls boutique multiculturalism, which is the pluralism of ethnic restaurants, weekend festivals, and high-profile flirtations with the other that the novelist Tom Wolfe once satirized as "radical chic." Boutique multiculturalists, wed to an essentialist anthropology, see difference not as basic to who and what women and men are but as exotic cuisines to be sampled and colorful locales to be visited—in short, as accessories to a standard model of universal humanity as defined by the technological regime of a world come of age. Such pluralism rejects the force of actual diversity at precisely the point where it makes the strongest claim on its most committed members, and prescribes instead a rational essence for the other that enforces a superficial respect that so many in our shrinking world rightly find insulting.[80]

There is another type of multiculturalism that is more serious because it seeks to value difference in and for itself. This postmodern version recognizes that the politics of equal dignity advocated by boutique multiculturalism is just too easy, too facile. Ascribing to everyone the identical basket of immunities and entitlements on the premise that "deep down" all of us are essentially the same (autonomous maximizers of self-interest) utterly fails to account for the particular and substantial ways in which persons, groups, and traditions differ. For these strong multiculturalists, nurturing particularity and diversity through tolerance, not adherence to some purported universal quality such as our status as autonomous rational agents, is a first principle of both personal morality and public policy.[81]

Nevertheless, says Fish, the time will always come for a serious pluralist when the other will act in a way that resists her or his proper place, that is, incorporation into the larger whole ordered by the nation-state and the global market: "Confronted with a demand that it surrender its view point or enlarge it to include the practices of its natural enemies—other religions,

80. Fish, "Boutique Multiculturalism," 382.

81. Ibid., 383.

other races, other genders, other classes—a beleaguered culture will fight back with everything from discriminatory legislation to violence." In such situations the dilemma for serious multiculturalists quickly becomes evident. Either they must stretch their tolerance so that it includes the intolerance of a group that they personally abhor, thus rejecting tolerance as their first principle, or they condemn the intolerance, in which case they no longer advocate difference at the point where it is most obviously at stake.[82] Whereas the boutique pluralism of the modernist is explicitly imperialist, the strong form of pluralism shows itself to be implicitly so, in spite of its best intentions to affirm difference and tolerance. To recall Raymond Williams, it betrays a slow reach for control on the part of the social order that animates liberal capitalism.

Multiculturalism simply *is* the culture of liberal capitalism, and as such it seeks to define what counts as permissible worldliness. Far from providing a viable solution to reconciling profound differences and disagreements, it represents yet one more comprehensive doctrine added to the fragmented, contentious mix, and thus it does not even name our present predicament accurately. It creates a banal façade of diversity masking an underlying and judgmental uniformity that sets human life in a world come of age apart from previous forms of social life. In some ways multiculturalism is a sign of the impatience of a liberal society in the face of seemingly intractable difference, hoping desperately that formal principles of equality and inclusion can transform themselves (and us) into meaningful substance through some sort of procedural alchemy.[83] An illiberal spirit haunts the noble aspirations of liberalism.

When defined by means of the culture-concept, the other, who is "merely" different, no longer makes a difference. In this regard the multiple senses of the concept—a general process of intellectual, spiritual, and aesthetic development (exemplified by the ethos of a world come of age), the particular way of life of a people or nation (delimited as a species of the genus), and artistic activity and production—though seemingly disparate, actually work hand in glove to keep the practices, customs, habits, and rites of other peoples in their proper places, rendering them politically and economically inert. Individuals, peoples, and whole societies are made to conform to the contours of production and consumption privileged by the technological regime of modernity. The sequestering of artistic expression in particular is unfortunate but completely understandable, for the grammar

82. Ibid.

83. The metaphor of alchemy to describe the modern belief that form can turn itself into substance I take from Mensch and Freeman, *Politics of Virtue*, 5.

of a world come of age restricts what counts as politics to the practice of statecraft. The state is invested with virtually unlimited sovereignty over society, privileging it as the fulcrum of all social order and change. Underwriting the practice of modern statecraft is the absence of any substantive conception of the common good, which effectively reduces politics to a set of procedures for protecting and promoting the individual pursuit of self-interest in the marketplace of desire and consumption.

The process of accounting for difference by the technological apparatus of the modern age is not limited to the concepts of religion and culture, for it takes an additional and even more pernicious form: racial reasoning and imagination. Though it is not a biblical concept, as a theological concept race continues to be an obstacle to the genuine worldliness that Bonhoeffer sees at the heart of Christian faith.

6

A Social Economy of Whiteness

"You are saved," cried Captain Delano, more and more astonished and pained; "you are saved; what has cast such a shadow upon you?"

"The negro."

—HERMAN MELVILLE, "Benito Cereno"

IN A RADICAL INVERSION of the way Christians are taught to read scripture, Dietrich Bonhoeffer concludes his argument in the crucial letter of April 30, 1944, with a strongly worded assertion: "God is the beyond in the midst of our lives. The church stands not at the point of where human powers fail, at the boundaries, but in the center of the village. That's the way it is in the Old Testament, and in this sense we don't read the New Testament nearly enough in light of the Old."[1] Bonhoeffer refers repeatedly to Old Testament texts in his prison correspondence as he critiques the *technische Organisation* that displaced God and discipleship from the center of human existence and relocated them to their "proper place" at the margins of life. These references provide us with important clues, first, to the continuing theological sense and significance of such concepts as a world come of age, religionless Christianity, and living unreservedly in this world; and second, to the need in our own time for an understanding of the church that can live faithfully before the God of Jesus Christ as a necessary condition for living unreservedly in a world that for several centuries has prided itself on having come of age, but that now seems to be growing older, more decrepit and less certain of itself every day.

1. *DBWE* 8:367.

Bonhoeffer's admonition to the church to interpret the New Testament in light of the Old touches on a perennial sore spot in Christian life and thought: supersessionism. This is a concept that holds, in its older and more familiar form, that the church has replaced Israel as the chosen people of God within the economy of redemption. The expropriation of Israel's scriptures by the post-apostolic Christian community was a critical move in support of the claim on the part of the church (and later on the part of the post-Carolingian *corpus Christianum*) to be the "new Israel," a phrase that is not found in the New Testament. Much like the capital vices (vainglory, avarice, wrath, sloth, envy, gluttony, and lust), expropriative supersessionism gives rise to other, equally pernicious forms of construing creaturely existence, one of which is the sordid history of racial existence and racial reasoning that came into being and flourished in connection with a world come of age. Europeans employed many social technologies to account for the new and strange peoples and lands they encountered in their colonial expeditions; in particular, the use of skin color as an instrument of differentiation and a measure of moral and developmental assessment was integral to these operations. That these modes of describing and evaluating the peoples of the "New World" emerged with the rise of the modern world was not coincidental, and in fact they comprise key components in the technological organization of life that has structured the vast diversity of humankind around its own distinctive ends. The legacy of racial reasoning, aptly summed up by the trope of "whiteness,"[2] is not just an unfortunate side effect of the world's coming of age but is part and parcel of its constitution, a situation that is nowhere more apparent than in the United States.

Whiteness in this context does not refer to a physical characteristic of peoples whose origins lie in Europe. Indeed, at the turn of the twentieth century many ethnic groups from Europe were excluded from this privileged category: Italians, Irish, Greeks, Armenians, Hungarians, Serbians, Slovenians, Poles, Jews, Montenegrins, Croatians, Russians, Bulgarians, Czechs, and Slovaks. People are members of this or that race, says Noel Ignatiev, "because they have been assigned to them."[3] David Roediger notes, for example, that federal officials in Minnesota tried to bar Finnish immigrants from naturalization on racial grounds, namely, that they were "Mongolian" and not white. The court hearing the case offered an ironic ruling: Finns

---

2. I refer to whiteness as a trope, and more specifically as a metonym, because it takes the characteristic of skin color that was singled out by the powers of Europe as the mark of differentiation and assessment, to represent the social, political, and economic project of colonization and all that came about as a result of it.

3. Ignatiev, *How the Irish Became White*, 1; cf. Budde, *Borders of Baptism*, 121.

may have been Mongols originally, but "are now among the whitest people in Europe."[4]

As a metonym, whiteness refers to a social economy and grammar that initially took shape late in the Middle Ages in association with the creation of "the Man of Reason" and came to the fore during the time of European colonization. It names both a sociological and theological way of imagining difference as part and parcel of the way the world has come to be organized and thus known. As a sociological and anthropological image it enabled conquistadors, traders, and colonists from the Old World to account for the astounding diversity of peoples and geographies that they encountered in the New. As a theological image it recapitulated the *sicut deus* of Genesis 3, the original and perpetual striving of humankind to usurp the divine powers of creation itself,[5] in order to transcend particularity and contingency and see all the peoples of the world in a universal gaze. Willie Jennings writes, "Whiteness was a global vision of Europeans and Africans but, more than that, a way of organizing bodies by proximity to and approximation of white bodies."[6] These habits of arranging the differences between the peoples of the world began as part of a corrupted theological imagination performed by theologians aligned with colonialist powers, but they subsequently migrated into the secular social imagination, putting being "white" at the top of a racial hierarchy.[7]

The situation with regard to the racial divide has changed in some respects since Bonhoeffer's two visits to the United States. Legally sanctioned segregation is for the most part a thing of the past (though tacit segregation continues in many places), and numerous efforts to integrate civil society continue to one degree or another. But in other ways the chasm is as great as it was when Bonhoeffer visited. Inequities in income, housing, education, the professions, healthcare, and percentage of the prison population have been exhaustively documented. With respect to the church, Michael Emerson and Rodney Woo argue that we have reached a troublesome stasis regarding the racial divide, such that blacks and whites represent the two indigenous American "cultures" (!) that set the tone for multiracial church life, to which all other ethnic and racial groups must accommodate themselves. Both maintain that they have "the right to practice their culture; have little interest in giving it up; have oppositional cultures, so that adopting one may

4. Roediger, *Working Toward Whiteness*, 61.

5. *DBWE* 3:111–14.

6. Jennings, *Christian Imagination*, 58–59.

7. A similar development has taken place with respect to gender. Sarah Coakley discusses how the generic male was established as the imagined sexless individual human subject. Coakley, "Feminism," 601–6.

be seen as denying the other; have cultures that have been institutionalized through, among other things, separate denominations and congregations; and have centuries of racial wounds."[8]

This is not to say that Christians are unmindful of the racial divide. The lament of Martin Luther King Jr., that "the most segregated hour of Christian America is eleven o'clock on Sunday morning, the same hour when many are standing to sing, 'In Christ there is no East or West,'"[9] is recalled time and again, but seemingly to no avail. In comparison with virtually all other institutions, says Michael Budde, the church has done much worse with regard to race: "We're more segregated than the public schools, than residential neighborhoods, than places of employment, than the military, than almost any other social force outside the Ku Klux Klan." There is deep disagreement as to the extent and causes of, as well as remedies for, this destructive rift in the body politic of Christ, which the church continues to tolerate to both its worldly shame and divine judgment. White Christians tend to think that it is largely a thing of the past, and when it does recur it is typically characterized as a matter of an individual's attitude or ignorance, whereas black Christians regard it as a living reality that is entrenched in the moral economy of America. Budde contends that racism functions as a permanent component in the stability of the nation. This will be a very difficult proposition for many, perhaps most, Americans to accept, because a racial equality syndrome that counsels us to "stay the course" has mesmerized us in spite of the chasm that separates blacks and whites.[10]

As I noted previously, one of the primary theological tasks of the church is to help a fallen world take its bearings here in the middle of things, in order to understand something of what went before, the ways things unfolded in the past that brought us to the place we are now. Instead of asking where to begin the work of theology, says Jennings, it is more appropriate to first ask a different set of questions: How did we get here, and how do we go on and go further? More concretely, how did we get to the point where humankind has been differentiated according to race? He gives a poignant response: "The here is outside Israel, outside the conversation between biblical Israel and its God, outside the continuing conversations living Israel has with the same God." This social location outside the historic life and ongoing struggles of the chosen people has proven to be disastrous for Christian existence, for that existence is finally unintelligible apart from

8. Emerson and Woo, *People of the Dream*, 139. David Anderson refers to these cultures as the "bookends" of life, with all other groups located somewhere in between, closer to one end or the other. D. Anderson, *Multicultural Ministry*, 18.

9. King, *Stride Toward Freedom*, 207.

10. Budde, *Borders of Baptism*, 113.

Israel as the *space* within which Christians can truthfully represent our *place* within the constitution of the people of God. Moreover, says Jennings, only when the church comes to terms with its Gentile existence in relation both to biblical Israel and to the Jewish people who comprise living Israel will the distortions of racial existence and thought both outside of and within the church's communion come more clearly into view.[11]

The questions of how the church has been formed in the past and how it needs to be formed now and for the future are high among Bonhoeffer's concerns in *Letters and Papers from Prison*. As we have seen in his critique of the concepts of religion and culture, he locates the sense and practical effect of these questions within a genealogical description. To address the historical connections between formation, supersessionism, and race in my constructive reading of Bonhoeffer, however, requires that I go on and go further with regard to the questions he raises and the descriptions and analyses he puts forward, for though he has significant things to say on these topics, he does not provide anything like a detailed analysis, certainly nothing like his assessments of religion or even of culture.

Bonhoeffer's distinctive contribution to the topic of race will become more evident in the next chapter, as I attend to the theological linkage between racial reasoning, supersessionism, and the interpretation of scripture. He accords a crucial role to the Old Testament in the formation of a profound this-worldliness that pertains to the questions of supersessionism and racial existence and reasoning. Before taking up this biblical hermeneutic in detail, however, I must first chart the ways that race joins with religion and culture as a technological instrument employed first by the colonial powers of Europe, and then in the United States, South Africa, and other locales, to describe and manage difference.

As with religion and culture, race is not only an unbiblical notion, it is also a theological misconception that has done incalculable damage to the worldliness of Christ that is to take form in the church. That said, a word of caution is in order. Though supersessionism and racism are inextricably connected, the precise ways in which they are linked must be parsed carefully. The use of racial imagining and reasoning in and by a world come of age was, to borrow an expression of Bonhoeffer, a historically conditioned and transitory form of human expression, as evidenced by the fact that for centuries in the life of the church it simply did not exist. Racial existence and reasoning is an utter distortion of human life, the catalyst for which was a form of supersessionism, a conceptually and historically complex phenomenon that evolved over time.

11. Jennings, *Christian Imagination*, 251–52.

Race and Supersessionism in Bonhoeffer's Writings

It is during his time at Union Theological Seminary in 1930 and 1931 that Bonhoeffer first encounters the racial division of America, not just in New York but also in the South and Southwest. A poem by Countee Cullen, a preeminent figure of the Harlem Renaissance, becomes emblematic of the damage done by and to the church in America. In "Essay about Protestantism in the United States," which he pens upon his return from a second trip to New York in 1939, Bonhoeffer writes, "The fact that today the 'black Christ' of a young Negro poet is pitted against the 'white Christ' reveals a destructive rift [*Zerstörung*] within the church of Jesus Christ."[12] Though he acknowledges that there were many white Christians working to improve relations between the races, and a growing recognition on the part of leaders in the black church of the serious problems before it, "today the general picture of the church in the United States is still one of racial fragmentation. Blacks and whites come separately to word and sacrament. They have no common worship."[13]

During his first visit to New York, writes Reggie Williams, Bonhoeffer comes to share the disdain that his new friends in Harlem held for the injustices suffered by African-Americans, and endorses their demands for the dignity that ought to be accorded to every human being. Here finally he encounters in the "New World" a form of Christianity that had not compromised with the racialized constitution of what counted as civilized society.[14] He also discovers an encounter with Jesus at odds with the Christ of white liberals who preached about virtually everything except "the gospel of Jesus Christ, the cross, sin and forgiveness, death and life." In place of this message, says Bonhoeffer, there is an "ethics and social idealism borne by a faith in progress that—who knows how—claims the right to call itself 'Christian.'"[15] When he returns his native Germany, says Williams, Bonhoeffer recognizes and translates his experience of whiteness in New York "as the National Socialist references to *die Herrenvolk*, the master race."[16]

---

12. Cullen, "The Black Christ."

13. *DBWE* 15:456–57.

14. R. L. Williams, *Bonhoeffer's Black Jesus*, 24.

15. *DBWE* 10:313. Bonhoeffer writes in a letter to Max Diestel that sermons in white America had been reduced to parenthetical remarks about newspaper events, and that he had heard only one sermon that contained a genuine proclamation, "and that was delivered by a Negro (indeed, in general I'm increasingly discovering greater religious power and originality in Negroes)." *DBWE* 10:266.

16. R. L. Williams, *Bonhoeffer's Black Jesus*, 24.

Together with his friendships with Jean Lasserre and others at Union Seminary, Bonhoeffer's time in Harlem contributes to what Bethge describes as "a momentous change" in his life.[17] Bonhoeffer characterizes his theological work prior to this time as unchristian and lacking in humility, driven principally by ambition. In a letter to Elisabeth Zinn he writes,

> I had often preached, I had seen a great deal of the church, had spoken and written about it—and yet I was not yet a Christian but rather in an utterly wild and uncontrolled fashion my own master. I do know that at the time I turned the cause of Jesus Christ into an advantage for myself, for my crazy vanity. I pray to God that will never happen again. Nor had I ever prayed, or had done so only very rarely.

It was during this difficult and lonely period that he first came to the Bible, stating that the Sermon on the Mount in particular liberated him from his self-satisfied smugness. "Since then," he writes, "everything has changed. I have felt this plainly and so have other people around me."[18]

Though his thoughts about his time in New York are powerful and demanding of consideration, Bonhoeffer's analysis of the concept of race is less detailed than his assessments of religion and culture. Part of the reason for this is that it had a somewhat different, though no less pernicious, range of meanings in Germany during the first third of the twentieth century than it had in the American setting, because skin color was not always a determining factor.[19] In "The Church and the Jewish Question," Bonhoeffer uses it at one point to refer to a group of human beings who share a line of descent. He adds that, when considered from a theological standpoint, Judaism is not a racial but a religious category. He goes on to distinguish between Jewish Christians and Gentile Christians by saying that all who see their participation in the church as determined by their observance of a divine law are a type of Jewish Christian, "regardless of whether they actually belong to the Jewish race or not." And in *Ethics* he states that the German pre-Christian ethnic past remains with the German people "by nature, as a species or, if one will, a race."[20] As Raymond Williams points out, when the

17. Bethge, *Dietrich Bonhoeffer*, 203.

18. *DBWE* 14:134.

19. We should not overstate the difference, because racial reasoning in Germany took in skin color when it was a factor. David Olusoga and Casper Erichsen have chronicled Germany's African colonial connection to racism that set the stage for the later atrocities against Jews and others during World War II. Olusoga and Erichsen, *Kaiser's Holocaust*.

20. *DBWE* 12:368–69; *DBWE* 6:109. In early drafts of the Bethel Confession Bonhoeffer speaks of "the origin of the human race in a common ancestor," in explicit rejection of Nazi racist ideology. *DBWE* 12:388.

concept of race is used, not just alongside *genus* and *species* in classificatory biology, but to differentiate a group within the human species for special consideration, the difficulties begin, and we can see here Bonhoeffer struggling with the terminology in use at the time.[21]

The notion of race, *Rasse*, during the first half of the twentieth century was closely paired with the concept of *Volk*, the (German) people. The racial purity of the *Volk*, as defined over against the corruption that was supposedly introduced into it by the presence of Jews, was a relatively new development. Moshe Zimmermann argues that the centuries-old anti-Semitism in Germany, which had been grounded principally in the difference of religion, was replaced by a racialized conception only in the second half of the nineteenth century. Zimmermann credits this momentous shift in part to *The Victory of Jewdom over Germandom Viewed from a Non-Confessional Standpoint*, an anti-Semitic pamphlet written by an obscure author named Wilhelm Marr. The impetus for this reconception evidently came from theories first proposed by the French racial theorist Joseph Arthur de Gobineau, and Marr took up this viewpoint to argue that the fundamental contrast was not that between Jews and Christians but between the two races: Jewish and German.[22] Michel Legaspi, drawing on the work of Jonathan Hess and Anna-Ruth Löwenbrück, pushes the time of racial reasoning's appearance back to the eighteenth century, contending that the racial contrast between Jews and Germans and not between Jews and Christians can be found in the writings of Hebraist and philologist Johann David Michaelis.[23]

With respect to supersessionism, Bonhoeffer explicitly deals with the topic in only one essay, again in "The Church and the Jewish Question" (an intriguing coincidence), and it is uncertain what to make of what we find there.[24] According to the text as it appeared in print, he seems to perpetuate the supersessionist claim that the Jewish people were cursed for having "hung the Redeemer of the world on the cross," and that their suffering will come to an end only with Israel's conversion to Christ.[25] I say "seems to" because there is material in the published version, including the offending paragraph, that does not appear in any of the drafts we have from Bonhoeffer's own papers. In addition, the style of that material does not fit well with the way he normally writes. The published essay, for example, begins and

21. R. Williams, *Keywords*, 248.

22. "It should be added that Marr, in his 1879 writings, consciously used the terms 'Judaism' and 'Germanism' as main terms." Zimmermann, *Wilhelm Marr*, 89; cf. Evans, *Coming of the Third Reich*, 27–28; Scholder, *Churches and the Third Reich*, 1:74–98.

23. Legaspi, *Death of Scripture*, 98.

24. See Barnett, "Dietrich Bonhoeffer's Relevance," 58–60.

25. *DBWE* 12:367.

ends with long quotes from Martin Luther, a stylistic trait that Bonhoeffer does not typically employ. Finally, nowhere else in the Bonhoeffer corpus do we find him voicing these sentiments. Larry Rasmussen rightly concludes that at present it is not possible to reconstruct the history of the published essay, to determine whether or not Bonhoeffer made these changes.[26]

Race and Displacement in a World Come of Age

Racial being and reasoning are intrinsic components of the world's celebrated coming of age, woven deeply into the fabric of society that now blankets virtually the entire globe, such that virtually no woman, man, or child escapes from its effects (though a disproportionate percentage of the world's population suffers inordinately from them). In close coordination with the concepts of religion and culture, racial being and reasoning constituted to a significant degree the technological organization of the world's vaunted coming of age, and they continue to do so in ways that elude the church's attention. Indeed, unless and until the church recognizes the interpenetration of racial being and the social grammar of a world come of age as a matter of dogmatic theology, Christians will not rightly understand either phenomenon.

One of the primary reasons for the obduracy of racial existence and reasoning, writes Jennings, is that they are the result, not just of the alteration of how we perceive human bodies, but of their displacement from their organic ties with particular places during the colonial and industrial eras, and their relocation within a very different economy. With the initial movements of colonialism and the beginnings of the slave trade, social identity for Europeans, Africans, Asians, and the indigenous peoples of the Americas was wrenched free from these indices (though again in disproportionate ways), leading to the intertwining of racial imagining with the logic of emerging capitalist markets. With the loss of the land (a category that embraces differences of topography, flora and fauna) as the decisive indicator of identity, racial designations came to constitute compelling grounds on which to identify corporate agency.[27]

---

26. *DBWE* 12:361 n. 1. Andreas Pangritz calls our attention to the ambiguities in this essay, noting that though Bonhoeffer rejects racial antisemitism, "his 'religious' concept of Jews and Jewish Christians is molded by the theological anti-Judaism lurking in the Lutheran confrontation of 'law' and 'gospel.' It implies a defamation of Judaism because of its alleged clinging to the 'law.'" Pangritz, "'To Fall within the Spokes,'" 102.

27. Jennings, *Christian Imagination*, 63.

A racial hermeneutic was first imagined in the fifteenth century in connection with colonial exploration and expansion, and subsequently realized in exemplary fashion in America (though by no means is the United States the only place in the world where the debilitating effects of racialized discourse and conduct are found).[28] Jennings puts the initial impulse succinctly: "Europeans enacted racial agency as a theologically articulated way of understanding their bodies in relation to new spaces and new peoples and to their new power over those spaces and peoples."[29] Much like the way the concept of culture was invented in the "Old World" to cope with the manifold changes in the conditions of common life in liberal industrial society, race became an operative category (working in concert with religion and culture) for the colonial powers dealing with new and strange peoples and lands.

The classification and assessment of the human world in racial categories, according to Jennings, took place in two related movements or processes, the first of which was displacement, which moved in two directions simultaneously. One of these directions was conceptual, crafting habits of mind that compared differences between peoples according to a racial and aesthetic scale that was ordered in a hierarchical ranking. For example, Alessandro Valignano, a sixteenth-century Jesuit, characterizes Africans as unintelligent, lacking culture, given to mean appetites, without an aptitude for self-governance, and thus born to serve. He devises in this regard a scale that places Japanese, Chinese, and Indians nearer the (white) top, and Jews and Muslims toward the (black) bottom.[30]

The penchant for creating hierarchical scales based on racial phenotypes was not limited to the Iberian Peninsula at the end of the Middle Ages. Immanuel Kant, in an essay titled "Of the Different Human Races," states that if we are to account for all the enduring distinctions in the human genus we must posit four distinct races: white, Negro, Hun (Mongol or Kalmuck), and Hindu (Hindustani). He eventually reduces this typology down to two base races: Negroes and whites.[31] As J. Kameron Carter notes, Kant locates all racial distinctions on a continuum between these two base races.[32] Kant then suggests the distinctions between the various races might be attributed to conditions in the different regions of the world in which they are found

---

28. I have taken this way of putting the matter from the subtitle to a book by Commager, *Empire of Reason*.

29. Jennings, *Christian Imagination*, 58.

30. Ibid., 79, 34–36.

31. Kant, "Of the Different Human Races," 11–12.

32. Carter, *Race*, 84.

(the most favorable being the zone between thirty-one and fifty-two degrees latitude), which causes certain characteristics to blossom and impedes others. It is in this zone (which in Kant's opinion deserves the name of Old World, i.e., Europe) where the greatest riches of earth are found, "and . . . also where human beings must diverge least from their original form, since the human beings living in this region were already well prepared to be transplanted into every other region of the earth." It is in this region we find "white, indeed, brunette inhabitants," and therefore we can safely conclude that "this form is that of the lineal root genus." All other races derive from this first race.[33]

Standing in the background of these "pigmentocracies," says Jennings, was a habit in the late Middle Ages on the part of the Spanish and Portuguese, who were obsessed with purity of blood with respect to converted Jews and Muslims. The perceived threat was that these *conversos* and *Moriscos* might return to Judaism and Islam, or even more worrisome, that they had secretly remained Jews and Muslims but were now "lodged deep in the Christian body," and thus in a position to "infect" the *corpus christianum*. This suspicion led many to doubt that these Jewish converts and Christian Moors were capable of the ministry, priestly orders, and ecclesiastical leadership (excluding Jews from church ministry was one of the first steps taken against them by pro-Nazi church synods in the fall of 1933[34]). It therefore seemed "natural" to extend this mode of differentiating between peoples to the heretofore unknown groups in Africa and elsewhere.[35]

The emerging racial aesthetic, which located bodies on a comparative scale ranging from white on one end to black on the other (with all others somewhere in between), was initially a theological operation that cannot be separated from the ambiguous legacy of Christendom. Long before secular anthropologists and ethnographers came along to develop it in more "rational" ways, theologians and court officials trained in theology, working in collaboration with imperial explorers and rulers, devised these aesthetic classifications in conjunction with their colonial exploits. The world of the church had for centuries been coextensive with that of the colonial powers, working in and through them to achieve its mission. Though the church was not in control of the situation by any means, it carried out its ministries and missions inside the social nexus created by these worldly powers—and did so willingly, even enthusiastically. Clerics provided temporal powers with a theological framework that designated them as the proper

---

33. Kant, "Of the Different Human Races," 19–20.

34. Cf. Bethge, *Dietrich Bonhoeffer*, 304–7.

35. Jennings, *Christian Imagination*, 79, 33–34.

subject of strategic choice and action in relation to the indigenous peoples they encountered in the course of their colonial expeditions. These powers thus saw themselves ordained to enact providential transitions on lands and peoples, imitating the creative power of God,[36] thus reprising the *sicut deus*, the desire of fallen humanity to be like God in its knowing and doing.

This theological operation has to do with the ability a particular group possesses to use, or in this case to abuse, the basic grammar of the church. Jennings contends, for example, that in the case of José de Acosta Porres, a Jesuit theologian of the sixteenth century who was sent from Spain to South America, the creedal substance of the classical doctrine of creation was not altered, but the way in which its logic would be performed was. In his efforts to shore up the authority of the Christian tradition in light of the new geographic discoveries, Acosta made key adjustments to Old World theories regarding the created order, discerning the providential hand of God in the way the Spanish were drawn to the "New World" through the technological advances (e.g., the compass) that made regular travel between continents possible, and the rich silver and mercury mines that made it economically desirable on the part of the temporal powers. Acosta also gave an account of the Andean peoples that afforded no place for their own self-understanding, but which located them firmly in the Christian history of salvation. "Acosta opened up a new performance of the doctrine of creation," writes Jennings, "and paved the way for the enfolding of theology inside racialized existence, inside whiteness."[37]

Mercantile and theological interests thus converged on Africa, Asia, and the Americas, giving birth to the concept of perpetual slavery and the resituating of indigenous bodies in their proper place, which was in relation to white bodies and modes of life. The evaluation of these new and strange peoples and lands, together with their inherited ways of life, their "cultures," were thus incorporated in the new economy of worldly power. Racial assessment becomes the means by which the Christian tradition must be articulated in the "New World," a social necessity dictated by the appetites of the colonial powers for gold, silver, sugar, and other sundries. The work of forming productive workers for the mines and fields thus merged seamlessly with the process of forming Christian hearts and minds.[38]

The second movement of displacement was material in character, as Europeans intruded upon new lands for exploration and development. In west Africa, much of the local population was either captured and sent

36. Ibid., 37, 60.
37. Ibid., 85, 90.
38. Ibid., 37, 107.

across the sea in slave ships or driven from their ancestral lands into the interior of the continent. The white sailors working the slave ships were taken principally from the most destitute classes, representing "an international and cosmopolitan group of impoverished laborers."[39] European and African bodies were thereby joined together in an asymmetrical arrangement within radically reconfigured space,[40] a process that was repeated in somewhat different forms on the Asian and American continents as well. A new reality for non-European flesh was thus created; tribal, dynastic, linguistic, and geographic coordinates that once determined social identity were erased, or at the very least occluded from view. Ecclesiastical and temporal powers conferred on themselves a godlike authority to reshape landscapes and peoples: "Church and realm . . . stand between peoples and lands and determine a new relationship between them, dislodging particular identities from particular places."[41]

As a result of conceptual and material displacement, whiteness became the principal concept in terms of which non-European bodies and their lands were understood, denoting refinement, civilization, a "just like us" designation. Whiteness as a performative description not only joined black to white flesh in distorted ways, but it also decoupled all flesh, regardless of pigmentation, from its connection with specific places on earth. Whiteness thus accurately names the "racial transcendental" that "alters reality, blowing by and through the specifics of identity bound to land, space, and place and narrating a new world that binds bodies to unrelenting aesthetic judgments. The European himself is the key to this theological act of displacement."[42]

In their formulation of racial existence to account for and contain the diversity and sociality of these new places and peoples, theologians made effective use of the modern concept of religion. According to Jennings, Acosta not only located the rites and customs of the Andean peoples within a Christian narrative (which, as Jennings says, is not problematic in and of itself) but also declared that they were both inferior and demonic: "The devil in his arrogance, and in competition with God, has taken over the things that God in his wisdom has ordained for his cult and honor, and for man's good and his salvation." Acosta finds virtually nothing but idolatry in Andean rites, which must therefore be rooted out completely.[43]

39. Ibid., 174.
40. Ibid., 37.
41. Ibid., 29.
42. Ibid., 30–31.
43. Ibid., 95, 98–99.

There were dissenting voices, to be sure, but not many. Bartolomé de las Casas, using natural law doctrines, recognizes a much greater degree of coherence and integrity in these practices.[44] Las Casas contends that all nations have at least some knowledge of God, however confused it might be; that "men are led to worship according to their capacities and in their own ways"; that "there is no better way to worship God than by sacrifice, which is the principal act of *latria*, which is owed to God alone"; and that though the act of sacrifice is mandated by natural law, what is to be offered is according to human law.[45] Though his approach to the rites, beliefs, and customs of the Indians does not solve many of the problems of whiteness, says Jennings, "Las Casas is able to grant conceptual space for native religious practices precisely on the ground of a Christian vision of creation in which such visions have their own integrity," without evacuating the substance of its theological claims.[46]

The comparativist hermeneutic that demonizes indigenous practices undergoes considerable refinement in the eighteenth and nineteenth centuries, but it was still tied to the colonialist project that separates human identity from particular forms of life. The new conceptual instruments of the Enlightenment allowed the comparison of the rites and customs of many different peoples in multiple colonialist sites. The procedures used to make these comparisons, however, were no longer undertaken from a theological standpoint, but according to ethnological taxonomies being developed at the time by the more "enlightened" thinkers of a world come of age. The ways of native peoples were no longer summarily dismissed as demonic, but employed as indicators of racial character and of civilization and cultural development.[47]

These refinements in the comparativist hermeneutic occurred in concert with control of land. In an important study of colonialism and comparative religion in southern Africa, David Chidester contends that when possession of the land was being violently contested the indigenous tribes of that region were said to lack any genuine religious sensibility and to be mired in irredeemable superstition. The archbishop of Dublin, Richard Whately, for example, says of the Xhosa in 1854 that "all savages are degenerated remnants of more civilized races."[48] Peoples who lack a true religious system

44. Ibid., 100–101.

45. Casas, *In Defense of the Indians*, 229.

46. Jennings, *Christian Imagination*, 101; cf. Gutiérrez, *Las Casas*.

47. Jennings, *Christian Imagination*, 133–34.

48. Richard Whately, "On the Origin of Civilisation," cited by Chidester, *Savage Systems*, 94.

do not possess the basics of civilization, with all that implies. Adopted as a strategy both by missionaries and by white settlers, the reasoning behind this way of putting matters was simple: if the indigenes lacked legitimate religion, they also lacked any recognizable claim to the land.[49]

A similar process had taken place in North America. John Winthrop, governor of the Massachusetts Bay Colony off and on from 1629 to 1649, states in a letter to his associate and successor John Endecott that the indigenous peoples had no defensible claim to the land: "That which is common to all is proper to none. This savage people ruleth over many lands without title or property; for they inclose no ground, neither have they cattell to maintayne it, but remove their dwellings as they have occasion, or as they can prevail against their neighbours. And why may not Christians have liberty to go and dwell amongst them in their waste lands and woods . . . as lawfully as Abraham did among the Sodomites?"[50] Winthrop also implies that God desired that the colonists take possession of the land, as large numbers of the local peoples were dying of disease, leaving them free to inhabit the land at their leisure. In a letter to Roger Williams, who defended the land rights of the native peoples against English expropriation, Winthrop writes, "If we had no right to this lande, yet our God hathe right to it, and if he be pleased to give it to us (takinge it from a people who had so long usurped upon him, and abused his Creatures) who shall control him or his termes?"[51]

Similar measures were later taken on the Great Plains of North America, as the horse tribes that roamed the area were forced onto reservations where they had to adopt ways of life antithetical to their nomadic ways. The buffalo were hunted to the point of extinction as a government policy in order to deprive the Comanches and other tribes of their primary means of subsistence and drive them off lands earmarked for white settlers. "There is no such thing as a horse Indian without a buffalo herd," writes S. C. Gwynne. "Such an Indian had no identity at all." The decimation of these peoples' food supply by the buffalo hunters was no accident; rather, "it was a deliberate political act." To ensure that these policies succeeded, the government of the United States sent the federal army, flush from its victory over the Confederate States, to take on these tribes with the weapons of modern warfare, and then to hound the scattered holdouts until they too

49. Chidester, *Savage Systems*, 94.

50. John Winthrop, "General Considerations for the Plantations in New England, with an Answer to Several Objections," cited by Freeman, "Alterity and Its Cure," 425, original spelling.

51. *Winthrop Papers*, 3:149, cited by Freeman, "Alterity and Its Cure," 425, original spelling.

were eliminated or driven onto reservations.[52] White farmers replaced these peoples of the High Plains, digging up the ground and removing the buffalo grass that for millennia had held the soil in place. The terrible years of the Dust Bowl were the result.[53]

Once control of the land in Africa was secured by European military power, white perceptions of indigenous religion changed virtually overnight. As soon as the Zulus were no longer able to resist European intrusions militarily, their "religion" gained recognition. "Contained and controlled under colonial administration," writes Chidester, "the Zulu had a religion." The Xhosa, by contrast, were still waging a losing war, and thus for a time were distinguished from the Zulu.[54] Jennings draws the appropriate conclusion: "Religion became a signifier within the loss of land control. Religion as a signifier for African identity grew in direct proportion to African alienation from their land, so that by the beginning of the twentieth century African life in Natal reflected a long history of geographic displacement and loss."[55]

The rites and customs of southern Africans were thus cast in a more positive light, but these refinements continued to function within the modern technologies of religion and culture, and only after the indigenes had been displaced from their traditional lands. These new ways of viewing indigenous peoples allowed missionaries to soften or reject older sentiments that unequivocally put those who died without Christian faith in hell undergoing eternal punishment. Europeans in colonialist settings, in an exercise of hubris, usurp divine prerogative by assigning to themselves decisions of eternal significance. It is a specifically colonialist hubris, concealed in theological formulas about the relationship between sin, damnation, and eternal punishment.[56]

Advocates of this new vision replace this hubristic conceit with a judgment that, again in keeping with the ironic logic informing the myth of a world come of age, cannot escape the same imperialist presumptions. John Colenso, an Anglican bishop assigned to South Africa in 1854, contends that all peoples have within them a revelation sufficient for their forgiveness and redemption. Colenso levels all peoples by positing a universal religious experience in the tradition of Schleiermacher, allowing him to discern a theological sameness in all people: "All people operate in the moral and spiritual light they have been given. Punishment is calibrated by their moral failure

---

52. Gwynne, *Empire of the Summer Moon*, 139, 260, 262.

53. Egan, *Worst Hard Time*.

54. Chidester, *Savage Systems*, 124.

55. Jennings, *Christian Imagination*, 135.

56. Ibid., 143.

or integrity in operating in their inherent sense of sin or righteousness."[57] What Colenso has done is to naturalize and domesticate Christianity, allowing him, as so many nineteenth-century theologians had done, to reconfigure it to serve as the grammatical structure of what counted as legitimate religious experience within the colonial economy.

Colenso accomplishes this feat, says Jennings, by rewriting salvation history as the history of religious consciousness. The missionary hubris shown by previous generations was actually an impediment to the proper cultivation of that consciousness and its possible (though not necessary) movement toward Christianity. Colenso thus makes religious experience the given within which all peoples operate: "In Colenso's hands, the message of the gospel becomes one of acceptance and awareness: acceptance of the gracious gift of God's righteousness and awareness of God's fatherly love, ultimately revealed in Jesus."[58] Though he offers an exquisite portrait of divine love, Colenso evacuates Christian identity of substantial content. Jewish, Christian, Zulu—all theological identity is essentially the same, consisting of "an internalized struggle of the religious consciousness to hear the word of love and acceptance from God the Creator-Father and his son, Jesus, and to follow the dictates of the moral universal inherent in all people."[59]

What looks initially like a decisively anti-racist, anti-ethnocentric vision of the Christian faith turns out to be intensely imperialist, as Colenso's universalism undermines all forms of social identity save that of the colonialist. Jennings acknowledges that this interpretation seems counterintuitive, particularly in light of his efforts to overcome misperceptions about the Zulus and a desire to build Christian civilization in South Africa on top of existing native conceptions and practices—for example, the exchange of property or cattle as part of arranged marriages, and the institution of polygamy. Nevertheless, his embrace of particularity is misleading, because he already knows what constitutes the telos of this universal religious consciousness, which Jeff Guy identifies with the "Christian way of life" as perceived by the Victorian middle class:

> The purpose of his mission was to produce the scrubbed, well-dressed, properly trained African family, living in a square house, separated from other households, faithful to the precepts of individualism, hard work and the Bible, the husband selling

57. Ibid., 143–44.

58. Colenso's description of the gospel bears an uncanny resemblance to Adolf von Harnack's summation of the teaching of Jesus: (1) the kingdom of God and its coming; (2) God the Father and the infinite value of the human soul; and (3) the higher righteousness and the commandment of love. Harnack, *What Is Christianity?*, 51.

59. Jennings, *Christian Imagination*, 145.

his labour, spending his income wisely, and thereby advancing the economic progress of the colony and his own social status, his wife in the home, his daughters in service, and his sons in training and preparing to marry monogamously, to reinforce and repeat the process.[60]

Once again what is touted as a form of liberation turns out to be a mode of social discipline.

Colenso's universalism is but the flip side of his colonialism, specifically, the ability to universalize the earth, to free it from the strictures of particular ways of life that had formed in geographically specific locales. The particularities of African peoples are resolved, says Jennings, virtually without remainder, into signposts for progress on the path of religious and cultural development, with an enlightened, domesticated Christianity as the normative pattern of religious consciousness, a design that reduces all other identities to a sublime futility. At the same time Colenso also deprives Christianity of its particularity. He speaks eloquently, for example, of Jesus' humanity as the ground of redemption, but then makes that ground merely symbolic, that is, no more than the bearer of the message about the Father's love for all peoples, a message whose content is derived from the *ethos* that informs this new economy of life. Faithful to his Enlightenment sensibilities, Colenso's universalism did not deny cultural particularity altogether, but it did deny that it mattered theologically, instead allowing it only an illustrative utility carefully contained within the colonialist project.[61]

In addition to making fruitful use of the modern concept of religion, the fabrication of racial being also develops in close coordination with the invention of culture—in the sense of an ethos or *habitus*, a set of practices and institutions whose end is the formation of a certain type of character—as an organizing and regulating technology. There is a deeply Christian impulse at work here, says Jennings, for Christianity is a teaching faith, obedient to the mandate to make disciples of all the earth. In the "New World," however, this impulse is subsumed into the colonialist logic. In Africa, Asia, and the Americas the level of morality and civilization was measured by the degree to which indigenes supported white interests, accepted European habits and sentiments, and willingly handed over land and labor to colonialist enterprises.[62]

To cite him again as an example (though he is far from being exceptional), Acosta divides the diversity of "barbarians" encountered in the "New

60. Guy, *Heretic*, 81.

61. Jennings, *Christian Imagination*, 146–47.

62. Ibid., 104–7.

World" into three classes. The first, which he regards as the most civilized and developed—the Chinese, the Japanese, and the peoples of eastern India—are those who have stable cities and governments, bureaucracies, commerce, and a knowledge of letters. These should be converted by persuasion and reason, not by force of arms. The second group—primarily Mexicans and Peruvians—lacks complex systems of writings, philosophy and civil wisdom but does display established forms of government, with leaders, custom, law, and a measure of social order. This class has innate abilities, seen in their simple writing and accounting skills, that can be cultivated, but illicit customs, rites, and rituals overshadow their common life. Once under the governance of Christian magistrates, however, they should be able to make progress in the Christian faith. The third class of barbarians resemble wild animals, hunting and gathering in packs and lacking all semblance of government or writing, with laws and customs that are childish and laughable. There are many such peoples in the "New World," and they may be dominated by force: "Since they are docile they may be 'attracted through flattery', and if that fails, then they must be constrained by force 'to enter the Kingdom of Heaven.'"[63] (It is interesting to note that Acosta's tripartite scheme divides peoples according to Plato's three parts of the soul—rational, spirited, and appetitive.[64])

The displacement of identity is not limited in its effect to human bodies but also organizes in new ways the lands of colonial conquest as well. Local sense and sensibility about land, derived from the interactions between humans and particular places, gives way to an imaginative vision that sees it as raw, untamed, but full of potential that the "natives" did not adequately understand, develop, or use to its full and proper extent. Jennings writes, "Everything—from peoples and their bodies to plants and animals, from the ground and the sky—was subject to change, subjects for change, subjected to change. The earth itself was barred from being a constant signifier of identity. Europeans defined Africans and all others apart from the earth even as they separated them from their lands."[65]

The organization of time is also caught up in the processes of racial displacement. The Christian history of salvation, subsumed within evolutionary metanarratives, is transformed into an immanent, observable reality of progress. The very designation of "primitive peoples" is a temporal concept devised by European thought to position them in relation to "modern" or "advanced" (i.e., white) civilization. Difference is thus imagined spatially,

63. Ibid., 102–3.

64. Plato, *Republic*, 436a.

65. Jennings, *Christian Imagination*, 43.

as a type of distance that the purveyors of progress need to overcome,[66] in order to render it allochronic, "belonging to a different time, and surviving into the present on false pretences," destined for extinction.[67] No group is more subject to this sort of scrutiny than the Jews, who were seen by Michaelis as "depraved and corrupt" in comparison to their ancestors the Hebrews, whom he describes as noble and inventive.[68]

The shared or coeval time of these "primitives" is thus problematized in favor of an ordering of time that permits the distancing of the observed peoples from the time of the observer. The purpose of this reordering of time is to show that "natural laws or law like regulations operate in the development of a human society and culture."[69] Peoples who do not participate in the progressive time of a world come of age, such as the Ju/wasi in southern Africa, become a transparent cipher, such that "looking through them, one sees the Paleolithic,"[70] which is to say, one sees "our" past.

Biblical Translation and Racial Reasoning

As noted earlier, the classification and assessment of the human world in racial categories took place in two related movements or processes, the first of which was the displacement of bodies and land. A second movement in the development of racial existence and reasoning was connected to the work of translation, of the Bible in particular and "Christian civilization" more generally. Translating scripture into native dialects in conjunction with the colonialist project effectively served the aims of that project, which was to "translate" indigenous customs and practices so that they could be "re-placed" within the ways and means of a "cosmopolitan" (white) human society.

In the background of this work of translation was the ugly specter of supersessionism, which Jennings labels as the most decisive and central theological distortion that exists in the church, growing in power and extension with each new generation.[71] If we are to understand the precise nature of this process, we need to sketch out more precisely both its origins and the ways it has not only grown in power and extension with the passage of time but has mutated as well. George Lindbeck contends that there are at least

66. Fabian, *Time and the Other*, 146.
67. Bauman, *Postmodern Ethics*, 38.
68. As cited by Sheehan, *Enlightenment Bible*, 215.
69. Fabian, *Time and the Other*, cited by Jennings, *Christian Imagination*, 46.
70. Jennings, *Christian Imagination*, 47.
71. Ibid., 32.

two distinct patterns of Christian supersessionism. In the older and more familiar type, dating back to the post-New Testament period, the church expropriates Israel's place as God's chosen people. The Christian community alone wears the mantle of "Israel," and the Old Testament promises and prophecies are fulfilled not only in Jesus (a conviction that Lindbeck rightly asserts is foundational to a coherent Christian identity) but also in the church, such that it is now the "New Israel" and thus sole heir to the rights and privileges of Israel's heritage. Through a type of figural interpretation in which an intrinsic relation is posited between seemingly unrelated events that in actuality constitute concrete moments in the working out of the divine economy in history, the early church imagined a form of supersessionism that remained tightly linked both to concrete history and to the church as in some sense the chosen people of Israel.[72]

A second type of supersessionism began to emerge in the sixteenth century in connection with the debate over how and when the church was founded. Catholics uniformly cited Jesus' comment to Peter, "On this rock I will build my church" (Matt 16:18), whereas Protestants pointed to a variety of events—Jesus' baptism, Pentecost, the call of the apostles—as their candidate for the point of origin. Regardless of how one resolved this matter, writes Lindbeck, a profound shift in ecclesiology had occurred, as the competing conceptions of the church shared one characteristic: they were no longer connected in any substantial and historical way to the peoplehood of Israel. Whereas the early form of supersessionism retained a link to Israel, we now begin to see mutated forms that learned to do without this connection.[73]

Add to these ecclesial questions the theological innovations that came about beginning in the fifteenth century, which decisively shifted attention away from the church and Israel as bodies of people "to Judaism and Christianity conceived of as religions that individuals believed in and/or practiced."[74] These shifts of attention gave rise to the theologies of replacement, which do more than neglect the identity of the church as Israel; they discard it. Liturgies and hymnody may still refer to Israel, Jerusalem, and Zion, applying these and many other Old Testament images and types to the church, but they function as illustrative figures of speech that are devoid of the typological realism that the older form possessed. The concept of fulfillment continues to be promoted, writes Lindbeck, but with a radically different meaning, one that is directly tied to the modern concept of religion:

72. Lindbeck, "What of the Future?," 358–60.

73. Ibid., 360.

74. Ibid.

"Fulfillment is no longer conceptualized in terms of the biblical narratives of God keeping and confirming promises and prophecies to persons and groups, but in terms of the impersonal patterns and evolutionary progress according to which one religion provides the conditions for the emergence of a better and higher one. Fulfillment now applies to religion, not peoples."[75] In Colenso's missionary work, for example, Christianity, when refitted as a religion, serves as the proper schema for interpreting other religious rites and customs.

This second type of supersessionism typically employs a *figurative* approach to the Old Testament, positing an *illustrative* correlation between a literary representation and a logically independent conceptual meaning. The exodus, for example, is frequently cited as a figure or type for which Christian baptism is the fulfillment. In a figurative interpretation the significance of baptism is established apart from the connection with the event of the exodus, and it becomes the primary meaning of that event: "Logical independence means that one can state the meaning apart from the representation without loss; the representation is, at best, a useful but dispensable illustration."[76] Unlike figural interpretation, figurative exegesis replaces the literal sense with a meaning that has no substantive connection to the people of Israel, but to poetic, moral, or historical sentiments that gained favor in the eighteenth and nineteenth centuries.

The modern form of supersessionism, by severing any meaningful connection between the church and Israel, leaves Christians free to commandeer this link for their nation. Lindbeck lists the British, Dutch, Swedes, Poles, South African Boers, and Americans as examples of those who at one time or another have asserted that their country is the new "city set on a hill" (cf. Matt 5:14).[77] In the early decades of European colonization the performance of scripture as an organizing technology for describing and containing difference within the sociopolitical economy of the times was for the most part simply an extension of the earlier supersessionist hermeneutic that had permeated Christian thought for centuries. The explorers, traders, and conquistadors of Spain, Portugal, England, and other countries had been trained to think of themselves as the true Israel, allowing them to see the peoples of Africa, Asia, and the Americas as idolatrous pagans who, "though they knew God . . . did not honor him as God or give thanks to him, but they became futile in their thinking, and their senseless minds were darkened" (Rom 1:21). The Christian nation, self-consciously acting as the

---

75. Ibid.; cf. Novak, *Talking With Christians*, 11.

76. Dawson, *Christian Figural Reading*, 16, 86.

77. Lindbeck, "What of the Future?," 361.

"new" Israel, played a very special role in God's providence as the bearer of the true vision of God to innately inferior people.[78] Tied to a racialized scale of existence, whiteness became the organizing frame of reference for the interpretation of the Bible in the colonial setting.

The work of biblical translation that took place in conjunction with the advent of a world come of age could not have taken place apart from developments that produced what Jonathan Sheehan calls the Enlightenment Bible. These developments brought about a transformation in the way scripture functions, says Sheehan, especially in Protestant Germany and England. The Enlightenment Bible was produced by "a complex set of practices whose most sophisticated instruments were *scholarship*—philological, literary, and historical—and *translation*." Though the roots of this transformation reach back to the Protestant Reformation, which from the outset sought to put vernacular translations into the hands of the Christian peoples, its most influential impetus came later, in the eighteenth and nineteenth centuries, with the emergence of a wide range of scholarly instruments for textual work. "If the answer to the question, 'Why should I read the Bible?' was, before 1700, overwhelmingly 'because it reveals the means to your salvation,'" writes Sheehan, "by the middle of the eighteenth century, Protestant answers began to proliferate, jostle, and compete with the standard one. In a sense, the Enlightenment Bible *was* this series of alternative answers."[79]

Sheehan identifies four scholarly disciplines in particular that collaborated to push the reading of scripture beyond theology, initially not as an explicitly secularizing project, but in conjunction with a series of ecclesial movements such as German pietism, which sought "to remove the theological blinders that confessional commitment had put on the Protestant world as a whole." At issue was the authority of a biblical text that, thanks to the Reformation, had been deprived of tradition and magisterium, and the responses to this question were distributed across four modes of study: philology, pedagogy, poetry, and history. Each of these disciplines, in the guise of new vernacular translations, offered its own answer to the question of why one should read the Bible, producing in the process not a unified text but "a panoply of Bibles."[80]

The redistribution of the authority of the biblical text around these scholarly disciplines resulted in what Sheehan labels the cultural Bible, "the familiar sense that the Bible is part of 'our' Western civilization." The catalyst

78. Jennings, *Christian Imagination*, 90–98.

79. Sheehan, *Enlightenment Bible*, xii–xiii, Sheehan's emphasis.

80. Ibid., 84, 217.

for this development takes place in Germany in the form of a romanticist reaction to the changes brought about by the Industrial Revolution. The idea
was subsequently exported to England, and from there it made its way to
the United States.[81] Sheehan traces the origins of the cultural Bible to Martin Luther's vernacular translation, which over time transformed scripture
from its alien origins in ancient Israel into "an originally German book."
Luther had initiated the transformation of the Bible into a fully German
text, "wresting it from its Oriental trappings and giving it to the German
people as the cornerstone of their cultural heritage . . . the German Bible
simultaneously created a German religion, a German culture, and a German nation."[82] It was a religion, culture, and nation, moreover, for which the
Reformation was "the first vital expression,"[83] helping create a sense of *Volk*,
Kultur, and *Rasse* essentially unrelated to their birth in paganism and, most
especially, in opposition to Judaism.

Jennings is quick to point out the significance of this development in
connection with the concepts of supersessionism and race. In Germany and
England, the cultural Bible became the sacred text not of the church but of a
nation and people. The primary use of scripture was the cultivation of a distinctly German or English society, the "Ur-text of civilization." At the heart
of the creation of the cultural Bible was the removal of Judaism and the
Jewish people from any claim they might have on any construal of cultural
heritage and tradition that might undermine the perception of scripture as
Christian literature: "The presence of Jewish people was hermeneutically
sealed off from the vision of the Bible as a national treasure, as the cultural
expression of the national spirit, and, in the case of Germany, the German
soul."[84]

This "re-placement" of scripture within the heritage and ethos of the
German nation takes a sinister turn when it is invoked by proponents of
the German Christian Church Movement to link National Socialism to
the workings of divine providence. According to a statement of principles
formulated in Thüringen in 1934, there are two sources of revelation for
German Christians, the first being the Bible. Here the distinction between
Old and New Testament is telling. The New Testament is described in a
fairly conventional way as "the holy testament of the Savior, our Lord, and
of his Father's kingdom." The Old Testament, however, is characterized
as "an example of the divine education of a people," which clearly echoes

81. Ibid., 220.

82. Ibid., 226–27.

83. Strauss, *Life of Jesus*, 1:11.

84. Jennings, *Christian Imagination*, 137.

developments connected to the cultural Bible of the nineteenth century. The full effect of this shift becomes clear in a subsequent affirmation: "As He has for every people, the eternal God has also created a unique law for our people. It has taken form in the Führer Adolf Hitler and in the National Socialist State formed by him."[85]

This transformation in the sense and reference of scripture converges time and again with the displacement of place and space by the colonial powers. We can discern in the writings of Bishop Colenso the ways that the markings of his enlightened scholarship play against the transformation of space that had been wrought in southern Africa, first by the Dutch and then by the British. At the heart of Colenso's refinement of a white aesthetic is the extensive use of a type of figurative exegesis often employed within the modern form of supersessionist hermeneutic. He has the Jews in Paul's Epistle to the Romans stand in for the English Christian settlers, while the Zulu are the Gentiles/heathens. By reading salvation history into settler-Zulu relations this way, Colenso draws on these racialized identities in order to transcend them. The key move in the entire process is to make Jewish particularity of no consequence to God, for all peoples are related to the divine, not in connection to Israel but, as we have seen, by a common religious consciousness. By evacuating the substantial differences between nations and peoples by means of shared religious experience, his ostensive universalism is a creature of colonialist power that has freed the earth from the strictures of particular ways of life tied to specific places, and put in their place a form of life that replicates what counts for civilization in England. "Indeed," says Jennings, "Colenso's own vision of civilization grants to Britannia what he refuses Israel, namely, the refashioning of a people's way of life for theological reasons."[86]

Neither Enlightenment scholarship nor colonialist transformation of space is an explicit theme in Colenso's commentary on Romans, says Jennings, "yet each enables the other. Together they display the modern abandonment of place-centered identity, an abandonment rooted in a particular theological vision." The result is a highly refined version of the whiteness hermeneutic, as the identities of indigenous tribes are dislodged from centuries-old ways of existing in and with particular places and relocated on the horizon of a soteriological vision that takes in all peoples. The problem is not that the social identity is located on this horizon, but the racialization

---

85. "Richtlinien der Kirchenbewegung 'Deutsche Christen,'" my translation.

86. Jennings, *Christian Imagination*, 141.

of that soteriological vision "such that racial existence is enfolded inside the displacement operation and emerges as a parasite on theological identity."[87]

The irony here is that while Enlightenment universalism of the sort that Colenso advocates liberates indigenous peoples from overt imperialist operations, it binds them and their efforts to do theology in and for their time and place to another, more subtle yet equally insidious form, that of cultural nationalism. Guy notes the irony of Colenso's lifework as one who was "as unaware of his ideological function in the colonial system and the springs of African resistance to missionary endeavor, as the very men he criticised."[88] Christian identity and witness is thus made to serve a sociopolitical economy to which the same powers that colonized the "New World" also gave birth. This also reflects a form of supersessionism that effectively extracts the gospel from its Jewish roots and relocates it in forms that are distinctly ahistorical in nature. Cultural nationalism is one of the signature realities of a world come of age, a reprise of *Kulturprotestantismus* that carries with it distinctive racial, social, political, and economic markers that cannot be divorced from the violence of nation-states.[89]

Colenso was certainly not the first to make such a grant for the centrality of Great Britain in divine providence, for it can also be seen in the way hymn writer Isaac Watts renders the Psalter in English. Watts' stated aim is to arrange a version more useful for singing and to prepare the way for hymn singing. At the same time, however, he also embeds in his translation of the Psalms an explicit, pronounced nationalistic sentiment. Jennings cites psalm after psalm in which Watts replaces the names of Israel and Judah with that of Great Britain, Israelite and Judean kings with British monarchs, and some of the more troublesome passages with themes taken from the New Testament. What he accomplishes is to take supersessionist thinking one step further. Like Acosta, Winthrop, Colenso, and many others, he removes Israel from its role in salvation history and places Great Britain at the center of the biblical drama, but in so doing he also casts a comprehensive vision of the relation of his Christology to the British land and nation. The story of Israel becomes simply a model for how God relates to a nation.[90] As Rochelle Stackhouse observes, the words "English" or "British" occur with regularity in Watts' translation of the Psalter, "making David sing not only as a Christian, but as an Englishman."[91]

87. Ibid., 138.

88. Guy, *Heretic*, 80.

89. Jennings, *Christian Imagination*, 161.

90. Ibid., 210–13.

91. Stackhouse, "Hymnody and Politics," 46. According to Stackhouse, Watts

The result of the efforts of Colenso, Watts, and many others was to reconstitute Christian theology as an instrument of nationalistic utility, that is, as a catalyst for articulating and reinforcing the cultural and racial identity of the nation-state. In place of a theology that contributes to a genuine universalizing of the particularity of Jesus, a form of thought emerges that is instead "a resource for the reiteration of cultural identities." Though this nationalistic bent can and does show itself in any number of ways, writes Jennings, the final result is the same: an invitation for peoples to look inward in search of a theological reiteration of the collective self.[92]

This movement reappears, says Jennings, in the emphasis on translation in the work of such eminent scholars as Lamin Sanneh and Andrew Walls.[93] While Sanneh and Walls are justly concerned to overcome the cultural and colonial imperialism of the West, their translation projects are nonetheless carried out within colonialist modalities, and therefore unwittingly and ironically reproduce them. "By drawing the incarnation so tightly inside translation," writes Jennings, "they eclipse a deeper historical movement with its concomitant theological scandal. Christians are, through Jesus the Christ, brought into the story of Israel, which is indeed God's story. What is at stake is not simply particularity and certainly not the dialectic between the particular and the universal, but rather the scandal of particularity."[94] This scandal cannot be divorced in a kernel-and-husk fashion from the Jewish people.

According to Jennings, Sanneh and Walls, in different ways, have imbibed the newer form of supersessionism, and in the process overlook the abiding connection between cultural nationalism and ethnocentrism. At the heart of their projects is the same assumption that we saw in the invention of religion, namely, that Christianity names a genus within which the various Christian nationalisms form the different species. What each envisions is "a God quickly clothed in multiple discourses and thereby clothed in multiple conceptualities throughout the historical process," which makes it possible to nationalize theological formation.[95] In a well-intentioned effort to extricate racial reasoning from the life and thought of the church, they unwittingly sink its roots deeper in that social formation.

---

intended for his hymn texts to underscore the fragility of the existing order, but they have been consistently used for the opposite purpose. Stackhouse, "Hymnody and Politics," 52.

92. Jennings, *Christian Imagination*, 154.

93. See, for example, Sanneh, *Whose Religion Is Christianity?*, and Walls, *Missionary Movement*.

94. Jennings, *Christian Imagination*, 160.

95. Ibid., 159, 157.

Reimaging Gentile Existence and Race

Racism is not a curable aberration in America, says Derrick Bell, but an integral, permanent, and indestructible component of this society.[96] The theological strategies that are typically put forward for tending to this open wound, such as contextualized theologies, actually prolong the dilemma, Jennings notes, by assimilating Christian existence within the religious and cultural formation of national identities, segregated theological mentalities, and social grammars that perpetuate, often unwittingly, the same senses and sensibilities that initially gave rise to racial reasoning. In addition, practices such as the Christian rite of reconciliation, if undertaken apart from a fuller accounting of the historic deformities that continue to shape Christian life and thought in the present, also fall short. Unless and until the members of Christ's body politic come to terms with the complex interactions between the displacements and relocations of a world come of age and the advent of racial being and thought, "every attempt to destabilize racial identity, argue for a common humanity, and claim race as fiction, social construction, or essentialized nonsense will be superficial at best."[97]

The disfigurement of whiteness on the body of Christ will not be resolved, writes Budde, by what is contained in the white evangelical toolkit, with its blend of accountable freewill individualism, focus on interpersonal relations as the basis for understanding social reality, and abiding and deep-seated antistructuralism, all of which leaves the social economy and grammar of racial reasoning virtually intact. Neither will the church be saved from its own failure by public policy, the preferred strategy of the mainline denominations, for it has been more than fifty years since the landmark civil rights legislation was passed by Congress, and eleven o'clock on Sunday morning is still the most segregated hour in America. Finally, shifting demographics will not heal the festering wound. Given the pressures to aspire to "the middle class," it may well be that many Asians and at least some Latinos, like the Irish, Italians, and Finns before them, will prefer to identify with the social and political status of the older white majority.[98]

There is no way back to a time before a racialized world, and the way forward will be *difficult*, to put it mildly. If the church is to be that place in the world where the form of Christ takes form in the center of the human village, a process that cannot take place without the displacement of racial reasoning, says Budde, it will have to happen "with the tools and gifts

96. Bell, *Faces at the Bottom of the Well*, ix; cf. Budde, *Borders of Baptism*, 113.

97. Jennings, *Christian Imagination*, 9–10, 63.

98. Budde, *Borders of Baptism*, 120–21.

that God gives his Church." This brings us "finally and fully into the area of formation, of making disciples, of the practices and ways in which Christians come to internalize the affections, dispositions and desires of Christ in their own times and places."[99] Formation is a practice that is spiritual but not religious (or "spiritual"), social but not "cultural." Above all it is not sequestered away from the "real" world where people earn bread and struggle to pay their bills, raise their children and bury their loved ones, suffer under murderous tyrants and vote for members of the local school board. It must take place in the midst of a racialized world come of age, or it cannot take place at all.

The formative practices of a profound this-worldliness presuppose the ecclesial discipline of unselfing, "of being unmade to be remade,"[100] whereby the *sicut deus* is remade in the form of the *agnus dei* (Lamb of God), that is, in Christ.[101] The gift of being unmade and then remade is a task that we must undertake, involving God's interpellation of us, an interrogation of our entire way of life. We must respond first to the "No" of divine judgment of that way of life, and only then receive the "Yes" of justification and reconciliation.[102] This practice interrupts the social grammar of whiteness and begins the process of cultivating a new self that participates in the reality of God united to the reality of the world in Christ. This gift of the new humanity is a task to be perfected in grace within the body of Christ, worked out in concert with last things, and lived out within the things before the last.

The sacrament of baptism begins the process of unselfing, as men and women are inducted into the body of Christ, an act that sets aside previous definitions of identity based on race, gender, and ethnicity. In concert with endowing each member of the community with her or his own distinctive role (the divine *charisma*), baptism establishes a new mode of social relations that supplants all others, particularly those conferred on us by the technologies of a world come of age. This sign is set in the context of the death and resurrection of Jesus, and thus in the context of the restoration of a *koinonia* disrupted time and again by human infidelity. To be buried and raised with Christ in baptism is to acknowledge the corrupt character of the present moment, and our complicity in it, but also to affirm and proclaim God's vindication of suffering in the "politics" of the crucified.[103]

99. Ibid., 121–22.

100. R. D. Williams, *Wound of Knowledge*, 8, 13.

101. *DBWE* 3:113.

102. *DBWE* 6:180; cf. R. D. Williams, *Wound of Knowledge*, 8, 13; Coakley, *Powers and Submissions*, 32–33, 35–36.

103. Harvey, "Post-Critical Approach," 54.

If a type of supersessionism was the catalyst for racial existence and imagination, and a reconfigured, more nuanced and "enlightened" type has carried it forward into our time and place, then the discipline of unselfing that is at the heart of Christian formation must reclaim Gentile identity as a central marker of our existence as members of Christ's ecclesial body (a task far easier to say than to do). To be a Gentile is to be outside of Israel and thus a stranger and an alien, excluded at one time from the covenants of promise, without hope and without God in the world (Eph 2:12). But as Jennings observes, to recognize that we are outside Israel is already to gesture to an entrance into the centuries-long conversation between God and the chosen people: "Someone allowed us to draw close enough to hear that there was a conversation going on between God and a people in the first place."[104] Christology, and more specifically the form of Christ taking form in us as his ecclesial body, thus lies at the heart of this process of unlearning whiteness. Recovering the social location out of which Gentile Christian life and thought first emerged, as people who were once far off but have now been brought near by Christ (Eph 2:13), is the crucial first step.

We should see the recovery of this ancient starting point as an inadvertent and therefore ironic gift of the world's coming of age. In his baptismal meditation for his godson Bonhoeffer states that in the future the church should give up its claims to privileges that it once exercised within the racial framework of post-Reformation Christendom, and in so doing it will recognize a certain historical justice at work.[105] As he sees so clearly, the church no longer has a seat within the inner circle that exercises authority in the social economy of a world come of age. This "demotion" can be a liberation for the church, for whenever it has seen itself as the spiritual form of the temporal order, it has invariably endeavored to be, as Vigen Guroian puts it, "not what it is but what it is not."[106] When this happens, it loses sight of itself as the sign and foretaste in this world of peace with God and with one another in God, and exchanges its birthright for an illusory pottage. Bonhoeffer puts the matter well when he writes, "The claim of the church-community of believers that it is building up the world with Christian principles ends, as a look at New York church bulletins amply shows, in the complete collapse of the church into the world."[107]

This is not a summary dismissal of the real accomplishments of Christendom (though its failures must also always be kept in view), or a

104. Jennings, *Christian Imagination*, 252.

105. *DBWE* 8:389.

106. Guroian, *Incarnate Love*, 146–47.

107. *DBWE* 6:127.

summons for the church to withdraw into a private enclave and await the end of the world. But the time has come, as Pope Benedict XVI observes, to say farewell to the notion that the church will be the form of life of a whole society.[108] As Bonhoeffer also comes to recognize, the body of Christ must learn to assume forms that identify less with great societies, which in a world come of age have been formed around the standard of whiteness. The church, as it participates in the worldly tasks of life, can no longer assume a dominant position, but must learn instead to help and to serve.[109]

In ironic fashion, the world's coming of age may well be providential, in that it provides the church with its best opportunity in centuries to revisit its *modus vivendi* with the earthly city and to fashion a distinctive and viable social identity that is not tethered to any temporal order, though it will always be engaged (indeed it must be, in one way or another, if it is to be the body of Christ) with every performance of the *civitas terrena*. How then can the church preserve its identity so it will see itself first and foremost in terms of the revealed economy of the triune God in and through the people of Israel and not as a function of the *saeculum*, but do so, not for its own sake alone, but for all made in God's image and called to be formed in God's likeness?

Bonhoeffer once again provides us with a promising way forward in the recovery of a generative Gentile space in his reflections on the crucial role that the Old Testament must play for our interpretation of the New Testament, and even more so in his reclamation of the ancient form of exegesis, figural interpretation. With his reclamation of figural exegesis he offers a way for Christians to reckon with the fact that church and Israel occupy the same divine economy.

108. Ratzinger, *Salt of the Earth*, 16, 164, 222.

109. *DBWE* 8:503; *DBWE* 11:265.

7

Reading the New in Light of the Old

At a UJA fund-raising workshop, people were asked why they thought it was important for Jews to get involved in Jewish causes. After typical answers had been given—"Jewish survival," "Israel's security," etc.—one man shyly stammered: "Why, to redeem the world."

—MICHAEL GOLDBERG, *Why Should Jews Survive?*

WHY IS IT, ASKS Dietrich Bonhoeffer, that in the Old Testament we routinely read of people killing, betraying, lying, robbing, divorcing, and even fornicating, all recounted to the glory of God? We seldom encounter anything of the kind in the New Testament.[1] The easy answer, given by many in the eighteenth, nineteenth, and early twentieth centuries, but which Bonhoeffer unequivocally rejects, is that the Old Testament embodies a primitive stage of "religion."[2] For him something far more significant is going on in connection with the Old Testament that bears directly and substantially on the performance of this-worldliness for a world come of age.

---

1. *DBWE* 8:214. Herbert McCabe points out that echoes of these events in the Old Testament reverberate in the genealogy of Jesus in Matthew (*God Matters*, 246–49). McCabe elsewhere observes that "the Hebrews were probably the only people in the world who even in their official propaganda about their own revolution took an entirely honest and realistic view of the events" (*Law, Love and Language*, 117).

2. *DBWE* 8:214. This view of religion as evolving from primitive to civilized is first posited in eighteenth-century Germany, though scholars were divided as to whether this evolution was a good thing (the enlightened view of Thomas Hobbes and Immanuel Kant) or bad (Jean-Jacques Rousseau and the Romantics). See Legaspi, *Death of Scripture*, 109–10, 115, 120, 127, 137; Sheehan, *Enlightenment Bible*, 131, 169–70, 219.

Scholars often comment at length on what Bonhoeffer says *about* the Old Testament in his prison correspondence, but few consider in much detail the specific passages that he actually cites or comments on *in* the Old Testament, or how he interprets them.[3] This is unfortunate, because these citations and commentaries, when read together with his use of Old Testament texts and themes in his previous writings, provide us with important clues, first, to the meaning of the contested concepts of a world come of age, religionless Christianity, and profound this-worldliness, and second, to the need of our own time for an understanding of the church that can live faithfully and truthfully before God while simultaneously living fully and completely in that irony known as the modern age.

My focus on Bonhoeffer's intense and persistent interest in the Old Testament in his prison writings continues the critique advanced in previous chapters. The technological organizations that facilitated the process of constructing useful, reliable, productive, and consuming "subjects" also enlisted the interpretation of the Bible to their cause. To this end the Old Testament was *displaced* from the ecclesial setting in which it played "an indispensable role in getting Christianity out of its diapers without breaking it off from its [Jewish] roots,"[4] and *re-placed* in a social complex constituted around the modern artifacts of religion, culture, and race. The Jewish scriptures were thus reconfigured to serve a new political order, one that Bonhoeffer repeatedly states cannot be left to its own self-understanding.

Bonhoeffer becomes increasingly aware over the course of his life of the importance of the Old Testament, and to a lesser extent the continued existence of the Jewish people, for grasping what is meant by the profound worldliness of Christianity, especially in view of the challenges posed to faith by a world come of age. Because God's transcendence dwells in our midst and not at the boundaries of our all too human existence, the church must learn to see itself where the Old Testament locates the chosen people of biblical and living Israel—in the center of the human village. Bonhoeffer provides a basis for this self-understanding in his reclamation of the

3. This is particularly surprising given the fact that much of Bonhoeffer's writings involve extensive biblical exegesis and commentary. Noteworthy exceptions to this general tendency include Kuske, *Old Testament as the Book of Christ*; Miller's brief but insightful comments on Bonhoeffer and the Psalter, "Dietrich Bonhoeffer and the Psalms"; and Hohmann, *Die Korrelation von Altem und Neuem Bund*, 74–116.

4. Lubac, *Scripture in the Tradition*, 6. Though helpful in many ways, Lubac's trope of Jewish roots is not without its problems, in large part because it represents a subtle yet crucial change in Paul's metaphor of having been grafted onto the cultivated olive tree of Israel (Rom 11:17–24) as the dominant image depicting the inclusion of Gentiles in the life of the covenant people. If we Gentiles have indeed been joined to the root, then perhaps we no longer need the cultivated tree itself.

method of figural exegesis of scripture, which he develops while teaching at the Confessing Church seminary in Finkenwalde and to which he returns in his prison writings.

Bonhoeffer's insights about the Old Testament do not stop there, for with his recovery of figural interpretation he also recognizes, though not always with sufficient emphasis, that Gentiles and Jews are participants in the same divine economy. He thus provides a way forward, in keeping with the testimony of scripture, for recognizing the *place* of Christians as *Gentiles* within the revelatory order of God's action in the world. In both the Finkenwalde period and during his imprisonment we also find that his thoughts are constituted to a significant degree by motifs associated with the "politics"[5] of diaspora, cultivated by Jews for centuries and now a reality that Christians must also develop, including those parts of the world once called Christendom.

Bonhoeffer undertakes three closely related tasks in connection with the emphasis he places on the Old Testament in *Letters and Papers* and in earlier works. First, he establishes the church as the primary context for interpreting scripture, which in turn deprives the state and its "culture" of that privilege, and emphasizes the christological sense of the Bible, such that it is read "as the book of the end, of the new [*vom Neuen*], of Christ."[6] Second, his frequent references to the tropes of diaspora and a colony of strangers and sojourners, together with his selection of Old Testament passages in the prison correspondence that draw on these same images, use figural interpretation to gesture to the "political" status of the church in a world come of age. Finally, these moves open the way for us to take the first few tentative steps toward remembering our Gentile existence within the diasporic space of biblical and living Israel.

If we are to benefit from his proposals and gestures regarding the role of the Old Testament in the formation of the congregation in the form of Christ, however, I must first trace the way the Bible was dislodged from its ecclesial context and resituated within the religious, cultural, and racial complex of a world come of age. This of course brings us back to the question of supersessionism, as the double displacement of church and scripture that occurred beginning in the seventeenth century only serves to transform, deepen, and make even more toxic the age-old separation of Gentile believers from both biblical and living Israel. If the church is to heed Christ's

5. As noted in the introduction, putting scare quotes around *politics* serves as a reminder that the church is distinct from the type of polity represented by the state, and yet it directly challenges the claim that the state makes on its inhabitants regarding the whole of life.

6. *DBWE* 3:22.

call to stand in the center of the village, Christians will need to remember what it means to be Gentiles who, solely by God's gracious initiative in Christ, have been swept up into the eternal covenants God has made with the chosen people of Israel to participate in the messianic suffering of Christ. This double relation to the chosen people of Israel and to the world in which Christians are called to participate and to which we are sent to bear witness turns in large part around the way we read the scriptures that Christians share with Jews.

From Christian Scripture to Cultural Bible

With an impressive array of scholarly tools and methods in hand, writes Jonathan Sheehan, English and German scholars in the eighteenth and nineteenth centuries separated the legitimacy and authority of scripture from the life and teaching of the church, and reassigned it to its proper place of culture, "that complex of literature, teaching, scholarship, and history." What had once served as the itinerary for each soul to follow to the beatific vision, and for the church as it made its way to the city of God, now became a synchronic treatment, *sub species aeternitatis*, of a foreign people and time. To this end the sense and significance of the Bible was redistributed across the new academic disciplines of philology, pedagogy, poetry, and history. In the hands of philologists the Bible became a document, the study of which was crucial to the perfection of the craft, and which effectively effaced theological commentary in favor of textual criticism and detailed annotations. A form of authority was conferred on the poetic Bible through its relocation in what was said to be the general literary heritage of humankind. In the pedagogical Bible enlightened souls sought timeless morals for all peoples everywhere, with Jesus reclassified as a teacher of a universal ethic. And in the historical Bible they discerned a valuable, if somewhat obscure, ethnological archive that preserves for later generations "an infinitely variegated library of human customs and origins."[7] Each of these "texts," by virtue of their new social and interpretive location, is formally distinct from the Jewish and Christian scriptures.

According to Sheehan, the production of this panoply of "Bibles" by means of a constellation of scholarly technologies makes possible the invention of the cultural Bible, "the familiar sense that the Bible is part of 'our' Western civilization."[8] In Germany, England, and the United States, arguably the three most prominent Protestant nation-states to date, the Bible

7. Sheehan, *Enlightenment Bible*, 92, 217.

8. Ibid., 220.

came to be regarded first and foremost as the Ur-text of nation and *Volk*. The values, aspirations, practices, and institutions of these national entities are what count as constitutive of civilization. Though it took decades and even centuries for the distinctively ecclesial and theological use of the Bible to be fully assimilated into its cultural meaning, eventually the sense of one's membership in the church as discontinuous with one's membership in the state largely fades from view, an unwitting consequence that Bonhoeffer discerns in Luther's own efforts.[9]

The production of the cultural Bible beginning in the eighteenth century has gone hand in glove with the removal of Israel as a social body, both in the Bible and in the continuing existence of the Jewish people, from their role in the Christian tradition as God's chosen nation. Both Christianity and Judaism were displaced as peoples and relocated as species of "religion" or "culture" within the new political institution of the state, a move that constituted a double supersession, such that the existence of both Jews and Christians is now incidental to human flourishing. One need not posit some kind of necessity at work in the use of these methods (the genetic fallacy) to note the way this line of thinking has unfolded over the past three centuries, and which continues to function in our time and place.

The principal laboratory for the invention of the cultural Bible, observes Sheehan, was Protestant Germany. The catalyst for this process was the convergence in the eighteenth century of the subjective religious zeal of Pietists, which grew out of their desire to "remove the theological blinders that confessional commitment had put on the Protestant world as a whole," with the philological sciences then being developed to produce biblical translations that would allow all to encounter God's word for themselves.[10] The scholars in these German universities did not accomplish this feat on their own, for they borrowed literary tools that had been originally forged in England. Michaelis's landmark project of creating a post-theological interpretation of the Old Testament depended to a significant degree on the insights developed in a series of lectures on Hebrew poetry delivered by Oxford University don Robert Lowth.[11] "If the English gave the Germans the tools to build the Enlightenment Bible," writes Sheehan, "the German philological, historical, and educational juggernaut exported the cultural Bible back to English scholars and literati as the eighteenth century faded from view."[12]

9. *DBWE* 14:432; *DBWE* 8:172–73.

10. Sheehan, *Enlightenment Bible*, xiii, 84.

11. Legaspi, *Death of Scripture*, 107–27.

12. Sheehan, *Enlightenment Bible*, xiv.

The invention of the cultural Bible was closely associated with the development of the state as the principal technological organization of society, and the instrument of that association was the emergence of the post-confessional university. Michael Legaspi notes that with the eclipse of confessional identities in Europe, the Bible had to find "a place in the new political order committed to the unifying power of the state." Through the use of the tools of scholarship that had been developed over the previous two centuries, beginning with vernacular translation during the Age of Reformation in the sixteenth century, "a new avenue for recovering the biblical writings as ancient cultural products capable of reinforcing the values and aims of a new sociopolitical order" was opened up.[13]

The fundamental purpose of the German university in the eighteenth century was to serve the interests of the state as a center for *Bildung*, which in this setting consisted in the formation of men who were "competent, public-minded, knowledgeable, and above all, socially adept." The university was to be reconstituted in order to play a crucial role in the new order, with statecraft (*Staatskunst*) as the ordering principle of the institution. Reason, utility, and taste were established as the formal norms for all subjects, with the expressed goal of forming individuals into useful, reliable, cultured citizens. The displacement of the Bible from its former confessional setting (to which the new universities such as Georgia Augusta in Göttingen gave only nominal attention in their founding) and its relocation in a new sociopolitical order was a significant project, the goal of which was the creation of a scholarly, nonconfessional Bible in accord with the canons of modern rationality.[14]

In addition to the displacement of the Bible from its ecclesial context, the continuing existence of Israel in the Jewish people is also denied any substantial role in the interpretation of scripture. According to Legaspi, Michaelis dismisses the Hebrew spoken and read by the Jews of his day as a corrupt and degraded language, and thus of virtually no use in the interpretation of the Old Testament. Moreover, the Jews did not posses the spirit of the ancient Israelites. The erudition of rabbinic and medieval Judaism, "untouched by the pleasant Muses, was scholastic to the highest degree," thus the Jews "have not, for hundreds of years, felt the impulses of that spirit which inspired the poets of old."[15] Chronopolitics once again raises its imperial head in connection with the development of modern methods of biblical study, its critical role in the technological organization of this new order made possible by the construction of a stadial account of history

13. Legaspi, *Death of Scripture*, 5.

14. Ibid., 35, 37, 43, 45.

15. Michaelis, *Beurtheilung*, §6, 29, cited by Legaspi, *Death of Scripture*, 88.

oriented to the normative status of what currently exists. The periodization of Israelite and Jewish history, and more specifically the separation between the pre-exilic and post-exilic periods, the latter culminating with the modern Jewish one, makes it possible for Michaelis to dispense with the latter.[16]

In light of this history it should come as no surprise to read what Bonhoeffer writes to Erwin Sutz a few months before taking over the directorship of the Confessing Church seminary, saying that he no longer believed in the university—indeed, never really had believed in it: "The next generation of pastors, these days, ought to be trained entirely in church-monastic schools, where the pure doctrine, the Sermon on the Mount, and worship are taken seriously—which for all three of these things is simply not the case at the university and under the present circumstances is impossible." He adds that it is time to break decisively with the theologically grounded reserve about whatever is being done by the state, which in the end comes down to fear.[17] Though in these comments he does not explicitly describe the university as a technological organization that seeks to master our fate in a world come of age, it nevertheless falls comfortably within that category.

Bonhoeffer words the break with the state more concretely and emphatically in his thesis paper in preparation for the Fanø Conference, in which he states in thesis seven that "the human will must be confronted with the commandment: Thou shalt not kill. God does not exempt us from obeying His commandments." In reply to objections that the state must be maintained and the nation (*Volk*) must defend itself, he writes, "The Church answers: Thou shalt not kill," and "Have you dared to entrust God, in full faith, with your protection in obedience to His commandment?" He then adds that the powers of evil will not be broken by means of organizations, asserting that prayer is stronger than organization and that it is easy to conceal the burden of evil and of struggle by organization![18] Yet again he restates in another context his constantly reiterated conviction that, in having been thrown back on ourselves in the fall, our efforts to safeguard ourselves by technological organization from the effects of fortune and fate come to naught.[19]

16. Legaspi, *Death of Scripture*, 88.
17. *DBWE* 13:217.
18. *DBWE* 13:305–6.
19. Cf. *DBWE* 8:500.

Learning the Unspeakable Name

Bonhoeffer repeatedly insists in *Letters and Papers* that the church needs to reappropriate the theological grammar of the Old Testament if Christians are to participate faithfully and fully in the messianic suffering of God. Six months prior to his comment about the need to interpret the New Testament in light of the Old, he reports to Bethge that he had read the Old Testament through two and half times.[20] The effect of that spiritual exercise erupts several times over the next few months. One of the more significant of these outbursts occurs in a letter in which he states that his thinking and perceiving were becoming more in line with the Old Testament and then makes four assertions that reveal the extent to which it had influenced him:

> Only when one knows not to utter the name of God may one dare to utter the name of Jesus Christ. Only when one loves life and the earth so much that with it everything seems to be lost and at its end may one believe in the resurrection of the dead and a new world. Only when one accepts the law of God as binding for oneself may one dare to speak of grace. And only when the wrath and vengeance of God against God's enemies are allowed to stand as inescapable realities can something of forgiveness and the love of enemies touch our hearts.[21]

Each of these assertions places central Christian convictions squarely within the grammatical framework established by the scriptures of Israel and the continuing existence of the chosen people in modern Judaism. In the first statement, faith in Christ is tied to the name of the God of Israel, a name that rabbinic Judaism has insisted should not be uttered or even written. The second assertion, recapitulating what Bonhoeffer discusses in *Ethics* regarding an authentic worldliness, comes directly from Jewish convictions regarding the inherent goodness of creation and of life itself, especially its embodied character. The connection of the third to Jewish

20. *DBWE* 8:181.

21. *DBWE* 8:213, translation altered. In the critical English edition the first, third, and fourth sentences read, "Only when one knows that the name of God may not be uttered may one sometimes speak the name of Jesus Christ. . . . Only when one accepts the law of God as binding for oneself may one perhaps sometimes speak of grace. . . . And only when the wrath and vengeance of God against God's enemies are allowed to stand can something of forgiveness and the love of enemies touch our hearts." The German reads, "Nur wenn man die Unaussprechlickkeit des Namens Gottes kennt, darf man auch einmal den Namen Jesus Christus aussprechen . . . nur wenn man das Gesetz Gottes über sich gelten lässt, darf man wohl auch einmal von Gnade sprechen . . . und nur wenn der Zorn und die Rache Gottes über seine Feinde als gültige Wirklichkeiten stehen bleiben, kann nur Vergebung und von Feindesliebe etwas unser Herz berühen." *DBW* 8:226.

teaching, having to do with the continuing significance of the Old Testament law for the reception of grace, is fairly obvious, though it is remarkable that it comes from the pen of a Lutheran theologian. The final assertion securely enfolds the Christian practice of reconciliation within the apocalyptic scope of God's wrath and judgment that pervades virtually every section of the Old Testament, and to which Bonhoeffer makes frequent reference in *Letters and Papers*.

Bonhoeffer summarizes his sentiments regarding the centrality of the Old Testament when he unequivocally declares at a critical juncture in *Life Together*, "The God of Abraham, Isaac, and Jacob is the God and Father of Jesus Christ and our God."[22] As revealing as these assertions are, however, they do not tell a complete story, for by themselves they could plausibly be read simply as affirmations of beliefs passed down to us from biblical Israel that do not need substantial connection to the continuing existence of the chosen people. This is a connection on which Bonhoeffer insists, as can be seen in several passages from both the Finkenwalde period and *Ethics*. This is not to claim that there are not important questions that must be pursued in this regard with respect to the subject of supersessionism, but unlike much of modern theology prior to Karl Barth, Bonhoeffer does not write them out of the picture of the divine economy.

In two Bible studies that we shall examine in more detail below, Bonhoeffer unequivocally states that the Jewish people are, by divine election, God's chosen people, and will remain so forever. His most telling assertions regarding the continuing significance of the Jewish people as God's chosen, however, come in two passages written several years apart. The first appears in a series of lectures on the visibility of the church in the New Testament, in which he states that what happens in Christ is the fulfillment of the promise given to David, and thus from its inception the New Testament church views itself as inextricably connected with the church of the promise, that is, with Israel, for God is one: "Any church that were to dissolve this unity would no longer be the church of the Holy Spirit, since the Spirit binds the church to Israel and to the Old Testament. Wherever the '*filioque*' falls, so also does this tie to the people of Israel fall."[23]

Bonhoeffer reiterates this same point a few years later: "The Jews keep open the question of Christ; they are the sign of God's free, gracious election and of God's rejecting wrath; 'see the kindness and the severity of God' (Rom. 11: 22). Driving out the Jew(s) from the West must result in driving

22. *DBWE* 5:62.

23. *DBWE* 14:440. Though this is not the venue for considering the theological legitimacy of the filioque controversy, Bonhoeffer offers here an interesting defense of what is typically considered the Western position.

out Christ with them, for Jesus Christ was a Jew."[24] Jewish theologian Michael Wyschogrod makes a virtually identical claim in *The Body of Faith*. The existence of the Jewish people, he states, is the earthly abode of God, "among or in whom God dwells." It is vital that this people live ethically, and if they do not God severely punishes them. Their sin does not drive God out of the world completely, however, for that would happen only with "the destruction of the Jewish people." Wyschogrod then states that Hitler "knew that it was insufficient to cancel the teachings of Jewish morality and to substitute for it the new moral order of the superman. It was not only Jewish values that needed to be eradicated but Jews had to be murdered."[25]

Old Testament and Figural Interpretation

Bonhoeffer's reclamation of figural exegesis of the Old Testament is a crucial first step for the church to take if it is to adequately see itself where the Old Testament locates the chosen people of Israel—in the center of the human village. Before I can examine in more detail the way he employs this approach to scripture, I need to say a bit more about this method of biblical interpretation, and in particular what distinguishes it from figurative exegesis. A figural interpretation posits an intrinsic relation between what might otherwise seem as unrelated persons, practices, or events, but which in actuality constitute concrete moments in the single divine utterance in and of history. For example, when Jesus is described as the fulfillment of Joshua in patristic and medieval texts, it is because both persons participate, each in his appointed way, in the enacted intention of God in history. If someone or some practice or event in the Old Testament is referred to as a type—for example, the offering of sacrifice, the antitype of which is found in Christ or in the church as the messianic community and witness—it is because this figure begins the extended divine performance that embraces subsequent persons, practices, and events. God thus becomes both the agent and the interpreter of what is depicted in scripture.[26] In figural interpretation, then, the plain or literal sense of the type must be preserved for the sake of the spiritual meaning and the historical continuity of the antitype. A reading of this sort, writes John David Dawson, "*extends without supplanting* the former Jewish meanings—that the spirit does not undermine but instead

24. *DBWE* 6:105. The translators and editors of this passage note an ambiguity in the abbreviated article Bonhoeffer uses in this passage, *Verstossung d. Juden*. They therefore translate it as "the Jew(s)" but point out that the meaning of this sentence is unaffected by the ambiguity. *DBWE* 6:105 n. 8.

25. Wyschogrod, *Body of Faith*, 223.

26. Auerbach, *Mimesis*, 73–76, 194–202; Dawson, *Christian Figural Reading*, 85.

draws out the fullest meaning of the letter; the letter must remain in the spirit because the spirit is the letter fully realized."[27] Both events are thus located within the one divine economy extended over time and space.

By contrast, figurative exegesis *displaces* the literal sense of the Old Testament, and *re-places* it with a meaning that has no intrinsic connection to either biblical or living Israel[28]—for example, when Jesus' parables are misinterpreted as illustrating universal truths.[29] The plots, characters, and settings that narrate the lives of the chosen people serve solely and simply as illustrative material to track the history of the soul's inner progress: "This theme and transfer of narrative continuity took place either directly, as in the Methodists' devout use of the Bible to aid in tracing and treading the path of sin to perfection, or indirectly as in the allegory of the Christian's journey to Mount Zion with the aid and admonition of Evangelist and Interpreter in *The Pilgrim's Progress.*"[30]

With respect to Bonhoeffer's use of figural methods of interpreting the Old Testament in the prison writings, virtually all of the passages he references in passing or comments on in more detail come from exilic or post-exilic texts. In the pivotal letter of April 30, 1944, which concludes with the assertion that Christians do not read the New Testament nearly enough in the light of the Old, he explicitly refers to a handful of biblical passages, but three from the Old Testament are most revealing. After stating that God would shortly accomplish something that could only be received with the greatest wonder and awe, he then says that the truth of Ps 58:11b ("surely there is a God who judges on earth") and Ps 9:19–20 ("Rise up, O LORD! Do not let mortals prevail; / let the nations be judged before you. / Put them in fear, O LORD; / let the nations know that they are only human") will be clear "for those who have eyes to see."[31]

As though to accentuate the apocalyptic tone of these passages, Bonhoeffer then states that "we shall have to repeat Jer 45:5 to ourselves every day."[32] This verse reads, "And you, do you seek great things for yourself? Do not seek them; for I am going to bring disaster upon all flesh, says the LORD; but I will give you your life as a prize of war in every place to which you may go." This is but one of five times in the prison correspondence in which he either cites or alludes to this short chapter in Jeremiah, more often

---

27. Dawson, *Christian Figural Reading*, 217, Dawson's emphasis.

28. Ibid., 16, 86.

29. *DBWE* 14:426.

30. Frei, *Eclipse of the Biblical Narrative*, 152–53.

31. *DBWE* 8:361.

32. Ibid.

than any other single biblical passage. Moreover, it is not just the frequency of quotation that makes this passage significant, for he often refers to it at critical points in his letters to Bethge.[33]

Bonhoeffer brings this letter to a close with a reference to two verses from Proverbs, a passage that "bars the way to all escapism in the guise of piety." His letter cites Prov 22:11–12, which reads, "Those who love a pure heart and are gracious in speech will have the king as a friend. The eyes of the LORD keep watch over knowledge, but he overthrows the words of the faithless." According to the editors of the critical edition of *Letters and Papers from Prison*, this is probably a mistaken reference, and he may well have intended to refer to Prov 24:11–12: "If you hold back from rescuing those taken away to death, those who go staggering to the slaughter; if you say, 'Look, we did not know this'—does not he who weighs the heart perceive it? Does not he who keeps watch over your soul know it? And will he not repay all according to their deeds?" If this is indeed the case, not only is it a powerful description of the events taking place in Nazi Germany, but it also reinforces the exilic and post-exilic tenor of his Old Testament references in the late prison correspondence.[34]

Bonhoeffer references a second set of Old Testament texts at the beginning of his letter of July 16, 1944, in which he suggests seven passages that Bethge might use as sermon texts. Only one, Matt 28:20b, is from the New Testament, and it reinforces the apocalyptic grammar of Bonhoeffer's theology: "And remember, I am with you always, to the end of the age." Of the other six, three are from the Psalter, all of which, in one way or another, exhort the soul to look to God for salvation (62:1; 119:94a; 42:5). Of the remaining passages, one is from Jeremiah, the other two from the later chapters of the book of Isaiah. The passage from Jeremiah has an explicitly exilic setting, as the God of Israel comforts the remnant of Israel that had survived the sword and found grace in the wilderness: "The LORD appeared to him [Israel] from far away. I have loved you with an everlasting love; therefore I have continued my faithfulness to you."[35] The two verses from the book of Isaiah are also set in the context of the exile. The first reads, "Do not fear, for I am with you, do not be afraid, for I am your God; I will strengthen you, I will help you, I will uphold you with my victorious right hand" (41:10). The other passage also addresses Israel, the people whom God had formed and knows by name, exhorting them not to fear, for God has redeemed

33. Ian Stockton documents Bonhoeffer's fondness for the book of Jeremiah in both his early work and sermons, and its reemergence in his prison writings. Stockton, "Bonhoeffer's Wrestling with Jeremiah," 50–58.

34. *DBWE* 8:367 and n. 30.

35. *DBWE* 8:475.

them (43:1). He then says to Bethge that he would "confine myself to a few fundamental and simple thoughts. One has to live in a congregation for a while to understand how 'Christ is formed' in it (Gal. 4:19), and that would be especially true for a congregation such as you would have."[36]

Bonhoeffer returns to Isaiah in the letter that he writes two days later, in which he discusses the participation of Christians in the messianic sufferings of God, "thus fulfilling Isa. 53" (the last of four Suffering Servant songs). He then explicates what it means to be caught up in these sufferings of God by referring to a series of events in the gospels and the book of Acts. None of these events—table-fellowship, healing stories, the shepherds in Bethlehem, the centurion in Capernaum, the rich young man, the encounters with the eunuch and Cornelius in Acts—is a "religious act," because "'faith' is something whole and involves one's whole life. Jesus calls not to a new religion but to life."[37]

A few days later, in a letter written the day after the failed assassination attempt, Bonhoeffer states that faith means "living fully in life's tasks, questions, successes and failures, experiences, and perplexities—then one takes seriously no longer one's own sufferings but rather the sufferings of God in the world." That, he states, is faith, the way one becomes a human being, and again he references Jer 45, once more relating his observations about a world come of age to the exilic and post-exilic periods.[38] He unpacks these comments further in his July 28, 1944 letter to Bethge, in which he links health, happiness, and physical strength to the Old Testament concepts of blessing, and then states that one should not make happiness and suffering, or blessing and cross, mutually exclusive. He speculates that the difference between the two testaments may well be that in the Old Testament the blessing includes the cross, and in the New the cross bears the blessing.[39]

Before turning to the letter that Bonhoeffer writes to his grandnephew on the occasion of his baptism, we should note a comment that he makes in "Outline for a Book." At the beginning of the third chapter he discusses what the church must do in a world come of age. He states that it must participate in the tasks of community life, "not dominating but helping and serving."[40] Though he gives no biblical reference for this comment, he does echo something that Jeremiah writes to the exiles in Babylon. The prophet

36. *DBWE* 8:475.

37. *DBWE* 8:482.

38. *DBWE* 8:486.

39. *DBWE* 8:492–93.

40. *DBWE* 8:503. The imperative not to dominate but to serve occurs virtually verbatim in "Draft for a Catechism," which Bonhoeffer coauthors with Franz Hildebrandt in 1932. *DBWE* 14:265–66.

tells them to get on with the daily necessities of building houses, planting gardens, marrying and giving in marriage, and raising sons and daughters. In addition, they were to attend to the task of securing the peace of the place to which God had sent them: "Seek the welfare of the city where I have sent you into exile, and pray to the LORD on its behalf, for in its welfare you will find your welfare" (29:7). Now of course it is impossible to say whether this passage crosses Bonhoeffer's mind as he writes this sentence (though he does cite it in a related context in his letter to his godson[41]), but it does fit with his comments about what constitutes profound this-worldliness in a world come of age.

The largest concentration of citations from the Old Testament in Bonhoeffer's prison correspondence is found in the meditation that he writes for his godson's baptism. In virtually every paragraph he strives to tell his grandnephew that he will grow up in a very different world than the one that he had known, but that his family will provide resources for coping with those changes. Unlike previous generations, "we have learnt by experience that we cannot plan even for the coming day, that what we have built up is being destroyed overnight, and that our life, in contrast to that of our parents, has become formless or even fragmentary." He then declares that he and his generation recognize more clearly than in previous times that the world rests in the wrathful and gracious hands of God.[42] Far from distancing himself from a supposedly "primitive" stage of religion in the Old Testament, Bonhoeffer embraces what most would regard as its most distasteful feature—its constant invocation of God's wrath and judgment.

The repeated recurrence of the theme of divine wrath and judgment in the prison correspondence underscores the apocalyptic hermeneutic that frames his interpretation of the scriptures in *Ethics* and elsewhere. In notes recorded after a meeting with Bonhoeffer in Sweden in 1942, George Bell, bishop of Chichester and Bonhoeffer's good friend from his time in England, states that Bonhoeffer had been talking to families in Germany who opposed the Nazis, and they wanted to know why their sons were killed fighting in Poland. Bell reports that Bonhoeffer told these grieving families, "our innocent ones suffer, as the innocent Poles suffer. Christians do not wish to escape repentance, or chaos if God wills to bring it on us. We must take this judgment as Christians."[43]

Returning to the baptismal sermon, Bonhoeffer then cites Jer 45 once again, with its emphasis on receiving one's life as a prize of war, and states

41. *DBWE* 8:389.
42. *DBWE* 8:387.
43. *DBWE* 16:300.

that the task of Bonhoeffer's generation will be not to seek great things but "to save and preserve our souls out of the chaos, and to realize that this is the only thing we can carry as 'booty' out of the burning building." He then quotes a proverb about vigilantly preserving the integrity of one's heart, saying that he and his generation "shall have to bear our lives more than to shape them, to hope more than to plan, to hold out more than to stride ahead," in the hope that they will preserve what is necessary for later generations, so that they might plan, build up, and shape a new and better life.[44]

In the penultimate paragraph of this letter, after referring to the need to accept humbly the verdict of history and renounce the privileges and rights they enjoyed within the framework of Christendom past, Bonhoeffer quotes three passages from the Old Testament, all of which are set in the exilic and post-exilic periods. The first comes from a statement that Jeremiah addressed to the last king of Judah, warning him that those who resist the rule of the Babylonian king will be punished by war, famine, and pestilence, but God would leave on their own land those who willingly serve Nebuchadnezzar (27:8–11). The second comes from the so-called Isaiah Apocalypse (Isa 24–27): "Come, my people, enter your chambers, and shut your doors behind you; hide yourselves for a little while until the wrath is past" (26:20). The final Old Testament quotation comes from a psalm connected to the dedication of the rebuilt temple, reminding the one who worships the God of Israel that "his anger is but for a moment; his favor is for a lifetime. Weeping may linger for the night, but joy comes with the morning" (30:5).[45]

In the concluding paragraph of the meditation Bonhoeffer states that the act of baptism drives Christians back to the beginnings of their understanding, the details of which are now so remote and difficult to comprehend, it is hard to know what to say about them anymore. He then once again quotes a passage from the book of Jeremiah, this one looking forward to the time when God will restore the chosen people in the promised land: "They [the nations] shall fear and tremble because of all the good and all the prosperity I provide for them" (33:9). Until then the Christian cause will be a silent and secret affair, with women and men who will pray, live justly and wait for God's own time. He then concludes with an exhortation and benediction drawn from the book of Proverbs (4:18): "May you be one of them, and may it be said of you one day: 'The path of the righteous is like the light of dawn, which shines brighter and brighter till full day.'"[46]

44. *DBWE* 8:387.
45. *DBWE* 8:389.
46. *DBWE* 8:389–90.

Pushback from the Biblical Studies Establishment

Bonhoeffer's use of figural interpretation in these examples from the prison correspondence are for the most part implied, though that does not make them any less significant. His reticence to make them more evident may be attributed to at least two factors, the first and more obvious being the occasional and ad hoc nature of letters in general. But there may be a more substantial reason he alludes to these typologies rather than making them explicit. During his tenure as head of the illegal seminary in Finkenwalde he teaches several Bible studies on Old Testament texts in which he explicitly develops extensive figural connections, for which professional biblical scholars publicly take him to task.

Before turning to these Bible studies, however, we must note something that Bonhoeffer says in a lecture on the topic of contemporizing New Testament texts, delivered in the summer of 1935. In comments dealing with the role of scripture as witness to the historical and living Christ he takes up the question of whether allegorical interpretations are permissible. His answer is remarkable, especially given his academic context: "The right of the allegorical interpretation consists in acknowledging the possibility that God does not allow his word to be exhausted in its grammat[ical], logical, unequivocal meaning, but rather that this word has even other perspectives and can serve better understanding." He remarks with some amusement that while Luther explicitly dismisses the medieval four- or sevenfold meaning of the Bible in favor of univocal meaning, he nonetheless goes on to allegorize his own lecture on the Psalm! He then asks, "Why should the word not *also* have symbolic or allegorical meaning? The decisive element and only criterion is whether something other than Christ is disclosed here." He sets two parameters for the use of allegorical interpretation, the first having to do with its *content*, that it discloses Christ alone, and the other specifying that the power of these forms to witness to Christ is attributed solely to the *word of the Bible*. He concludes by linking allegorical readings of scripture with the freedom of the church, not to somehow prove the unity between the two testaments, but as a way of allowing the whole of the Bible to testify to the historical and risen Christ.[47]

In a Bible study presented two months later to leaders of the Confessing Church in Pomerania on chapters 11–19 of 2 Samuel, Bonhoeffer puts this hermeneutical approach to the test, describing King David as the type and shadow (*Vorbild*[48] *und Schatten*) of the crucified Christ. *Vorbild*

47. *DBWE* 14:428–29, Bonhoeffer's (emphatic!) emphases.

48. Bonhoeffer uses this term most extensively during his time at Finkenwalde, though he does return to it in the third chapter of "Outline for a Book" when he writes

has a range of meanings and can be variously translated as "example," "model," and "type." Though it can signify a moral exemplar, in the sense that Bonhoeffer sees Gandhi as an example of nonviolent resistance to be emulated,[49] when he uses it to exegete the Old Testament it almost always signifies a typological relation between persons or events. In the paragraph just prior to the one in which Bonhoeffer describes David as the *Vorbild* and *Schatten* of Christ, for example, he states that "the Messiah is prefigured [*vorgebildet*] in David,"[50] a term that clearly invokes the figural relationship between antitype and type.

Bonhoeffer's reclamation of typological interpretation is consistent with his overall theological approach with respect to the Bible, as his rejection of principles and ideals as the primary mode of theological ethics, when taken together with his emphasis on participating in the revelatory action of God in Christ, makes something like this approach necessary. In *Life Together*, he depicts scripture as a living whole, placing the listening congregation in the midst of the world of biblical Israel "with their prophets, judges, kings, and priests, with their wars, festivals, sacrifices, and sufferings." The liturgical reading draws the community of believers into the story of Jesus' birth, baptism, miracles, teachings, suffering, death and resurrection. Through this way of reading scripture the congregation participates now in past events for the salvation of the whole world.[51]

With respect to David, the anointed king, as messianic type, Bonhoeffer states that he occupies this role not because of his personal moral qualities or holiness but entirely because of God's faithfulness to the divine election, anointing and grace. As the one who is humbled and punished for his sins by God, and who bears this punishment as the justified sinner, he is the type and shadow of the crucified Christ.[52] In an allegorical allusion

---

that the church should not understate the significance of human example (*die Bedeutung des menschlichen "Vorbildes"* [*DBW* 8:560]), beginning with the humanity of Jesus. It is not abstract argument that gives the church's words its power and emphasis, but example. According to the editors of the critical translation, in the background of this formula stands a pair of concepts from Augustine's *De Trinitate*, which Bonhoeffer quotes for a seminar paper on Luther's understanding of the Holy Spirit. *DBWE* 8:503 n. 31; *DBWE* 9:338 n. 72.

49. *DBWE* 13:152; with regard to his use of *Vorbild* in the sense of a moral example, see *DBWE* 4:286–87; *DBWE* 8:503; *DBWE* 15:325, 333.

50. *DBWE* 14:873 (*DBW* 14:881).

51. *DBWE* 5:61. Those who would downplay what Bonhoeffer says in *Life Together* because it is a "devotional" work and not a "real" (i.e., academically accredited) work of theology are assuming a false dichotomy predicated on pre-twentieth-century ideas that have long since lost credibility. For his part Bonhoeffer makes no such assumption.

52. *DBWE* 14:877, 891. In his little book *Prayerbook of the Bible* Bonhoeffer states

to David as a shadow of Christ, Bonhoeffer states that we see shadows only where bodies are found: "Biblically this means that there is a shadow only because there is also the incarnation, only because the word of God became flesh. David is the shadow of the incarnate Messiah." The Word made human, because it is that which casts a shadow on David, must therefore be understood as the *prius*, that is, the first, the antitype.[53]

Bonhoeffer then extends the figural connection between David and Christ to include David's household as the type of the church. As one who had shed innocent blood, David is told that the sword would never leave his house. This passage proclaims the struggle between violence brought by the sword and the church of God, which would remain forever. The seed of David, which is Christ and his church, will be struck by violence, and yet the sword will not destroy the promise of God. In the mystery of God's chastisement of David, the image of the sword brings both life and the promise once again to the church, as grace is included in the punishment. Out of the church of the Messiah itself arises the son, Absalom, who profanes the church in full view before the entire world. Absalom is the shadow or type of all who from David's time until now have as the offspring of the church also been its desecrators. They must do this dreadful work under the menacing promise of God, though by doing so they bring judgment and ruin upon themselves.[54]

The allusion to the ongoing church struggle in Germany is readily apparent. The house of David is the type for the Protestant church in Germany, caught up in the violence of the sword, and Absalom is the figure for those within the church who desecrate it through their involvement in the violence of the Nazi regime and the German Christian movement. Bonhoeffer draws the typological connection between David's house and the church under the cross for his students to help them follow God's ongoing action in the world, not only to find Christ in this passage, but also themselves and their historical situation.[55] God judges the church, then and now, but through bearing that judgment it receives new life according to the promise.

Bonhoeffer offers another figural interpretation of the Old Testament in a Bible study concerning the rebuilding of Jerusalem in the books of Ezra and Nehemiah. At the end of the study he declares in unequivocal terms

---

that David is the *Vorbild* of Christ. DBW 5:110; cf. Bonhoeffer's lecture "Christ in the Psalms," *DBWE* 14:386–93.

53. *DBWE* 14:873. Bonhoeffer contends that in David as the anointed king of Israel, Christ is prefigured "as something temporally prior" in the course of the history of salvation. *DBWE* 14:874.

54. *DBWE* 14:886–88.

55. Clements, *What Freedom?*, 146.

that the church of God, both then and now, is one, and that both then and now God leads the one community to restoration through a distinctive pattern of judgment, punishment, and destruction. He thus connects the two times and places within the one history of divine activity, according to which the church then and today hears the call and promise of God, in which the dominant theme has less to do with judgment and more with restoration after judgment.[56]

Bonhoeffer makes an interesting observation in this study, stating that God uses the pagan Cyrus to create space for the church when the Persian king frees the people of Israel and instructs them to rebuild the temple in Jerusalem. He notes that Cyrus does not come to faith by converting to Judaism, nor does he truly comprehend the significance of his actions. Nevertheless, God uses his pagan notions to create space for the church, for the people of God, and that, he emphatically adds, is enough. Just as Nebuchadnezzar once served God by acting as the rod of discipline against a disobedient Israel, now Cyrus allows God's chosen to serve their God "in freedom and in a fashion pleasing to God."[57]

The two studies—of David and of Ezra and Nehemiah—are significant because in both cases Bonhoeffer uses figural exegesis to posit a real connection grounded in the revelatory activity of God in Christ between the people and events narrated in the Old Testament and those in the Germany of his day. Through these interpretations he endeavors to show the way that these people and events, separated in time and space, nonetheless belong together as two aspects of a single economy or pattern orchestrated around the one divine utterance made incarnate in Christ. Though events never repeat themselves identically, there is the contention that a nonidentical repetition is at work in God's redemptive activity in the world, a repetition articulated through typological interpretation.

These studies were sharply criticized at the time by biblical scholars, above all by Friedrich Baumgärtel, an Old Testament scholar from the University at Greifswald. Baumgärtel accuses Bonhoeffer of interpreting the Old Testament arbitrarily and states that should this method prevail in the church, "The Old Testament will be surrendered and lost to the church."[58] Baumgärtel also pens a letter of protest to Eberhard Baumann, a theologian associated with one of the Confessing Church groups, calling into question Bonhoeffer's qualifications to teach at a Confessing Church seminary. Both

56. *DBWE* 14:930.

57. *DBWE* 14:919.

58. Baumgärtel, *Die Kirche ist Eine*, 17, cited by Kuske, *Old Testament as the Book of Christ*, 82.

Martin Kuske, who describes the criticism in some detail, and Bethge agree with Baumgärtel to the extent that his interpretation was arbitrary when viewed from a historical-critical perspective.[59] But as Hans Pfeifer observes, Bonhoeffer is not constructing a historical theory of these texts but is offering a theological judgment on present time and circumstance on the basis of figural readings.[60] Such judgments are only possible by retaining the distinction between the literal or historical and figural readings of the text.[61]

Bonhoeffer becomes more circumspect with regard to figural interpretation after these attacks, but as Bethge observes, he "would not admit that the wealth of a text is exhausted in its literal meaning."[62] At no point does he shy away from his basic conviction that the events in scripture and those in which he and his friends are caught up are both located in the one divine economy. As for Baumgärtel's contention that these sorts of interpretations deprive the church of the Old Testament, the opposite is in fact the case, for as David Steinmetz observes, "The church which is restricted in its preaching to the original intention of the author is a church which must reject the Old Testament as an exclusively Jewish book."[63] When done well (which is a condition that applies to any exegetical method or technique), figural interpretations help preserve it precisely *as scripture*, that is, as the primary medium for the ongoing counterpoint of revelation and not simply as a relatively small anthology of documents from an ancient people group.

The "Politics" of Profound Worldliness: Dwelling as Strangers among the Godless

Reading the New Testament in the context of the Old, says Bonhoeffer, is vital to the summons for Christians to participate in God's reality revealed in Christ and made real among God's creatures, and thus in the reality of the world. That the passages he selects from the Old Testament to exegete while in prison as he reflects on what it means to be Christian in a world come

59. Kuske, *Old Testament as the Book of Christ*, 83–84; Bethge, *Dietrich Bonhoeffer*, 526–29.

60. *DBWE* 14:917 n. 1.

61. In the afterword to the English translation of *Prayerbook of the Bible*, Gerhard Müller and Albrecht Schönherr note that Bonhoeffer does not contest the validity of the historical-critical method of biblical interpretation, for it confirms the historicity of revelation. At the same time, however, he recognizes the theological meaning of scripture that overlaps the interests of that method, and uses christological, tropological, and typological methods to disclose that meaning. *DBWE* 5:179–80.

62. Bethge, *Dietrich Bonhoeffer*, 528.

63. Steinmetz, "Theology and Exegesis," 27.

of age are largely drawn from texts set in exilic and post-exilic contexts is especially telling. When taken together with his choice of psalms that typically exhort the reader to look to God alone for salvation, the biblical studies at Finkenwalde, and the emphasis on diaspora in *Life Together*, this selection of passages points to a typological connection between the fate of the people of Israel during and after the Babylonian exile and the social character of the church in the modern world. As he expresses it in his study of Ezra and Nehemiah, "The people of Israel must now dwell as strangers among the godless."[64]

The figural connection between Israel's exilic and post-exilic fortunes and those of the church now at the very least demonstrates that the history and heritage that Christians share with the Jewish people has much to teach us of what the "politics" of profound this-worldliness looks like in this time after Christendom. David Novak observes that in situations where Christian spiritual and even physical survival is at stake, there is much to be learned from the fact not only *that* the Jews have survived but also *how* they survived, both physically and spiritually: "Learning how God has not abandoned us to oblivion can greatly help you appreciate how God has not abandoned you to oblivion either. Learning what God has done for us in the past enables us to have faith in what God is yet to do for us in the future. By doing that for you, we Jews can fulfill God's assurance to Abraham that he and his progeny will 'be a blessing' (*berakhah*) for the other peoples of the world (Gen 12:3)."[65]

It is not my claim that we find in Bonhoeffer a fully developed, "political" ecclesiology in the figural connections he makes between his time and circumstances and those of the Babylonian exile and Second Commonwealth Judaism. What these links do offer, however, are generative images that retrieve and rework traditional forms of scriptural interpretation for existence in a world come of age, a retrieval and reworking that I propose the church take up and take further in connection with the question of what it means, in our time and place, to be Gentiles gathered up into the contrapuntal spiral of the apocalypse of God in Christ. What follows in the remainder of this chapter and into the next, then, is a series of constructive proposals that extends Bonhoeffer's assumptions, descriptions, and assertions about religionless Christianity, a world come of age, and the Old Testament discussed thus far.

---

64. *DBWE* 14:918. As noted in chapter 2, the reference to the godless is not for Bonhoeffer a disparaging term.

65. Novak, *Talking With Christians*, 12–13.

Something of the political significance that Bonhoeffer invests in the figural interpretation of these texts for the life and activity of the church-community in diaspora has been insightfully recapitulated in an article by Walter Brueggemann provocatively titled, "The Legitimacy of a Sectarian Hermeneutic." In his analysis of the passages detailing the Assyrian siege of Jerusalem in 701 BCE (Isa 36:1—37:36 and 2 Kgs 18:13—19:35), Brueggemann draws our attention to a dramatic confrontation that takes place at the city wall between the spokesmen of the Assyrian king, sent to persuade the inhabitants of the city to surrender, and the besieged representatives of King Hezekiah of Judah. Two conversations occur simultaneously in this story, the first of which is conducted in Aramaic, taking place with the head of the Assyrian delegation standing outside the wall. The Assyrian envoy alternately taunts, threatens, and stipulates terms of surrender to the Judeans. The gist of his diatribe is that the city's inhabitants have "no real alternative to surrender; certainly, Judah's trust in [their God] is not an alternative, for imperial reason makes clear the falseness of such reliance."[66]

At the same time, however, another conversation takes place "behind the wall, inside the city, [where] a different language is spoken by a different set of people with a different agenda." This other conversation, principally between King Hezekiah and the prophet Isaiah, remains "out of sight and range of the imperial negotiators," and it is this conversation that ultimately determines the response of the city. In fact, says Brueggemann, if not for this secret conversation,[67] in which "a different set of assumptions, a different perception of the world, [and] a different epistemology are at work," imperial perceptions of reality would prevail, and everything that matters would already be conceded. "If the conversation with the empire at the wall is either the only conversation or the decisive one, Israel will decide that [their God] is indeed like all the other impotent gods and consequently endorse imperial policies as nonnegotiable realities. The ground for any alternative will have been forfeited."[68]

Israel's distinctive way of speaking and communicating enables the inhabitants of the city to take part in the discussion that occurs with the imperial spokesmen at the wall with a measure of critical discernment:

66. Brueggemann, "Legitimacy of a Sectarian Hermeneutic," 41–42.

67. Brueggemann's reference to a conversation that takes place "out of sight and range of the imperial negotiators" calls to mind the references Bonhoeffer makes to the ancient practice of the arcane discipline in *Letters and Papers from Prison. DBWE* 8:365, 373.

68. Brueggemann, "Legitimacy of a Sectarian Hermeneutic," 43–44, 46.

> Israel's elemental suspicion regularly notices that what appears
> to be *rational* is in fact *interested*, that what appears to be objec-
> tive is in fact *self-serving*. The empire wants its claims to appear
> rational and objective. [God's] critical presence enables Israel
> to notice the reality of Assyria's self-interest. Israel's alternative
> memory notices that what passes for public discourse is in fact a
> new sectarian proposal of an ideological kind.[69]

In the end, says Brueggemann, the primary effect of the deliberations that
go on behind the wall "is *to authorize* those who join the public conversation on the wall to be present freely, imaginatively, and critically. Had there
been no conversation behind the wall . . . the conversation on the wall would
have been preempted by an Assyrian reading of reality that appeared to be
absolute, accounted for all the recognized evidence, and faced no serious
criticism."[70] In other words, the city's inhabitants are *liberated* by their facility
in this other language, a skill that is critical to the practice of "politics."

Bonhoeffer understands that without this alternative conversation,
predicated on a different set of assumptions, a different perception of the
world, and a different understanding of how knowledge is achieved, Christians (along with everyone else) will, as Brueggemann says, "only submit to
and echo imperial perceptions of reality," or as Bonhoeffer puts it, "follow
merely human paths."[71] The guises behind which the interests of a world
come of age conceal themselves are effective if they keep most people from
noticing the narrow base of real interest. Unless there is a standpoint, a
"place" that lends critical distance to these interests and perceptions that are
the product of the technological organization of a world come of age, there
is no possibility for an alternative assessment of reality, or of a distinctive
mode of living.

The Gentile Place of the Church

The figural connection Bonhoeffer posits between Israel's exilic and post-
exilic fortunes and those of the church, together with his scattered comments about the importance of Israel to the gospel and the need to read the
New Testament in light of the Old, are but a starting point for reclaiming
Gentile existence. For centuries Christians have been formed by expropriative supersessionist theologies that locate faith "outside Israel, outside the
conversation between biblical Israel and its God, outside the continuing

69. Ibid., 54.
70. Ibid., 50, my emphasis.
71. *DBWE* 4:40.

conversations living Israel has with the same God." The result, says Jennings, has been "a *sicut deus* form of communion in place of an *imago dei* form of communion," the destructive effects of which reverberate to our day and place. Only by "recapturing the original situation out of which Gentile Christian faith must always think and imagine itself"[72] can we begin to recognize how we got to this place at this time, and then how to go on and go further with our witness to the reconciliation of the world in Christ.

Several angles of perception are involved in this process, says Jennings, the first being the need to recognize that we are Gentile readers of Israel's scripture, and thus we must read the Old Testament as first and foremost the story of Israel, the offspring of Abraham and Sarah through whom God promises to bless all humankind. Though we narrate it differently than do Jewish exegetes, it is still Israel's story, and it must remain so, because only in that way can it possibly become our story as those who have been grafted onto the cultivated branches of God's people. Second, we can never forget that we have been summoned to read this story solely as a result of the life, death, and resurrection of Jesus of Nazareth, a member of the people of Israel. It is Jesus and Jesus alone who, as it were, allows us to eavesdrop on the conversation going on between God and Israel. Third, "we are Gentile readers who should perceive living Israel through the lens provided by biblical Israel." In other words, God remains faithful to the covenants with Israel and does not dispose of the chosen ones. Finally, as Gentile readers we properly interpret our own existence through the lens provided by the Jewish Jesus, and not through the lenses of religion, culture, or race. These closely coordinated angles of vision all presuppose that we need to learn again for the very first time to see the world and ourselves from within the place established by God for us in relation to both biblical and living Israel.[73]

To recall what I said in chapter 3, a world come of age works diligently to bring about a mastery of both time and space by means of technological organizations of all kinds. At the heart of this project is the designation of a subject as the proper locus of choice and action, which need not be an individual person but can include businesses, laboratories, and armies, and for us it definitely includes the nation-state and global market. Once the place of this subject is secured, it serves as the base from which all other persons, institutions, and events are assigned their proper places. As we have seen, Christians have at the very least been complicit with this project, and too often we have been at the forefront of its operations. In so doing we have forgotten, in a centuries-long fit of self-induced amnesia, that the

72. Jennings, *Christian Imagination*, 251–52, 292.

73. Ibid., 252.

decisive subject is not the state, not the market, not democracy or Western civilization, but a first-century Jewish man in whom the reality of God and the reality of the world have been united, to whom the church is called to bear testimony. It is in relation to *this* subject, together with his people, their land and their God, encompassing a mountain in the wilderness, a royal city, a stable, a carpenter's shop, a well in Samaria, and finally a hill with three crosses and containing an unused tomb, that we find our proper place. Though we were once far off from this place, the suffering of Christ has brought us near (Eph 2:13).

8

Polyphonic Worldliness

In the Darkness something was happening at last. A voice had begun to sing.
… One moment there had been nothing but darkness; next moment a thousand, thousand points of light.

—C. S. Lewis, *The Magician's Nephew*

In J. R. R. Tolkien's creation saga, "Ainulindalë," Ilúvatar sings the world into
existence, setting forth for the Ainur, the first offspring of the creator's song,
the leitmotif to which the angelic beings were to add their voices. "Of the
theme that I have declared to you," Ilúvatar said to the divine ensemble, "I
will now that ye make in harmony together a Great Music. And since I have
kindled you with the Flame Imperishable, ye shall show forth your powers
in adorning this theme, each with his own thoughts and devices, if he will.
But I will sit and hearken, and be glad that through you great beauty has
been wakened into song." And a glorious counterpoint arose, composed of
endless melodies woven together that the heavens could not contain, "and
the music and the echo of the music went out into the Void, and it was not
void."

Numbered among the Ainur was Melkor, to whom Ilúvatar had granted the greatest gifts of power and knowledge, including a share in the gifts of
his siblings. After the music had progressed for a time without flaw, it came
into Melkor's heart to add themes of his own imagination that were not in
accord with that of Ilúvatar, "for desire grew hot within him to bring into
Being things of his own, and it seemed to him that Ilúvatar took no thought
for the Void, and he was impatient of its emptiness." He began to conceive

234

thoughts unlike those of his cohort, which he wove into his music. Some were distracted by these thoughts such that their own singing faltered, while others began to attune their music to his voice.

In response to the discord there arose from Ilúvatar a new theme, like and yet unlike the first, with power and beauty, but Melkor's discord rose up against it as well, resulting in a war of sound even more violent than before, such that many of the Ainur stopped singing altogether. Ilúvatar arose from his throne with a stern countenance and lifted up his hand. A third theme emerged that "seemed at first soft and sweet, a mere rippling of gentle sounds in delicate melodies; but it could not be quenched, and it took to itself power and profundity." Though they were at variance with each other, the two songs unfolded side by side for a time, one "deep and wide and beautiful, but slow and blended with an immeasurable sorrow," the other loud, vain, and repetitious. Melkor's song consisted of clamorous unison comparable to the sound of many trumpets braying on a few notes. His music sought to drown out that of Ilúvatar by violence, "but it seemed that its most triumphant notes were taken by the other and woven into its own solemn pattern." Ilúvatar then said to his angelic servants,

> Mighty are the Ainur, and mightiest among them is Melkor; but now that he may know, and all the Ainur, that I am Ilúvatar, those things that ye have sung, I will show them forth, that ye may see what ye have done. And thou, Melkor, shalt see that no theme may be played that hath not its uttermost source in me, nor can any alter the music in my despite. For he that attempteth this shall prove but mine instrument in the devising of things more wonderful, which he himself hath not imagined.

Ilúvatar then took the Ainur into the Void and said to them, "Behold your Music!" And they saw what previously they had only heard: a new World made visible before them, surrounded by the Void but not partaking of it. Ilúvatar said to them again,

> This is your minstrelsy; and each of you shall find contained herein, amid the design that I set before you, all those things which it may seem that he himself devised or added. And thou, Melkor, wilt discover all the secret thoughts of thy mind, and wilt perceive that they are but a part of the whole and tributary to its glory.[1]

Once again it may seem strange to introduce an aspect of Dietrich Bonhoeffer's thoughts on this-worldliness with something that at first

---

1. Tolkien, "Ainulindalë," 15–17.

glance appears unrelated, in this case, a creation myth by Tolkien that serves as the backdrop for his acclaimed trilogy *The Lord of the Rings*. There is, however, something discussed by Bonhoeffer, a German Lutheran theologian, pastor, seminary principal, and conspirator, in three prison letters to Eberhard Bethge that resonates with this story by Tolkien, an English Catholic literary author and Oxford don, making it a suitable introduction to and commentary on the subject matter of this chapter. In these letters Bonhoeffer develops the idea of the polyphony of life as "the musical image . . . of our *vita christiana*" (Christian life) flowing from our participation in the uniting of God's reality with that of the world in Christ.[2]

Bonhoeffer primarily uses the metaphor of the polyphony of life to describe the shape and direction of personal life before God and with others, but it also provides us with a generative image for representing the church's life and witness in a world come of age. The church interrupts the clamorous monophony orchestrated by the social technologies of modernity with the Spirit-led counterpoint of life in Jesus Christ. These two songs are not sung in separate domains or spheres—the one private and otherworldly, the other public and this-worldly—but are performed on the same stage, the world. Both performances are concerned with the origin, essence, and goal of life, the one keyed to the motif of death, the other to the joyous triumph over death, through death, to resurrection and the new creation. Through prayer and just action, the body of Christ interacts with performers of the monophony of a world come of age as voices in the counterpoint of creation, reconciliation, and redemption.

Bonhoeffer's comments about the polyphony of life are not the only times he invokes musical imagery as the basis for theological reflection. Jeremy Begbie observes that music seems to influence the way he envisions the basic tasks of theology.[3] Andreas Pangritz and John de Gruchy have made similar observations,[4] though they do not delve into the elements of musical composition that make the polyphony of life an apt imaginary for theology. No one to my knowledge, however, has developed the idea of

2. *DBWE* 8:394. Bonhoeffer asserts that he is "at home" with polyphony in music, a passion that he shares with Martin Luther: "It is most remarkable that one single voice continues to sing the tenor, while at the same time many other voices play around it, exulting and adorning it in exuberant strains and, as it were, leading it forth in a divine roundelay, so that those who are the least bit moved know nothing more amazing in this world." Luther, "Preface to Georg Rhau's *Symphoniae Iucundae*," 324. That said, it should be noted that in *Life Together* Bonhoeffer expresses a preference for unison singing in congregations, because it is free from "musical excess." *DBWE* 5:67.

3. Begbie, *Resounding Truth*, 158.

4. Pangritz, *Polyphonie des Lebens*; Pangritz, "Point and Counterpoint"; de Gruchy, *Christianity, Art and Transformation*, 136–68.

polyphony as an image for construing the church's multifaceted relationship to a world come of age as it seeks in communion with the triune God to cultivate a profound this-worldliness.

As we saw in chapter 1, Bonhoeffer leaves little doubt that the church's profound this-worldliness is distinct from, and stands in permanent tension with, the way worldliness is understood and performed in and by a world come of age. It is consonant with his life and thought to say that there are two distinctive ways or performances of being worldly in our circumstances, one staged and enacted by the social technologies of modernity, which as he says take "the world seriously only to the extent to which it can be *calculated* and *exploited*,"[5] the other revealed (though not always well) through the worship and activity of the church. The figure of the polyphony of life, its contrapuntal voices interacting with each other at multiple levels, beautifully represents the dynamic interactions on the part of the members of Christ's body with the same goods that the technological organizations of modernity use, and therefore with those whose performance is orchestrated within these technologies. At times the result is stridently dissonant; at others it harmonizes more readily with the form of Jesus Christ.

Through their involvement in the polyphony of the church's life and witness, men and women are drawn into the never-ending series of relations and transformations that takes form around Jesus Christ, in whom God gathers together time and space through the uniting of the reality of the world with the triune reality. The reconciliation of God and the world accomplished by Christ repeats or realizes itself time and again in the members of Christ's body through the power of the Holy Spirit, allowing the distinctive rhythms and progressions of profound this-worldliness to be heard anew in every time and place. The contrapuntal relation between Christ and the Spirit, enacted in and through the church, displays for all to see the constantly developing relation between reality and becoming real, between past, future and present, and between history and event or faith.[6]

Bonhoeffer on the Polyphony of Life

An accomplished musician whose tastes were initially shaped by classical and romantic music, and then by the gospel music he heard at the Abyssinian Baptist Church in Harlem, Bonhoeffer makes frequent use of musical tropes and analogies in his prison writings. In his lamentation about the way the personal and professional lives of his generation were fragmented,

5. *DBWE* 13:360, Bonhoeffer's emphasis.
6. *DBWE* 6:59, 50.

for example, he asserts that what matters is that they discern in these bits and pieces what the whole was intended and designed to be, and from what material that whole is made. Though some fragments are good only for the garbage heap, others remain significant for centuries, because God can perfect them. He has in mind here the *Art of the Fugue*, in which J. S. Bach explores the contrapuntal possibilities inherent in a single, very carefully composed musical subject.[7] "If our life is only the most remote reflection of such a fragment," he writes,

> in which, even for a short time, the various themes gradually accumulate and harmonize with one another and in which the great counterpoint is sustained from beginning to end—so that finally, when they cease, all one can do is sing the chorale "Vor Deinem Thron tret' ich allhier" ("I come before thy throne")— then it is not for us, either, to complain about this fragmentary life of ours, but rather even to be glad of it.[8]

He introduces the idea of polyphonic music, in which "more than one melody [is] played or sung simultaneously, each moving to some extent independently of the others,"[9] in a response to a letter from Bethge, who was stationed at the time in Italy with the German army. Bethge confesses that the missionary fervor he had as a seminary student in Finkenwalde had waned, and all his thoughts and feelings were now concentrated on his love for his wife, Renate. He then tells about one evening in particular, when he had sat up late with three comrades. Just before they retired for the night one of them said to the others that they had to remain positive about the end of the war, otherwise "we wouldn't experience what would come later; we'd just get together somewhere, 'dig in' like hedgehogs, and hold out until the last man falls." This attitude, he adds without elaboration, is considered to be "the true soldiery, the highest honor."[10]

Bonhoeffer rebukes Bethge for these last comments, telling him that he had no right to talk as he did with his comrades about the last man and the like, and that one should never follow that course of action out of some personal emotion. He then assures his friend that his desire to live and to be with his wife and child is natural, and indeed obligatory. "When you are in love," he writes, "you want to live, above all things, and you hate everything that represents a threat to your life." Bethge had every right to want to live

---

7. Wolff, *Johann Sebastian Bach*, 433.

8. *DBWE* 8:306. The first printed edition of *Art of the Fugue* included this chorale at the end.

9. Begbie, *Resounding Truth*, 160.

10. *DBWE* 8:369–70.

with Renate and his son and to be happy. Indeed, he must live, for the sake of his family and even for Bonhoeffer himself![11]

There is nevertheless a danger involved in any passionate erotic love, he adds, which can cause us to lose the polyphony of life. God desires to be loved with our whole heart and being, "not to the detriment of earthly love or to diminish it, but as a sort of cantus firmus to which the other voices of life resound in counterpoint."[12] Where the cantus firmus is clearly and distinctly heard, "the counterpoint can develop as mightily as it wants. The two are 'undivided and yet distinct,' as the Definition of Chalcedon says, like the divine and human natures in Christ." Is this why polyphonic music is so important to them, he asks, "because it is the musical image [*Abbild*] of this christological fact and thus also our *vita christiana*?"[13] That Bonhoeffer connects the relationship between our love for God and our earthly loves to the Chalcedon formula comes as no surprise, given his christological focus: "Human beings are not called to realize ethical ideals, but are called into a life that is lived in God's love, and that means lived in reality."[14]

The intimate affection shared between husband and wife, Bonhoeffer continues, is one of the contrapuntal themes that needs to be arranged around the cantus firmus that is our love for God, for only in doing so can it keep its full independence while at the same time stay firmly grounded. He encourages his friends to let the cantus firmus be heard clearly in their life together, for "only then will it sound complete and full, and the counterpoint will always know that it is being carried and can't get out of tune or be cut adrift, while remaining itself and complete in itself." Only a polyphonic counterpoint in concert with Christ is able to give life its wholeness.[15]

Bonhoeffer's comments are focused in this letter on the loves and passions that each of us possesses and that are a constitutive part of being human, and by implication of the marriage relationship itself. He notes that the Bible contains the Song of Solomon, and observes that one "really can't imagine a hotter, more sensual, and glowing love than the one spoken of here (cf. 7:6)!" Such passages, Bonhoeffer writes, contradict all those who insist that being a Christian consists in the "tempering" of one's passions, a requirement that is nowhere to be seen in the Old Testament. If the love that marks life together in marriage is related to the cantus firmus, then the

11. *DBWE* 8:393.

12. The cantus firmus is the lead melody in a polyphonic song, to which the other melodies relate to form constantly unfolding harmonic patterns. Counterpoint refers to the technique that orchestrates the independent melodic lines to form harmonies.

13. *DBWE* 8:393–94.

14. *DBWE* 6:232.

15. *DBWE* 8:393–94.

counterpoint will know that it is being borne, carried along, and cannot get out of tune or be cut off from the cantus firmus, all the while remaining itself and complete in itself.[16]

Implicit in Bonhoeffer's comments about the polyphony of life is an ontological surmise regarding the relationship between God and the world that is central to his understanding of the basic grammar of theology. He confesses God as both the first and the final reality (*die erste und letzte Wirklichkeit*), but in no way does this sublimate the world.[17] When he states that God desires to be loved with our whole heart and being, and yet that does not take anything away from our other loves, he makes no allowance for the erroneous conception of God as *a* being among beings, "the First of Creatures," as Friedrich von Hügel puts it, occupying a place alongside of them and thus competing with them for our love. According to this misconception, when we give our love to other creatures, we must take it from our love for God. God is only loved perfectly in this zero-sum game when God is loved alone. In the representation that Bonhoeffer puts forward, which is the more rare and difficult conception, God does not stand alongside other creatures, for God's "space" is not ours. God is, as it were, "behind" creatures, "as the light which shines through a crystal and lends it whatever lustre it may have." The love of God, writes Hügel, "is the 'form,' the principle of order and harmony; our natural affections are the 'matter' harmonized and set in order; it is the soul, they are the body, of that one Divine Love whose adequate object is God in, and not apart from, His creatures."[18]

Bonhoeffer returns to the idea of the polyphony of life in a letter he writes the next day, noting that as a prisoner he is in less danger than Bethge, a soldier on the front lines of battle. As he sees it, Bethge is experiencing all sides of life—its happiness in his marriage and in the birth of his son, but also its dangers. Bethge's situation is better than "having the breath of life choked off,"[19] as Bonhoeffer describes his own circumstances, quickly add-

---

16. *DBWE* 8:394; regarding the polyvalent meaning of the phrase "the love of God," see *DBWE* 6:232. What counts as "tempering" the passions, of course, may be debated. The ordering of one's loves to the cantus firmus of Christ, having to do with the virtue of temperance, is in fact what "tempering" is all about. See in this regard the first stanza of the poem "Stations on the Way to Freedom," subtitled "Discipline," *DBWE* 8:512.

17. *DBWE* 6:48; cf. Aquinas, *Summa Theologica* Ia.2.Prol.

18. Hügel, *Mystical Element of Religion*, 2:353; cf. Lash, *Beginning and the End of "Religion"*, 173.

19. In his poem "Who Am I?" Bonhoeffer gives elegant expression to the sense of having his breath choked off: "Restless, yearning, sick, like a caged bird, / struggling for life breath, as if I were being strangled, / starving for colors, for flowers, for birdsong, / thirsting for kind words, human closeness, / shaking with rage at power lust and pettiest insult, / tossed about, waiting for great things to happen, / helpless fearing for

ing that he is not seeking pity or wanting Bethge to worry about him. He encourages Bethge to be glad for what he has, "which is truly the polyphony of life." He adds in a brief but powerful conclusion that sorrow and joy belong equally to this polyphony and can exist independently side by side.[20]

This second reference to the polyphony of life extends the image to take in the actions of persons and events beyond one's personal life. Serving under fire on the front lines, or enduring the bombing of a city, are equally occasions in which we are to let the cantus firmus form and direct our thoughts and actions. The things that bring us joy, and the things that cause us sorrow, are aspects of life lived before God and in the midst of the world. His thoughts in this regard are very similar to what he says in connection to the psalms of lamentation in *Prayerbook of the Bible*. He notes that in these psalms suffering is not ignored, nor do the faithful deceive themselves with pious words, for suffering always comes with struggle, anxiety, and doubt. In such circumstances the faithful address their complaints to God, not only or even primarily in relation to their own suffering, but in view of the anguish of the whole community throughout time. Suffering causes our confidence in God's righteousness and hope in God's gracious will to be shaken, but the psalms of lament do not attempt to give a theoretical answer any more than the New Testament does. "The real answer," he writes, "is Jesus Christ." This is the *telos* of these psalms, to pray about the one who took upon himself our sickness and bore our infirmities: "They proclaim Jesus Christ as the only help in suffering, for in Christ God is with us."[21]

A final reference to the polyphony of life comes a week later, in a letter dated May 29, the Monday after Pentecost. He returns to the theme of living in dangerous times, observing that events that are life-threatening should be taken in as part of the totality of human life. Few people, however, seem to be able to hold many things together at the same time. When the bombers come they are overcome by fear; when there is something good to eat, they are obsessed with eating; when they do not receive what they wish for they fall into despair, and if it comes their way they see nothing else. What such people miss is the fullness of life and the wholeness of their existence. "Everything," Bonhoeffer writes, "whether objective or subjective, disintegrates into fragments." By contrast, Christianity "puts us into many different dimensions of life at the same time; in a way we accommodate God and the whole world within us." We weep or rejoice with those who mourn

---

friends so far away, / too tired and empty to pray, to think, to work, / weary and ready to take my leave of it all . . ." *DBWE* 8:459–60.

20. *DBWE* 8:397.

21. *DBWE* 5:170; cf. *DBWE* 8:479.

or celebrate; we are fearful when there are threats to our well-being, but nevertheless recognize that there are more important matters than our lives: "Life isn't pushed back into a single dimension, but is kept multidimensional, polyphonic." He adds that it is faith alone that makes a polyphonic life possible, allowing Christians to celebrate Pentecost in situations such as those he and his colleagues were enduring at the time.[22]

Bonhoeffer shares the sense of personal fragmentation and danger to which his fellow prisoners have fallen victim, but is not overwhelmed by them. When women and men live in a single dimension, seeing only the want or need immediately before them, they are unable to discern the many dimensions of human existence in play at a given time or the moments and movements of the past that led up to the present, and thus they are unable to anticipate what is to come in the future beyond what will satisfy their appetites and assuage their fears. They are realists of the brutely (and in the case of these prisoners, brutally) given,[23] held captive as much by their own passions as by the walls and bars behind which they are imprisoned. They are unable to see in the fragments of their lives the whole that God wills, or perceive that these bits and pieces are the material from which God composes that whole.

Taking (and Taking in) Time

What is it, then, about polyphonic music in particular that makes it a generative image not only for personal life lived before God but also for the church as it seeks to truthfully take in and faithfully respond to the many and various possibilities and challenges of a world come of age? A credible answer to that question begins with what Rowan Williams calls a bedrock fact about music, which is that "it takes time, and it arrogantly imposes *its* time on us. It says, 'There are things you will learn only by passing through this process, by being caught up in this series of relations and transformations.'" It is this characteristic that makes listening to and performing music one of the most potent ways of learning what it is to live before God and with our fellow creatures. We learn that things change, actions have consequences, and nothing in the temporal order of creation lasts forever. Music teaches us these lessons by extending itself through time, constantly transforming positions and relations, creating possibilities, some of which are realized immediately, others of which are delayed or left unrealized, but which are always opening up possibilities for change. Christians celebrate

22. *DBWE* 8:405.
23. I take this expression from Milbank, "Magisterial . . . and Shoddy?," 31.

this gift because "this is how we learn what we are, how we learn the wisdom of creatures." We experience what it means to work *with* the grain, "in the stream of God's wisdom."[24]

Williams further states that music is the most fundamentally contemplative of all the arts,[25] not because it transports us to an otherworldly sphere beyond time but because it compels us to rethink time, and in so doing to discern in the midst of time the origin, essence, and goal of all things, most especially of human beings. Music keeps and is kept by time, its performance and reception accomplished in and through the appropriation of *our* time, our life, our flesh and blood. Because it takes time and will not be rushed, music helps us recover the ethics of time. When performing or listening to music, time is no longer available for action, achievement, and power, or for calculating strategies of domination and exploitation. Music, in other words, does not easily lend itself to the ways and means of technological organization (which is a prime reason for its confinement within the realm of culture). It is a transformative event, able to remind us of "what we are and what we are not, creatures, not gods, creators only when we remember that we are not the Creator, and so are able to manage the labor and attention and expectancy that belongs to art." Music insists that we be receptive, that we allow ourselves to be changed, enlarged, and transformed by what happens, not at the boundaries where our abilities and projects play out, as Bonhoeffer puts it, but here, in the middle of things.[26]

Music keeps and is kept by time by keeping and being kept by us. It is impossible to sing a Mozart opera or listen to a Beethoven concerto in a timeless instant. Our being and bearing in the world are formed by what we hear, sing, or play. We can only listen to and perform music by giving ourselves over to what is occurring *at* the time, *in* that moment, by being receptive to and formed by the movements and expectations, delays and resolutions and surprises generated by it. That fundamental receptivity does not, however, render us passive or inert, for as we are caught up in the rhythms and progression of music our thoughts, actions, and passions are always drawn into the process.[27]

24. R. D. Williams "Keeping Time," 214–15, 217. In Bonhoeffer's words, this is how we learn to be a human being, "to have faith by living in the full this-worldliness of life." *DBWE* 8:487–88.

25. This is not a new idea, for Boethius in the sixth century reflected on the relations between the *musica mundana* (the harmony of the celestial spheres), *music humana* (the harmony of the human body in relation to the soul), and *musica instrumentalis* (the music that is played on earth). See Faulkner, *Wiser Than Despair*, 93–94.

26. R. D. Williams "Keeping Time," 214–15.

27. Begbie, *Resounding Truth*, 278.

One of the characteristic temporal features of Western tonal music is this forward movement toward the goal of gathering together the various musical elements, generated by multiform patterns of tension and resolution. "Tension" describes any musical event that produces a sense of anticipation that matters cannot and will not be left as they are: "All that is necessary is the generation of a sense of incompleteness, implying a later disclosure." "Resolution" in turn consists of a musical event that in some way, either partially or finally, satisfies that sense of incompleteness and expectation. These patterns of tension and resolution, which take time to unfold and be resolved, confer on music its distinctive dynamic in and with time, catching us up into an insistent movement that is neither circular nor strictly linear.[28]

The introduction of tension into a prior state of equilibrium creates an expectation of, and typically a desire for, resolution in the future. Tension is also generated through partial fulfillments, such that the sense of anticipation in the future comes from the plentitude and power of what came before it. One thinks here of the opening bars of Beethoven's Fifth Symphony, surely the most famous twenty-one measures in musical history. Upon reaching the cadence at the end of the twenty-first measure we sense there is much more to come; our desire for what is to follow is only intensified by the partial resolution. It would be a mistake, therefore, to assume that tension is solely a function of dissonance, though certainly that is one of its sources. Bonhoeffer notes in *Sanctorum Communio* that tension (*Spannung*) or conflict (*Kampf*) is often dismissed as entirely evil but contends that it has a productive aspect that arises from a common love of God, and exists even in the community of love (*Lebensgemeinschaft*):

> It is in the nature of the will as activity to function in community. Will comes into being where there is "resistance." However, resistance in the fullest sense of the word can only be that of another spirit's will. . . . Will itself experiences resistance only in the will of a person who wills something different. Only in strife with other wills, in subjecting these to one's own will or being subjected, is strength and richness of will developed.[29]

28. Ibid., 38.

29. *DBWE* 1:60–61, 84, 86, 72 (*DBW* 1:223). As the editors of this volume observe, Bonhoeffer here is echoing a position held by his mentor Reinhold Seeberg and others, defining social synthesis as the unity of the reality of will, feeling, and thought in their mutual opposition, culminating in the progress of culture toward the kingdom of God as the final goal of history (*DBWE* 1:86 n. 88; cf. 84 n. 81). The constructive role it has in *Sanctorum Communio* does not often reappear in subsequent writings, and when it does on occasion appear Bonhoeffer typically links it to the suffering of the Christian (cf. *DBWE* 15:336, 414).

The most common source of tension in music occurs through the element of harmony, working in concert with meter and rhythm. The unfolding pattern of tension and resolution generated by harmonic progressions and transpositions drives the music toward a goal that is then resolved, at times in partial, incomplete, or unexpected ways, creating new moments of tension and expectations of resolution, and at other times in a final and complete way, with the concluding notes. Tonal music depends on these multiple, overlapping, and interactive sequences or waves of tension and resolution. These waves seldom occur in a simple linear sequence, with one following after the other, but unfold on many levels at the same time. This is achieved through the element of meter, which refers to the pattern of beats arranged in numerical groups called measures or bars. A waltz has three beats to a measure, with an emphasis given to the first beat, called the downbeat. These measures are then grouped together into phrases that last two or more bars, which can in turn be grouped in longer phrases. These phrases are arranged in overlapping patterns such that the resolution of one generates the beginning of another, and propels the forward movement of a third. One phrase ends while others progress toward their respective resolutions, which then generate new phrasings.

The insistent forward movement of Western music in and through time toward a future goal regularly involves repetition of some sort, but never in ways that are identical. Even if the same theme is played or sung a second time in the same key or arrangement, it comes at a different time in the music, with different antecedents (e.g., recapitulating earlier themes rather than transitioning to a new section) and consequents. Repetition thus always includes an element (often quite pronounced) of variation, and thus of both temporal movement forward and return, to one degree or another. It is therefore necessary to speak of nonidentical repetition.

Complicating Space

Music's relationship to time is generally recognized; what is not as widely acknowledged is the way it also invites us to radically rethink space. When we take in the spatial dimension according to visual images alone, our perception of it is confined within tight parameters. Painters, for example, know that in any given space on a canvas there can be only one specific color, say, red or yellow. Either one color covers the other or, if they mix, a third color emerges, in this case, orange. In the same way any distinct object cannot be in two spaces at one time, or two objects in exactly the same space. "Things in our visual field occupy discrete, bounded locations—spaces with edges," writes Begbie. In the visual world, things are either here *or* there; two things cannot be in the same place at the same time in the same way.[30]

The visual construal of space is a key feature in the grammar of a world come of age. The concrete and differentiated habitations of space in premodern societies (which are dismissed as restrictive and obstructionist practices) are displaced in favor of an abstract and uniform configuration. The abstracted space can then be subdivided into identical units and assigned as "proper places," each carefully situated side by side as on a map, and each unit containing but one object, person, or event. As noted in chapter 3, the external imposition of proper places on indigenous space makes possible the strategic logic of action that informs the imaginaries of modern science, statecraft, and military strategy.

A visual construal of space as a series of concentric circles also informs Karl Barth's representation of the relationship between church and state, with the church functioning as the hidden center of the state and civil society.[31] A residual effect of Christendom past, this way of looking at this relationship presupposes what is in effect a static way of taking in as a unity what is whole and universal in reality, one that abstracts from the actual activity of seeing in time. Once this move is made, a picture is created in which every part of what is seen becomes simultaneously co-present to the knowing subject with every other part. The timeless subjects, in this case, the state and the church, exist within a finite, static, and timeless spatial relationship, the parts of which are simultaneously co-present in that timeless space. The temporal movements of history are thus reconfigured into the timeless abstractions of historicity, with little or no room for historical developments, ethical transpositions, or social inversions.[32]

This visually constituted logic also underwrites the default conception of human freedom in our time. The buffered, self-determining subject exists by itself within a technological cocoon that secures its independence from all other realities, including God. Freedom can only be the absence of external constraint, and thus every relationship must be voluntary if our freedom is to be preserved, at least to the extent of the conferral of meaning on everything and everybody that the self encounters. Every relation is set in a zero-sum, contrastive game, in which an individual's personal "space" necessarily excludes the presence or activity of another. Even should two individuals voluntarily enter into an agreement, it is only because they have chosen to restrict their freedom by allowing the other to intrude on their

---

30. Begbie, *Resounding Truth*, 286.

31. Barth, "Christian Community and the Civil Community," 146–89.

32. Poteat, *Polanyian Meditations*, 57.

space. The zero-sum game is then safeguarded by the contract, keeping the respective spaces distinct. The irony is that this conception of freedom as absolute self-determination underwrites popular democracy *and* unfettered capitalism, the dignity of the individual *and* the will to mastery.

As noted previously, the grammatical reach of this imaginative venture or wager extends to divine matters. Without instruction most people envision God as the First of Creatures, taking up space in the way that human beings, physical objects, and events do. Should God then act in relation to me, this action would invariably encroach on my individual "space." To the degree that God is active, it reduces to that same degree a person's ability to act in freedom. God must therefore withdraw from my personal space, must in effect leave me alone, if I am to be truly free. Paul's contention that we must work out our salvation in fear and trembling, at the same time and in the same space we perceive God also at work (Phil 2:12–13), can only seem incoherent.

Our perception of space is significantly different when it is "viewed" in acoustic terms. When I play two different notes on a piano at the same time and volume—for example, a middle C and the E immediately above it—both notes occupy the same space and yet remain distinct. They do not exist in discrete, "proper" places but overlap, augment, interpenetrate, and intensify each other without either swallowing up the other in the process. In the visual register there is only the space of mutual exclusion, with each thing in its own place and nowhere else. In the world of sound, by contrast, we are able to perceive space as allowing for realities to interact in the same place while simultaneously retaining their distinctiveness.[33]

We also think about freedom differently when we envision space in acoustic terms. When I play the middle C while silently depressing the key for the C an octave above, the higher note vibrates even though it has not been struck (an example of the phenomenon of overtones). "And the *more* the lower string sounds," writes Begbie, "the *more* the upper string sounds in its distinctiveness." They are not competing with one another, nor is the one simply making room for the other to vibrate: "The lower string enhances, brings to life the upper string, frees it to be itself, compromising neither the integrity of the upper string nor its own."[34] Multiple agencies, each having its own integrity, nonetheless interact in a way that can legitimately be called causal. The zero-sum game that reigns in visually construed space no longer rules in acoustic space.

---

33. Begbie, *Resounding Truth*, 286–87.
34. Ibid., 287–88.

Polyphonic music exploits to the fullest the complex character of acoustic space. Each melody line is independent, while at the same time being played or sung in concert with the others. These voices blend to create multiple layers of sound that have their own integrity, and yet which are dependent on the individual melodies. Finally, each voice is also dependent on the others for its harmonic and rhythmic coherence and direction, above all on the cantus firmus. Neither the distinct melodic lines nor the harmonic structure is either temporally or logically prior to the other. The harmony is generated through the interweaving of the melodic lines, while the contours of these melodies arise from, with, and in the harmonic key established by the cantus firmus.

Intimations of the Polyphony of Life

The imaginative grasp on being human, both personally and communally, in terms of the polyphony of life is anticipated in *Sanctorum Communio*, where Bonhoeffer identifies the reality of lived time as a dividing point between his thought and the idealist philosophy of the previous two centuries. He singles out Immanuel Kant in particular, who posits time as a pure form of the mind's intuition, not as a feature of experienced reality itself.[35] Idealism thus projects a timeless way of thinking about thinking,[36] but in actuality persons only arise and pass away in time, and thus in history. The I or subject is not a timeless, self-enclosed, "buffered" self; to be a person is to keep and be kept by time. Persons only exist in relation to others, as they are addressed in the midst of time, understood not in terms of a sequence of identical moments flowing as though through empty space, but in the value-related moment: "*In the concept of the moment, the concept of time and its value-relatedness [Wertbezogenheit] are co-posited.*" This moment is not a quantitative measurement, the shortest span of time, "a mechanically conceived atom, as it were. The 'moment' is the time of responsibility, value-related time, or, let us say, time related to God; and most essentially, it is concrete time."[37]

It is within the tensional setting of personal and social being that one person encounters another, not as an identical I, but as a You. Human beings do not exist as "unmediated" metaphysical units "qua spirit in and of themselves" (as if they were gods), but always and only as historically extended, socially embodied, and geographically located beings. There is therefore no

35. *DBWE* 1:47.
36. *DBWE* 6:174.
37. *DBWE* 1:77, 47–48, Bonhoeffer's emphasis.

individual without "others."[38] To be a person is to exist, as Bonhoeffer puts it in *Creation and Fall*, "over-against-one-another, with-one-another, and in-dependence-upon-one-another."[39] Others therefore comprise a porous[40] barrier or limit to our formation as persons, such that to be a person is to be both structurally open and closed. Open, because thinking, self-conscious willing, and feeling can only be conceived from, with, and in sociality; closed, because the person is not dissolved into a sea of surrounding spirits, but retains its own unity and integrity (though this is too often violated). This relation between the I and the You can therefore not be mapped onto the subject-object relation that is presupposed by the strategic logic governing the technological organizations of a world come of age.[41]

It would be a mistake, however, to conclude that for Bonhoeffer the "person-creating efficacy" of the You is identical with the personhood of the You, for as he asserts, "One human being cannot of its own accord make another into an I."[42] He locates the human spirit in "the web of sociality," within which there are both social and theological aspects. He explicitly cites language as constituting the social matrix, "hence the ordering of language before thought, and word before spirit."[43] Moreover, only as God, in the person of the Holy Spirit, joins the concrete You "does the other become a You to me from whom my I arises." It is because of God's activity that the human You is an image of the divine You, and since the human You is willed and created by God, "it is a real, absolute and holy you, like the divine You." That person as I is not holy as such, for that is God's attribute alone; that holiness does become visible in the concrete You of social life. The claim of this You rests solely with God. It is only through the activity of the Holy Spirit, then, that the You becomes a holy image of the divine You.[44]

---

38. *DBWE* 1:50–51.

39. *DBWE* 3:64; cf. *DBWE* 6:393–94.

40. Taylor, *Secular Age*, 35–43.

41. *DBWE* 1:67, 69, 73, 75. Bonhoeffer states that he does not intend to dispute the epistemological understanding of time as a pure form of intuition, and therefore he is not calling into question the epistemological endeavor as such (*DBWE* 1:47). His thought, however, tends toward the kind of radical critique of epistemology made by MacIntyre, *First Principles*, 12–13, and Taylor, "Overcoming Epistemology," 1–19, among others.

42. *DBWE* 1:54.

43. *DBWE* 1:65, 69, 157–58.

44. *DBWE* 1:54–55. Marsh's claim that Bonhoeffer's understanding of personhood in *Sanctorum Communio* is strictly dialogical is not entirely correct (*Reclaiming Dietrich Bonhoeffer*, 76–80). That said, Bonhoeffer does emphasize to a greater extent the mediation of Christ in subsequent writings.

The encounter between persons takes place, says Bonhoeffer, within a "real historical dialectic" in which personal existence and social existence constantly interact and modify the other.[45] This dialectic is possible because personal and social being have the same basic structure. Like an individual person, social being has a unified center of action from which it operates: "such unity is self-conscious and has a will of its own, though only in the form of its members." Individuals necessarily participate in social being that transcends them, but which can only be comprehended through them. As members of this concrete unity, persons are organically bound to the community or communities that form the center of activity shared by them: "This unity must be the starting point for a concept of community, for there is no way from the many to the one. Thus an individualistic starting point precludes understanding community."[46]

Bonhoeffer articulates his understanding of the relation of responsibility between the I and the You in a construal of history that sets the context in which the moment of responsibility is staged. We must first grasp the concept of person in the state of humankind after the fall, "for history in the true sense only begins with sin and the fate of death that is linked with it." The unbroken and direct communion with God that primal humanity had has been ruptured, and sin and death become the mediating point between human beings and God and between persons. The form of the collective person of humanity, and therefore of the social basic relations between persons, exists with Adam's rebellion in status corruptionis, as love is replaced by selfishness and communion with God and the other is broken.[47] We exist, paradoxically, in a state that isolates us from all other persons and yet binds us in a deep and immediate bond with them. This state is humanity-in-Adam, a collective person composed of isolated individuals that are at the same time one. All humanity thus falls with each sin, and each person is in principle no different from Adam. Everyone is therefore both herself or himself and the "first" sinner.[48]

God does not leave the sociality of Adam to its own devices, for there is another, "Christ existing as church-community [*Christus als Gemeinde existierend*]," who supersedes without destroying it. In the person of Christ the whole of humanity is concentrated in this one historical event, in which

45. *DBWE* 1:62. According to the editors of the critical edition, the concept of "real historical dialectic" implies a critique of the formal dialectic that pervades nineteenth-century idealist philosophy, and which Bonhoeffer regards as alien to reality (*DBWE* 1:62 n. 2).

46. *DBWE* 1:77-78.

47. *DBWE* 1:63, 107, 146.

48. *DBWE* 1:115, 121, 145-46.

God restores communion, on the one hand, between God and human beings, and on the other, between human beings.[49] Bonhoeffer reiterates this process in *Discipleship*, stating that Christ breaks the immediacy that characterizes Adam, in order to become the medium through whom everything should happen: "He [Christ] stands not only between me and God, he also stands between me and the world, between me and other people and things. *He is the mediator* [i.e., the cantus firmus], not only between God and human persons, but also between person and person, and between person and reality. Because the whole world was created by him and for him (John 1:3; 1 Cor. 8:6; Heb. 1:2), he is the sole mediator of the world."[50]

The difference between Adam, who exists only in isolated individuals, each one comprehending the essence of Adam in herself or himself, and Christ consists precisely in the latter's sacrificial life and suffering. While Adam's actions are self-centered and egocentric, the life, death, and resurrection of Christ constitute the new humanity, bringing all men and women at one and the same time into communion with God and with one another. A new dynamic erupts in history with the suffering of Christ on our behalf, as those who participate in him similarly accept responsibility for others.[51] In and through Christ's life, suffering, and resurrection, repeated time and again through the work of the Spirit in the church-community, the fate of Adam is transformed by the polyphony of life.[52]

Though death as the wages of sin constitutes history, the life that abides in the love of God in Jesus Christ breaks the continuity of the historical process, "not empirically, but objectively."[53] Here then is the beginning of a perception of reality markedly different from that imagined and promoted by the technological regime of a world come of age, a first sketch that as it develops allows women and men to regard "the redeeming mystery of the sinless bearing of guilt by Jesus Christ" as the uniting of the divine reality with the reality of the fallen world. As Bonhoeffer expands on this point in *Ethics*, to see "reality *as* it is," to see "into the depth of things," one must

49. *DBWE* 1:121, 145–47, 157 (*DBW* 1:76).

50. *DBWE* 4:94.

51. *DBWE* 1:146–47; *DBWE* 6:220.

52. *DBWE* 1:213.

53. *DBWE* 1:146. Though one could read this statement as creating a sharp break between the invisible and visible church, Bonhoeffer rejects any such interpretation, stating that this distinction is dangerous because it denies that the visible church is actually church. The notion of invisible "is in fact not used here as the opposite of what is visually perceptible or an object of thought. The 'essential' church becomes literally visible in the empirical church. . . . The 'invisible' church is visible from the outset" (*DBWE* 1:220–21, n. 92). This emphasis on the visibility of the church becomes more pronounced in *Discipleship* (*DBWE* 4:225–52).

recognize that "the world of things receives its full freedom and depth only where it is seen as oriented toward the world of persons in its origin, essence, and goal" in Christ.[54]

The Contrapuntal Form of Creation and Reconciliation

Bonhoeffer's description of the real historical dialectic between social and personal being in *Sanctorum Communio* anticipates his description of the polyphony of life. Just as the harmonic structure of polyphonic music only becomes audible through the melodic lines of the individual voices, so the structure of the collective person "only becomes visible in the individual intention to action"; at the same time the interactions between the different voices are only possible through the harmonic and rhythmic organization of the piece, just as the intention of an individual becomes intelligible only as we see it arising from, with, and in human sociality. The irreducible distinction *and* the inextricable relationship between social structure and personal intention cannot be overcome: "Individual personal spirit lives solely by virtue of sociality, and 'social spirit' becomes real only in individual formation; thus genuine sociality itself presses toward personal unity." It is only in our relations with others within a community that one discovers one's reality, one's "I-ness." God relates to human persons not as isolated individuals but in and through a natural state of communication with other human beings. God desires a history not of individuals but of the human community, not in the sense that the community absorbs the individual within its structure, but as a community of *human beings*.[55]

The striving of the world in time toward its destined conclusion by means of developing relationships of tension and resolution, and the complex nature of space that allows for both the integrity and interdependence of distinct voices operating at multiple levels: these are defining marks of polyphonic music, and they also describe the shape of this-worldliness in a world that has been created, judged and reconciled in the life, death, and resurrection of Christ. As a metaphor for construing the life of faith, polyphonic music allows us to see both persons and communities as contrapuntal elements in the *musica humana* that is both divine and creaturely.[56]

54. DBWE 6:234, 81, 260, 59, my emphasis.

55. *DBWE* 1:75, 62, 67 n. 3, 79–80; cf. Milbank, *Theology and Social Theory*, 74. Though misplaced, Bonhoeffer's reservations about the doctrine of theosis, expressed most fully in his Christology lectures, are anticipated here.

56. I am using the medieval notion of *musica humana* here to refer not just to the individual human body and soul but to social being as well.

Jews and Christians have recognized (to one extent or another) over the centuries the abiding tension between, on the one hand, the demands and challenges of being a "peculiar people" (Exod 19:5; 1 Pet 2:9[57]), and on the other, the need to live responsibly in the world as it is presently ordered. Bonhoeffer rejects both the radical and the compromise approach to this tension, each of which seeks a decisive resolution to this defining characteristic of the church. There is instead "a lasting and irremovable tension" between God's word of judgment and of reconciliation, between the divine Yes and No, between the last things and the things before the last, that is generative for the Christian life.[58] God's becoming human marks the apocalyptic intrusion of the final reality (*die letzten Wirklichkeit*), which is also the first reality (*die erste Wirklichkeit*), into history, transforming it into the time before the end.[59] God's rectifying action in Christ redeems time from the futility of sin and death, making possible a profound this-worldliness. The world is headed somewhere, and on the journey God desires that it flourish in concert with that end. It is precisely because there is an intended end that beckons to us from the future that the present is to be taken seriously *as* history.

Without the forward movement in time that is generated by the contrapuntal encounter between the last things and the things that come before the end, says Bonhoeffer, a movement that is neither uniform nor strictly linear, there is no future and no past. There is only the present moment that we must rescue from the nothingness, followed by the need to grasp the next moment. The result is a world that is perfectly set up for consumption as the exclusive occupation of the buffered self: food, drink, sex, celebrity, spiritual experiences, fashion, and sports (just to name a few possibilities). These things, taken by themselves, are but isolated bits and pieces thrown together in the monophony of acquisition and consumption. The loss of past and future leaves men and women vacillating between private enjoyment of the moment and the calculation of risk about the possibilities for enjoying the next moment. "Every inner development, every process of slow maturing in personal and vocational life," writes Bonhoeffer, "is abruptly broken off. There is no personal destiny and therefore no personal dignity." Serious tensions, which make times of waiting necessary, are no longer endured in the modern world, a fact that becomes evident, he writes, when one looks at the domains of work and erotic life. (This latter reference recalls the

57. Authorized or King James Version.

58. *DBWE* 6:104.

59. *DBWE* 6:149, 48–49 (*DBW* 6:140, 32–34).

potential danger he sees in our earthly loves when they are not keyed to the polyphony of life.)[60]

The description that Bonhoeffer gives of his fellow prisoners provides a microcosm of what takes place more generally when all sense of past and future, of destiny and dignity, are dissolved. When bombers come they are paralyzed by fear; when they have something to eat they take notice of nothing else; when what they long for is not forthcoming they fall into despair, and if it comes their way nothing else matters. Time is closed down and history is little more than one thing after another, one more appetite for which we seek momentary satisfaction, one more threat we try to escape or destroy. The wholeness and fullness of life, which as Bonhoeffer notes operates at multiple levels, goes unheeded. By contrast, the polyphony of life in Christ is multidimensional, accommodating God and the whole world at the same time. It is necessary, therefore, to "dislodge people from their one-track thinking—as it were, in 'preparation for' or 'enabling' faith, though in truth it is only faith itself that makes multidimensional life possible."[61]

Bonhoeffer's approach to space is a bit more ambiguous. His frame of reference for personal and social life is often spelled out in visually construed images. For example, in a letter to his parents from Tegel prison he notes that our lives are interwoven with the lives of others, and then marvels at the fact that "the center of one's own life lies outside oneself."[62] And in both his lectures on the nature of the church and on Christology he adopts Barth's static alignment of Christ, the church and the state in concentric circles. In the former he states that "the church is the center of the world and is the church-community of God," and in the latter he affirms with Barth that "the church must be understood to be the center, the hidden center, of the state."[63] His proposals in *Ethics* regarding the mandates can also be read in this way, with each mandate having its "proper place" and therefore a carefully delineated and distinct role to play in the one society of Christendom.

On other occasions, however, he pushes against a visual construal of social space, nowhere more forcefully than in his critique of the dominant conception of "two realms [Räume] [that] bump up against each other: one divine, holy, supernatural, and Christian; the other worldly, profane, natural, and unchristian." Subdividing the world in this manner is a marker of the imaging of space within the technological organization of modernity. Only within such a construal can one accept as a given the description of

60. *DBWE* 6:128–29.

61. *DBWE* 8:405.

62. *DBWE* 8:149.

63. *DBWE* 11:281; *DBWE* 12:326.

modernity as "characterized by an ever-progressing independence of the worldly over against the spiritual." Because of the eternal conflict between the two realms, women and men can no longer take in, as it were, the whole of reality, and thus they are told they must choose between the world and Christ.[64]

Bonhoeffer's rejection of the division of reality into separate domains readily lends itself to a dynamic and complex construal of space from an acoustic standpoint. Imaging the world in terms of separate realms positions the paired concepts of worldly-Christian, natural-supernatural, profane-sacred, rational-revelational in fundamental opposition to each other, existing as mutually exclusive places within a unitary space. This way of envisioning the world is oblivious to the original unity of these terms in the reality of Christ, and "*replaces* this with a forced unity provided by a sacred or profane system that overarches them." In Christ, in whom the reality of God and the reality of the world are united, nature, reason, and the profane do not exist in and for themselves but are included in God from the beginning: "It belongs to the real concept of the worldly that it is at all times seen in the *movement* of the world's both having been accepted and becoming accepted by God in Christ."[65]

Over against the static division of reality into separate domains, that is, proper places, Bonhoeffer envisions in this passage a complex and tensile conception of space in accord with the acoustic imaging of space, in which what is Christian is only to be found "in the worldly, the 'supernatural' only in the natural, the holy only in the profane, the revelational only in the rational." At the same time, however, he does not merge into a simple unity what was once separated, for what is Christian is not identical with what is worldly, the natural is not to be conflated with the supernatural, and the revelational is not to be equated with the rational. The unity of these aspects of reality exists in the Christ-reality and must be accepted by faith in this ultimate reality. They must not be set in "static independence" over against each other, for they relate to each other "polemically." Luther polemically led the worldly against Rome's sacralizing tendencies, and what is "Christian" and "sacred" must now polemically contradict what is counted as worldliness as soon as it seeks to establish its independence, "as happened soon after the Reformation, reaching its high point in cultural Protestantism." He adds that it is only in this sense of a polemical unity that Luther's two

64. *DBWE* 6:56–58.

65. *DBWE* 6:58–59, my emphasis.

kingdoms doctrine may rightly be used, and that this is probably its original meaning.[66]

A performative construal of time also enters into the tensile formation of complex space, as the reconciliation of the realities of God and the world in Christ "(repeats itself, or, more exactly) realizes itself again and again in human beings." The sacramental site of this nonidentical repetition (a hallmark of Western music) is the work of the Holy Spirit in the church. If we are to see "reality as it is," to see "into the depth of things," says Bonhoeffer, we must recognize that "the world of things receives its full freedom and depth only where it is seen as oriented toward the world of persons in its origin, essence, and goal."[67]

Bonhoeffer labels the static thinking that informs the division of the world into separate spheres as a form of legalism. When the world establishes itself as autonomous space, it denies the fact of its being accepted in Christ and of its grounding in the reality of revelation (*Offenbarungswirklichkeit*). When this occurs the world is not seen as reconciled by God in Christ, but as a sphere that is either subject to the extrinsic demands of Christianity, or as a domain that opposes its own law against the law of Christ. When what is Christian is portrayed as an autonomous sector, the world is deprived of the communion (*Gemeinschaft*) that God has established with it in Christ. A Christian law of some sort that simply condemns the law of the world is thus established, giving rise to a battle against a world that God has already reconciled to himself. Thusly separated into discrete spatial domains, the world falls prey to arbitrariness, and Christianity to unnaturalness, irrationality, and triumphalism, as well as arbitrariness.[68]

To be sure, there are those who would contest Bonhoeffer's conclusions at this point. Ludwig Feuerbach asserts that it does not follow "that goodness, justice and wisdom are chimaeras because the existence of God is a chimaera."[69] While Feuerbach is technically correct in his logic, it also does not follow that humankind can turn its back on some sort of substantive relation to transcendence and continue to act as if its moral compass will function as it has functioned. We denizens of a world come of age are the unwitting victims of a self-induced amnesia; or, to continue with the

---

66. *DBWE* 6:59–60. According to the editors of the critical edition of *Ethics*, for Bonhoeffer a "polemical" relation is one in which two adversaries strive to uncover each other's deficiencies (*DBWE* 6:59 n. 47). In *Letters and Papers* he rejects a polemical approach to the modern world, though it is not clear that he is using the term in the same sense in which he uses it here (*DBWE* 8:431).

67. DBWE 6:59, 64, 81, 260.

68. *DBWE* 6:60–61 (*DBW* 6:46).

69. Feuerbach, *Essence of Christianity*, 21.

metaphor of music, we are for the most part tone-deaf to that counterpoint of life whose origin, essence, and goal is the triune God.

A Musical Imaginary for the Church's Witness

The imaginary of the polyphony of life allows us to re-envision in important ways the church's engagement with the world that has been organized by the social technologies of the last few centuries. First, the complex patterns of equilibrium, tension, and resolution that are intrinsic to tonal music have deep affinities with the overall shape and direction of the biblical story. Beginning with the story of creation and fall, and continuing through the call of Abraham and Sarah, the exodus, the entrance into and then exile and dispersion from the Promised Land, a narrative progression unfolds at many overlapping levels through a series of promises, partial fulfillments, delays, inversions and transpositions, all of which revolves around the chosen people. At each stage a sense of anticipation is generated and a type of resolution is achieved in one or more of these levels, but typically with a sense that God will not leave things as they are, that more is forthcoming from the mysterious design of providence. A recurring pattern of expectation, delay and fulfillment, and further expectation gradually emerges, taking the form of a nonidentical repetition of events, places, and characters. As Begbie puts it, the providential activity of God moves in mysterious waves.[70]

These waves are arranged in the New Testament around the cantus firmus that is the apocalypse of Christ, in and through whom God gathers the people of Israel, together with the whole of creation, past, present and future, into the triune life of God. In Christ, says Bonhoeffer, nothing is lost: "All things are taken up, preserved, albeit in transfigured form, transparent, clear, liberated from the torment of self-serving demands. Christ brings all this back, indeed, as God intended, without being distorted by sin."[71] Sarah Coakley notes in Gregory of Nyssa's book on his sister St. Macrina that she bore on her breast a little scar from a miraculous healing of a tumor. As with the scarred body of the crucified and risen Christ, says Coakley, "nothing is lost that represents suffering confronted and overcome."[72]

Bonhoeffer and Coakley both gesture to the essence of Ilúvatar's response to Melkor's attempt to refashion, quite apart from the mediation of the creator's song, the music of the spheres. Ilúvatar tells him that no creature can play a theme that does not have its source in him, nor can any

---

70. Begbie, *Resounding Truth*, 282.

71. *DBWE* 8:229–30.

72. Coakley, *Powers and Submissions*, 166; cf. Gregory, *Life of Saint Macrina*, 47–48.

alter the creator's music, and to attempt to do so will only confirm Ilúvatar's intention to create things more wonderful than he or anyone else could imagine. Tolkien also alludes to Christ's suffering on our behalf when he states that the third song sung by Ilúvatar is "deep and wide and beautiful, but slow and blended with an immeasurable sorrow."

Bonhoeffer associates the gathering together of creation through Christ to Irenaeus's doctrine of recapitulation, which he calls "a magnificent and consummately consoling thought." The restoration of all things includes all earthly desire, and thus is not the same thing as sublimation, which he regards as belonging to the realm of σάρξ, the flesh ("and pietistic?!").[73] Restoration has instead to do with spirit, "not in the sense of 'spiritualization' (which is also σάρξ), but of καινὴ κτίσις [new creation] through the πνεῦμα ἅγιον [the Holy Spirit]." No one, writes Bonhoeffer, expresses this consoling thought with such childlike simplicity as Paul Gerhardt does in the hymn "Fröhlich soll mein Herze springen" ("All my heart this night rejoices"), putting in the mouth of the Christ child the phrase "I will restore it all."[74]

But as Bonhoeffer is well aware, all creation still awaits the eschaton, the final reality. The gathering together of heaven and earth in Christ did not reach a final and perfected cadence with his crucifixion and resurrection; instead it initiated a new phrasing that continues on in his body, the church. Christians believe in the last things, witness to them, live from them, and consider all things from that standpoint, but are called by Christ to live completely and fully in this time before the end.[75] As with the performance of music, the church's participation in the profound mystery of history that springs from and flows into God's guidance demands our time, our flesh and blood, in a process that cannot be rushed, and therefore must also be passed through.[76] The counterpoint of revelation—the reality of God breaking into history and taking form in us through the power of the Holy Spirit—generates in us both an expectation of an imminent end and the patience to wait for "God to speak in God's own time."[77] The activity of the Spirit weaves the members of Christ's body into this polyphonic movement of God in

---

73. *DBWE* 8:231. As Michael Legaspi notes, the notion of the sublime in the eighteenth century was instrumental in shifting the emphasis in biblical studies from an objective to a subjective understanding. Robert Lowth's revealing definition of the sublime, having to do with that force of composition that strikes and overpowers the mind and excites the passions, shows perfectly the parturition and development of the buffered self. Legaspi, *Death of Scripture*, 111.

74. *DBWE* 8:230.

75. *DBWE* 3:21; *DBWE* 8:213.

76. *DBWE* 6:226.

77. *DBWE* 6:152.

the world, transforming our bodies into voices in the counterpoint of God's suffering for the world. The church awaits a final fulfillment that has been delayed through diversions, digressions, and repetitions, including those moments when God is seemingly absent and we hear only silence. Waiting is seldom easy, especially when lives are broken into fragments, bits and pieces that are disconnected for the time being from the whole that is God's intention for the new creation.

The significance of the polyphony of life for the church's existence and calling in a world come of age involves the liberation of time and space from the constraints and divisions implemented by the technological organizations of modernity, which deceive humankind with, among other things, the illusion of immediacy with and mastery over the world.[78] When men and women are principally formed by these technologies, they no longer experience the temporal and spatial stage of their lives as participants in God's created order and redemptive design that mediates all that they see, do, and say, but see other people and things as threats to be met, opportunities to exploit, and targets to conquer. Our existence as human beings is caught up in the illusory sense that, as buffered selves existing within a comprehensive cocoon of knowledge, time and space are immediately subject to our control.

A theological imaginary that takes its cues from the acoustic sphere of music gives rise to a substantially different construal of the human relationship to both time and space. A distinctive picture of personal agency in particular emerges that allows for a richer conception of freedom than simply the absence of external constraint in simple space. Personal freedom does not require God to withdraw, to leave us alone. On the contrary, this imaginary allows us to grasp the true nature of creaturely freedom, which is only possible because God is acting in the same "space" as we do. God, who creates all things *ex nihilo*, is the direct cause of human freedom: "We are not free in spite of God, but because of God."[79] With God there is no zero-sum game.

For Bonhoeffer, created freedom is not a property or potentiality of human existence, but a relationship in which we are set by the divine act of justification.[80] He ties the structure of personal freedom in *Ethics* to responsible life, which "is determined in a twofold manner, namely, by life's bond to human beings and to God, and by the freedom of one's own life. It

78. *DBWE* 4:94. In *Act and Being* Bonhoeffer states, "When conscience is said to be an immediate relation to God, Christ and the church are excluded, because God's having bound the divine self to the mediating word is circumvented." *DBWE* 2:141.

79. McCabe, *God Matters*, 14–15.

80. *DBWE* 3:65.

is this bond of life to human beings and to God, constituted in Christ, which establishes the freedom of our own life. Only the life that, within this bond, has become selfless has the freedom of my very own life and action." We can either acknowledge or reject the responsibility that springs from this bond with God and other human beings, but we are decisively formed by it as persons.[81]

A This-Worldly Polyphony

Owing to its participation in the polyphony of life, the body of Christ does not identify itself with any configuration of temporal power, nor does it seek to withdraw into some illusory sphere of spiritual purity. Instead, it is called by Christ to live and act in tension with the forms of human association—family, language, state, people, culture, nation, and civilization—that the modern world would have us take as givens. At certain times and in certain places the tension will be less, the affirmation of the divine Yes will be the dominant motif,[82] and opportunities for collaboration in pursuit of the goods required for human existence will be numerous and substantial. Christians are then able to receive as gifts what others regard as givens,[83] and respond to them as voices in the counterpoint of the triune God. In other circumstances the degree of friction with respect to these givens increases. At these times and in these places the two performances of worldliness, regrettably, can become increasingly dissonant, the divine No comes to the fore, and the church may need to decide to act as a body of resistance. In either case, however, should the church cease to cultivate its own distinctive habits, rites, and institutions, it will to one extent or another be absorbed into the forms of temporal power within the technological regime of modernity.

The summons to a profound this-worldliness is never a command to change the world,[84] which in any case has already occurred in the apocalypse of Christ's life, death, and resurrection, nor is it to stand by as the world drifts further into the abyss. In *Ethics* Bonhoeffer writes, "No one has the responsibility of turning the world into the kingdom of God, but only of taking the next necessary step that corresponds to God's becoming human in Christ. . . . The task is not to turn the world upside down but in a given place to do what, from the perspective of reality, is necessary

81. *DBWE* 6:257; 1:51, 54–55.

82. *DBWE* 6:224.

83. Wells, *Improvisation*, 125.

84. Hunter, *To Change the World*.

objectively [sachlich] and to really carry it out."[85] He continues to hold to this opinion in the prison correspondence, stating in "Outline for a Book" that the church does not participate in worldly tasks by dominating but by helping and serving. And in his baptismal meditation for his godson he appeals to the word of Jeremiah to the exiles: "Seek the welfare of the city . . . and pray to the Lord on its behalf," for it is indeed in its welfare that we find our own (29:7).[86]

There are any number of voices that Christians, both as individual persons and together with other members of Christ's body, encounter as they sing the polyphonic song of life. Some are perennial features of the world, starting with the activities that Bonhoeffer discusses in his doctrine of the mandates. These mandates are four tasks—work, marriage and the family, government, and the church—that God has imposed upon the world to bind all human beings to their beginning and end in Christ. The theological warrants that he offers for the mandates are the incarnation of God in Christ, in whose ecclesial body "all humanity is accepted, included, and borne, and the church-community of believers is to make this known to the world by word and life," and second, the doctrine of creation, explicated from the standpoint of the incarnation, however, and not as "determinate forms of being" (John 1:10; Col 1:16).[87]

There is profound wisdom in Bonhoeffer's account of the mandates. With them he decisively rules out any suggestion of an autonomous secular sphere that lies beyond the authority of God's self-disclosing activity in Christ. Our everyday activities, relationships, and habits find their significance only in their origin, continuance, and goal in Jesus Christ, and thus there can be no retreat from a "worldly" into a "spiritual" sphere, for the whole human being stands indivisibly before the world (*coram hominibus*) and before God (*coram Deo*). He also condemns in his discussion of the mandates the concept of the orders of creation that can lead "all too easily to a divine sanctioning of all existing orders per se, and thus to a romantic conservatism" that is entirely at variance with the purposes of God.[88] Bonhoeffer is seeking to find a way to indicate that the life and language of the church do not operate at the margins of life, where the institutions of state and market would love to consign them to their proper place, but impinge on the practices, habits, and relationships that occur "in the center of the

85. *DBWE* 6:224–25.
86. *DBWE* 8:503, 389.
87. *DBWE* 6:67–69, 388.
88. *DBWE* 6:389.

village."[89] For example, with respect to the mandate of work, the globalization of capitalism has introduced some very discordant notes into the *musica humana* to which the church must respond.

That said, Bonhoeffer's inclusion of the church among the mandates suggests that at this point in the development of his thought he is still working with assumptions held over from the time of post-Reformation Christendom, first and foremost that there exists one integrated social space called "society" in the singular, within which the church functions as a subsystem. The emergence of the modern concept of the nation-state is key here, for with it the ideas of state and society are merged into a single unit. As Anthony Giddens states, "the nation-state is a power container whose administrative purview corresponds exactly to its territorial delimitation,"[90] and as William Cavanaugh says, "the nation-state is simply what sociologists mean when they say 'society' in contemporary life."[91] On this model the church is not yet a distinctive performance of this-worldliness, but a cast member within a more comprehensive production.

Matters begin to change in *Letters and Papers from Prison*. First, the concept of the mandates explicitly appears but once,[92] and when it does it is to take note of crucial limitations. Second, Bonhoeffer states that he is unsure how to relate to the mandates the goods of culture and spiritual formation, education, play, friendship, and the sphere of freedom, all of which are important human goods. He then makes a crucial distinction in connection with the good of friendship, "the rarest" and "most precious" within the realm of freedom, asking where it is to be found "in our world, which is defined by the *first three* mandates?"[93] This is a crucial qualification, for rather than continuing to group the church with state, labor, and family that together define what it means for the world to be world, he explicitly distinguishes it from them. This statement gives us an opening (though admittedly not much more than that) to see the church not as serving an increasingly marginal function within a unitary society but as engaging in a distinctive *performance* of these worldly tasks, treating them not as social givens but as contrapuntal voices in the divine polyphony. The church is not

---

89. *DBWE* 8:367.

90. Giddens, *Nation-State and Violence*, 172.

91. Cavanaugh, *Migrations of the Holy*, 30.

92. *DBWE* 8:268. Though Bonhoeffer does not explicitly return again to the subject of the mandates in *Letters and Papers* (which is a curious omission about which we can only speculate), in the poem "The Friend" he alludes to aspects of life for which he employs the terminology of mandates in *Ethics*, but he is again focused on the question of how friendship and freedom relate to regularities of life. *DBWE* 8:526–27.

93. *DBWE* 8:268, Bonhoeffer's emphasis.

an institution that exists and works in its own separate space but a living body politic that seeks to find ways to attune elements of the monophony of a world come of age to the triune counterpoint of life.[94]

Other voices in the polyphony of life show up only at certain times and places, some of which are harmonious, life-affirming goods (friends, neighbors, music, play), others of which are more dissonant (war, enemies, famine, natural disasters, betrayals, sickness). As Bonhoeffer has pointed out, the Spirit gathers these voices together in the eschatological counterpoint of Christ's life, death, and resurrection, such that nothing from the things before the last is lost, though neither are they left as is, but preserved, transfigured, and liberated from self-serving demands: "Christ brings all this back, indeed, as God intended, without being distorted by sin."[95]

The polyphony of life becomes even more rich and complex as the church encounters other peoples and forms of life, including their intellectual achievements, beginning with Greek and Roman philosophies during the first few centuries of Christianity. It is here that a second aspect of Bonhoeffer's thought in *Ethics*, the idea of the natural, relates to the question of the interaction between the church and a world come of age. He defines the natural, which he develops as a mediating concept in connection with the discussion of the last things and the things before the last, as distinct from the created, in order to take into account humankind's fall into sin, and from the sinful, in order to take into account the created. The distinction is crucial, given the tendency on the part of some theologies to conflate what is created and what is fallen, and thus the original splendor of the natural "was completely lost in the darkness of general sinfulness." This perspective, which holds that we remain sinners "even in the best of lives," and thus Christians should live the same way as the world does, underwrites the deception of cheap grace.[96]

The idea of the natural is also at odds with those who contend that aspects of creation were not corrupted in the fall and thus to some extent are knowable; for these the concept of nature "took on the brightness of the primal creation."[97] The context for this debate is a series of developments in the late medieval world, when an understanding of human nature developed that eventually led to the claim that the social mediation of transcendence was no longer needed to discern and achieve what made and kept human life human. In our day and time it is thus widely assumed that nothing vital

94. Cf. Cavanaugh, *Migrations of the Holy*, 65.

95. *DBWE* 8:229–30.

96. *DBWE* 6:171; *DBWE* 4:43–44.

97. *DBWE* 6:171.

is lost when the surplus baggage of "religion" is removed from the domain of what is purely human, what Charles Taylor calls an immanent humanism.[98]

In *Sanctorum Communio* Bonhoeffer dismisses the possibility of a speculative knowledge of the primal state of human nature. Given that the grammar of theology as a whole is eschatological, this doctrine must be derived from revelation as "hope projected backward."[99] He reiterates this stance in *Creation and Fall*, stating that the desire to conceive of the beginning is the innermost passion of our thinking. This insatiable appetite to take in and take hold of the beginning does not arise from mere curiosity but, as Williams puts it, "from the impulse to look for a ground in the discussion of justice and injustice in political affairs," that is, from the shared need for an "idea of intelligible action in a world of diverse agents."[100] Yet the beginning is closed off to us, and every attempt to breach this barrier constitutes "the bold and violent action of enthroning reason in the place of God." Human beings no longer live in the beginning, but in the middle, "knowing neither the end nor the beginning, and yet knowing that it [humankind] is in the middle."[101] All human thought and action take place within this middle, and somehow we must make our way through it.

As a mediating concept the natural denotes all that is open to the coming of Jesus Christ (*das Kommen Jesu Christi*) here "in the middle,"[102] while its opposite, the unnatural, designates everything that has closed itself off against the coming of Christ. In musical terms, the natural names all that acts in concert with the cantus firmus of Christ, while the unnatural refers to all that is dissonant with it. Natural and unnatural thus function typologically as anticipations and refusals respectively of justification, salvation, and renewal. In terms reminiscent of Aquinas's understanding of the relationship between nature and grace,[103] Bonhoeffer asserts that "the natural does not compel the coming of Christ," and hence it is truly unmerited grace,

---

98. Taylor, *Secular Age*, 242–59. According to Bonhoeffer, "There is no human being as such" (*DBWE* 6:155). The current debate over the concept of "pure nature" is a complex and contested one that cannot be discussed here. For an overview and an attempt to reconcile the various positions, see Swafford, *Nature and Grace*.

99. *DBWE* 1:58–60.

100. R. D. Williams, "Between Politics and Metaphysics," 5–6.

101. *DBWE* 3:25.

102. Though the Luther Bible typically translates the Greek παρουσία as *die Zukunft*, on occasion it uses the verb *kommen*, e.g., "Wahrlich ich sage euch: Es stehen etliche hier, die nicht schmecken werden den Tod, bis daß sie des Menschen Sohn kommen sehen in seinem Reich" (Matt 16:28); "Ein jeglicher aber in seiner Ordnung: der Erstling Christus; darnach die Christo angehören, wenn er kommen wird" (1 Cor 15:23; *Lutherbibel 1912*).

103. Aquinas, *Summa Theologica* I.1.8.

nor does "the unnatural make it [the coming of Christ] impossible; in both aspects the real coming is an act of grace," an act that *is* the ultimate or eschatological.[104]

Bonhoeffer pairs the concept of the natural with the idea of preservation, a concept he introduces in *Creation and Fall* to denote God's action in the world in the aftermath of the fall:

> All orders of our fallen world are God's orders of preservation that uphold and preserve us for Christ. They are not orders of creation but of preservation. They have no value in themselves; instead they find their end and meaning only through Christ. God's new action with humankind is to uphold and preserve humankind in its fallen world, in its fallen orders, for death—for the resurrection, for the new creation, for Christ.[105]

As such they participate in the forward movement of this time before the end that drives the polyphony of life.

The destruction of the natural, by contrast, "is, according to Holy Scripture, among the signs of the approaching end of the world." Bonhoeffer does see a limit to this destruction, stating that the organization that overpowers the natural breaks down in the long run, because life is on the side of the natural. There is thus reason for optimism, though it is a thoroughly immanent type that is grounded in the natural and has nothing to do with the nineteenth-century optimism that sin can be gradually overcome. Such optimism has its limits in the approaching end of the world, "indeed, scriptural prophecy drives this optimism from the role of a historical principle and pacifier once and for all."[106] As with the concepts of the end time and the time before the end, natural and unnatural, the preservation of the natural and its destruction through organization, are grounded in the christological and eschatological grammar of his theology.

In "After Ten Years" Bonhoeffer offers a similar interpretation of optimism, calling it a power of life and of hope when others have resigned themselves, a power to hold one's head high when all seems lost and to tolerate setbacks, "a power that never abandons the future to the opponent but lays claim to it." Christians who think it impious to hope for a better future on earth advocate a flight from the world. "It may be that the day of judgment will dawn tomorrow," he writes, but "only then and no earlier will we readily lay down our work for a better future."[107] This is but one instance of the

104. *DBWE* 6:173, 163.
105. *DBWE* 3:140 (*DBW* 3:129); cf. *DBWE* 6:224–25.
106. *DBWE* 6:177–78.
107. *DBWE* 8:50–51.

fundamental difference between those who argue that there is a substantial conceptual shift in his theological outlook between *Ethics* and his prison writings, and those (myself included) who believe that though we can see development and change in emphasis in his thought over time, they do not constitute a radical departure from what he has written previously. In the end how one views this difference rests as much on the assumptions one brings to the reading of Bonhoeffer as what is in his writings.[108]

Bethge and others have argued that he drops the concept of the orders of preservation after *Creation and Fall* due to its misuse by others,[109] but this is misleading. It is true that Bonhoeffer no longer employs *Erhaltungsordnungen* in subsequent writings, but the idea of preservation continues to pervade his thinking. He states in *Ethics* that government is not creative, which is to say that by itself it cannot produce life or values, but instead functions to preserve (*halten*) what is created. "By establishing justice and by the power of the sword," he writes, "government preserves [*bewahren*] the world for the reality of Jesus Christ." And the notion of preservation is implied when he states that through the mandate of work "a world should emerge that—knowingly or unknowingly—expects Christ, is directed toward Christ, is open for Christ, and serves and glorifies Christ."[110] Once again the forward motion that is characteristic of tonal music and especially polyphony resonates with these observations.

The emphasis on preservation is most evident in the link between the concepts of the natural and reason. Formally the natural is determined by God's intention to preserve the world and direct it toward justification, salvation, and renewal through Christ, and hence this aspect can only be discerned in relation to Christ. Materially the natural is itself the form of preserved life, embracing the whole of humanity. Reason belongs to the material dimension as the source of knowledge itself. It is not a divine principle of knowledge and order that can raise human beings above the natural but is itself a facet of the creation that has been preserved by God, and thus wholly embedded in the natural. Its function is to take in as a unity that which in reality is whole and universal. The natural and reason are thus correlated with each other, the former as the form of being of the preserved life, the latter as the form of its awareness. Reason is fully implicated in the fall, and

---

108. For an insightful discussion of the relationship between hope, optimism, and the Christian proclamation of the resurrection from the dead, see de Gruchy, *Led into Mystery*, 174–214.

109. Bethge, *Dietrich Bonhoeffer*, 459.

110. DBWE 6:72–73 (DBW 6:58–59).

thus on its own it "perceives only what is given in the fallen world, and, indeed, exclusively according to its content."[111]

Bonhoeffer's description of the natural and unnatural as dimensions of an ongoing and dynamic interaction between the apocalypse of Christ and the world spells out in more detail the performative tension that drives the church's participation in the power of the Spirit in the polyphony of life. With its complex interweaving of voices, each of which is independent of and yet dependent on the others for its harmonic and rhythmic coherence and direction, this imaginary brings to the fore the eschatological reserve with respect to the way that these technological organizations configure what counts as worldliness that neither the radical nor the compromise position is able to do.

The aim of maintaining the tension on the part of the church between the last things and the things before the last, as I have already noted, is not to separate itself from the human race as such, but from all communities and kinships whose boundaries fall short of the human race, past, present and future.[112] The independence and distinctiveness of the church is a sacramental sign in and to the world that it has its unity only in Christ, in whom the whole of reality "has already been drawn . . . and is held together."[113] As noted above, the idea of tension in music describes an event that signifies a sense of anticipation that matters cannot and will not be left by God as they are. A sharp or jarring dissonance is only one type, and it is not the most common.

There are also sources of tension that are internal to the church, legacies of the past with which the current generation must deal. The division of the church is one discordant note, as is the racial imagination that has fractured the body of Christ, especially in North America. Finally, the continued existence of Israel in the Jewish people is a voice that reminds the church, first, that the body of Christ may never regard the triune polyphony of life as its possession, and second, that much more is forthcoming and things will not remain as they are presently. For much of its history the church has responded to this tension badly, and even when efforts to get beyond the expropriative supersessionism of the early centuries were attempted, they often had the effect of making the dissonance worse.

In the final chapter I offer an example of the church's participation in the polyphony of life in connection with the dissonance that dominated much of Bonhoeffer's life, thought, and death: Adolf Hitler and the Third

---

111. *DBWE* 6:174–75.

112. R. D. Williams, *On Christian Theology*, 228, 233.

113. *DBWE* 6:58.

Reich. For his part Bonhoeffer is often remembered for his participation in the conspiracy against Adolf Hitler and National Socialism, though his contribution to that series of events culminating in the failed attempt on Hitler's life was minimal. I want to suggest that our theological assessment of his involvement in that endeavor needs to be put into a broader context, both historically and ecclesially. To that end I compare the context that Bonhoeffer inherits in Germany with that of a contemporary in France, with whom Bonhoeffer has much in common, and yet their efforts yielded very different results.

9

A Tale of Two Pastors

We National Socialists and Christianity resemble each other in only one respect: we claim the whole man!

—ROLAND FREISLER, President of the People's Court (*Volksgerichtshof*)[1]

WHEN ASKED ABOUT THE victory against Napoleon at Waterloo, the Duke
of Wellington is said to have replied, "The battle of Waterloo was won on the
playing fields of Eton." It was the habits and dispositions that the officers and
soldiers of the British army learned in boarding school that enabled Great
Britain to prevail in the encounter. Samuel Wells contends that Eton and
Waterloo exemplify two distinct aspects of ethical thought and behavior, the
first the long period of preparation, the second "the tiny episode of imple-
mentation—the moment of decision, or 'situation.'" Of the two, says Wells,
the time of preparation is the more significant.[2]

Those familiar with the life and thought of Dietrich Bonhoeffer know
about his involvement in the German resistance during World War II, which
came to an abrupt end with the failed attempt on the life of Adolf Hitler and
eventually led to his execution just prior to the end of war in Europe. Bonhoeffer had sought by his participation in the conspiracy to help bring to an
end to the horrific acts perpetrated by the Nazi regime, in which the social
technologies of race, culture, and religion converged in a perfect storm of
tyranny and genocide. What makes his decision intriguing is the fact that
he had previously embraced a form of pacifism. The decision to join the

1. Cited by Schlingensiepen, *Dietrich Bonhoeffer*, 115.
2. Wells, *Improvisation*, 73.

conspiracy stands in tension with his articulation of a peace ethic, which has left many to conclude that he had renounced it in favor of something more "realistic."

The decision to cast his lot with the conspirators is for many the signature event for what Bonhoeffer describes as acting responsibly for others. Debates about this fateful decision have gone on since the publication of *Letters and Papers from Prison* and Eberhard Bethge's biography. Most of these debates focus on whether Bonhoeffer made the right decision, and a recent book challenges the widely held assumption that Bonhoeffer knew or approved of the plot to kill Hitler. But if the time of preparation is more significant, these debates may well be misplaced. The lesson to be learned from Bonhoeffer's participation in the conspiracy, regardless of its extent, should not be limited just to this one decision, or even to his context and upbringing alone, but adjudicated within the typological juxtaposition of "Eton" and "Waterloo."

Bonhoeffer understands the importance of preparation, noting that while the entry of grace into the world is the *Letzte*, the last times, the church must first speak of preparing the way of the Lord in this time before the last if people are to be made ready to receive Jesus Christ. An intervention must be made, involving visible deeds of humility and repentance, "the concrete changing of one's ways." Though it must be as tangible as hunger and nourishment, "everything depends on this action being a spiritual reality, since what is finally at stake is not the reform of worldly conditions but the coming of Christ." Only preparations of this sort create the conditions for the gracious coming of Christ, conditions that he describes as being human and being good.[3]

In taking up this topic I do not wish to demean what the conspiracy to rid the world of Hitler has come to symbolize in Germany and elsewhere. It serves as a reminder that a vestige of natural goodness and humanity remained in a dark and evil time, and that should never be taken lightly. Christians, especially those who embrace some form of pacifism or peace ethic, should never dismiss or belittle the memory of what was attempted by these opponents of National Socialism. If, however, we are to learn the lessons not only of the events of that day but from all that led up to that fateful time, as well as what occurred in its aftermath, we must critically examine the larger setting on which the tragic drama was staged.

Bonhoeffer provides criteria for deliberations in our time and place by his own implicit rationale for participating in the conspiracy. In a given situation, he writes, "it is necessary to observe, weigh, evaluate, and decide, and

3. *DBWE* 6:163–65 (*DBW* 6:155–56).

to do all that with limited human understanding. We must have courage to look into the immediate future; we must seriously consider the consequences of our actions; and we must attempt seriously to examine our own motives and our own hearts."[4] Several things here are worth noting, beginning with the limits on human understanding, particularly with regard to what might follow from any action we take in the short term as members of Christ's body.

Such matters are part of any inquiry into the good, which is inseparable from the question of life and thus from the question of history. We cannot ignore the wisdom that hindsight offers. In what follows I focus on the ethical significance of hindsight as we observe, weigh, evaluate, and decide, and do all that with limited human understanding. More specifically, we must face the fact that the conspiracy not only failed to accomplish its primary goal of removing Hitler and the National Socialists from power, but almost certainly made matters much worse. A critical assessment of Bonhoeffer's actions must reckon with this failure, and do so in the terms he sets forth in his own writings. This assessment is necessary if we are to think more generally about what we should learn from this particular episode in the past, not only with respect to our ethical reflections on what it means to act responsibly in concert with reality, but with regard to the time of preparation. Any decision we make depends on the ability to observe, weigh and evaluate, and this ability in turn depends on hindsight in the form of memory, which is the wellspring of imagination and foresight. The ability to perceive the world truthfully and to envision the possibilities for acting in concert with reality must be carefully cultivated, which can only happen if there is time to prepare.

There must also be a space in which the preparation of memory and imagination can take place. Though Bonhoeffer's insistence that the church needs its own living space can be commandeered to support a two-spheres conception of Christian life and witness, we cannot avoid spatial imagery in our descriptions of the church. The church-community does occupy a certain space in the world determined by its worship, its order, and its congregational life, and this is how it should be. Rightly understood, worship is not a "religious" act but, as William Stringfellow describes it, "a living, political event. The very example of salvation, it is the festival of life which foretells the fulfillment and maturity of all of life for all of time in *this* time. The liturgy *is* social action because it is the characteristic style of life for human beings in this world."[5] The church occupies space in the world, not

4. *DBWE* 6:268.

5. Stringfellow, *Dissenter in a Great Society*, 154, Stringfellow's emphasis.

primarily for itself, but first and foremost to testify to the world that it is the world, that is, that it is loved, judged, and reconciled to God in Jesus Christ. The church has no need to claim all space for Christ, but only what allows it to fight for the salvation of the world. One of the many things for which the church needs to repent, Bonhoeffer writes, is the barrenness of its worship, the loss of holidays, the contempt for Sunday rest, all of which contributes to the restlessness and discontent of workers.[6]

Bonhoeffer's actions during the war were grounded in his desire to bring the violence and injustice of the Nazi regime to a halt. As he puts it in a letter to Reinhold Niebuhr, he must wish for the defeat of Germany in order that Christian civilization may survive.[7] The time had come for what he had earlier called "direct political action."[8] It is a mistake, however, to limit such action to involvement in a conspiracy against a tyrannical regime. That he and his co-conspirators could not envision other possibilities suggests, among other things, that both the time and the space to prepare for alternative courses of action had been lacking for generations. The church in Germany had allowed religious, cultural-political, and racial concerns to determine the place where the confrontation would play out. Because of this neglect, the conspirators were forced to "do battle" on the ground chosen by the Nazis. The polyphony of Christ, performed through the contrapuntal "politics" of the Spirit, had effectively been muted almost to the point of silence.

As a backdrop to my examination of the setting in which Bonhoeffer lived and worked, I contrast his involvement in the conspiracy with the ministry of a contemporary, a pastor of a small church in the French village of Le Chambon-sur-Lignon named André Trocmé. What the inhabitants of that village accomplished during World War II should also be considered direct political action, but one that is only possible when the church has not surrendered its self-understanding as a type of "polis" or "society" in its own right, with a distinctive "political ethics," which was not the case for the most part in Germany. The Huguenots, as French Protestants are called, had suffered through a period of persecution in the aftermath of the age of Reformation in France, and it is their memory of this time that constituted their playing fields of Eton, preparing them for the remarkable feat they accomplished during World War II.[9]

6. *DBWE* 6:62–64, 139.

7. *DBWE* 15:210.

8. *DBWE* 12:366.

9. David Gushee contends that of the small minority of Christians who were active in the rescue of Jews during the war, the memory of having been persecuted was often one of the motivating factors. Gushee, *Righteous Gentiles*, 112.

Finally, Bonhoeffer states that different ethical problems and circumstances require us to use different terminology, but that we must be aware that when we do so there is a very real danger of slipping away from the real subject matter, which for Christians is being accountable for our witness to Jesus Christ.[10] There is an ambiguity connected to the concept of responsibility that has led some to misinterpret what Bonhoeffer says in this regard. A careful examination of this misinterpretation brings us back full circle to the technological organization of individual and social life in the modern world.

Bonhoeffer's Role in the Conspiracy

Bonhoeffer was among the first in Germany to recognize that the ascension of Hitler to power constituted a political problem of the first order, and not just one having to do with the church.[11] On the day after Hitler was appointed chancellor Bonhoeffer gave a radio address in which he declares that the ideology of the leader "cannot be rationally based."[12] In contrast, many other church pastors and theologians welcomed Hitler's plan to revitalize Germany in the aftermath of a devastating war and in the midst of economic woes and political upheaval, protesting only when the government stepped beyond its proper limits to interfere in what had traditionally been the independent affairs of the church.

On one side of the ensuing struggle over the nature and mission of the church in the world were the so-called German Christians. These were enthusiastic supporters of the Nazis who boldly declared that "in the *Führer* Adolf Hitler" God was creating a law that spoke to the German people "in the history of our people, which arises from blood and soil. Fidelity to this law demands from us the struggle for honor and freedom."[13] They took advantage of a desire on the part of the twenty-eight provincial Protestant churches in Germany to unite together in a closer-knit fellowship (up to this point they comprised a loose federation) to campaign passionately for a single "German Reich Church in the national socialist spirit."[14]

Hitler and his inner circle understood that the support of the Catholic and Protestant churches was crucial to their early success. They skillfully played on widespread fears of communism and lingering anti-Semitism to

10. *DBWE* 6:256–57.

11. Schlingensiepen, *Dietrich Bonhoeffer*, 125.

12. *DBWE* 12:274.

13. "Richtlinien der Kirchenbewegung 'Deutsche Christen,'" 131, my translation.

14. Schlingensiepen, *Dietrich Bonhoeffer*, 122.

win the support of many Christians, or at the very least to convince them to adopt a wait-and-see stance in the hope that a *modus vivendi* with the new government could be found. In his speech announcing the passing of the Enabling Act, according to which the German parliament essentially gave up its right to govern, Hitler declared, "The National Government perceives in the two Christian confessions the most important factors for the preservation of our national heritage [*Volkstum*]. . . . It will respect any contracts concluded between these Churches and the provincial governments [*Länder*]."[15]

The German Christians, however, proved to be more inept than Hitler and Goebbels, alienating many who were otherwise sympathetic when they called for synchronization of Protestantism with the new Germany, which entailed adopting the *Führer* principle and dismissing non-Aryan (Jewish) pastors from church pulpits. Many pastors who were otherwise open to the Nazi program saw this as an unwarranted intrusion of the state on the rights of the church. The result was a prolonged struggle for the soul of Protestantism in Germany, leading finally to the formation of a dissenting group of churches called the Confessing Church.[16]

Bonhoeffer is fully involved in this struggle, seeking to awaken those who were outraged by the moves engineered by the German Christians to the full scope of Hitler's plans. He works tirelessly with the fledgling Confessing Church and later with his seminarians at Finkenwalde to develop the kind of theological judgment that could recognize the Nazi state for the atrocity it was. As war drew nearer, however, he grows increasingly frustrated with the Confessing Church, which at every turn had backed down from open confrontation with the regime and sought principally its own independence from the state.[17] He would later complain in a prison letter that in the end the Confessing Church was interested only in its own preservation, lapsing finally into efforts for a conservative restoration.[18] Moreover, many of those who personally opposed Hitler, particularly among Lutherans who had been formed to think about such matters according to Luther's two kingdoms doctrine, could not imagine acting against the fatherland.[19] For a time Bonhoeffer considers refusing conscription into the armed forces on the basis of conscientious objection, which would most likely have led directly

15. Ibid., 124.

16. Schlingensiepen notes that this tradition of church independence from the intrusions of the state still exercised an influence on Bonhoeffer (ibid., 122–24).

17. Barnett, *For the Soul of the People*, 35.

18. *DBWE* 8:429.

19. Schlingensiepen, *Dietrich Bonhoeffer*, 125.

to his death. He knows, however, that such a move would not be understood or affirmed either by the rank and file of the Confessing Church or by his own seminarians.[20] The only hope for disrupting Hitler's murderous plans, it would seem, was direct action against the *Führer* and his government.

As I have already noted, this decision stands in tension with Bonhoeffer's earlier commitment to and advocacy for pacifism. In spite of the efforts of some to hide or downplay this aspect of his theology, Clifford Green rightly states that it is "an ingredient and an implication of his theology as a whole."[21] In a lecture delivered in 1932 titled "Christ and Peace," and again in an address to the ecumenical conference in Fanø, Denmark, in 1934, he declares that the commandment of Jesus in the Sermon on the Mount for Christians to be witnesses of peace is simple and unmistakable: "The commandment 'You shall not kill,' the word that says, 'Love your enemies,' is given to us simply to be obeyed. For Christians, any military service, except in the ambulance corps, and any preparation for war, is forbidden."[22] A few years later, in a letter to Elizabeth Zinn, in which he admits that prior to his trip to the United States, "I was not yet a Christian but rather in an utterly wild and uncontrolled fashion my own master," he unequivocally embraces pacifism: "The Bible, especially the Sermon on the Mount, freed me from all this. Since then everything has changed. . . . Christian pacifism, which a brief time before—at the disputation where Gerhard [Jacobi] was also present!—I had still passionately disputed, suddenly came into focus as something utterly self-evident."[23]

Efforts to reconcile this tension typically fall into two categories. On the one side there are those who argue that Bonhoeffer abandons his peace ethic in favor of something approximating Niebuhr's "Christian realism."[24] On the other side a recent book contends that Bonhoeffer never leaves his pacifism behind,[25] and remains committed to what he disparages as "doctrinaire pacifism" during a class discussion at Finkenwalde.[26] But one looks in vain for any evidence that he embraces an absolute principle of nonviolence (though he does state on more than one occasion that Christianity "stands or falls with its revolutionary protest against violence"[27]) or that he moves

20. Ibid., 222.

21. Green, "Pacifism and Tyrannicide," 35.

22. *DBWE* 12:260; cf. *DBWE* 13:307–8.

23. *DBWE* 14:134.

24. Kelly and Nelson, *Cost of Moral Leadership*, 108.

25. Nation et al., *Bonhoeffer the Assassin?*

26. *DBWE* 14:766.

27. *DBWE* 13:402.

decisively away from his earlier peace ethic toward an endorsement of the principle of self-defense grounded in a nontheological conception of realism.[28] His pacifism, as Green summarizes it, is an explicitly Christian and theological commitment that regards pacifism as central to and inseparable from the gospel; it is rooted in his distinctive and thoroughly theological reading of scripture, with an emphasis on the Sermon on the Mount; and it is intrinsic to the church, to discipleship, and to faith itself.[29]

Bonhoeffer was drawn into the plot against Hitler principally through members of his family. The key player here was his brother-in-law Hans von Dohnanyi, who before the war had been a key figure in the Ministry of Justice but who with the outbreak of hostilities found his way into the *Abwehr*, the military intelligence office, which became a rallying point for anti-Nazi conspirators. It was not until after Germany's triumph over France in the spring and early summer of 1940, however, that Bonhoeffer was enrolled as an unpaid agent for the *Abwehr*. His clandestine efforts with military intelligence protected him from conscription into the army and also allowed him to continue his church work and his writing. His primary responsibility was to meet with people abroad who had contacts with their respective governments and to persuade them that the conspirators should be taken seriously and helped in any way possible.

For many, at the heart of the moral question of Bonhoeffer's participation in the resistance is whether he agreed with the need to assassinate Hitler. According to Eberhard Bethge, Dohnanyi asked Bonhoeffer at a meeting of the conspirators about the passage in the Gospel of Matthew in which Jesus says that "all who take the sword will perish by the sword" (26:52). Was it was permissible for Christians be involved in the murder of the dictator? According to Bethge, Bonhoeffer replied that the passage did indeed apply to their circle, and thus they would be subject to judgment, "but there was now a need for such people who would take the responsibility for deciding its validity for themselves."[30] Bethge states that Bonhoeffer was willing to carry out the deed should he ever get close enough to Hitler.[31]

Not all of the conspirators thought it necessary to kill Hitler. One of the resistance cells known as the Kreisau Circle included members who did not agree with those in Berlin who were plotting the coup d'état. One in particular, Count Helmuth von Moltke, who accompanied Bonhoeffer on

---

28. Kelly and Nelson, *Cost of Moral Leadership*, 116.
29. Green, "Pacifism and Tyrannicide," 40.
30. Bethge, *Dietrich Bonhoeffer*, 625.
31. Ibid., 751–52.

an *Abwehr*-sponsored mission to Norway, consistently expressed strong reservations against tyrannicide.[32]

Nevertheless, though Mark Nation, Anthony Siegrist, and Daniel Umbel offer a close and careful reading of the relevant texts that in many ways is exemplary, their effort to distance Bonhoeffer from involvement in the attempt on Hitler's life is finally unpersuasive. Even if one questions Bethge's recollection that Bonhoeffer was prepared to carry out the deed of assassinating the *Führer* should the opportunity present itself,[33] as these three do, Bonhoeffer was not naïve. He had to have inferred that at least some, and probably most, of those with whom he was conspiring were contemplating tyrannicide. Moreover, we know that he regarded those who seek above all to maintain their innocence in times such as these as incurring an even greater degree of guilt.[34] It seems safe to conclude, therefore, that he makes no effort to harmonize, either theoretically or practically, the profound tension between his peace ethic and his cooperation with those who sought with all the means at their disposal to bring the regime to an end. From 1940 on his life unfolds and then ends on a dissonant note.

Bonhoeffer on Responsible Action

Bonhoeffer begins to formulate what would become his rationale for participating in the conspiracy in the essay "The Church and the Jewish Question." Alerted by Dohnanyi about forthcoming state action that would exclude Jews in Germany from civil service, he asserts that the church has three options for action. First, it can question whether the state's actions are legitimate, that is, whether they genuinely create law and order and not a lack of rights and disorder either through excessive or deficient actions. Second, the church can bind up the wounds of the victims, whether or not they are Christian, when it fails to defend these rights and establish a proper order. The third and most radical possibility is for the church "to fall within the spokes of the wheels."[35] This colloquial expression refers to stopping a

---

32. Even the case of Moltke is disputed. According to Schlingensiepen, Moltke's widow reported after the war that her husband eventually set aside his principled objection to tyrannicide as evidence of Nazi atrocities came to light. Nation, Siegrist, and Umbel dispute this assertion, citing a line from his last letter to his wife to the effect that he wished to "remain free from all connection with the use of violence." Schlingensiepen, *Dietrich Bonhoeffer*, 286; Nation et al., *Bonhoeffer the Assassin?*, 7.

33. Nation et al., *Bonhoeffer the Assassin?*, 92–93.

34. *DBWE* 6:80, 275–76; *DBWE* 8:40.

35. In past English translations this phrase *dem Rad in die Speichen fallen* has been translated either as "to put a spoke in the wheel" or "to seize the wheel," but according to

runaway vehicle that is causing or threatening to cause injury to people. "Such an action," writes Bonhoeffer, "would be direct political action on the part of the church. This is only possible and called for if the church sees the state to be failing in its function of creating law and order, that is, if the church perceives that the state, without any scruples, has created either too much or too little law and order."[36]

The need to stop the regime forms the background for Bonhoeffer's later and more developed reflections on responsible action in the section of *Ethics* titled "History and the Good," for which we have two drafts. He begins by noting that our relationship to the question of the good is as creatures that are already living, not as those who create life anew and good. We therefore ask about the good not in the abstract *sub species aeternitatis* but immersed in life as it is given to us: "The question about the good is asked and decided in the midst of a situation of our life that is both determined in a particular way and yet still incomplete, unique and yet already in transition; it happens in the midst of our living bonds to people, things, institutions, and powers, that is, in the midst of our historical experience."[37] As historical beings we always find ourselves in the midst of a narrative that sets definite parameters on the way the story can continue, but within which there is an indefinite number of ways it can continue from that time and place.[38] Our inquiry into the good is inseparable from the question of life in a particular time and place, which must be articulated in terms of a historical narrative of one sort or another.

Walker Percy gives us a helpful way of differentiating between these two ways of thinking about the good in terms of a distinction between making assertions that require that we withdraw from the day-to-day affairs of life in order to discern underlying constancies amid the flux of physical and historical phenomena, and assertions uttered in the course of our immersion in the contingencies of the day to day. The former category Percy calls "science," in which he includes metaphysics and poetry as well as mathematics and physics; the latter he labels "news," and encompasses utterances such as "The British are coming" and "The market is up $2.00." The two types of assertions signify two kinds of postures on the basis of which we hear or read them, two types of verification procedures by which we act on them, and two kinds of responses to what they assert. The mistake that

---

Andreas Pangritz, neither renders the implicit personal emphasis of throwing oneself into the spokes of the wheel to stop it that is implied in the German. Pangritz, "'To Fall within the Spokes,'" 102–3.

36. *DBWE* 12:365–66 and n. 12.

37. *DBWE* 6:246–47.

38. MacIntyre, *After Virtue*, 216.

modern human beings regularly make, says Percy, is to assume that "science" sentences are intrinsically superior to "news" sentences.[39]

Due to his unwillingness to examine the concept apart from the uniting of God's reality with the reality of the world in the person of Jesus Christ, Bonhoeffer locates the question of our inquiry into the good firmly in the category of news. In response to this good news that informs us of the mystery of history, those who act in the dangerous freedom of their own responsibility see their action both flowing into and springing from God's guidance and initiative. Free human action in history is shown to be God's action, and thus the purest action is passivity.[40] Because only the triune God is good,[41] it is God alone who accomplishes good in history, and makes human action good by incorporating it into God's hidden plan in pursuit of the goal of history that has been revealed in Christ. Human historical action can be called good only as God draws it into this hidden plan, "and as the human agent completely surrenders all to God's action without claiming any other justification."[42]

Bonhoeffer displays a robust conception of both divine providence and human freedom consistent with the "news" character of the gospel, setting up a tension that best makes sense in terms of something like the polyphonic depiction of time and space as the context of Christian life. What follows epistemically from the mysterious counterpoint of historical existence, however, is that we must live and act "in the twilight [*Zwielicht*] that the historical situation casts over good and evil." Within this sphere of contingent historical action we cannot know with any degree of certainty how and to what extent our actions help bring about the goal of history, which is the good. Those who act in concert with reality as defined by the uniting of the reality of God and of the world in Christ, and who offer up to God their actions, "have to console themselves with faith in the forgiving and healing grace of God." They have no way of ensuring that their actions

---

39. Percy, *Message in the Bottle*, 122–25, 133, 211.

40. For Bonhoeffer passivity is a theological and not a psychological concept, and does not exclude our thoughts, words, or deeds: "To be loved by God certainly does not prohibit human beings from thinking powerful thoughts and doing joyful deeds. It is as whole human beings, as thinking and acting human beings, that we are loved by God in Christ, that we are reconciled with God. And as whole human beings, thinking and acting, we love God and our brothers and sisters" (*DBWE* 6:226, 336–37; cf. 147). As I noted before, such a conception implicitly entails a noncontrastive relationship between God and human beings, such that God's action is the cause of our own and not its antithesis.

41. *DBWE* 4:255.

42. *DBWE* 6:226–27; cf. 284.

are the right ones to take, because living reality does not provide an unambiguous standard for particular times and places.[43]

Bonhoeffer here recapitulates themes previously introduced in *Creation and Fall*. The desire to ask about the beginning, to long for that sense of certainty, is the fundamental impulse of human thinking, imparting "reality to every genuine question we ask." It is a basic impulse, because we want to believe what is true; few things are more distressing to us than the thought that we have assented to what is false. But as soon as we pose the question about the beginning, our thinking comes to an end, because we live and act in the middle, "knowing neither the end nor the beginning, and yet knowing that [we are] in the middle," that is, in the twilight in which what is created and what is evil cannot be separated without damaging something crucial. Faced with this situation, who can speak of the beginning? One possibility is the evil one, who has been a liar from the beginning and who summons us to worship him, so that we will imagine ourselves with him in the beginning and thereby be the lord of the truth that comes out of his lie. The other is to turn to the one who was in the beginning, the very God, Christ, the Holy Spirit, who has been the truth from the beginning.[44]

Faith in the triune God does not, however, make matters clearer, either with respect to dogmatic questions such as the oneness of God that we share with our Jewish neighbors,[45] or to the course of providence within history. With regard to the latter, we are faced with a deep and mysterious abyss, says Bonhoeffer, for God uses both good and evil to accomplish the divine plan. When we consider with our limited knowledge and wisdom what humans do, we learn (often only after the fact) that God often acts in ways such that "the 'good' causes harm and the 'evil' brings benefits." It is through the deed of Judas Iscariot that God makes Christ the redeemer of the world. God cuts across the grain of our good and evil, for only God seeks to do the good, and thus we must surrender our actions to God's wrath and grace.[46]

If God alone does the good, and if our actions cannot simply accomplish God's good, which is nothing other than Christ and the guidance of history toward God, what then constitutes the good in our historical actions? It consists first in "allowing our actions to be determined by the knowledge that it is not us but indeed God alone who accomplishes good in history." This knowledge allows us to abandon the search for absolute and certain standards by which to judge our actions in the contingencies of

43. *DBWE* 6:222, 284, 227 (*DBW* 6:221); cf. *DBWE* 3:104.

44. *DBWE* 3:25–29.

45. R. D. Williams, *On Christian Theology*, 138.

46. *DBWE* 6:227.

history,[47] and accept "the intrinsically hopeless predicament" that is placed on all who seek to act responsibly, which is the quandary of having to do the good without being able to do it. Only those who can renounce any self-justification are those who are able to act with the eschatological freedom of the wager to do the good, that is, to live in concert with reality, and trusting God's grace to do what is necessary and commanded.[48]

Bonhoeffer once again posits a christological basis for his argument. In *Creation and Fall* he states that God alone tells us that God is in the beginning, testifying to that fact by means of a word that comes to us wholly from the middle and not from the beginning. "This word," he writes, "spoken and heard as a human word, is the form of a servant in which from the beginning God encounters us and in which alone God wills to be found."[49] In *Ethics* the question of the good, bound as it is to the question of life and thus of history, find its appropriate expression not in the query, *what* life is, for in light of the incarnation that question changes into the answer of *who* life is.[50] For Bonhoeffer, life is not a thing, an abstract essence or concept, but a particular and unique person. This person does not just possess life among other attributes, for it subsists "as an I, the I of Jesus."[51] This life that is identical with this person is life itself, not just as an abstract metaphysical entity, for "he is precisely *my* life, our life. . . . My life is outside myself, beyond my disposal. My life is another, a stranger, Jesus Christ."[52]

Because both the good and life subsist in Christ, and "it is no longer possible to conceive and understand humanity other than in Jesus Christ, nor God other than in the human form of Jesus Christ," concepts such as the human being as such are empty abstractions. This means, among other things, that there is no relation to other women and men without a relation to God, nor a relation to God without other persons: "Again, only the relation to Jesus Christ is the basis for our relation to other human beings and to God." And just as Christ is our life, so also is he the life of all that is created:

47. As Aristotle had already noted two and a half centuries earlier, such expectations are simply not reasonable. Aristotle, *Nicomachean Ethics*, 1094a, 1098a.

48. *DBWE* 6:228. The German reads, "Verzicht auf jede Selbstrechtfertigung bei letzter Freiheit des Wagnisses, das Gute, das heißt das der Wirklichkeit Gemäße, das Notwendige und Gebotene zu tun, auf Gottes Gnade hin" (*DBW* 6:227).

49. *DBWE* 3:30.

50. This distinction follows the pattern Bonhoeffer set in his 1933 Christology lectures. *DBWE* 12:302–3.

51. Here Bonhoeffer avails himself of the well-established grammar of divinity that Aquinas lays out in his theology, such that God does not possess goodness as creatures do, for goodness is identical to God's being. Aquinas, *Summa Theologica* 1a.6.

52. *DBWE* 6:249–50, Bonhoeffer's emphasis.

"Jesus Christ is life itself. And what is thus true of my life is true of all that is created. 'What has come into being—in it he was life' (John 1:4)."[53]

In this word of life that God addresses to us we must hear and accept both the divine No and the divine Yes. The No is spoken over our fallen life that we live in contradiction to Christ, who is the origin, essence, and goal of our life. This fallen life cannot become the life of Christ without first suffering its own end, annihilation, and death, which is brought about by the divine No. This No then becomes the condition for God's Yes to us in Christ, who gives us the life we cannot give ourselves, but comes from beyond ourselves. We now live stretched between the No—the judgment and death that rules over life that has fallen away from its origin, essence, and goal—and the Yes to what is created, to health, happiness, achievement, success, greatness, honor.[54]

To live, therefore, means that in our dealings with other persons and with God, whether in the ordinary events of everyday life or in moments of crisis, the divine No and Yes are bound inextricably together in a contradictory unity (*widerspruchsvollen Einheit*), taking the form of a selfless self-assertion that is at its base a surrender of oneself to God and other human beings: "The life that encounters us in Jesus Christ as the Yes and the No to our life must be answered by a life that incorporates and unites this Yes and No." We come to live in this contrapuntal tension of the Yes and the No by responding to the word that God has addressed to us in Christ, which addresses every aspect of our life, and to which our answer must also be with the whole of our life as it is realized in particular acts.[55]

Our understanding of and participation in the good cannot take the form of isolated individuals applying abstract principles, because this understanding of the moral life fails to connect with real life, a failing that in turns tends in one of two extremes. One such extreme understands the good exclusively as following principles without concern for other human beings, leading to the complete privatization of the moral life in the form of either bourgeois existence or the monastery. The second is the path of *die Schwärmer*, the enthusiasts and fanatics, a category that includes political extremists and ideologues of all sorts, and the nosy, crazy reformers of every shade and color. Action that is in concert with the divine Yes and the No that is at the heart of created reality originates instead in the person of Jesus Christ and "is directed to concrete neighbors in their concrete reality."[56]

53. *DBWE* 6:155, 253–54, 250.
54. *DBWE* 6:250–51.
55. *DBWE* 6:253–54 (*DBW* 6:252).
56. *DBWE* 6:248–49, 231, 261.

Any attempt to understand the reality of the world apart from Christ means living in an abstraction, "detached from reality and vacillating endlessly between the extremes of a servile attitude toward the status quo and rebellion against it."[57] As the origin, essence, and goal of all reality, of all things, conditions, and values as well as of human beings, Christ is the lord and law of the real. His sayings, above all the Sermon on the Mount, are the interpretation of his life and actions, and thus they interpret that reality in which history finds its fulfillment. They constitute the divine commandment for responsible action in history insofar as they are the reality of history that has been fulfilled in Christ, "that is, insofar as they are the responsibility for human beings that has been fulfilled in Christ alone." These sayings are not an abstract ethic for individuals but are intelligible only within the reality of history, for it is there that they find their source: "Only when rooted in their origin do they possess the power to gain control of reality."[58]

Acting in concert with Christ allows the world to be the world, and only on that basis are we able to reckon with it *as* world, that is, as that which is loved, judged, and reconciled by God in Christ. Precluded is any kind of distinction between a "Christian principle" and a "worldly principle," which can only lead us in one of two erroneous directions. On the one hand it leads to various forms of secularism, and in particular to the establishment of "autonomous spheres of life," and on the other, to religious enthusiasm. Dividing the world into autonomous spheres posits a very different reality for it, embodied in a number of irreconcilable laws, which is the view of reality in Greek tragedy. It is also wrong, says Bonhoeffer, to see the Christian and the worldly as a unity in the form of a principle. The reconciliation of God and the world takes place solely in Christ, who as God incarnate acts and suffers on behalf of and as representative for all humanity. Human action springs from this already accomplished reconciliation, such that neither what is worldly nor Christian is defined in distinction from the other but only within the concrete responsibility of action grounded in the reconciliation that has taken place in Christ.[59]

Responsible action is undertaken within definite limits, the first of which is the limitation of creatureliness, especially human understanding: "Ultimate ignorance of one's own goodness or evil, together with dependence upon grace, is an essential characteristic of responsible historical action." A second limitation is the recognition that other people who inhabit the sphere of historical action should also be regarded as responsible. This

57. *DBWE* 6:259–62.
58. *DBWE* 6:263–64.
59. *DBWE* 6:264–66.

requires recognizing others as responsible, and making them aware of it. The responsibility that one has as a parent or a statesman encounters its limit in the responsibility of the other in that relationship, the child or the citizen. "Indeed," writes Bonhoeffer, "the responsibility of the father or the statesman consists precisely in raising to a conscious level the responsibility of those entrusted to their care, in strengthening their responsibility." In other words, there is a component of spiritual and moral formation that subsists in the mutual relationship between persons in the context of responsible action. This relationship is derived from the responsibility of Jesus Christ for all humanity as the origin, essence, and goal of all reality.[60]

At the heart of Bonhoeffer's implicit argument for participating in the conspiracy against Hitler is the question of what constitutes the appropriate (*sachgemäß*) relationship between the person who seeks to act responsibly and technological organizations such as the state. He says, first, that in their origin, essence, and goal these organizations are related both to God and to human beings, establishing the objective standpoint (*Sachlichkeit*) from which to assess them. A proper knowledge of this relationship both purifies and intensifies our dedication to the matter at hand in that it frees us from secondary personal agendas. When the ultimate personal sacrifice must be made, it must be to restore this relationship of social institutions and human persons grounded in the responsibility that is derived from Jesus Christ.[61]

Second, Bonhoeffer posits the existence of an intrinsic law (*Wesengesetz*) for these institutions that is based in their origin, that is, having to do with their essential function or purpose. "To be in accord with reality," writes Bonhoeffer, "responsible action has to discern and comply with these laws." In some areas of life (he cites as an example the manufacture of electronic goods), it is almost completely a matter of technology, but when human beings are involved, as in the practice of statecraft (*Staatskunst*), more is required. The task of discerning the intrinsic law for these institutions is more difficult since they are tied to the historical contingencies of human existence. The intrinsic law of the state extends beyond the definitions that constitute its technological basis in the practices of administration and diplomacy, but also in instruments such as legal codes, treaties, and the rules of national and international political existence that have received historical sanction. Appropriate action will typically be carried out in the context of these laws.[62]

60. *DBWE* 6:260–70.

61. *DBWE* 6:270–71.

62. *DBWE* 6:271–72.

The key word here is "typically," for whenever strict observance of these laws clashes with the basic and irreducible necessities of life, responsible action moves beyond the domain of these laws and principles, beyond what is normal and regular, and confronts the extraordinary situation of these necessities. These necessities have to do with primordial facts of life, which can never be comprehended by formal laws and techniques, nor can they become laws themselves: "They create an extraordinary situation, and are in essence borderline cases. They no longer permit human reasoning [*ratio*] to come up with a variety of exit strategies, but pose the question of the ultima ratio." In politics (i.e., statecraft), this is war, engaging in deception, or breaking a treaty for the sake of these necessities. The ultima ratio does not fit into the technological canons of rationality, and thus in that sense is "irrational."[63] It would be a complete misunderstanding if the attempt were made to take what is a borderline case and turn it into a rational law.[64]

Responsible action in situations of extraordinary necessity grows out of the freedom of those who act in these circumstances. This freedom is constituted not by the principle of buffered self-determination but by the bond we have with God and other human beings.[65] There is, however, no law, no rule, that justifies our conduct or ensures that this rather than that course of action is the appropriate one to take. What we do, we do as a free wager, but in these extraordinary circumstances it must be undertaken in full acknowledgment that the law is being violated, thereby affirming the legitimacy of the law in the act of breaking it. "In thus giving up the appeal to any law, indeed only so," Bonhoeffer writes, "is there finally a surrender of one's own decision and action to the divine guidance of history."[66]

The question in this context that can never be answered in the abstract is "whether in historical action the ultimate is the eternal law or free responsibility that is contrary to all law but before God."[67] This eschatological

---

63. I have qualified Bonhoeffer's assertion about the irrationality of responsible action with scare quotes, because without them it perpetuates a false conception of rationality, and of human intellect more generally, which reduces it to a matter of following rules. As the ability "to 'take in' [*vernehmen*] as a unity, the whole and the universal in reality," that is, to take in the world *as* world, *as* some kind of ordered, intelligible whole that we did not create, but to which we must respond, reason subsists in communal practices and projects, for which particular sets of metaphors, analogies, concepts, and rules of procedure form working cross-sections. *DBWE* 6:174; see Toulmin, *Human Understanding*, 133, 478.

64. *DBWE* 6:272–73.

65. *DBWE* 6:226–28, 257.

66. *DBWE* 6:274.

67. Bonhoeffer does not consider another possibility here, which emerges precisely in the tension between the eternal law and the positive law of particular human

and ethical question remains open, for in either case those who act become guilty and must therefore rely solely on God's grace and forgiveness. Those who act in accordance with the law and those who act in free responsibility must also accept the indictment from the other side of the question, and neither can judge the other, for such judgment belongs to God alone.[68]

The structure of responsible action for Christians within its own distinctive "politics" (i.e., churchcraft) involves both the willingness to become guilty, and freedom. If we are to understand what it means to be willing to incur guilt in the act of living responsibly, however, we must turn our focus back to the origin, essence, and goal of all responsibility, which is to return our attention back to Christ. Jesus does not concern himself with establishing a new set of ethical ideals or with preserving his own goodness but acts solely out of love for human beings. Indeed, his entire life, all that he said, did, and suffered, was at its foundation the sacrificial offering of himself on our behalf before God and on God's behalf to us: "In Christ we see humanity as a humanity that is accepted, borne, loved, and reconciled with God. In Christ we see God in the form of the poorest of our brothers and sisters."[69]

As the advocate of God before humanity and of human beings before God, Jesus enters into the community of human guilt to stand in our place, assume our burden, and act on our behalf. This love for human beings is the historical embodiment of God's No and Yes spoken to and over humanity. Because he acts solely out of his selfless love for real human beings, Jesus does not desire to be thought of as the only perfect or guiltless one, or acquit himself of our guilt that leads to death: "A love that would abandon human beings to their guilt would not be a love for real human beings. As one who acts responsibly within the historical existence of human beings, Jesus becomes guilty." He takes human guilt upon himself, linking in his person sinlessness and bearing guilt. Here then is the origin of all responsible action on behalf of and in the place of others. Springing as it does from the selfless love for the real brother or sister, such action cannot seek to withdraw from the community of human guilt.[70]

Those who wish to act responsibly but at the same time try to avoid becoming guilty have no part in the reality of history, that is, in the redeeming mystery that is the sinless bearing of guilt by Jesus Christ. Placing one's personal innocence above responsibility for other human beings

---

societies. It is to this conflict that Martin Luther King Jr. refers in "Letter from Birmingham Jail": "To put it in the terms of St. Thomas Aquinas: An unjust law is a human law that is not rooted in eternal law and natural law." King, *Why We Can't Wait*, 82.

68. *DBWE* 6:274–75.

69. *DBWE* 6:275, 258, 253.

70. *DBWE* 6:235, 275.

unwittingly results in one becoming even more egregiously guilty. Such individuals are blind to the fact that genuine guiltlessness is shown in one's entering into community with the guilt of other human beings for their sake. In the context of the Third Reich, those who seek to avoid guilt and maintain their innocence became bystanders, averting their gaze from the evil going on around them and failing to recognize the connection between themselves and the victims of the regime.[71] "Because of Jesus Christ," Bonhoeffer writes, "the essence of responsible action intrinsically involves the sinless, those who act out of selfless love, becoming guilty."[72]

Bonhoeffer is aware of how this statement can be quickly distorted, and he immediately adds that those who seek to find in what he has written a blanket license to do evil acts commit a sacrilege and an outrageous perversion. Only those who become guilty out of love and responsibility for the sake of others participate in the justifying act of Christ's bearing the sin and guilt of humankind. He also maintains the qualitative difference between the action of Jesus and our action, "between the essential sinlessness of Jesus' willingness to become guilty and the universal contamination of all human action by original sin." Taking responsibility for the life and wellbeing of others is never the action of the sinless, but that action does participate indirectly in the action of Jesus Christ and should be contrasted with any self-righteous action based on abstract principles. Bonhoeffer calls it a relative sinlessness that is shown in taking on another's guilt.[73]

André Trocmé and the Church at Le Chambon-sur-Lignon

On a Saturday evening in late summer of 1942 a convoy of police cars, motorcycles, and buses pulled into Le Chambon-sur-Lignon, a village of about three thousand people on the Plateau Vivarais-Lignon in southeastern France. According to Philip Hallie, the district police chief, an official with the Vichy government collaborating with the Nazis following France's defeat in 1940, summoned the pastor of the local Protestant church to the town hall. When André Trocmé arrived, he was informed that they knew that under his leadership the town was engaged in suspect activities, specifically, that they were hiding Jews. Trocmé was ordered to hand over a list of these persons and where they were hiding so that they could be deported to extermination camps in the east.[74]

71. Barnett, *Bystanders*, 5–8, 159.

72. *DBWE* 6:276.

73. *DBWE* 6:234–35, 279.

74. Hallie, *Lest Innocent Blood Be Shed*, 107–9. As Richard Unsworth notes, after

Trocmé refused to cooperate, telling the official (truthfully, as it so happened) that he had no such list. But even if he had such a list, these people had sought protection from the church in this region. He was therefore their pastor, their shepherd, and it was not the role of a shepherd to betray the sheep committed to his keeping. The chief warned Trocmé that he could be arrested and deported for his refusal, and set a deadline for compliance. Trocmé afterwards went to his office and set into motion a plan worked out in the weeks leading up to this fateful day. Messengers were sent to outlying farms where the Jews were staying to warn them to flee into the woods under the cover of darkness. "Under a starlit night," writes Philip Hallie, "it was as if ghosts were purposefully making their respective ways through the square and the streets while the police waited for their ultimatum to expire, sleeping upon straw."[75]

The next morning Trocmé ascended the high pulpit in the big gray church of Le Chambon and preached to the townspeople gathered for worship. According to some accounts, he cited a passage in the book of Deuteronomy that established cities of refuge for the innocent in Israel and declared that their village must become a city of refuge for all those sought by the Vichy government, "lest innocent blood be shed" (Deut 19:10). His parishioners responded to their pastor's charge, and with the charge in the Sermon on the Mount that Jesus' followers were to be a city set on a hill as their model, they began to hide Jews and other refugees (coming eventually from all parts of Europe), smuggling them to safety in Switzerland when possible. Though the police remained in town for three weeks, only two Jews were arrested, and one was later released because he was only "half Jewish," which at the time was sufficient to avoid deportation.

The actions that were subsequently taken by the Chambonnais under the leadership of André Trocmé and his wife, Magda, resulting in the rescue of somewhere between twenty-five hundred and five thousand refugees,[76] most of them Jewish, surely meets Bonhoeffer's specifications for responsible action, including the willingness to enter into the sinfulness of the world. Their rescue of the lives of Jews and other refugees involved deceit, subterfuge, and all kinds of moral shortcuts on the part of most of the villagers,[77] and showed little interest in preserving a pretense of inno-

---

many years one encounters conflicting accounts of the details of this event, though the main thread of the story remains the same. Unsworth, *Portrait of Pacifists*, 179 n. 2.

75. Hallie, *Lest Innocent Blood Be Shed*, 109–12; Henry, *We Only Know Men*, 25.

76. Suckau, "Christian Witness," 94. Because the Chambonnais wisely kept no written records, the estimated number of people rescued varies.

77. According to Patrick Henry, teachers enrolled children as students who possessed blatantly forged papers, civil servants handed out extra food tickets to families

cence (unless, of course, one makes the only measure of that willingness the use of lethal violence). Nor is there any indication they acted from an abstract principle. Their motivation, says Victoria Barnett, was a certain type of *vision*, the way they had been formed to understand what was happening in their midst. This imaginary was of a different kind of society and of themselves as citizens of that alternative society. It compelled them to be attentive to those who were being unjustly treated, to see that they had "a personal stake in what was happening around them."[78]

The events that occurred in Le Chambon were not the actions of isolated individuals who demonstrated an uncommon courage for brief moments of time. The region was involved to one degree or another in a complex rescue effort that took place over several years. Their involvement, however, did not come cheaply. Some were imprisoned in concentration camps and a few were executed. The hospitality shown to refugees during the war was not something new for the Chambonnais. During the Spanish Civil War, which took place in the three years leading up to the start of the Second World War, the citizens of Le Chambon organized to provide shelter and other assistance to those fleeing Spain for political reasons. And prior to the outbreak of hostilities between Germany and the Allies in 1939 they welcomed a number of Communists, Socialists, and other left-leaning individuals from Austria and Germany. Their actions during the war were simply the continuation of the hospitality they had extended to refugees for decades, some of whom were being persecuted for their political or religious stances, others of whom were simply seeking to survive the hardships of poverty and the destruction of war.[79]

The resistance of the Chambonnais grew out of a distinctive pattern of life together that had been formed by the common life and language of a community over several generations. Trocmé's admonition that their village should transform itself into a city of refuge so that innocent blood would not be shed reveals a deep and abiding sense of who they were and a source of power such that, when the crisis came, their life together generated possibilities of direct "political" action that effectively and successfully disrupted the designs of a foe that others regarded as irresistible. And they did so during a time when virtually every other village, town, and city in Europe claimed that they were powerless to do anything about their situation.

---

who were sheltering refugees, and shopkeepers conveniently forgot to ask for rationing cards. Henry, *We Only Know Men*, 23–24.

78. Barnett, *Bystanders*, 159, 172.

79. Suckau, "Christian Witness," 31–32.

The playing fields of Eton for the Huguenots was their shared memory of having been a despised and persecuted minority beginning in sixteenth-century France. The most memorable event in this history, though not the only one by any means, was the St. Bartholomew's Day massacre, which took place on August 24, 1572. Thousands were killed in Paris that night, and countless others were compelled to renounce their Protestant faith. The persecution and killings continued and intensified over the next two centuries until Louis XVI issued a decree of tolerance. During this time the Huguenots were not allowed to own church buildings, and so they gathered at night in secret in fields and wooded areas (much like slaves in the antebellum South[80]) to read scripture, preach, confess and celebrate the Eucharist. They referred to these gatherings as "Assemblée du Désert," an assembly in the desert, with typological connections to the exodus wanderings of the children of Israel.[81] When the Chambonnais led refugees on a three-hundred-kilometer trek to the safety of Switzerland, they followed the same route their ancestors had taken centuries before.[82]

The "crime" for which the Huguenots were persecuted was neither their religious practice nor their occasionally treasonable political activity, says G. A. Rothrock, but their resistance to a national consciousness, not only in France but throughout Europe, that demanded conformity and submission.[83] It was due to their "religious" practice (obviously not limited to private, "spiritual" matters) that the Chambonnais recognized the idolatry of national consciousness. Laboring in quiet anonymity down through the centuries, a handful of saints developed a nonviolent but nevertheless disruptive form of reasoning and acting that served their descendants well. It allowed them to stand fast against the demands of an idolatrous regime precisely at the point where Christians elsewhere succumbed to religious, cultural, and racial technologies.

80. See Raboteau, *Slave Religion*, x, 138, 141; Rawick, *From Sundown to Sunup*, 40; Cone, *Speaking the Truth*, 88.

81. Bost, "Le désert des Huguenots," 177–206; Garrison, "Assemblée du Musée du Désert," 109–12.

82. Henry, *We Only Know Men*, 28. Unsworth notes that the tactics used on these trips were similar to those of the Underground Railroad prior to the Civil War in the United States. Unsworth, *Portrait of Pacifists*, 187.

83. Rothrock, *Huguenots*, 189–90. Actually, it was only due to their "religious" practice that French Protestants resisted the idolatry of national consciousness.

Assessing Bonhoeffer and Trocmé

What makes the comparison of Bonhoeffer and Trocmé particularly in-triguing are the many similarities between the two men. Born four years apart, both were members of relatively well-to-do and privileged families who first educated them at home and who communicated to them a sense of responsibility to history. Trocmé's mother was German, which gave him a sense of empathy for the German people. Both attended Union Seminary in New York, and both found the theological offerings there lacking. Both embraced a form of pacifism (a remarkable coincidence given that they be-longed to traditions—Lutheran and Reformed—that had not made room for such an ethic). In an ironic twist, Bonhoeffer was convinced to embrace pacifism by a Frenchman he met at Union, Jean Lasserre, while it was a German soldier named Kindler, whom Trocmé met during the German occupation of Saint-Quentin during the First World War, who persuaded him. Finally, in the days and weeks leading up to the start of the war Trocmé contemplated using his facility with German to slip into Hitler's entourage and assassinate him.[84]

Trocmé also understands the challenge of the ultima ratio to which Bonhoeffer refers, and articulates the rationale for acting as Bonhoeffer did: "People argue, 'Our nation is about to be exterminated; or the future of our civilization, or our moral values, or true religion is threatened; or yet, our institutions violate human rights, and to save human rights we must suspend our scruples and use violence, sacrificing human lives to destroy unjust structures, and thus saving the poor from oppression.'"[85] He clearly has a profound sense of what is at stake in the decision before Bonhoeffer.

Though Trocmé was not the trained theologian Bonhoeffer was, they shared a good deal in common in this regard, beginning with a similar christological framework.[86] As suggested by the title to his most frequently cited book, *Jesus and the Nonviolent Revolution*, Trocmé describes Jesus as a revolutionary figure who sought to bring in the kingdom of God, though what he denotes with this concept is not the same thing that Bonhoeffer has in mind when he warns against a revolutionary understanding of Jesus.[87] Trocmé also does not qualify the concepts of politics or the church as polis

84. Unsworth, *Portrait of Pacifists*, 35–36, 40–51, 101–03; Suckau, "Christian Wit-ness," 52, 128.

85. Trocmé, *Jesus and the Nonviolent Revolution*, 128.

86. In what follows I am indebted to Suckau's helpful summation of Trocmé's theol-ogy. Suckau, "Christian Witness," 57–70.

87. When Bonhoeffer rejects the idea of the revolutionary as a description of Christ he has something different in mind, viz., the blessing of every revolution. *DBWE* 6:224.

as Bonhoeffer does with scare quotes, preferring instead to let these notions stand in straightforward juxtaposition to the practice of Roman statecraft. He asserts that Jesus had a definite political program, consisting of the messianic reestablishment of Israel, a reconstitution that would permit the chosen people to serve as the light of the nations: "The body of Christ today is the new Israel, formed by those who have responded to Jesus' call of discipleship. The contemporary church has thus inherited Jesus' revolutionary program."[88]

At the center of Trocmé's portrait of Christ's revolutionary life and mission is the image of the Jubilee, the time set aside in the Torah for debts to be forgiven and lands to be returned to their original owners, to which Jesus appears to refer in his Nazareth sermon (Luke 4:16–21). Trocmé emphasizes the political context of Jesus' life and ministry, that it claims, as Bonhoeffer puts it, the whole person: "Jesus came to bring a revolution, one that would impact every sphere of existence, including social and power relations. His message of repentance called for an about-face on the part of both individuals and entire cities. He did not want to reform political structures but wanted everything to come under God's rulership."[89]

Trocmé, like Bonhoeffer, places considerable emphasis on history as the arena of God's apocalypse and is therefore uninterested in any kind of properly "religious" place for Christ's life and ministry. He states explicitly in the preface to *Jesus and the Nonviolent Revolution* that Jesus Christ is the central event in history, "because de facto his coming changed humankind." His understanding of the nature and character of history as the arena of God's judging and redeeming activity, again like Bonhoeffer, is apocalyptic, for "at a given place and time, God intervened in history, rendering all subsequent happenings on this planet as of divine importance." And Trocmé expresses this apocalyptic take on history in figural readings of scripture— for example, in an interpretation of the exodus, which when viewed through the hermeneutical lens of the church announces "the supreme liberation at the end of history."[90]

Because they are aware of the tension between the present and the future aspects of God's reign, Bonhoeffer and Trocmé place similar emphasis on the significance of the cross, and reject any effort to understand Jesus' ministry solely in terms of either incarnation or resurrection, or in the confidence that any action that is undertaken will be successful. Trocmé writes, "Jesus came proclaiming the kingdom of God, inaugurated by a

88. Trocmé, *Jesus and the Nonviolent Revolution*, xiv, 156.

89. Ibid., 53.

90. Ibid., xiii, 55.

Jubilee. This Jubilee upset both human tradition and religious scruples. Consequently, Jesus' adversaries tried to kill him. They were determined to prevent a dangerous revolution that would usurp their influence and power." In view of Christ's own apparent failure, says Trocmé, disciples must prepare themselves as well for failure and for physical death, which will lead the enemy to conclude that he is the victor: "God alone will change the cross into a victory."[91] As Bonhoeffer states, "The form of the crucified disarms all thinking aimed at success, for it is a denial of judgment."[92]

Trocmé also shares Bonhoeffer's reticence about abstract principles, though he puts the matter in his own terms. He uses a mathematical trope, stating that when Jesus told his disciples that they were the salt of the earth and the light of the world, "he was not teaching them the 'arithmetic' of the kingdom of God, that is, the technique of performing operations on absolute values. Rather, he was revealing the 'algebra' of the kingdom of God, that is, the 'functions and relations' between unknown values." These "algebraic formulas" include the fruition of God's plan of redemption in history through the chosen people of Israel, the refusal to separate justice and forgiveness, and Jesus' refusal to abandon the way of nonviolence.[93]

Finally, Bonhoeffer and Trocmé share a vision of reality that is disclosed in Christ, though they articulate it differently. As one would expect with a Lutheran, Bonhoeffer connects the intersection of the last things and the things before the last with the doctrine of justification. In this one event, "The past and future of the whole of life flow together in Gods presence. The whole of the past is embraced by the word 'forgiveness'; the whole of the future is preserved in the faithfulness of God." Through their justification women and men are free for God and for one another, able to realize that "there is a God who loves and accepts them, that alongside them stand others whom God loves equally, and that there is a future with the triune God and God's church-community." Faith is nothing other than basing life on a foundation outside the self, "on an eternal and holy foundation, on Christ."[94] At the same time, however, we are still in the time before the last, which means, as Bonhoeffer puts it in a prison letter, that we cannot speak the last word prior to the next to last. Belief in the last things does not relieve us from living in the time before; indeed, it refers us back to our life on earth in a completely new way, to take on earthly tasks and difficulties.[95]

91. Ibid., 93, 141; cf. McCabe, *God Matters*, 218.

92. *DBWE* 6:90.

93. Trocmé, *Jesus and the Nonviolent Revolution*, 155.

94. *DBWE* 6:146–47.

95. *DBWE* 8:213, 447–48.

Trocmé unpacks the intersection of the reality of the world and the reality of God's apocalypse by means of an ocular metaphor. He compares our ability to envision the present reality of God's reign to the stereoscopic vision that gives depth perception to our eyesight. Thus when we view the world with one eye closed, we lose our sense of depth. He then applies this metaphor to our understanding of reality, stating that those who do not have the ability to superimpose stereoscopically the present and the future are seriously handicapped. When present and future are viewed separately, "Each image is flat. Indeed, the world 'as it is' has no depth; it is a sequence of phenomena with no rhyme or reason, without origin or end. Similarly the world 'as it should be and will be,' the kingdom, is flat. Isolated from the sensible world, it remains an 'ideal' without substance, because ideas need the support of matter to become realities." However, when present and future, actuality and possibility are performatively juxtaposed in prayer, liturgy, and action, those with eyes to see and ears to hear are able to "take in" the reality of the world, a seeing and hearing that incites a revolution.[96]

A Failure to Prepare

In spite of the many personal and theological similarities, Bonhoeffer and Trocmé came to opposite conclusions regarding the kind of action to take against the Nazi regime, with Bonhoeffer casting his lot with the conspiracy against Hitler, and Trocmé deciding to proceed nonviolently in concert with his parishioners and neighbors in Le Chambon. What are the lessons for our time and place in this tale of two Christians, whose convictions were so similar yet whose lives took such different paths?

The historical context for our consideration is, first of all, the utter failure of the conspiracy. One cannot dismiss the advantage of hindsight in this regard, for as Bonhoeffer observes in *Ethics*, in our actions we must observe, weigh, evaluate, and decide, and do so with limited human understanding. One of the factors in that process, he writes, is to "seriously consider the consequences of our actions."[97] The only source of foresight for such consideration available to us, living as we do in the middle of things, is

---

96. Trocmé, *Jesus and the Nonviolent Revolution*, 162–63. Trocmé's stereoscopic analogy is reminiscent of Bonhoeffer's comment in *Sanctorum Communio* to the effect that the life that abides in love breaks the continuity of the historical process that was constituted by death as the wages of sin, "not empirically but objectively. Death can still completely separate past and future for our eyes, but not for the life that abides in the love of Christ." *DBWE* 1:146.

97. *DBWE* 6:268.

what occurred in the past, and as the oft-cited adage reminds us, if we fail to learn from the past we are doomed to repeat it.

It is not sufficient to simply to acknowledge that the abortive attempt on Hitler's life did not bring down the Third Reich or shorten the war, for as Richard Evans argues, it brought about "the most disastrous possible consequences for almost everybody involved in it, for a variety of reasons, both specific and general."[98] The failed attempt revived support for Hitler personally and gave the regime a new lease on life at a crucial juncture of the war. The fact that high-ranking officers undertook the coup d'état meant that the other officers had to go to great lengths to prove their loyalty to Hitler and disavow any connection to the conspirators, thus eliminating any possibility of the armed forces bringing about a regime change. "At a time when Germany was rocked by disastrous military defeat and soaring anxieties over the superiority of enemy forces, Hitler's war leadership and the prospects for Germany's future," Ian Kershaw concludes, "the assassination attempt and uprising had the effect of strengthening the regime—at least in the short term."[99] In the final analysis it provided convenient scapegoats for past military defeats and further incited the regime's paranoid determination to fight on to the bitter end.

What are we to make theologically of this bit of hindsight, which in connection with the contrapuntal movement of historical action with its nonidentical repetitions must be considered our most substantial source of foresight? I have no interest in using hindsight either to condemn or condone Bonhoeffer's decision, but it would be foolish for us not to take it into account when considering our own time and place, particularly in view of the limitations of human reasoning about the future. What the villagers accomplished on the Plateau Vivarais-Lignon serves as a reminder that there is almost always more than one way to take direct political action, provided that there is a community that has adequately prepared to do so. Those who rescued even one innocent life foiled the dark plans of the Nazis.

There is another aspect to this matter that must be considered. Bethge observes that the certainty and clarity of judgment and bearing that distinguished Bonhoeffer even at a young age cannot "be acquired in a single

---

98. Evans, *Third Reich at War*, 644.

99. Kershaw, *The End*, 34, 44, 48, 51. This is not the only case in which the judgment that violence was the only or best course of action resulted in utter failure. John Yoder points to the Colombian priest-sociologist Camilo Torres: "He joined the guerrillas, he explained, as a simple work of love, since it would do away with social oppression. Not only were Torres and his fellow militants killed, but there is no way to measure any positive contribution which their campaign made to their cause." Yoder, *What Would You Do?*, 14.

generation. He grew up in a family that believed that the essence of learning lay . . . in the deeply rooted obligation to be guardians of a great historical heritage and intellectual tradition."[100] Much of what made him an influential theologian and pastor is due to his family's legacy, but is there a sense in which Bonhoeffer's upbringing in an upper-class, professional, and highly "cultured" setting, while it instilled in him the virtues that served him so well over the course of his life, also led him and others of his social class to interpret "acting responsibly" as needing to take charge of the situation? Did this upbringing restrict their ability to think imaginatively about the different ways they might have responded to Hitler and National Socialism? It is possible to act responsibly and in a worldly manner in accord with the reality of God becoming human without assuming that they alone were responsible for the outcome of events. The Chambonnais acted as Bonhoeffer says one should: "No one has the responsibility of turning the world into the kingdom of God, but only of taking the next necessary step that corresponds to God's becoming human in Christ."[101]

This caveat around the notion of responsibility points to a vexing ambiguity in the way it has been interpreted in recent moral theology. The vexation, as Bernd Wannenwetsch puts it, has to do with the confusion of Bonhoeffer's understanding of responsibility and responsible action with conceptions such as that posited by H. Richard Niebuhr, who offers the notions of responsible self and man-the-answerer as guiding tropes for interpreting moral agency. Implicit in the idea of responsibility, Niebuhr writes, is the image of a human being engaged in dialogue with herself or himself, of a human being acting in response to action upon her or him. Whereas previous conceptions of moral agency asked what should I do, or which law, rule, or virtue governs my conduct, "man-the-answerer" asks, "What is going on?"[102] What, in other words, is happening to me, and what are the impulses to which I need to react?[103]

Locating the fulcrum of responsible action within the self represents both a continuation of the forensic context in which the concept of responsibility was historically set in Christian moral thought and also a radical departure from that tradition. In the Middle Ages men and women saw themselves standing ultimately before the judgment seat of God, to whom it would be required at some point to give an account for their actions. As such, the notion of responsibility was not ethical in the modern sense of the term

100. Bethge, *Dietrich Bonhoeffer*, 13.

101. *DBWE* 6:224–25; cf. 267.

102. Niebuhr, *Responsible Self*, 56.

103. Wannenwetsch, "'Responsible Living,'" 128.

but soteriological and eschatological. Within the technological organization of the modern world, however, the forensic understanding of responsibility is reconfigured as a moral concept operating within an imminent frame of reference. Now, instead of standing before Christ, the act of responding has been displaced from its theological context and relocated in the *forum internum* of the human conscience.[104] This displacement is part and parcel of the shift from a transcendent to a transcendental locus of authority, that is, from the revealed truth of a transcendent Being to purportedly self-evident truths known to the sovereign subject. The I is now responding not to a You but to its "higher" self, with the role of the other recast as the occasion of responsibility to one's higher self. To view responsibility in this way, as Bonhoeffer says, is to attempt to justify oneself.[105]

Christian basic-relations, writes Bonhoeffer in *Sanctorum Communio*, are properly theological and not ethical in nature.[106] But when "Christian ethics" is cut loose from doctrine, "Christian behavior . . . is no longer aware of its Christian character. Only recently have people begun to ask again about the foundation of their own behavior and therefore have come back to doctrine and the church. The issue at stake is to unite the two, to lead back to faith."[107] His unease with the modern discipline of ethics is thus yet another thread that ties all of his writings together into a coherent whole: "The source of a Christian ethic is not the reality of one's own self, not the reality of the world, nor is it the reality of norms and values. It is the reality of God that is revealed in Jesus Christ." With regard to the concept of responsibility he writes, "I take responsibility and answer for Jesus Christ, and with that I naturally take responsibility for the commission I have been charged with by him (1 Cor 9:3)."[108]

Niebuhr's forensic conception of responsibility, by locating it securely within the buffered self, gives us something very different from what Bonhoeffer calls responsible action.[109] Niebuhr contends that "we respond as we interpret the meaning of actions upon us." Our actions, in other words, become responsible "not only insofar as they are reactions to interpreted actions upon us but also insofar as they are made in anticipation of answers to our answers."[110] If my interpretations include my anticipation of how the

104. Ibid., 133, 136.

105. *DBWE* 6:255.

106. *DBWE* 1:156.

107. Bonhoeffer, *Zettelnotizen*, 32, cited in *DBWE* 6:49–50 n. 20.

108. *DBWE* 6:49, 255–56.

109. Wannenwetsch, "'Responsible Living,'" 136–37.

110. Niebuhr, *Responsible Self*, 63–64.

other will answer my answers, the You as an ethical barrier disappears and is replaced by my construct of the other as identical to myself. For Niebuhr's responsible self, there is no You that stands over against and alongside the I, no engagement with an other, but only with another I. He substitutes the *actus reflexus*, the radical reflexivity of the buffered self, for the *actus directus*, in terms of which the act of faith is directed outward in grateful response to God's revelation in Christ. For Bonhoeffer this displacement signifies a refusal of what is "yet to come," as the direct relation to Christ is set aside in favor of "a reflection upon the I."[111]

In a related question, does Bonhoeffer's intellectual struggle with the transcendental and idealist thought that dominated the German academy of his day lead him to draw an overly rigid dichotomy between acting in accordance with principles and acting in concert with reality? There is something fundamentally sound about his contention that our actions as Christians are not ordered by a set of principles that we must somehow enforce against the reality of the world, but done in obedience to what is necessary or commanded. These commands are communicated to us in the sayings of Jesus Christ, above all in the Sermon on the Mount, which interpret the reality of this person in whom history finds its origin, essence, and goal.[112] That said, is the problem with principles per se, or is it with the way certain forms of ethical reflection have used them? At times his opposition to abstract principles sounds, well, abstractly principled. If received as the accumulated wisdom of those who have genuinely engaged reality and the good in the concrete stuff of life as they encountered it, rules and principles can play a very important role, as he puts it, as tools in God's hands.[113]

I also question whether those who appeal to Bonhoeffer's decision regarding the conspiracy to justify the use of lethal violence, whether in war or in other circumstances, not only ignore his repeated statements that we can never justify our actions in such matters but also run afoul of his own suspicions about the way past precedents are used. In the famous passage in *Discipleship* where he deals with the difference between cheap and costly grace, he makes a crucial distinction between grace as presupposition, which makes of it a cheap thing, and as conclusion, which acknowledges its true worth and price. He offers an interesting analogy: "When Faust says at the end of his life of seeking knowledge, 'I see that we can know nothing,' then that is a conclusion, a result. It is something entirely different than when a

---

111. *DBWE* 2:157, 158.

112. *DBWE* 6:261, 263–64.

113. *DBWE* 6:82.

student repeats this statement in the first semester to justify his laziness."[114] He says something similar in a lecture at Finkenwalde. Luther could call on grace because he had sought to live for years under the law, and only then came to know Christ in the call to follow him. What is true as a result, is false as a supposition. True obedience is a result of hearing Christ's call to discipleship. The failure to heed this distinction leads to a conception of grace that sanctifies the ordinances of the world, serving only to confirm Constantine's covenant with the church and give birth to a minimalist ethic.[115] Does not a similar danger lurk in an appeal to Bonhoeffer to justify the use of violence? His decision to cast his lot with the conspirators was not undertaken lightly, and it should not be lightly cited as justification for violence.

When it comes to Bonhoeffer's decision to participate in the conspiracy, we must assess his actions in a broader historical and social context that includes the question of preparation. The legacy that Bonhoeffer's family bequeathed to him the church failed to provide for most Christians in Germany. Unlike the situation in Le Chambon, there was little or no ecclesial space to supply the means and media needed to prepare a distinctively Christian form of action. The fate of the Confessing Church had largely been decided by its religious, cultural-political, and racial (i.e., *völkisch*) captivity that had become entrenched over the centuries. There were few structures, practices, and skills of "political" life in Germany capable of resisting Nazi totalitarianism, and as a consequence Christians there, with a few exceptions, never had the chance to be formed in the moral habits and reasoning adequate to the needs of the time.[116]

In Le Chambon, by contrast, there was a church-community that, thanks to the quiet but steady life of faith of previous generations, prepared women and men to respond to the Nazi regime in ways that were not available to Bonhoeffer. When Trocmé told his congregation that they must create a city of refuge for Jews and other so-called undesirables, his summons did not fall upon ears that could hear but not understand. In interview after interview that he conducted with the rescuers of Le Chambon, Hallie was told, "Things had to be done, that's all, and we happened to be there to do them. You must understand that it was the most natural thing in the world to help these people."[117] These responses exemplify what Bonhoeffer calls the hiddenness of discipleship, which is not hidden from the world but from

114. *DBWE* 4:51.
115. *DBWE* 14:431–33.
116. See McClendon, *Ethics*, 210–11.
117. Hallie, *Lest Innocent Blood Be Shed*, 21.

the disciples themselves: "The righteousness of the disciples is hidden from themselves. . . . The only required reflection for disciples is to be completely oblivious, completely unreflective in obedience, in discipleship, in love."[118]

The Chambonnais could think of what they did as natural and not heroic because they had been formed in a profound this-worldliness over many generations to hear the call of God in Jesus Christ, and thus to heed "what the Spirit is saying to the churches" (Rev 2:7). A theological tradition forged by generations of French Protestants who suffered through their own persecutions had fashioned a people who did not confuse being members of the body of Christ with being citizens of France. A handful of unarmed men and women were prepared to arrest the forward motion of the wheel of a diabolical enemy that others regarded as unstoppable. In ways that Bonhoeffer could only imagine, they were in a position to make a genuinely free wager about their Jewish neighbors because they had been formed never to lose sight of the tension between being French nationals and being Christian disciples.

Should we consider Bonhoeffer a martyr? Some do,[119] but for others this is a contested issue that will not soon be resolved to everyone's satisfaction.[120] He most likely would have been as uncomfortable with that designation as he was with the notion of saint, and would have preferred to be known as simply a human being.[121] Nevertheless, a definition offered by William Cavanaugh in an article on Óscar Romero would seem to fit Bonhoeffer as well:

> For Christians, what makes a martyr is whether or not the church as a whole is able to discern the body of Christ, crucified and glorified, in the body broken by the violence of the powers. The point is not the heroism of the individual; martyrdom is not a heroic self-giving, for our lives are not ours to give. What makes martyrdom possible is the eschatological belief that nothing depends on the martyr's continued life; if he or she dies, that death is not ultimate, for Christ lives on in the multitude of foolish and sinful people like us, who make Christ present by remembering the martyrs. As such, martyrdom recalls into

---

118. *DBWE* 4:149–50; cf. *DBWE* 6:318, 381, *DBWE* 11:442. Henry observes that while some have written about the banality of evil during the Holocaust, he refers to what happened in Le Chambon as the "ordinariness of goodness." Henry, *We Only Know Men*, 24.

119. Leahy, "'Christ Existing as Community,'" 32–59.

120. Heffernan, "Martyrdom, Charisma, and Imitation," 263–67.

121. *DBWE* 8:485.

being a people, the people of God, and makes their life visible to themselves, to the powers, and to the whole world.[122]

If he was not a martyr, and if heroic self-giving does not fit, could we nonetheless say that he exhibits some of the traits of a tragic hero? According to Aristotle, a tragic hero is someone, usually of noble stature, who possesses outstanding virtues and performs great acts but who comes to an unfortunate end, or at least fails in some significant way, due to an error in judgment: "a person who is neither perfect in virtue and justice, nor one who falls into misfortune through vice and depravity, but rather, one who succumbs through some miscalculation."[123] This definition does at least partial justice to the way his life ended, which is ironic given the critique of tragedy that he develops in many of his writings.

Whether tragic hero, martyr, or just a human being, Dietrich Bonhoeffer is a theologian whose insights continue to serve as a resource and catalyst for our own reflections into the nature of profound this-worldliness, and also a remarkable example of a faithful response to the reality of a world united to its creator in the person of Jesus Christ. It is fitting, therefore, to give him the last word, taken from the conclusion to *Discipleship*:

> But now the final word about those who as disciples bear the image of the incarnate, crucified, and risen Jesus Christ, and who have been transformed into the image of God, is that they are called to be "imitators of God." The follower [Nachfolger] of Jesus is the imitator [Nachahmer] of God. "Therefore be imitators of God, as beloved children" (Eph. 5:1).[124]

---

122. Cavanaugh, "Dying for the Eucharist?," 181–82. As I was completing this book a decision was made in the Vatican to officially recognize Romero as a Christian martyr. According to news reports, the case for Romero was delayed for decades as the Congregation for the Doctrine of the Faith debated whether his death should be attributed to his faith or to his political involvement. I would suggest that in the cases of Romero and Bonhoeffer in particular this distinction is unhelpful and misleading. West, "Archbishop Oscar Romero Was a Martyr."

123. Aristotle, *Poetics* 13.

124. *DBWE* 4:288.

Bibliography

Allison, Dale C. *Constructing Jesus: Memory, Imagination, and History*. Grand Rapids: Baker, 2010.

———. *The Historical Christ and the Theological Jesus*. Grand Rapids: Eerdmans, 2009.

American Piety in the 21st Century: New Insights to the Depth and Complexity of Religion in the US; Selected Findings from The Baylor Religion Survey. Baylor Institute for Studies of Religion, September 2006. http://www.baylor.edu/content/services/document.php/33304.pdf.

Anderson, Benedict. *Imagined Communities: Reflections on the Origin and Spread of Nationalism*. Rev. ed. New York: Verso, 1991.

Anderson, David. *Multicultural Ministry: Finding Your Church's Unique Rhythm*. Grand Rapids: Zondervan, 2004.

Aquinas, Thomas. *Summa Theologica*. Translated by Fathers of the English Dominican Province. Rev. ed. New York: Benziger, 1948.

Ardrey, Robert. *The Territorial Imperative: A Personal Inquiry into the Animal Origins of Property and Nations*. New York: Atheneum, 1966.

Aristotle. *Nicomachean Ethics*. Translated by Martin Ostwald. Englewood Cliffs, NJ: Prentice Hall, 1999.

———. *Poetics*. In *The Basic Works of Aristotle*, edited by Richard McKeon, 1455–87. New York: Random House, 1941.

Arnold, Matthew. *Culture and Anarchy*. Edited by Samuel Lipman. New Haven: Yale University Press, 1994.

Asad, Talal. *Genealogies of Religion: Discipline and Reasons of Power in Christianity and Islam*. Baltimore: Johns Hopkins University Press, 1993.

———. "Reading a Modern Classic: W. C. Smith's *The Meaning and End of Religion*." *History of Religions* 40 (2001) 205–22.

Auerbach, Erich. *Mimesis: The Representation of Reality in Western Literature*. Translated by Willard R. Trask. Princeton: Princeton University Press, 1953.

Augustine. *The City of God Against the Pagans*. Edited by R. W. Dyson. New York: Cambridge University Press, 1998.

———. *The Confessions*. Translated by Maria Boulding. Hyde Park, NY: New City, 1997.

———. *Of True Religion*. In *Augustine: Earlier Writings*, edited by John J. S. Burleigh, 225–82. Philadelphia: Fortress, 1953.

———. *Teaching Christianity*. Edited by Edmund Hill. Hyde Park, NY: New City, 1996.

Aurelius, Marcus. *Meditations*. Translated by Gregory Hays. New York: Modern Library, 2002.

Bacon, Francis. *The Oxford Francis Bacon*. Vol. 4, *The Advancement of Learning*. Edited by Michael Kiernan. Oxford: Clarendon, 2000.

Balthasar, Hans Urs von. *Theo-Drama*. Vol. 2, *The* Dramatis Personae: *Man in God*. Translated by Graham Harrison. San Francisco: Ignatius, 1990.

Barnett, Victoria J. *Bystanders: Conscience and Complicity during the Holocaust*. Westport, CT: Praeger, 1999.

————. "Dietrich Bonhoeffer's Relevance for Post-Holocaust Christian Theology." *Studies in Christian-Jewish Relations* 2 (2007) 53–67.

————. *For the Soul of the People: Protestant Protest against Hitler*. New York: Oxford University Press, 1992.

Barth, Karl. "The Christian Community and the Civil Community." In *Community, State, and Church: Three Essays*, edited by Will Herberg, 149–89. Gloucester, MA: Peter Smith, 1968.

————. *Church Dogmatics I/2: The Doctrine of the Word of God*. Translated by G. T. Thomson and Harold Knight. Edited by G. W. Bromiley and T. F. Torrance. Edinburgh: T. & T. Clark, 1956.

————. *Church Dogmatics II/2: The Doctrine of God*. Translated by J. C. Campbell et al. Edited by G. W. Bromiley and T. F. Torrance. Edinburgh: T. & T. Clark, 1958.

————. *From Rousseau to Ritschl*. Translated by H. H. Hartwell. London: SCM, 1952.

————. *The Theology of Schleiermacher: Lectures at Göttingen, Winter Semester of 1923/24*. Translated by Geoffrey W. Bromiley. Grand Rapids: Eerdmans, 1982.

Batnitzky, Leora. *How Judaism Became a Religion: An Introduction to Modern Jewish Thought*. Princeton: Princeton University Press, 2011.

Bauman, Zygmunt. *Postmodern Ethics*. Cambridge, MA: Blackwell, 1993.

Beaudoin, Tom. *Witness to Dispossession: The Vocation of a Postmodern Theology*. Maryknoll, NY: Orbis, 2008.

Begbie, Jeremy S. *Resounding Truth: Christian Wisdom in the World of Music*. Grand Rapids: Eerdmans, 2007.

————. *Theology, Music and Time*. New York: Cambridge University Press, 2000.

Beker, J. Christiaan. *Paul's Apocalyptic Gospel*. Philadelphia: Fortress, 1992.

Bell, Daniel M., Jr. *The Economy of Desire: Christianity and Capitalism in a Postmodern World*. Grand Rapids: Baker, 2012.

Bell, Derrick. *Faces at the Bottom of the Well: The Permanence of Racism*. New York: Basic Books, 1992.

Benjamin, Walter. *Illuminations*. Translated by Harry Zohn. New York: Schocken, 1969.

Berman, Lila Corwin. *Speaking of Jews: Rabbis, Intellectuals, and the Creation of an American Public Identity*. Berkeley: University of California Press, 2009.

Bernstein, Richard J. "What Is the Difference That Makes a Difference? Gadamer, Habermas, and Rorty." In *Philosophical Profiles: Essays in a Pragmatic Mode*, 331–59. Philadelphia: University of Pennsylvania Press, 1986.

Bethge, Eberhard. *Bonhoeffer: Exile and Martyr*. Edited by John W. de Gruchy. New York: Crossroad, 1975.

————. *Dietrich Bonhoeffer: A Biography*. Edited by Victoria J. Barnett. Minneapolis: Fortress, 2000.

Bock, Brian. *Christian Ethics in a Technological Age*. Grand Rapids: Eerdmans, 2010.

Bonaventure. *The Journey of the Mind to God*. Translated by Philotheus Boehner. Indianapolis: Hackett, 1956.

Bonhoeffer, Dietrich. *Act and Being: Transcendental Philosophy and Ontology in Systematic Theology*. Edited by Wayne Whitson Floyd Jr. Translated by H. Martin Rumscheidt. Dietrich Bonhoeffer Works 2. Minneapolis: Fortress, 1996.

———. *Akt und Sein*. Edited by Hans-Richard Reuter. Dietrich Bonhoeffer Werke 2. Munich: Kaiser, 1988.

———. *Barcelona, Berlin, New York, 1928-1931*. Edited by Clifford J. Green. Translated by Douglas W. Stott. Dietrich Bonhoeffer Works 10. Minneapolis: Fortress, 2008.

———. *Berlin, 1932-1933*. Edited by Carsten Nicolaisen and Ernst-Albert Scharffenorth. Dietrich Bonhoeffer Werke 12. Munich: Kaiser, 1997.

———. *Berlin, 1932-1933*. Edited by Larry L. Rasmussen. Translated by Isabel Best et al. Dietrich Bonhoeffer Works 12. Minneapolis: Fortress, 2009.

———. *Conspiracy and Imprisonment, 1940-1945*. Edited by Mark S. Brocker. Translated by Lisa E. Dahill. Supplementary material translated by Douglas W. Stott. Dietrich Bonhoeffer Works 16. Minneapolis: Fortress, 2006.

———. *Creation and Fall: A Theological Exposition of Genesis 1-3*. Edited by John W. de Gruchy. Translated by Douglas Stephen Bax. Dietrich Bonhoeffer Works 3. Minneapolis: Fortress, 1997.

———. *Discipleship*. Edited by Geffrey B. Kelly and John D. Godsey. Translated by Barbara Green and Reinhard Krauss. Dietrich Bonhoeffer Works 4. Minneapolis: Fortress, 2001.

———. *Ecumenical, Academic, and Pastoral Work, 1931-1932*. Edited by Victoria J. Barnett et al. Translated by Anne Schmidt-Lange et al. Dietrich Bonhoeffer Works 11. Minneapolis: Fortress, 2012.

———. *Ethics*. Edited by Clifford J. Green. Translated by Reinhard Krauss et al. Dietrich Bonhoeffer Works 6. Minneapolis: Fortress, 2005.

———. *Ethik*. Edited by Ilse Tödt et al. Dietrich Bonhoeffer Werke 6. Munich: Kaiser, 1998.

———. *Gemeinsames Leben/Das Gebetbuch der Bibel*. Edited by Eberhard Bethge et al. Dietrich Bonhoeffer Werke 5. Munich: Kaiser, 1987.

———. *Illegale Theologenausbildung: Finkenwalde, 1935-1937*. Edited by Otto Dudzus et al. Dietrich Bonhoeffer Werke 14. Munich: Kaiser, 1996.

———. *Letters and Papers from Prison*. Edited by John W. de Gruchy. Translated by Lisa E. Dahill et al. Dietrich Bonhoeffer Works 8. Minneapolis: Fortress, 2010.

———. *Life Together and Prayerbook of the Bible*. Edited by Geffrey B. Kelly. Translated by Daniel W. Bloesch and James H. Burtness. Dietrich Bonhoeffer Works 5. Minneapolis: Fortress, 1996.

———. *London, 1933-1935*. Edited by Hans Goedeking et al. Dietrich Bonhoeffer Werke 13. Munich: Kaiser, 1994.

———. *London, 1933-1935*. Edited by Keith Clements. Translated by Isabel Best. Supplementary material translated by Douglas W. Stott. Dietrich Bonhoeffer Works 13. Minneapolis: Fortress, 2007.

———. *Nachfolge*. Edited by Martin Kuske and Ilse Tödt. Dietrich Bonhoeffer Werke 4. Munich: Kaiser, 1994.

———. *Ökumene, Universität, Pfarramt, 1931-1932*. Edited by Eberhard Amelung and Christoph Strom. Dietrich Bonhoeffer Werke 11. Munich: Kaiser, 1994.

———. *Sanctorum Communio: A Theological Study of the Sociology of the Church*. Edited by Clifford J. Green. Translated by Reinhard Krauss and Nancy Lukens. Dietrich Bonhoeffer Works 1. Minneapolis: Fortress, 1998.

———. *Sanctorum Communio: Eine dogmatische Untersuchung zur Soziologie der Kirche*. Edited by Joachim von Soosten. Dietrich Bonhoeffer Werke 1. Munich: Kaiser, 1986.

————. *Schöpfung und Fall.* Edited by Martin Rüter and Ilse Tödt. Dietrich Bonhoeffer Werke 3. Munich: Kaiser, 1989.

————. *Theological Education at Finkenwalde, 1935–1937.* Edited by H. Gaylon Barker and Mark S. Brocker. Translated by Douglas W. Stott. Dietrich Bonhoeffer Works 14. Minneapolis: Fortress, 2013.

————. *Theological Education Underground, 1937–1940.* Edited by Victoria J. Barnett. Translated by Claudia D. Bergmann et al. Dietrich Bonhoeffer Works 15. Minneapolis: Fortress, 2011.

————. *Widerstand und Ergebung.* Edited by Christian Gremmels et al. Dietrich Bonhoeffer Werke 8. Munich: Kaiser, 1998.

————. *The Young Bonhoeffer, 1918–1927.* Edited by Paul Duane Matheny et al. Translated by Mary C. Nebelsick with the assistance of Douglas W. Stott. Dietrich Bonhoeffer Works 9. Minneapolis: Fortress, 2002.

————. *Zettelnotizen für eine "Ethik".* Edited by Ilse Tödt. Munich: Kaiser, 1993.

Bossy, John. *Christianity in the West, 1400–1700.* Oxford: Oxford University Press, 1985.

————. "Some Elementary Forms of Durkheim." *Past & Present* 95 (1982) 3–18.

Bost, Hubert. "Le désert des Huguenots: Une Poetique de l'Épreuve." *Revue des Sciences Humaines* 258 (2000) 177–206.

Boyarin, Daniel. *Border Lines: The Partition of Judaeo-Christianity.* Philadelphia: University of Pennsylvania Press, 2004.

Boyle, Nicholas. *Who Are We Now? Christian Humanism and the Global Market from Hegel to Heaney.* Notre Dame: University of Notre Dame Press, 1998.

Brueggemann, Walter. "The Legitimacy of a Sectarian Hermeneutic." In *Interpretation and Obedience: From Faithful Reading to Faithful Living,* 41–69. Minneapolis: Fortress, 1991.

Bruford, W. H. *The German Tradition of Self-Cultivation: "Bildung" from Humboldt to Thomas Mann.* New York: Cambridge University Press, 1975.

Buber, Martin. "What Is Man?" In *Between Man and Man,* translated by Ronald Gregor-Smith, 140–244. New York: Routledge, 2002.

Budde, Michael L. *The Borders of Baptism: Identities, Allegiances, and the Church.* Eugene, OR: Cascade, 2011.

————. *The (Magic) Kingdom of God: Christianity and Global Culture Industries.* Boulder, CO: Westview, 1997.

Budde, Michael L., and Robert W. Brimlow. *Christianity Incorporated: How Big Business Is Buying the Church.* Grand Rapids: Brazos, 2002.

Bultmann, Rudolf. *Jesus Christ and Mythology.* New York: Scribner, 1958.

Burrell, David B. *Freedom and Creation in Three Traditions.* Notre Dame: University of Notre Dame Press, 1993.

Calvin, John. *Institutes of the Christian Religion* [1559]. Edited by John T. McNeill. Translated by Ford Lewis Battles. 2 vols. Philadelphia: Westminster, 1960.

Carnes, Natalie. *Beauty: A Theological Engagement with Gregory of Nyssa.* Eugene, OR: Cascade, 2014.

Carpenter, Humphrey. *The Inklings: C. S. Lewis, J. R. R. Tolkien, Charles Williams and Their Friends.* London: HarperCollins, 1997.

Carter, J. Kameron. *Race: A Theological Account.* New York: Oxford University Press, 2008.

————. "An Unlikely Convergence: W. E. B. Du Bois, Karl Barth, and the Problem of the Imperial God-Man." *CR: The New Centennial Review* 11 (2011) 167–224.

Casas, Bartolomé de las. *In Defense of the Indians: The Defense of the Most Reverend Lord, Don Fray Bartolomé de las Casas, of the Order of Preachers, Late Bishop of Chiapa, against the Persecutors and Slanderers of the Peoples of the New World Discovered Across the Seas.* Translated by Stafford Poole. DeKalb: Northern Illinois University Press, 1974.

Cavanaugh, William T. "Dying for the Eucharist?" *Theology Today* 58 (2001) 177–89.

———. *Migrations of the Holy: God, State, and the Political Meaning of the Church.* Grand Rapids: 2011.

———. *The Myth of Religious Violence: Secular Ideology and the Roots of Modern Conflict.* New York: Oxford University Press, 2009.

———. *Theopolitical Imagination: Discovering the Liturgy as a Political Act in an Age of Global Consumerism.* New York: T. & T. Clark, 2002.

Certeau, Michel de. *The Mystic Fable.* Vol. 1, *The Sixteenth and Seventeenth Centuries.* Translated by Michael B. Smith. Chicago: University of Chicago Press, 1992.

———. *The Practice of Everyday Life.* Translated by Steven Rendall. Berkeley: University of California Press, 1984.

Chidester, David. *Savage Systems: Colonialism and Comparative Religion in Southern Africa.* Charlottesville: University Press of Virginia, 1996.

Cicero. *Tusculan Disputations.* Translated by J. E. King. Cambridge, MA: Harvard University Press, 1927.

Clark, Adam, and Michael Mawson, eds. *Ontology and Ethics: Bonhoeffer and Contemporary Scholarship.* Eugene, OR: Pickwick, 2013.

Clements, Keith W. *What Freedom? The Persistent Challenge of Dietrich Bonhoeffer.* Bristol: Bristol Baptist College, 1990.

Coakley, Sarah. "Feminism." In *A Companion to Philosophy of Religion,* edited by Philip L. Quinn and Charles Taliaferro, 601–6. Malden, MA: Blackwell, 1997.

———. *God, Sexuality, and the Self: An Essay "On the Trinity."* New York: Cambridge University Press, 2013.

———. *Powers and Submissions: Spirituality, Philosophy and Gender.* Malden, MA: Blackwell, 2002.

Coles, Romand. *Beyond Gated Politics: Reflections for the Possibility of Democracy.* Minneapolis: University of Minnesota Press, 2005.

Commager, Henry Steele. *The Empire of Reason: How Europe Imagined and America Realized the Enlightenment.* New York: Oxford University Press, 1982.

Cone, James H. *Speaking the Truth: Ecumenism, Liberation, and Black Theology.* Grand Rapids: Eerdmans, 1986.

Correll, Mark R. *Shepherds of the Empire: Germany's Conservative Protestant Leadership, 1888–1919.* Minneapolis: Fortress, 2014.

Cranmer, Frank. "The Archbishop and Sharia." *Law & Justice* 160 (2008) 4–5.

Cullen, Countee. "The Black Christ." In *The Black Christ & Other Poems,* 69–110. New York: Harper, 1929.

Cusa, Nicholas de. *De pace fidei.* In *Unity and Reform: Selected Writings of Nicholas De Cusa,* edited by John Patrick Dolan, 195–237. Notre Dame: University of Notre Dame Press, 1962.

Dawkins, Richard. *The Selfish Gene.* 2nd ed. New York: Oxford University Press, 1989.

Dawson, John David. *Christian Figural Reading and the Fashioning of Identity.* Berkeley: University of California Press, 2002.

Day, Dorothy. *The Long Loneliness: An Autobiography*. San Francisco: Harper & Row, 1952.

De Gruchy, John W. *Christianity, Art and Transformation: Theological Aesthetics in the Struggle for Justice*. New York: Cambridge University Press, 2001.

———. *Led into Mystery: Faith Seeking Answers in Life and Death*. London: SCM, 2013.

DeJonge, Michael P. "Bonhoeffer's Concept of the West." In *Bonhoeffer, Religion and Politics*, edited by Christiane Tietz and Jens Zimmermann, 37–52. Frankfurt am Main: Peter Lang, 2012.

———. *Bonhoeffer's Theological Formation: Berlin, Barth, and Protestant Theology*. Oxford: Oxford University Press, 2012.

Deneen, Patrick J. "Would Someone Just Shut That Pope Up?" *The American Conservative*, December 5, 2013. http://www.theamericanconservative.com/would-someone-just-shut-that-pope-up/.

Dewey, John. *A Common Faith*. New Haven: Yale University Press, 1934.

Dilthey, Wilhelm. *Gesammelte Schriften*. Vol. 2, *Weltanschauung und Analyse des Menschen seit Renaissance und Reformation*. 6th ed. Stuttgart: B. G. Teubner, 1960.

Dionysius of Halicarnassus. *Roman Antiquities*. Translated by Earnest Cary. Cambridge, MA: Harvard University Press, 1945.

Dostoevsky, Fyodor. *The Brothers Karamazov*. Translated by Richard Pevear and Larissa Volokhonsky. New York: Vintage, 1991.

Douglas, Mary. *Risk Acceptability According to the Social Sciences*. New York: Russell Sage, 1985.

Dreyfus, Herbert L. "Knowledge and Human Values: A Genealogy of Nihilism." *Teachers College Record* 82 (1981) 507–20.

Dreyfus Hubert L., and Paul Rabinow. *Michel Foucault: Beyond Structuralism and Hermeneutics*. 2nd ed. Chicago: University of Chicago Press, 1983.

Dumas, André. *Dietrich Bonhoeffer: Theologian of Reality*. Translated by Robert McAfee Brown. New York: Macmillan, 1971.

Dunn, James D. G. *Jesus Remembered*. Christianity in the Making 1. Grand Rapids: Eerdmans, 2003.

———. *The Theology of Paul the Apostle*. Grand Rapids: 1998.

Eagleton, Terry. *Culture and the Death of God*. New Haven: Yale University Press, 2014.

———. *The Meaning of Life: A Very Short Introduction*. New York: Oxford University Press, 2007.

———. *Reason, Faith, and Revolution: Reflections on the God Debate*. New Haven: Yale University Press, 2009.

Egan, Timothy. *The Worst Hard Time: The Untold Story of Those Who Survived the Great American Dust Bowl*. Boston: Houghton Mifflin, 2006.

Emerson, Michael O., with Rodney M. Woo. *People of the Dream: Multiracial Congregations in the United States*. Princeton: Princeton University Press, 2006.

Evans, Richard J. *The Coming of the Third Reich: A History*. New York: Penguin, 2003.

———. *The Third Reich at War*. New York: Penguin, 2008.

Fabian, Johannes. *Time and the Other: How Anthropology Makes Its Object*. New York: Columbia University Press, 1983.

Faulkner, Quentin. *Wiser Than Despair: The Evolution of Ideas in the Relationship of Music and the Christian Church*. Westport, CT: Greenwood, 1996.

Feil, Ernst. *The Theology of Dietrich Bonhoeffer*. Translated by Martin Rumscheidt. Philadelphia: Fortress, 1985.

Feuerbach, Ludwig. *The Essence of Christianity*. Translated by George Eliot. New York: Harper, 1957.

Fish, Stanley "Boutique Multiculturalism, or Why Liberals Are Incapable of Thinking about Hate Speech." *Critical Inquiry* 23 (1997) 378–95.

Foucault, Michel. *Discipline and Punish: The Birth of the Prison*. Translated by Alan Sheridan. New York: Random House, 1979.

———. *Technologies of the Self: A Seminar with Michel Foucault*. Edited by Luther H. Martin et al. Amherst: University of Massachusetts Press, 1988.

Fowler, James W. *Stages of Faith: The Psychology of Human Development and the Quest for Meaning*. San Francisco: Harper & Row, 1981.

Francis, Pope. *Evangelii Gaudium*. http://www.vatican.va/holy_father/francesco/apost_exhortations/documents/papa-francesco_esortazione-ap_20131124_evangelii-gaudium_en.html.

Freeman, Curtis W. "Alterity and Its Cure." *Cross Currents* 59 (2009) 404–41.

Frei, Hans. *The Eclipse of Biblical Narrative: A Study in Eighteenth and Nineteenth Century Hermeneutics*. New Haven: Yale University Press, 1974.

———. *Types of Christian Theology*. Edited by George Hunsinger and William C. Placher. New Haven: Yale University Press, 1992.

Freud, Sigmund. *The Future of an Illusion*. Translated by James Strachey. New York: Norton, 1961.

Fukuyama, Francis. "The End of History?" *The National Interest* 16 (1989) 3–18.

Garrison, Janine. "Assemblée du Musée du Désert, 1er Septembre 1985." *Bulletin de la Société de l'histoire du Protestantisme Français* 132 (1986) 109–12.

Gaventa, Beverly Roberts, and Richard B. Hays, eds. *Seeking the Identity of Jesus: A Pilgrimage*. Grand Rapids: Eerdmans, 2008.

Geertz, Clifford. *The Interpretation of Cultures*. New York: Basic Books, 1973.

Gellner, Ernest. *Nations and Nationalisms*. Ithaca: Cornell University Press, 1983.

Giddens, Anthony. *Consequences of Modernity*. Stanford: Stanford University Press, 1990.

———. *Modernity and Self-Identity: Self and Society in the Late Modern Age*. Stanford: Stanford University Press, 1991.

———. *The Nation-State and Violence*. Berkeley: University of California Press, 1987.

Gides, David M. *Pacifism, Just War, and Tyrannicide: Bonhoeffer's Church-World Theology and His Changing Forms of Political Thinking and Involvement*. Eugene, OR: Pickwick, 2011.

Gierke, Otto. *Associations and Law: The Classical and Early Christian Stages*. Translated by George Heiman. Toronto: University of Toronto Press, 1977.

Gillespie, Michael Allen. *The Theological Origins of Modernity*. Chicago: University of Chicago Press, 2008.

Goldberg, Michael. *Why Should Jews Survive? Looking Past the Holocaust Toward a Jewish Future*. New York: Oxford University Press, 1995.

Gorman, Michael J. *Inhabiting the Cruciform God: Kenosis, Justification, and Theosis in Paul's Narrative Soteriology*. Grand Rapids: Eerdmans, 2009.

Gracchi [pseud.]. "Civil and Religious Law in England: Contra Canterbury!" *Liberal Conspiracy*, February 8, 2008. http://liberalconspiracy.org/2008/02/08/civil-and-religious-law-in-england-contra-canterbury/.

Grant, George. *Technology and Justice*. Notre Dame: University of Notre Dame Press, 1986.

Green, Clifford J. "Pacifism and Tyrannicide: Bonhoeffer's Christian Peace Ethic." *Studies in Christian Ethics* 18 (2005) 31–47.

Greggs, Tom. *Theology Against Religion: Constructive Dialogues with Bonhoeffer and Barth.* New York: T. & T. Clark, 2011.

Gregory, Bishop of Nyssa. *The Life of Saint Macrina.* Translated by Kevin Corrigan. 1989. Reprint, Eugene, OR: Wipf & Stock, 2005.

Gregory, Brad. *The Unintended Reformation: How a Religious Revolution Secularized Society.* Cambridge: Belknap Press of Harvard University Press, 2012.

Griffiths, Paul J. *Intellectual Appetite: A Theological Grammar.* Washington, DC: Catholic University of America Press, 2009.

Guardini, Romano. *The Church and the Catholic.* Translated by Ada Lane. New York: Sheed & Ward, 1935.

Guroian, Vigen. *Incarnate Love: Essays in Orthodox Ethics.* 2nd ed. Notre Dame: University of Notre Dame Press, 2002.

Gushee, David P. *The Righteous Gentiles of the Holocaust: A Christian Interpretation.* Minneapolis: Fortress, 1994.

Gutiérrez, Gustavo. *Las Casas: In Search of the Poor of Jesus Christ.* Translated by Robert R. Barr. Maryknoll, NY: Orbis, 1993.

Guy, Jeff. *Heretic: A Study of the Life of John William Colenso, 1814–1883.* Johannesburg: Raven, 1983.

Gwynne, S. C. *Empire of the Summer Moon: Quanah Parker and the Rise and Fall of the Comanches, the Most Powerful Indian Tribe in American History.* New York: Scribner, 2010.

Hahn, Roger. "Laplace and the Mechanistic Universe." In *God and Nature: Historical Essays on the Encounter between Christianity and Science,* edited by David Clindberg and Ronald L. Numbers, 256–76. Berkeley: University of California Press, 1986.

Hallie, Philip P. *Lest Innocent Blood Be Shed: The Story of the Village of Le Chambon and How Goodness Happened There.* New York: HarperPerennial, 1994.

Hanke, Lewis. *All Mankind Is One: A Study of the Disputation between Bartolemé de Las Casas and Juan Ginés de Sepúlveda in 1550 on the Intellectual and Religious Capacity of the American Indians.* DeKalb: Northern Illinois University Press, 1974.

Hardy Daniel W., and David F. Ford. *Praising and Knowing God.* Philadelphia: Westminster, 1985.

Harnack, Adolf von. *What Is Christianity?* Translated by Thomas Bailey Saunders. New York: Harper , 1957.

Harrison, Peter. *"Religion" and the Religions in the English Enlightenment.* New York: Cambridge University Press, 1990.

Harvey, Barry. "Accounting for Difference: Dietrich Bonhoeffer's Contribution to a Theological Critique of Culture." In *Mysteries in the Theology of Dietrich Bonhoeffer,* edited by Kirsten Busch et al., 81–109. Göttingen: Vandenhoeck & Ruprecht, 2007.

———. *Another City: An Ecclesiological Primer for a Post-Christian World.* Harrisburg, PA: Trinity, 1999.

———. "The Body Politic of Christ: Theology, Social Analysis, and Bonhoeffer's Arcane Discipline." *Modern Theology* 13 (1997) 319–46.

———. *Can These Bones Live? A Catholic Baptist Engagement with Ecclesiology, Hermeneutics, and Social Theory*. Grand Rapids: Brazos, 2008.

———. "Life in Exile, Life in the Middle of the Village: A Contribution of Dietrich Bonhoeffer to a Post-Christendom Ecclesiology." In *Dietrich Bonhoeffer's Theology Today: A Way between Fundamentalism and Secularism?*, edited by Christiane Tietz et al., 229–43. Gütersloh: Gütersloher, 2009.

———. "The Path of the Church's Decision: Bonhoeffer on Church, 'Politics' and the State." In *Bonhoeffer, Religion and Politics*, edited by Christiane Tietz and Jens Zimmermann, 81–98. New York: Peter Lang, 2012.

———. "A Post-Critical Approach to 'Religionless Christianity.'" *Union Seminary Quarterly Review* 46 (1992) 39–58.

———. "Ransomed from Every Language: The Church as a Community of Word-Care." *Review and Expositor* 112 (2015) 104–18.

———. "Re-Envisioning the Wall of Separation, or One and a Half Cheers for Secularization: Toward an Ecclesial Identity after Christendom." In *Questions of Identity: Studies in Honour of Brian Haymes*, edited by Anthony R. Cross and Ruth M. B. Gouldbourne, 50–66. Oxford: Centre for Baptist History and Heritage, Regent's Park College, 2011.

———. "Religion, Race and Resistance: Extending Dietrich Bonhoeffer's Critique of Religion." In *A Spoke in the Wheel: The Political in the Theology of Dietrich Bonhoeffer*, edited by Kirsten Busch Nielsen et al., 150–63. Gütersloh: Gütersloher, 2013.

———. "The Wound of History: Reading Bonhoeffer after Christendom." In *Bonhoeffer for a New Day: Theology in a Time of Transition*, edited by John W. de Gruchy, 72–93. Grand Rapids: Eerdmans, 1997.

Hauerwas, Stanley. "Abortion, Theologically Understood." In *The Hauerwas Reader*, edited by John Berkman and Michael Cartwright, 603–22. Durham: Duke University Press, 2001.

———. *Dispatches from the Front: Theological Engagements with the Secular*. Durham: Duke University Press, 1994.

Hays, Richard B. *The Moral Vision of the New Testament: Community, Cross, New Creation; A Contemporary Introduction to New Testament Ethics*. San Francisco: HarperSanFrancisco, 1996.

Heffernan, Thomas J. "Martyrdom, Charisma, and Imitation: Paths to Christian Sanctity." *Greek Orthodox Theological Review* 55 (2010) 251–67.

Heidegger, Martin. *Being and Time*. Translated by John Macquarrie and Edward Robinson. New York: Harper & Row, 1962.

———. *Nietzsche*. Vol. 1, *The Will to Power as Art*. Translated by David Farrell Krell. San Francisco: HarperSanFrancisco, 1979.

———. "The Question Concerning Technology." In *Basic Writings from Being and Time (1927) to The Task of Thinking (1964)*, edited by David Farrell Krell, 283–317. New York: Harper & Row, 1977.

Henry, Patrick. *We Only Know Men: The Rescue of Jews in France during the Holocaust*. Washington, DC: Catholic University of America Press, 2007.

Hobsbawm, E. J. *Nations and Nationalism since 1780: Programme, Myth, Reality*. Cambridge: Cambridge University Press, 1990.

Hohmann, Martin. *Die Korrelation von Altem und Neuem Bund: Innerbiblische Korrelation statt Kontrastkorrelation*. Berlin: Evangelische Verlagsanstalt, 1978.

Horkheimer, Max, and Theodor W. Adorno. "The Culture Industry: Enlightenment as Mass Deception." In *Dialectic of Enlightenment: Philosophical Fragments*, edited by Gunzelin Schmid Noerr, translated by Edmund Jephcott, 94–136. Stanford: Stanford University Press, 2002.

Hügel, Friedrich von. *The Mystical Element of Religion.* 2 vols. New York: Crossroad, 1999.

Hunter, James Davison. *Culture Wars: The Struggle to Define America.* New York: Basic Books, 1991.

———. *To Change the World: The Irony, Tragedy, and Possibility of Christianity in the Late Modern World.* New York: Oxford University Press, 2010.

Ignatiev, Noel. *How the Irish Became White.* New York: Routledge, 1995.

Inwood, Michael. *A Heidegger Dictionary.* Malden, MA: Blackwell, 1999.

James, William. *The Varieties of Religious Experience.* New York: Mentor, 1958.

Jenkins, Philip. *The Next Christendom: The Coming of Global Christianity.* New York: Oxford University Press, 2011.

Jenks, Chris. *Culture.* 2nd ed. New York: Routledge, 2004.

Jennings, Willie James. *The Christian Imagination: Theology and the Origins of Race.* New Haven: Yale University Press, 2010.

Josephson, Jason Ānanda. *The Invention of Religion in Japan.* Chicago: University of Chicago Press, 2012.

Julian of Norwich. *Revelations of Divine Love.* Translated by Elizabeth Spearing. New York: Penguin, 1958.

Jünger, Ernst. *The Forest Passage.* Translated by Thomas Friese. Candor, NY: Telos, 2013.

Kant, Immanuel. "Of the Different Human Races." In *The Idea of Race*, edited by Robert Bernasconi and Tommy L. Lott, 8–22. Indianapolis: Hackett, 2000.

Kelly, Geffrey B. *Liberating Faith: Bonhoeffer's Message for Today.* Minneapolis: Augsburg, 1984.

Kelly, Geffrey B., and F. Burton Nelson. *The Cost of Moral Leadership: The Spirituality of Dietrich Bonhoeffer.* Grand Rapids: Eerdmans, 2002.

Kershaw, Ian. *The End: The Defiance and Destruction of Hitler's Germany, 1944–1945.* New York: Penguin, 2011.

King, Martin Luther, Jr. *Stride Toward Freedom: The Montgomery Story.* New York: Harper & Row, 1958.

———. *Why We Can't Wait.* New York: New American Library, 1964.

Kuske, Martin. *The Old Testament as the Book of Christ: An Appraisal of Bonhoeffer's Interpretation.* Translated by S T Kimbrough Jr. Philadelphia: Westminster, 1976.

Lash, Nicholas. *The Beginning and the End of "Religion".* New York: Cambridge University Press, 1996.

———. *Easter in Ordinary: Reflections on Human Experience and the Knowledge of God.* Charlottesville: University Press of Virginia, 1988.

———. *Theology on the Way to Emmaus.* London: SCM, 1986.

Leahy, Brendan. "'Christ Existing as Community': Dietrich Bonhoeffer's Notion of Church." *Irish Theological Quarterly* 73 (2008) 32–59.

Legaspi, Michael C. *The Death of Scripture and the Rise of Biblical Studies.* New York: Oxford University Press, 2010.

Lehmann, Paul L. *Ethics in a Christian Context.* New York: Harper & Row, 1963.

———. "Evanston: Problems and Prospects." *Theology Today* 11 (1954) 143–53.

Lentricchia, Frank. *Criticism and Social Change*. Chicago: University of Chicago Press, 1983.

Lepenies, Wolf. *The Seduction of Culture in German History*. Princeton: Princeton University Press, 2014.

Levinas, Emmanuel. "Ethics as First Philosophy." In *The Levinas Reader*, edited by Seán Hand, 75–87. Cambridge, MA: Blackwell, 1989.

Lewis, C. S. "The Magician's Nephew." In *The Chronicles of Narnia*, 7–105. New York: HarperCollins, 2004.

Lindbeck, George. *The Nature of Doctrine*. Philadelphia: Westminster, 1984.

———. "What of the Future? A Christian Response?" In *Christianity in Jewish Terms*, edited by Tikva Frymer-Kensky et al., 357–66. Boulder, CO: Westview, 2000.

Lubac, Henri de. *Scripture in the Tradition*. Translated by Luke O'Neill. New York: Herder & Herder, 2000.

Luther, Martin. *The Freedom of a Christian*. Translated by Mark D. Tranvik. Minneapolis: Fortress, 2008.

———. "Preface to Georg Rhau's *Symphoniae Iucundae*." In *Luther's Works*, vol. 53, *Liturgy and Hymns*, edited by Ulrich S. Leupold, 321–24. Philadelphia: Fortress, 1965.

MacIntyre, Alasdair. *After Virtue*. 3rd ed. Notre Dame: University of Notre Dame Press, 2007.

———. *First Principles, Final Ends, and Contemporary Philosophical Issues*. Milwaukee: Marquette University Press, 1990.

———. *Whose Justice? Which Rationality?* Notre Dame: University of Notre Dame Press, 1988.

Macquarrie, John. *Christian Hope*. New York: Seabury, 1978.

Malinowski, Bronisław. "Introductory Essay: The Anthropology of Changing African Cultures." In *Methods of Study of Culture Contact in Africa*, edited by Bronislaw Malinowski, vii–xxxviii. New York: Oxford University Press, 1938.

Marlé, René. *Bonhoeffer: The Man and His Work*. Translated by Rosemary Sheed. New York: Newman, 1967.

Marsh, Charles. *Reclaiming Dietrich Bonhoeffer: The Promise of His Theology*. New York: Oxford University Press, 1994.

———. *Strange Glory: A Life of Dietrich Bonhoeffer*. New York: Knopf, 2014.

Martin, Calvin Luther. *The Way of the Human Being*. New Haven: Yale University Press, 1999.

Martyn, J. Louis. *Galatians*. New Haven: Yale University Press, 2004.

———. *Theological Issues in the Letters of Paul*. Nashville: Abingdon, 1997.

Marx, Karl, and Frederick Engels. "The Communist Manifesto." In *Economic and Philosophic Manuscripts of 1844; and The Communist Manifesto*, translated by Martin Milligan, 203–43. Buffalo, NY: Prometheus, 1988.

Masuzawa, Tomoko. *The Invention of World Religions, or, How European Universalism Was Preserved in the Language of Pluralism*. Chicago: University of Chicago Press, 2005.

Mathewes, Charles T. *A Theology of Public Life*. New York: Cambridge University Press, 2008.

McCabe, Herbert. "Comment." *New Blackfriars* 48 (1967) 226–29.

———. *God Matters*. London: Geoffrey Chapman, 1987.

———. *Law, Love and Language*. New York: Continuum, 2003.

————. *The New Creation*. New York: Continuum, 2010.

McCarraher, Eugene. "Love Covers a Multitude." October 19, 2014. http://syndicatetheology.com/love-covers-a-multitude/.

McClendon, James Wm., Jr. *Biography as Theology: How Life Stories Can Remake Today's Theology*. Nashville: Abingdon, 1974.

————. *Systematic Theology*. Vol. 2, *Ethics*. Rev. ed. Nashville: Abingdon, 2002.

McCormack, Bruce. *Orthodox and Modern: Studies in the Theology of Karl Barth*. Grand Rapids: Baker, 2008.

McGrane, Bernard. *Beyond Anthropology: Society and the Other*. New York: Columbia University Press, 1989.

Melville, Herman. "Benito Cereno." In *Billy Budd, Sailor and Other Stories*, 159–258. New York: Penguin, 1986.

Mensch, Elizabeth, and Alan Freeman. *The Politics of Virtue: Is Abortion Debatable?* Durham: Duke University Press, 1993.

Metaxas, Eric. *Bonhoeffer: Pastor, Martyr, Prophet, Spy*. Nashville: Thomas Nelson, 2010.

Meyendorff, John. *Byzantine Theology: Historical Trends and Doctrinal Themes*. 2nd ed. New York: Fordham University Press, 1979.

Milbank, John "Magisterial . . . and Shoddy?" *Studies in Christian Ethics* 7 (1994) 29–34.

————. *Theology and Social Theory: Beyond Secular Reason*. 2nd ed. Malden, MA: Blackwell, 2006.

————. *The Word Made Strange: Theology, Language, Culture*. Cambridge, MA: Blackwell, 1997.

Miller, Kevin D. "Reframing the Faith-Learning Relationship: Bonhoeffer and an Incarnational Alternative to the Integration Model." *Christian Scholar's Review* 43 (2014) 131–38.

Miller, Patrick D. "Dietrich Bonhoeffer and the Psalms." *Princeton Seminary Bulletin* 15 (1994) 274–82.

Moberly, Jennifer. *The Virtue of Bonhoeffer's Ethics: A Study of Dietrich Bonhoeffer's Ethics in Relation to Virtue Ethics*. Eugene, OR: Pickwick, 2013.

Moltmann, Jürgen. *Theology of Hope: On the Ground and the Implications of a Christian Eschatology*. Translated by James W. Leitch. New York: Harper & Row, 1967.

Mulhall, Stephen. "Wittgenstein on Faith, Rationality, and the Passions." In *Faith, Rationality, and the Passions*, edited by Sarah Coakley, 197–208. Malden, MA: Wiley-Blackwell, 2012.

Müller, Hanfried. *Von der Kirche zur Welt: Ein Beitrag zu der Beziehung des Wort Gottes auf die Societas in Dietrich Bonhoeffers Theologischer Entwicklung*. Hamburg: Herbert Reich Evangelischer Verlag, 1966.

Nation, Mark Thiessen, et al. *Bonhoeffer the Assassin? Challenging the Myth, Recovering His Call to Peacemaking*. Grand Rapids: Baker, 2013.

Neuhaus, Richard John. *The Naked Public Square: Religion and Democracy in America*. Grand Rapids: Eerdmans, 1984.

Newman, John Henry. "The Nature of Faith in Relation to Reason." In *Fifteen Sermons Preached Before the University of Oxford between AD 1826 and 1843*, 202–21. Notre Dame: University of Notre Dame Press, 1977.

Niebuhr, H. Richard. *Christ and Culture*. New York: Harper & Row, 1951.

————. *The Responsible Self: An Essay in Moral Philosophy*. San Francisco: Harper & Row, 1963.

Nietzsche, Friedrich. *The Antichrist*. In *The Portable Nietzsche*, translated by Walter Kaufmann, 568–656. New York: Penguin, 1954.

———. *Human, All Too Human: A Book for Free Spirits*. Rev. ed. Translated by Stephan Lehmann. Lincoln, NE: Bison, 1996.

Nongbri, Brent. *Before Religion: A History of a Modern Concept*. New Haven: Yale University Press, 2013.

Northcott, Michael S. *A Political Theology of Climate Change*. Grand Rapids: Eerdmans, 2013.

Novak, David. *Talking With Christians: Musings of a Jewish Theologian*. Grand Rapids: Eerdmans, 2005.

O'Connor, Flannery. "A Good Man Is Hard to Find." In *Flannery O'Connor: Collected Works*, 137–53. New York: Library of America, 1988.

O'Donovan, Oliver. *Church in Crisis: The Gay Controversy and the Anglican Communion*. Eugene, OR: Cascade, 2008.

O'Hanlon, Gerard. "Theological Dramatics." In *The Beauty of Christ: An Introduction to the Theology of Hans Urs von Balthasar*, edited by Bede MacGregor and Thomas Norris, 92–110. Edinburgh: T. & T. Clark, 1994.

Olusoga, David, and Casper W. Erichsen. *The Kaiser's Holocaust: Germany's Forgotten Genocide and the Colonial Roots of Nazism*. London: Faber and Faber, 2010.

Ott, Heinrich. *Reality and Faith: Theological Legacy of Dietrich Bonhoeffer*. Translated by Alex. A. Morrison. Philadelphia: Fortress, 1972.

Pangritz, Andreas. *Karl Barth in the Theology of Dietrich Bonhoeffer*. Translated by Barbara Rumscheidt and Martin Rumscheidt. Grand Rapids: Eerdmans, 2000.

———. "Point and Counterpoint—Resistance and Submission: Dietrich Bonhoeffer on Theology and Music in Times of War and Social Crisis." In *Theology in Dialogue: The Impact of the Arts, Humanities, and Science on Contemporary Religious Thought*, edited by Lyn Holness and Ralf K. Wüstenberg, 28–42. Grand Rapids: Eerdmans, 2002.

———. *Polyphonie des Lebens: Zu Dietrich Bonhoeffers "Theologie der Musik"*. Berlin: Alektor, 1994.

———. "'To Fall within the Spokes of the Wheel': New-Old Observations concerning 'The Church and the Jewish Question.'" In *A Spoke in the Wheel*, edited by Kirsten Busch Nielson et al., 94–108. Gütersloh: Gütersloher, 2013.

———. "Who Is Jesus Christ, for Us, Today?" In *The Cambridge Companion to Dietrich Bonhoeffer*, edited by John W. de Gruchy, 134–53. New York: Cambridge University Press, 1999.

Paul VI, Pope. *Lumen Gentium*. http://www.vatican.va/archive/hist_councils/ii_vatican_council/documents/vat-ii_const_19641121_lumen-gentium_en.html.

Percy, Walker. *The Message in the Bottle: How Queer Man Is, How Queer Language Is, and What One Has to Do with the Other*. New York: Farrar, Straus and Giroux, 1975.

Phillips, Jacob. "Dispossessed Science, Dispossessed Self: Dilthey and Bonhoeffer's Christology Lectures of 1933." In *Ontology and Ethics: Bonhoeffer and Contemporary Scholarship*, edited by Adam Clark and Michael Mawson, 57–71. Eugene, OR: Pickwick, 2013.

Pieper, Josef. *Faith, Hope, Love*. San Francisco: Ignatius, 1997.

———. *The Four Cardinal Virtues*. Notre Dame: University of Notre Dame Press, 1966.

————. *Reality and the Good*. In *Living the Truth*, translated by Stella Lange, 107–79. San Francisco: Ignatius, 1989.

Plato. *The Republic*. Translated by C. D. C. Reeve. Indianapolis: Hackett, 2004.

Polanyi, Michael. *Personal Knowledge: Toward a Post-Critical Philosophy*. Corrected ed. Chicago: University of Chicago Press, 1962.

Poteat, William. *Polanyian Meditations: In Search of a Post-Critical Logic*. Durham: Duke University Press, 1985.

Pseudo-Dionysius. "The Mystical Theology." In *Pseudo-Dionysius: The Complete Works*, translated by Colm Luibheid, 133–41. New York: Paulist, 1987.

Raboteau, Albert J. *Slave Religion: The "Invisible Institution" in the Antebellum South*. Updated ed. New York: Oxford University Press, 2004.

Radner, Ephraim. *A Brutal Unity: The Spiritual Politics of the Christian Church*. Waco, TX: Baylor University Press, 2012.

Rasmussen, Larry. *Dietrich Bonhoeffer: His Significance for North Americans*. Minneapolis: Fortress, 1990.

Ratzinger, Joseph Cardinal. *Salt of the Earth: Christianity and the Catholic Church at the End of the Millennium; An Interview with Peter Seewald*. Translated by Adrian Walker. San Francisco: Ignatius, 1997.

Rawick, George P. *From Sundown to Sunup*. Westport, CT: Greenwood, 1972.

"Richtlinien der Kirchenbewegung 'Deutsche Christen' in Thüringen (vom 11 Dezember 1933) über die 'Deutsche Christliche Nationalkirche.'" In *Der Nationalsozialismus: Dokumente 1933–1945*, edited by Walther Hofer, 131. Frankfurt am Main: Fischer, 1962.

Ricoeur, Paul. *The Symbolism of Evil*. Translated by Emerson Buchanan. New York: Harper & Row, 1967.

Rieger, Joerg, and Kwok Pui-lan. *Occupy Religion: Theology of the Multitude*. Lanham, MD: Rowman & Littlefield, 2012.

Ritschl, Albrecht. *The Christian Doctrine of Justification and Reconciliation: The Positive Development of the Doctrine*. Translated by H. R. Mackintosh and A. B. Macaulay. 3 vols. Edinburgh: T. & T. Clark, 1900.

Robinson, Marilynne. "Dietrich Bonhoeffer." In *The Death of Adam: Essays on Modern Thought*, 108–25. New York: Picador, 1998.

Roediger, David R. *Working Toward Whiteness: How American's Immigrants Become White*. New York: Basic Books, 2005.

Rosen, Stanley. *Hermeneutics as Politics*. New York: Oxford University Press, 1987.

Rothrock, G. A. *The Huguenots: A Biography of a Minority*. Chicago: Nelson-Hall, 1979.

Rouse, Joseph. *Knowledge and Power: Toward a Political Philosophy of Science*. Ithaca: Cornell University Press, 1987.

Rousseau, Jean-Jacques. *Discourse on the Origin of Inequality*. Translated by Donald A. Cress. Indianapolis: Hackett, 1992.

Sanders, E. P. *Paul and Palestinian Judaism*. Philadelphia: Fortress, 1977.

Sanneh, Lamin. *Whose Religion Is Christianity? The Gospel Beyond the West*. Grand Rapids: Eerdmans, 2003.

Schlabach, Gerald W. "Deuteronomic or Constantinian: What Is the Most Basic Problem for Christian Social Ethics?" In *The Wisdom of the Cross: Essays in Honor of John Howard Yoder*, edited by Stanley Hauerwas et al., 449–71. Grand Rapids: Eerdmans, 1999.

Schleiermacher, Friedrich. *On Religion: Speeches to Its Cultured Despisers.* Edited by Richard Crouter. New York: Cambridge University Press, 1996.

Schlingensiepen, Ferdinand. *Dietrich Bonhoeffer, 1906–1945: Martyr, Thinker, Man of Resistance.* Translated by Isabel Best. New York: T. & T. Clark, 2010.

Schmemann, Alexander. *Church, World, Mission: Reflections on Orthodoxy in the West.* Crestwood, NY: St. Vladimir's Seminary Press, 1979.

———. *For the Life of the World: Sacraments and Orthodoxy.* Crestwood, NY: St. Vladimir's Seminary Press, 2000.

Schmitz, Florian. *Nachfolge: Zur Theologie Dietrich Bonhoeffers.* Göttingen: Vandenhoeck & Ruprecht, 2013.

———. "Reading *Discipleship* and *Ethics* Together: Implications for Ethics and Public Life." In *Interpreting Bonhoeffer: Historical Perspectives, Emerging Issues,* edited by Clifford J. Green and Guy C. Carter, 147–53. Minneapolis: Fortress, 2013.

Scholder, Klaus. *The Churches and the Third Reich.* Vol. 1, *Preliminary History and the Time of Illusions, 1918–1934.* Translated by John Bowden. Philadelphia: Fortress, 1988.

Seligman, Adam B. *Modernity's Wager: Authority, the Self, and Transcendence.* Princeton: Princeton University Press, 2000.

Sen, S. R. *The Economics of Sir James Steuart.* Cambridge, MA: Harvard University Press, 1957.

Shakespeare, William. *Hamlet.* Edited by E. R. Hibbard. New York: Oxford University Press, 1987.

Sheehan, Jonathan. *The Enlightenment Bible: Translation, Scholarship, Culture.* Princeton: Princeton University Press, 2005.

Skinner, Quentin. *The Foundations of Modern Political Thought.* Vol. 2, *The Age of Reformation.* London: Cambridge University Press, 1978.

Smith, Adam. *An Inquiry into the Nature and Causes of the Wealth of Nations.* Edited by R. H. Campbell and A. S. Skinner. 2 vols. Indianapolis: Liberty Fund, 1981.

Smith, Christian, with Melinda Lundquist Denton. *Soul Searching: The Religious and Spiritual Lives of American Teenagers.* New York: Oxford University Press, 2005.

Smith, Janet E. "Plato's Myths as 'Likely Accounts,' Worthy of Belief." *Apeiron* 19 (1985) 24–42.

Smith, Wilfred Cantwell. *The Meaning and End of Religion: A New Approach to the Religious Traditions of Mankind.* New York: Macmillan, 1962.

Sopko, Andrew J. "Bonhoeffer: An Orthodox Ecclesiology?" *Greek Orthodox Theological Review* 28 (1983) 81–88.

Sorkin, David Jan. *Moses Mendelssohn and the Religious Enlightenment.* Berkeley: University of California Press, 1996.

Southern, Richard William. *Western Society and the Church in the Middle Ages.* Harmondsworth: Penguin, 1985.

Southwold, Martin. "Buddhism and the Definition of Religion." *Man* 13 (1978) 362–79.

Stackhouse, Rochelle A. "Hymnody and Politics: Isaac Watts's 'Our God, Our Help in Ages Past' and Timothy Dwight's 'I Love Thy Kingdom, Lord.'" In *Wonderful Words of Life: Hymns in American Protestant History and Theology,* edited by Richard J. Mouw and Mark A. Noll, 42–66. Grand Rapids: Eerdmans, 2004.

Steinmetz, David C. "Theology and Exegesis: Ten Theses." In *A Guide to Contemporary Hermeneutics: Major Trends in Biblical Interpretation,* edited by Donald K. McKim, 27. Grand Rapids: Eerdmans, 1986.

Strauss, David Friedrich. *The Life of Jesus, Critically Examined*. Vol. 1. Translated by George Eliot. Bristol: Thoemmes, 1998.

Strauss, Richard. *Ariadne auf Naxos*. Libretto by Hugo von Hofmannsthal. Translation by Christopher Cowell. http://www.chandos.net/pdf/CHAN%203168.pdf.

Stockton, Ian. "Bonhoeffer's Wrestling with Jeremiah." *Modern Believing* 40 (1999) 50–58.

Stout, Jeffrey. *Democracy and Tradition*. Princeton: Princeton University Press, 2004.

———. *Ethics After Babel: The Languages of Morals and Their Discontents*. Boston: Beacon, 1988.

Stringfellow, William. *Dissenter in a Great Society*. Nashville: Abingdon, 1966.

Suckau, Krishana Oxenford. "Christian Witness on the Plateau Vivarais-Lignon: Narrative, Nonviolence, and the Formation of Character." PhD diss., Boston University School of Theology, 2011.

Surin, Kenneth. "A Certain 'Politics of Speech': 'Religious Pluralism' in the Age of the McDonald's Hamburger." *Modern Theology* 7 (1990) 67–100.

———. "*Contemptus mundi* and the Disenchanted world: Bonhoeffer's 'Discipline of the Secret' and Adorno's 'Strategy of Hibernation.'" In *The Turnings of Darkness and Light: Essays in Philosophical and Systematic Theology*, 180–200. New York: Cambridge University Press, 1989.

Swafford, Andrew Dean. *Nature and Grace: A New Approach to Thomistic Ressourcement*. Eugene, OR: Pickwick, 2014.

Tanner, Kathryn. *Theories of Culture: A New Agenda for Theology*. Minneapolis: Fortress, 1997.

Taylor, Charles. "Overcoming Epistemology." In *Philosophical Arguments*, 1–19. Cambridge, MA: Harvard University Press, 1995.

———. *A Secular Age*. Cambridge, MA: Belknap Press of Harvard University Press, 2007.

———. *Sources of the Self: The Making of the Modern Identity*. Cambridge, MA: Harvard University Press, 1989.

Tillich, Paul. *Systematic Theology*. 3 vols. Chicago: University of Chicago Press, 1951–63.

———. *Theology of Culture*. Edited by Robert C. Kimball. New York: Oxford University Press, 1959.

Tolkien, J. R. R. "Ainulindalë." In *The Silmarillion*, edited by Christopher Tolkien, 15–22. 2nd ed. Boston: Houghton Mifflin, 2001.

Toulmin, Stephen. *Human Understanding*. Princeton: Princeton University Press, 1972.

Trocmé, André. *Jesus and the Nonviolent Revolution*. Edited by Charles E. Moore. Rifton, NY: Plough, 2011.

Turner, Bryan S. *Religion and Social Theory*. 2nd ed. Thousand Oaks, CA: Sage, 1991.

Turner, Denys. *The Darkness of God: Negativity in Christian Mysticism*. New York: Cambridge University Press, 1995.

———. *Faith, Reason and the Existence of God*. Cambridge: Cambridge University Press, 2004.

Unsworth, Richard P. *A Portrait of Pacifists: Le Chambon, the Holocaust, and the Lives of André Trocmé and Magda Trocmé*. Syracuse: Syracuse University Press, 2012.

Virgil, *The Aeneid*. Translated by Robert Fagles. New York: Viking, 2006.

Vischer, Robert K. "The Dangers of Anti-Sharia Laws." *First Things* 221 (2012) 26–28.

Walls, Andrew. *The Missionary Movement: Studies in the Transmission of Faith.* Maryknoll, NY: Orbis, 2000.

Wannenwetsch, Bernd. "'Responsible Living' or 'Responsible Self'? Bonhoefferian Reflections on a Vexed Moral Notion." *Studies in Christian* Ethics 18 (2005) 125–40.

Ward, Graham. *True Religion.* Malden, MA: Blackwell, 2003.

Weber, Max. *The Protestant Ethic and the Spirit of Capitalism.* Translated by Talcott Parsons. Boston: George Allen & Unwin, 1930.

Wells, Samuel. *Improvisation: The Drama of Christian Ethics.* Grand Rapids: Brazos, 2004.

Werntz, Myles. *Bodies of War and Peace: Ecclesiology, Nonviolence, and the Witness against War.* Minneapolis: Fortress, 2014.

West, Charles C. Review of *Dietrich Bonhoeffer: His Significance for North Americans,* by Larry Rasmussen. *Theology Today* 47 (1991) 471–72.

West, Ed. "Archbishop Oscar Romero Was a Martyr, Declare Vatican Theologians." http://www.catholicherald.co.uk/news/2015/01/09/archbishop-oscar-romero-was-a-martyr-declare-vatican-theologians/.

Wiegele, Katharine L. *Investing in Miracles: El Shaddai and the Transformation of Popular Catholicism in the Philippines.* Honolulu: University of Hawai'i Press, 2005.

Williams, A. N. "The Future of the Past: The Contemporary Significance of the *Nouvelle Théologie.*" *International Journal of Systematic Theology* 7 (2005) 347–61.

Williams, Raymond. *Culture and Society, 1780–1950.* New York: Columbia University Press, 1958.

———. *Keywords: A Vocabulary of Culture and Society.* Rev. ed. New York: Oxford University Press, 1983.

Williams, Reggie L. *Bonhoeffer's Black Jesus: Harlem Renaissance Theology and an Ethic of Resistance.* Waco, TX: Baylor University Press, 2014.

Williams. Rowan D. "Between Politics and Metaphysics: Reflections in the Wake of Gillian Rose." In *Rethinking Metaphysics,* edited by L. Gregory Jones and Stephen E. Fowl, 3–22. Cambridge, MA: Blackwell, 1995.

———. "Civil and Religious Law in England: A Religious Perspective." *Islamic Studies* 47 (2008) 99–112.

———. *The Edge of Words: God and the Habits of Language.* New York: Bloomsbury, 2014.

———. "Keeping Time." In *A Ray of Darkness: Sermons and Reflections,* 214–17. Boston: Cowley, 1995.

———. *On Christian Theology.* Malden, MA: Blackwell, 2000.

———. *Resurrection: Interpreting the Easter Gospel.* New York: Pilgrim, 1984.

———. "The Suspicion of Suspicion: Wittgenstein and Bonhoeffer." In *Grammar of the Heart: New Essays in Moral Philosophy and Theology,* edited by Richard Bell, 36–53. San Francisco: Harper & Row, 1988.

———. *The Wound of Knowledge: Christian Spirituality from the New Testament to St. John of the Cross.* 2nd ed. Cambridge, MA: Cowley, 1991.

Wind, Renate. *Dietrich Bonhoeffer: A Spoke in the Wheel.* Translated by John Bowden. Grand Rapids: Eerdmans, 1990.

Wittgenstein, Ludwig. *Philosophical Investigations.* Translated by G. E. M. Anscombe. 3rd ed. New York: Macmillan, 1958.

Woelfel, James. *Bonhoeffer's Theology*. Nashville: Abingdon, 1970.

Wolff, Christoph. *Johann Sebastian Bach: The Learned Musician*. New York: Norton, 2000.

Wright, N. T. *Justification: God's Plan and Paul's Vision*. Downers Grove, IL: IVP, 2009.

————. *Surprised by Hope: Rethinking Heaven, the Resurrection, and the Mission of the Church*. New York: HarperOne, 2008.

Wright, Robert. *The Evolution of God*. New York: Little, Brown, 2008.

Wüstenberg, Ralf K. "Philosophical Influences on Bonhoeffer's 'Religionless Christianity.'" In *Bonhoeffer and Continental Thought*, edited by Brian Gregor and Jens Zimmermann, 137–55. Bloomington: Indiana University Press, 2009.

Wyschogrod, Michael. *The Body of Faith: God in the People Israel*. San Francisco: Harper & Row, 1983.

Yoder, John Howard. *What Would You Do? A Serious Answer to a Standard Question*. Expanded ed. Scottdale, PA: Herald, 1992.

Ziegler, Philip G. "Dietrich Bonhoeffer—an Ethics of God's Apocalypse?" *Modern Theology* 23 (2007) 579–94.

Zimmermann, Jens. *Incarnational Humanism: A Philosophy of Culture for the Church in the World*. Downers Grove, IL: IVP Academic, 2012.

Zimmermann, Moshe. *Wilhelm Marr: The Patriarch of Anti-Semitism*. New York: Oxford University Press, 1986.

Žižek, Slavoj. *The Puppet and the Dwarf: The Perverse Core of Christianity*. Cambridge, MA: MIT Press, 2003.

Scripture Index

❦

Index of Names and Subjects

Index of Greek Terms